ALPENGLÜHN

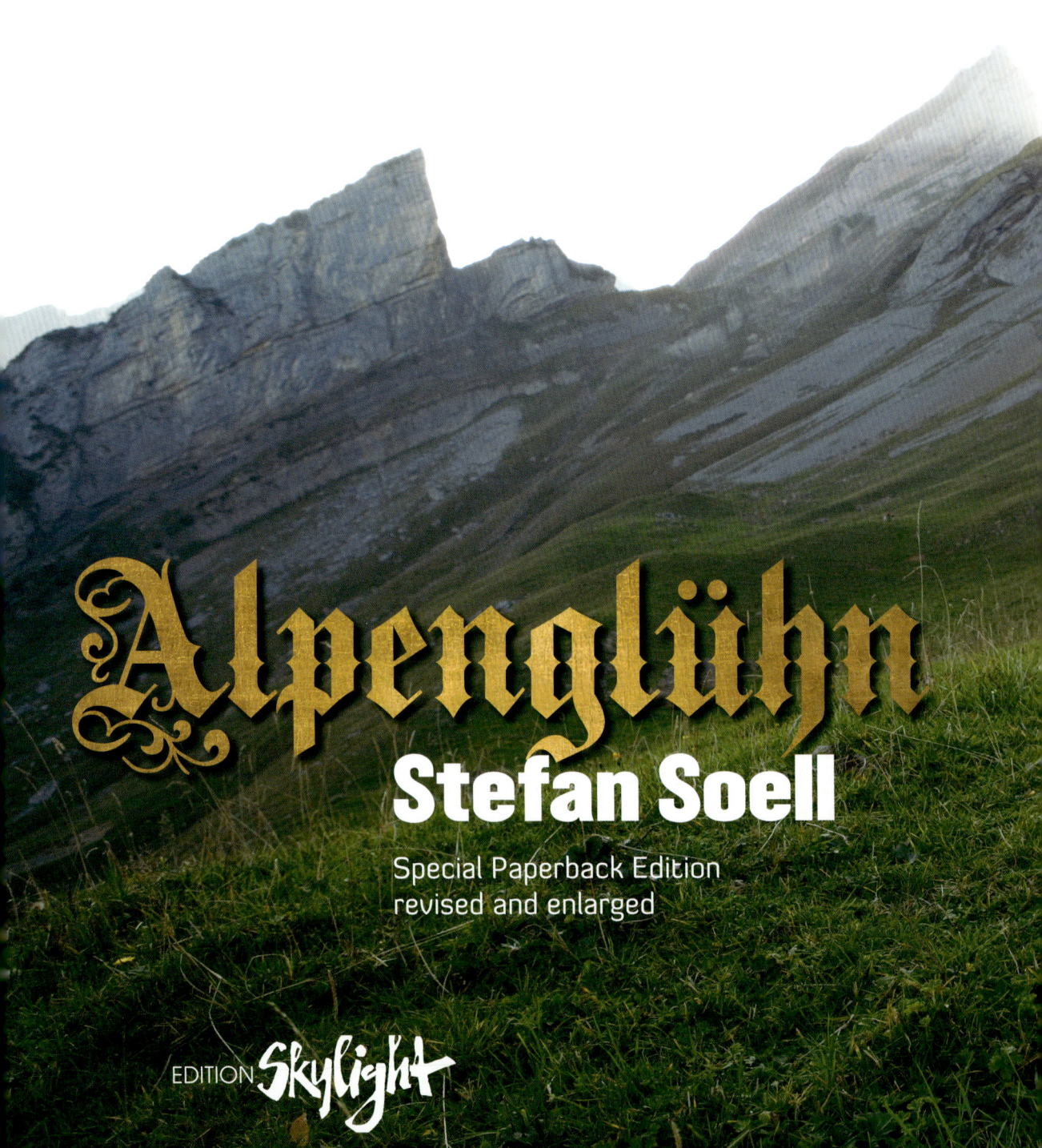

Alpenglühn

Stefan Soell

Special Paperback Edition
revised and enlarged

EDITION Skylight

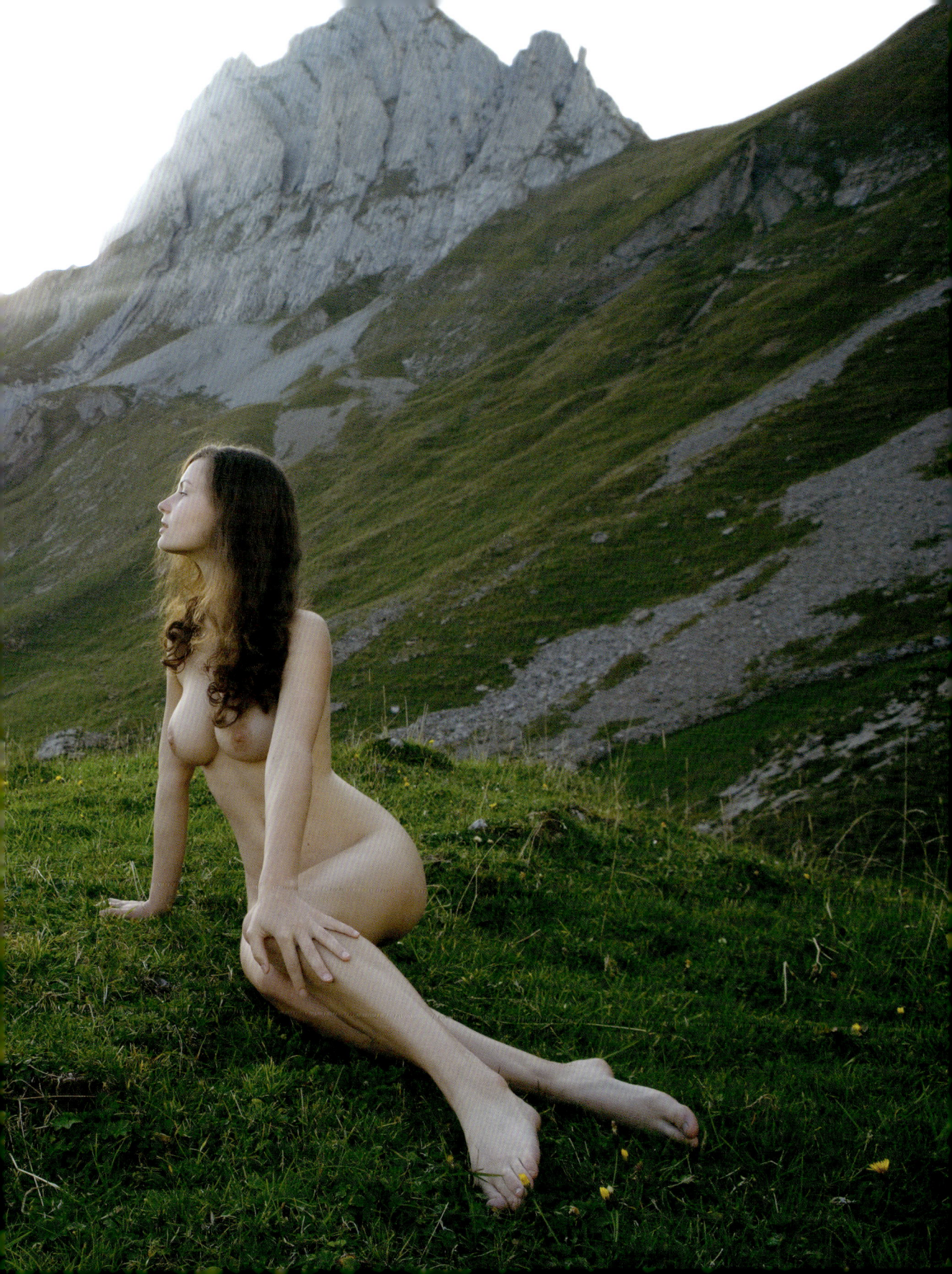

Cover/Umschlag:
Olga (47°3'25.94"N, 9°45'59.02"E)
Main title/Frontispiz:
Susann (47°16'17.81"N, 9°23'17.36"E)
Opposite page/Gegenüber:
Shasta (47°06'02.0"N, 9°24'43.6"E)

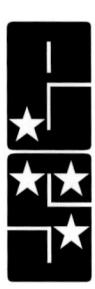

Special Paperback Edition revised and enlarged
2nd Edition 2023
1st Edition 2020
Copyright © Edition Skylight 2010

EDITION SKYLIGHT
Rosengartenstr. 13B
CH-8608 Bubikon / Zürich
Switzerland

info@edition-skylight.com
www.edition-skylight.com

ISBN 978-3-03766-673-9

Bibliographic information published by Die Deutsche Bibliothek
Die Deutsche Bibliothek lists this publication in the
Deutsche Nationalbibliografie; detailed bibliographic data
are available in the Internet at http://dnb.ddb.de.

Übersetzungen: Eugene Edwards

Printed in Slovenia

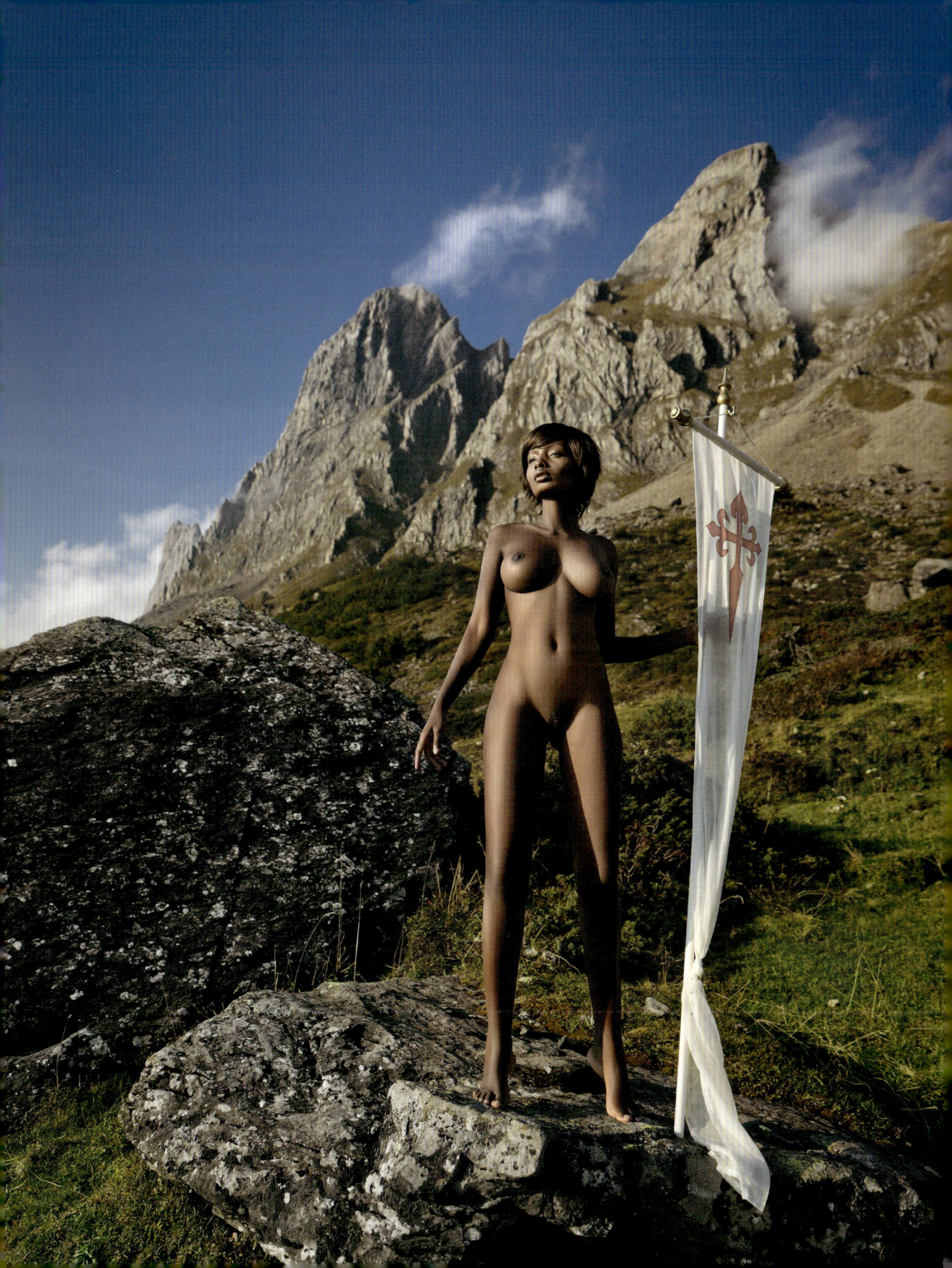

Interview with/mit Stefan Soell

1. What first got you interested in photography? I have always thought it was my interest in displaying the female subject.
2. What kind of professional training have you had? I haven't had any professional training. I am a self-educated photographer. Photography has always been my muse and there has been no day in my life without it. **3. How did you get into nude photography?** I started shooting my girlfriends at the age of 14. It's funny because at that time we didn't really know what we were doing but these images are still beautiful. **4. What is your casting process like and what do you look for in a model?** My casting process has miscellaneous forms. I am constantly scouting models on the street, searching on model-sites on the internet or getting enquiries from models all over the world. I am looking for natural models, full of character and beauty.
5. When you approach a model on the street, how do you go about convincing her to pose nude for you? It's a long-winded process to find a nude model on the street. When I am „street casting" I never ask new models to pose nude. We arrange a portrait shooting and the model gets to know my method of photography. But the number of models that will pose nude in from „street casting" is very low. **6. What artistic elements make a Stefan Soell photograph unique?** First it's the exposure to light and the strong association between the model and the location. Second it's a trustful, intimate and relaxed atmosphere in coherence with my models. **7. Do you consider what you do to be erotica or art?** I think I do both, art and erotica. There are several different styles in my work. My B&W work is more art than my color work. There are artistic as well as classical poses in my imagery. But in all my images one recognizes they have been created from one artistic source **8. How have your photographic goals and artistic methods changed over the years?** To associate my models with dreamier landscapes and locations has always been my goal. A radical change in my methods was the turning to digital photography 12 years ago. Before this switch I used a medium format camera due to image quality reasons. I only used B&W films and processed all films and prints in my own darkroom. It was VERY time-consuming! After changing to digital photography I got more and more into color photography. **9. Who do you admire and why?** / I have a very strong respect for ALL my nude models. They are not only a body. Every single model has her own personal character. To any of my images they donate a part of their soul.

10. Tell us about the process you go through in deciding where and how to shoot a model? It's a complicated process. Hiking around in my country I am always in search of particular locations that include a „special" aura. Depending on the change of the seasons there are multiple factors that contribute to an exact match for a „good" location. I don't know why, but I must feel a special mood to decide a „good" location. Sometimes it's exhausting to reach this locations and I am happy when my models are not tired from hiking ;-) My models always get in a close relationship with the places I am shooting, and I try to infuse this into my perspectives. **11. What artists have most influenced you?** There is no special artist that has influenced me. I have been influenced by photographers who worked in the beginning of photography. But now my imagination is fired by legends, fairytales and mythologies. **12 Tell us about what you say to your models while you're shooting them. Do you talk a lot, suggest poses, or do you let them do their own thing?** It depends on how often I have worked with a model. At the beginning i talk A LOT ;-) to get the full concentration of the model. We are joking and kidding and suddenly there is an invisible alliance between the model and me - shooting starts to be self-controlled and I only give short instructions to correct the pose. **13. Is there any particular part of a woman's body that most interests you?** I have always appreciated beautiful women. It's odd but all through my career I have most been fascinated by the face and character of a model. **14. If you had to give three tips to someone interested in becoming a great erotic photographer like yourself, what would they be?** — Listen to your own fantasy and try to transform your dreams and wishes into photography. — You do not need expensive equipment. — Do not copy other photographers images. Only use these images to enhance your own creativity. — and...try to stay strong-headed :-)

→ **www.stefansoell.de**

1. Was hat Ihr Interesse an der Fotografie geweckt? Ich denke, es war die Darstellung des Weiblichen, die mich gereizt hat. **2. Welche Berufsausbildung haben Sie durchlaufen?** In Sachen Fotografie: gar keine, ich bin Autodidakt. Die Fotografie war immer meine Muse. Bis jetzt gab es keinen Tag in meinem Leben, an dem sie keine Rolle gespielt hätte. **3. Wie sind Sie zur Aktfotografie gekommen?** Mit 14 fing ich an, meine Freundinnen zu fotografieren. Und obwohl wir damals eigentlich noch gar nicht wussten, was wir taten, sind die Fotos immer noch schön. **4. Wie casten Sie Ihre Modelle und was suchen Sie in ihnen?** Mein Casting-Prozess hat ganz verschiedene Formen. Ich halte auf der Straße die Augen auf, durchforste Model-Seiten im Internet und bekomme Bewerbungen aus aller Welt. Ich suche natürliche Modelle, Schönheiten mit viel Charakter. **5. Wenn Sie ein Modell auf der Straße ansprechen, wie gehen Sie vor, um sie dazu zu überreden, dass sie nackt vor Ihnen posiert?** Es ist ein weiter Weg von der Entdeckung auf der Straße bis zum Aktmodell. Beim „Straßen-Casting" bitte ich die Modelle nie, nackt vor mir zu posieren. Wir vereinbaren zunächst eine Porträt-Session, bei der die Modelle meine Arbeitsweise kennenlernen. Von den Frauen, die ich von der Straße weg gecastet habe, lassen sich nur ganz wenige nackt fotografieren. **6. Welche künstlerischen Elemente machen ein Stefan-Soell-Foto einzigartig?** In erster Linie die Belichtung und die starke Verbindung zwischen dem Modell und der Location. Zum Zweiten ist es die vertraute, intime und entspannte Atmosphäre der Bilder. **7. Betrachten Sie das, was Sie tun, als erotische Fotografie oder Kunst?** Ich denke, es ist beides, Kunst und erotische Fotografie. Es gibt unterschiedliche Stille in meiner Arbeit. Meine Schwarz-Weiß-Fotos sind näher an Kunst als die Farbfotos. Meine Bildsprache enthält künstlerische wie klassische Posen. Aber all meinen Bildern ist anzusehen, dass sie denselben künstlerischen Ursprung haben **8. Wie haben sich Ihre fotografischen Ziele und künstlerischen Methoden im Laufe der Jahre verändert?** Es war immer mein Ziel, meine Modelle mit noch traumhafteren Landschaften und Locations zu verbinden. Ein radikaler Schritt war der Umstieg auf digitale Technik vor zwölf Jahren. Davor benutzte ich aus Gründen der Bildqualität eine Mittelformatkamera. Ich verwendete ausschließlich Schwarz-Weiß-Filme und entwickelte alle Filme und Abzüge in meiner eigenen Dunkelkammer. Das war SEHR zeitaufwendig. Nach dem Wechsel zur Digitalfotografie kam ich nach und nach zur Farbfotografie.

9. Wen bewundern Sie und warum? Ich habe großen Respekt vor all meinen Aktmodellen. Sie sind nicht nur schöne Körper: Jedes einzelne Modell hat seinen eigenen persönlichen Charakter. Jedem meiner Bilder schenken sie einen Teil ihrer Seele. **10. Verraten Sie uns, wie Sie entscheiden, wo und wie ein Modell fotografiert wird?** Der Entscheidungsprozess ist kompliziert. Ich durchstreife die Gegend, immer auf der Suche nach besonderen Orten mit einer „speziellen" Aura. Je nach Jahreszeit gibt es viele Faktoren, die eine „gute" Location ausmachen. Ich weiß nicht warum, aber ich muss mich in einer besonderen Stimmung befinden, um eine „gute" Location auch als solche zu erkennen. Manchmal sind die Orte schwer zu erreichen und ich bin froh, wenn meine Modelle vom langen Wandern nicht völlig erledigt sind ;-). Meine Models bauen immer eine enge Verbindung zu den Orten auf, an denen ich sie fotografiere, und das versuche ich, in meine Bilder mit hineinzubringen. **11. Welche Künstler haben Sie am stärksten beeinflusst?** Es gibt keinen speziellen Künstler, der mich geprägt hätte. Ein wichtiger Einfluss waren die Fotografen aus der Anfangszeit der Fotografie, aber heute sind es die Mythen, Märchen und Legenden, die meine Phantasie beflügeln. **12. Verraten Sie uns, was Sie zu Ihren Modellen sagen, wenn Sie sie fotografieren? Reden Sie viel, schlagen Sie Posen vor oder lassen Sie sie ihr eigenes Ding machen?** Das hängt davon ab, wie oft ich schon mit einem Modell zusammengearbeitet habe. Am Anfang rede ich SEHR viel, um die komplette Aufmerksamkeit des Modells zu bekommen. Wir albern herum und lachen viel, und plötzlich ist da ein unsichtbares Band zwischen dem Modell und mir – von da an übernimmt das Shooting die Kontrolle und ich gebe nur noch kurze Anweisungen, um eine Pose zu korrigieren. **13. Gibt es einen bestimmten Teil des weiblichen Körpers, der Sie besonders interessiert?** Ich habe schöne Frauen schon immer geliebt. Es ist komisch, aber während meiner gesamten Fotografenlaufbahn war ich immer vor allem vom Wesen und Gesicht eines Modells fasziniert. **14. Wenn Sie jemandem, der ein großer Erotik Fotograf werden will, drei Tipps geben müssten, was würden Sie ihm raten?** – Hör auf deine Phantasie und versuche, deine Träume und Wünsche in Fotografien zu verwandeln. – Du brauchst kein teures Equipment. – Kopiere nicht die Bilder anderer Fotografen. Benutze deren Bilder nur, um deine eigene Kreativität zu stimulieren. – Und versuche, hartnäckig zu bleiben :-)

→ **www.stefansoell.de**

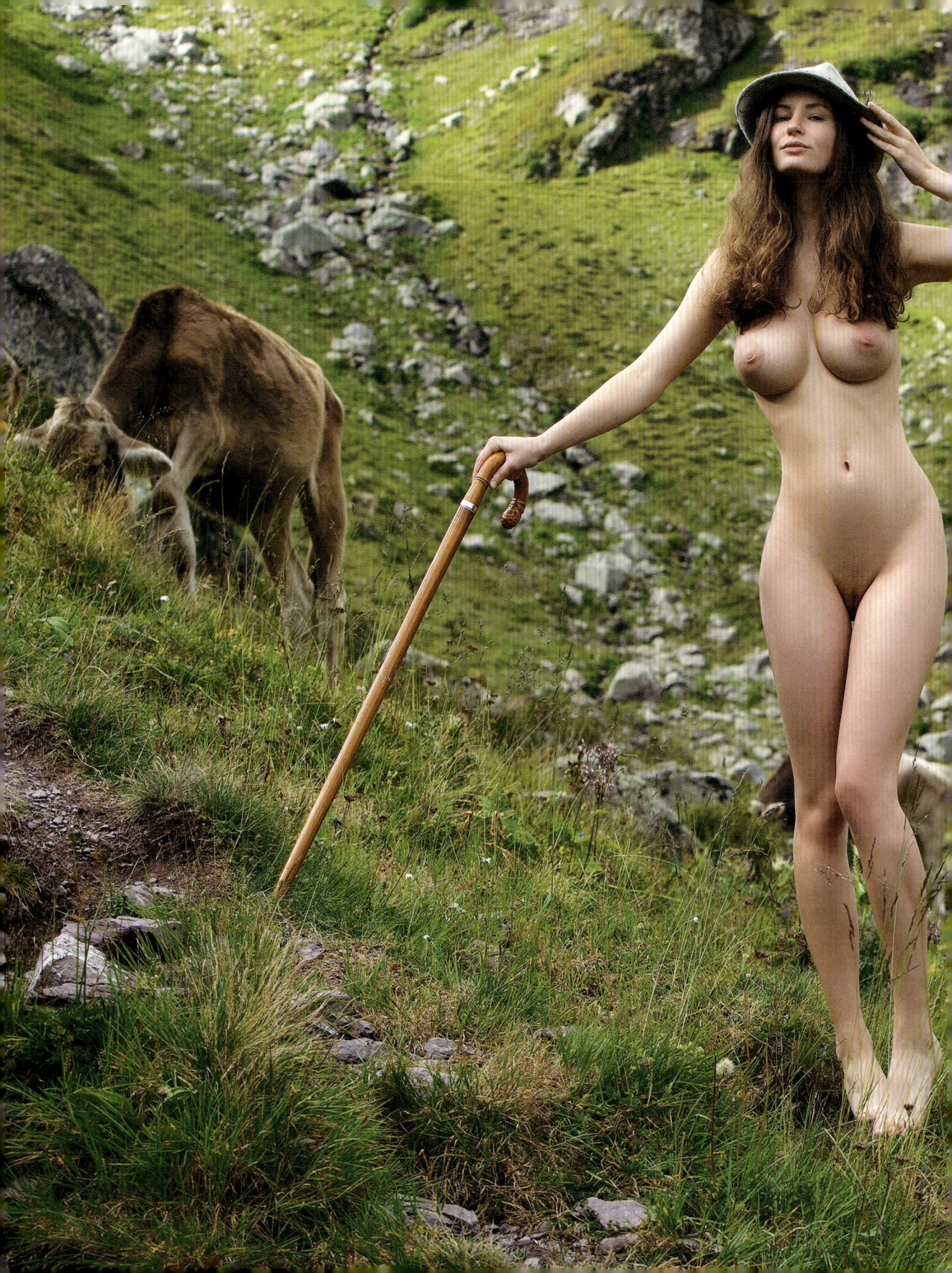

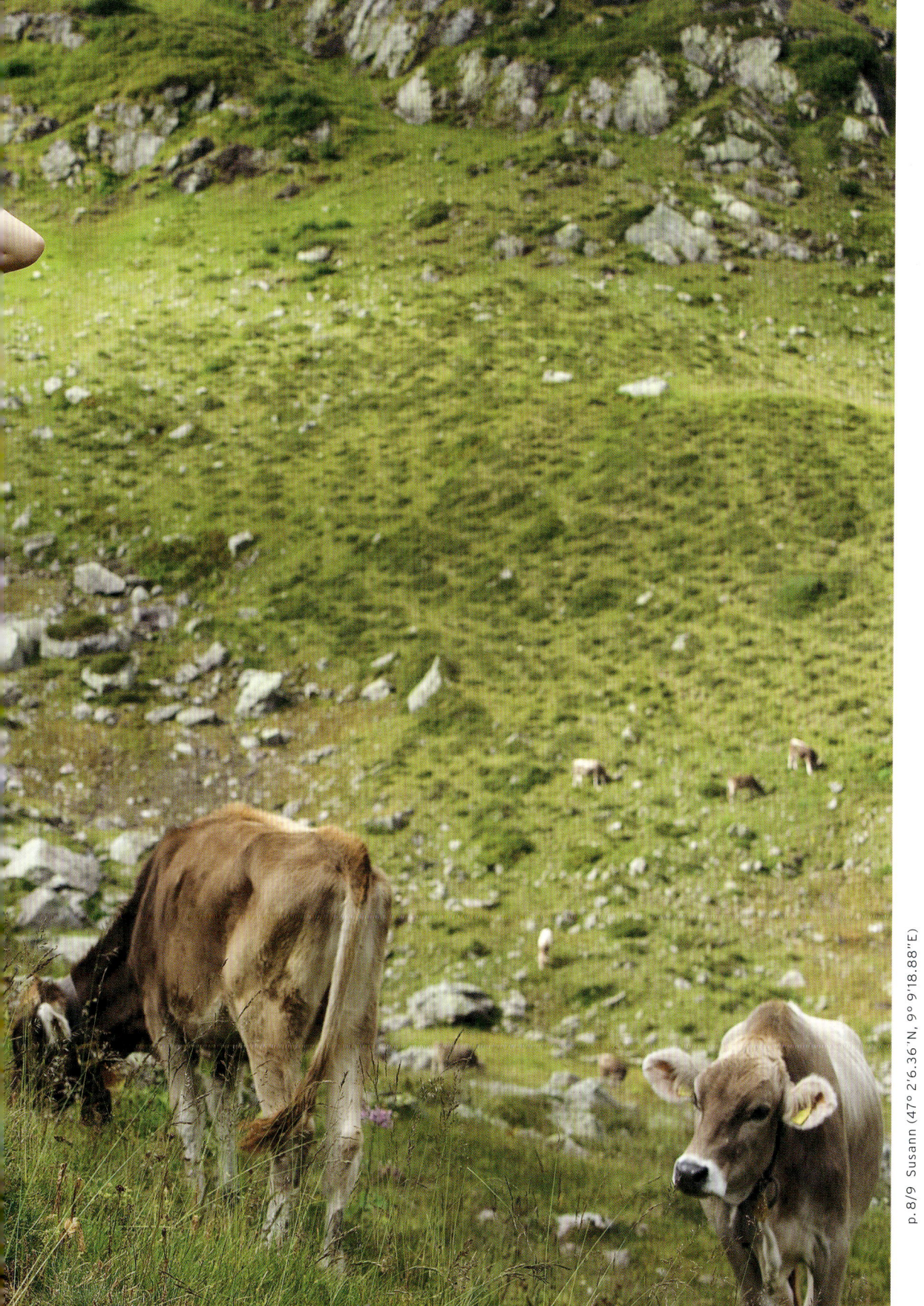

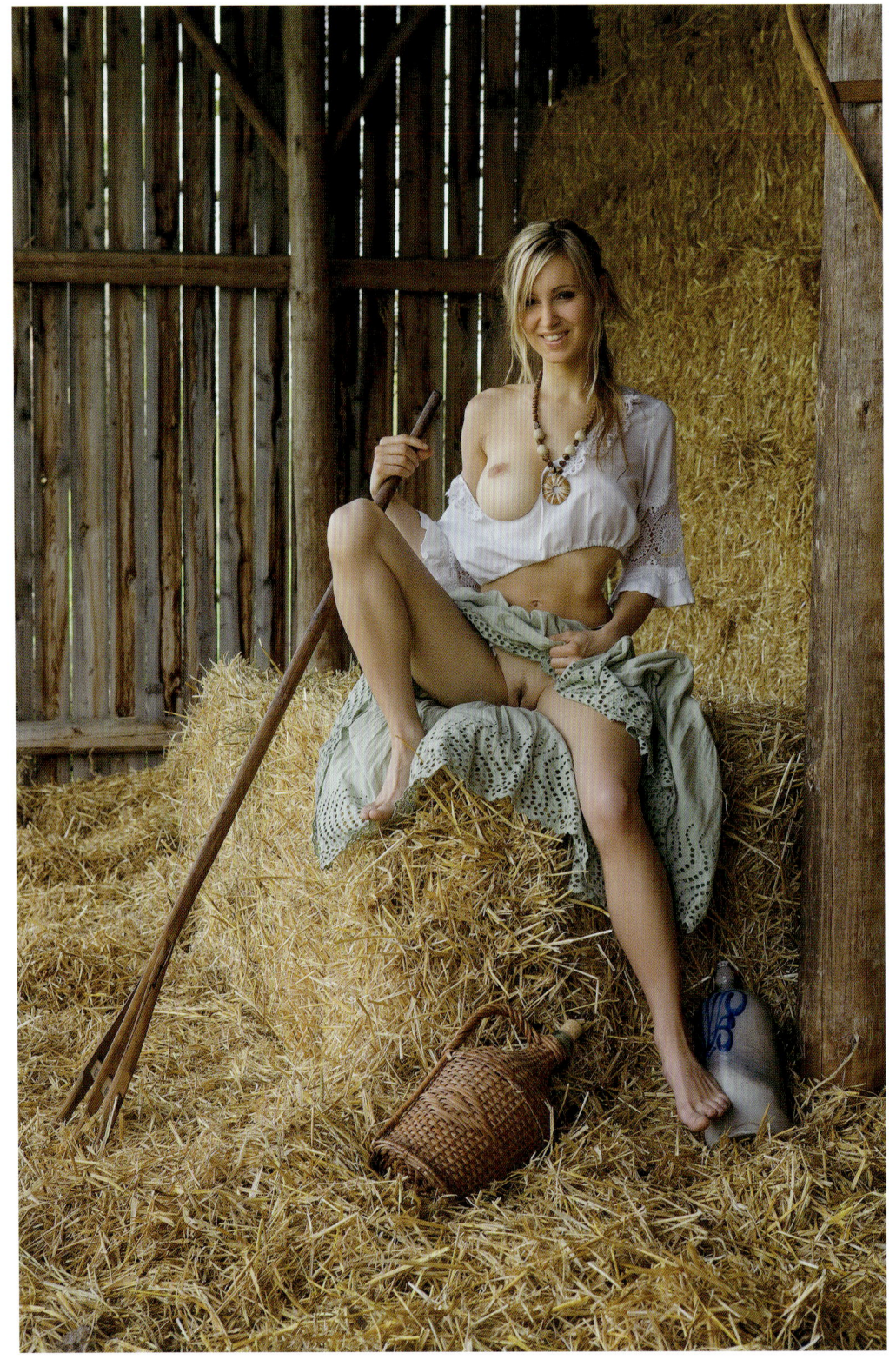

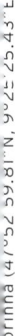

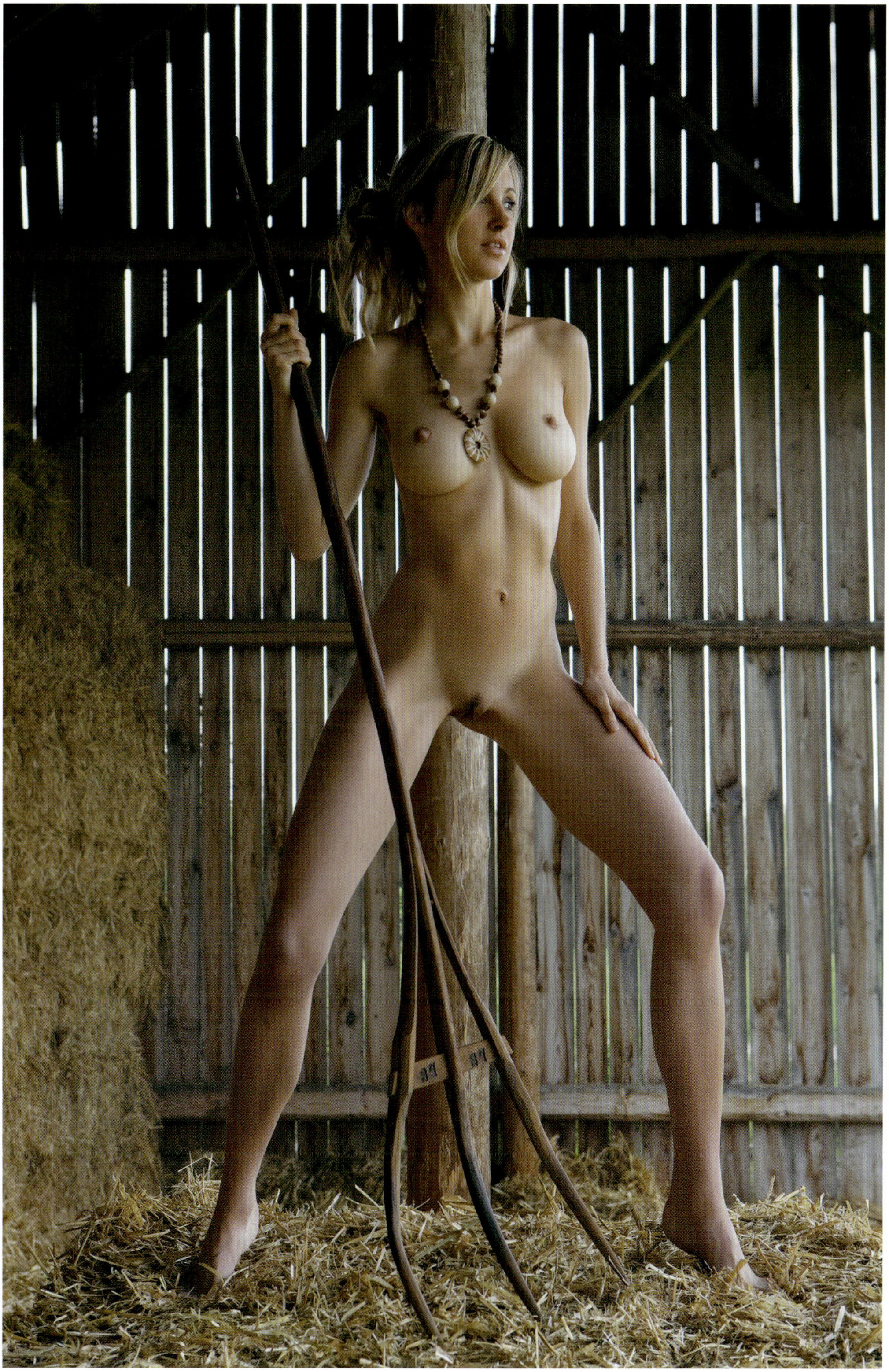

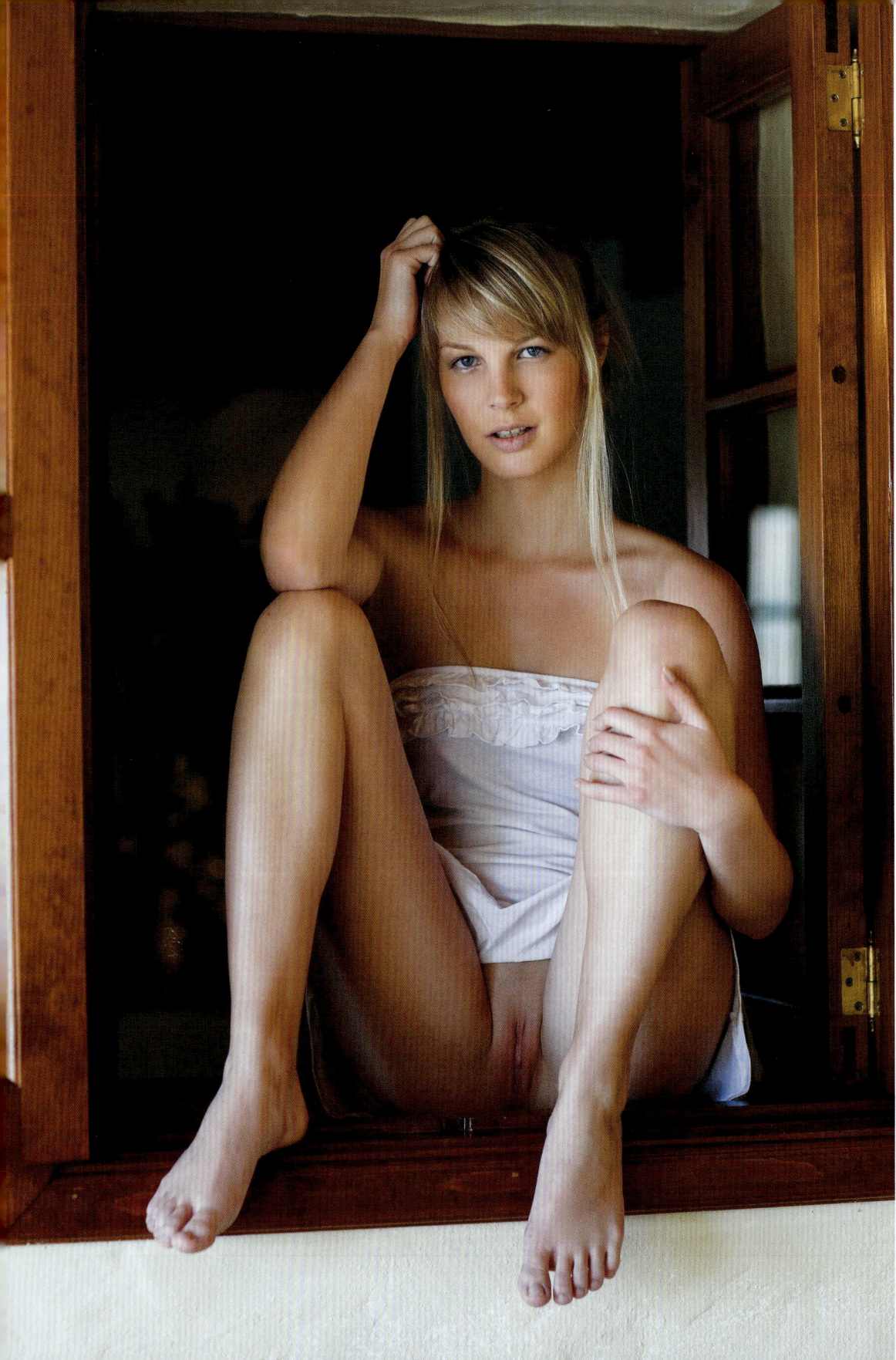

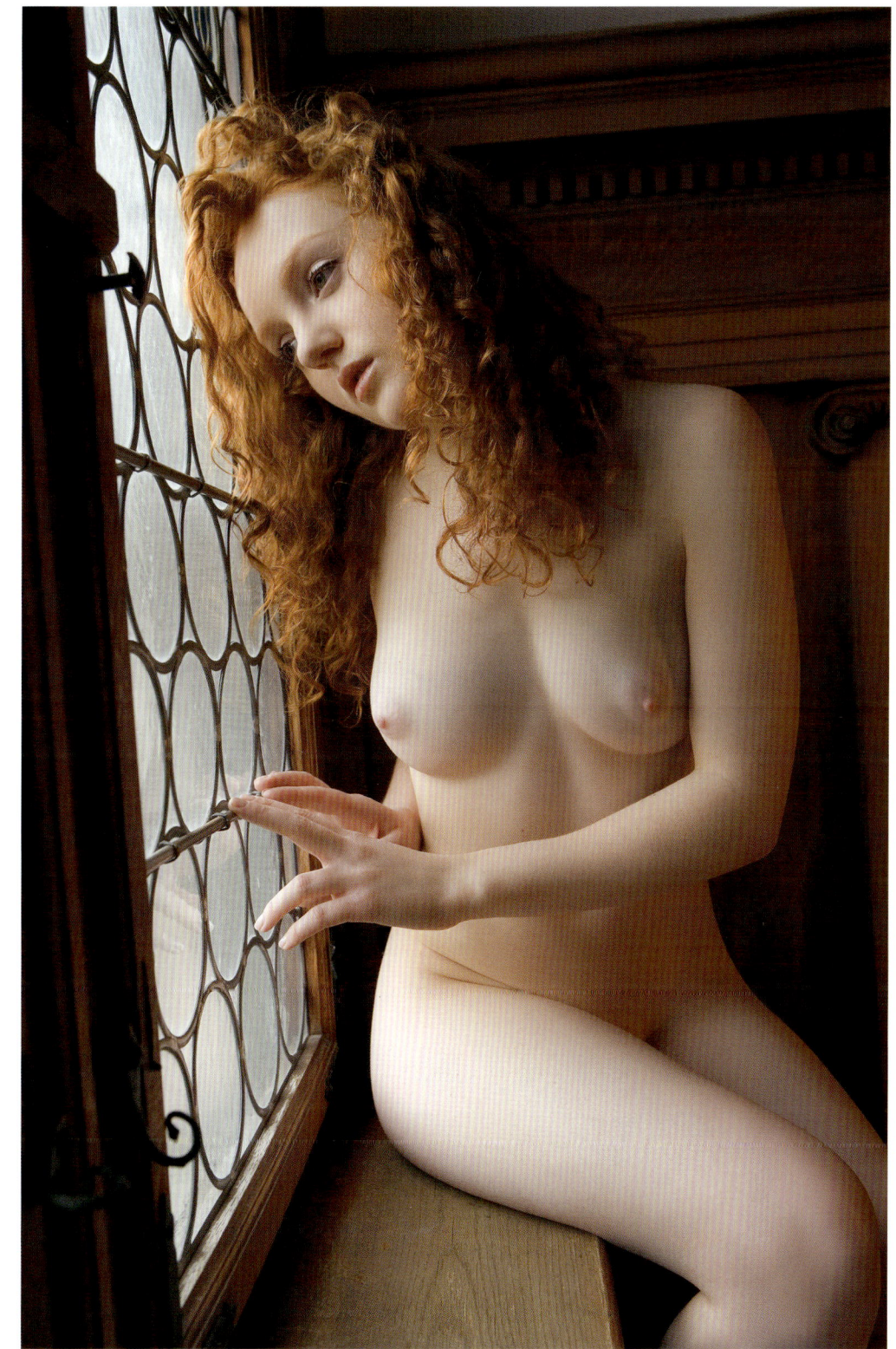

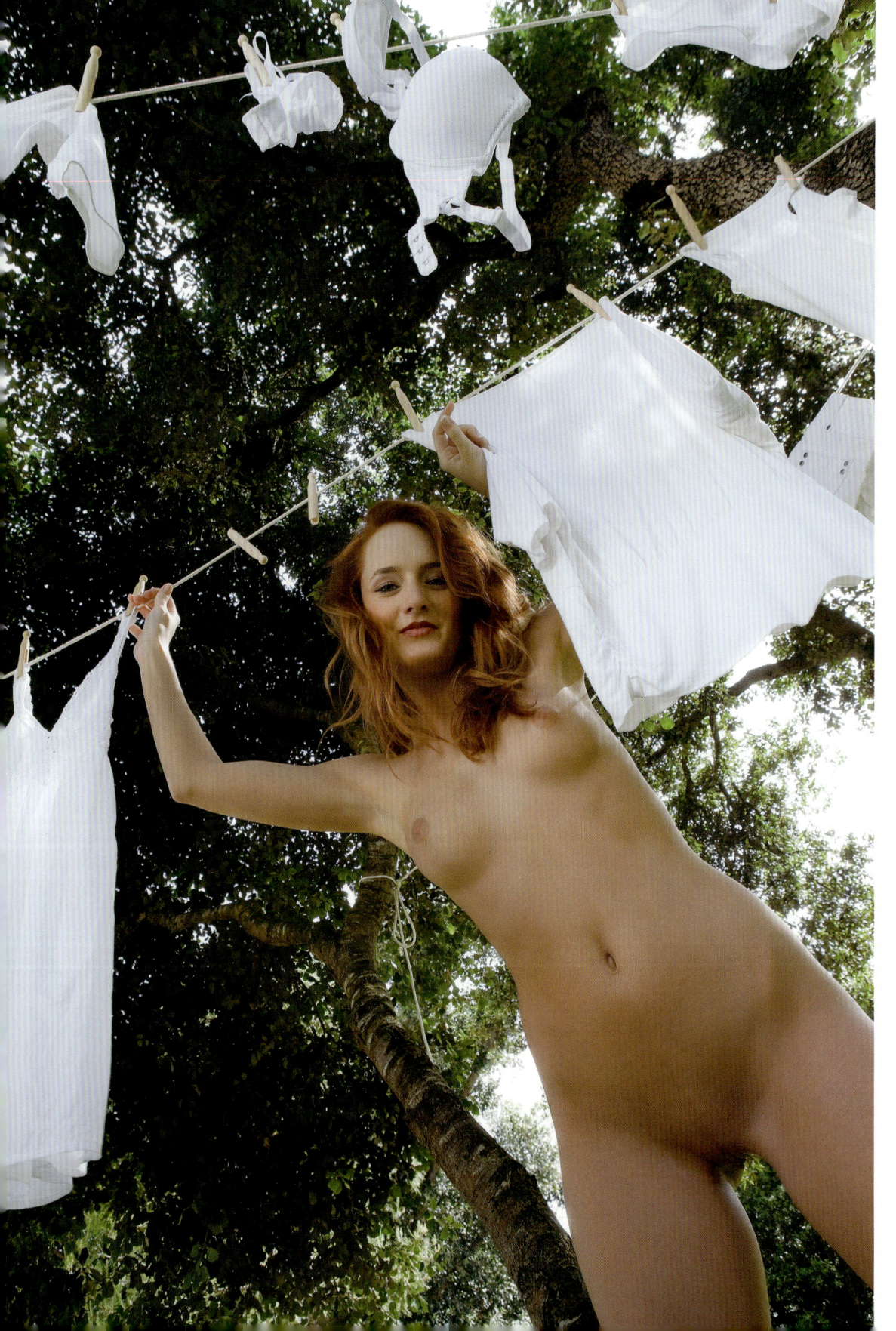

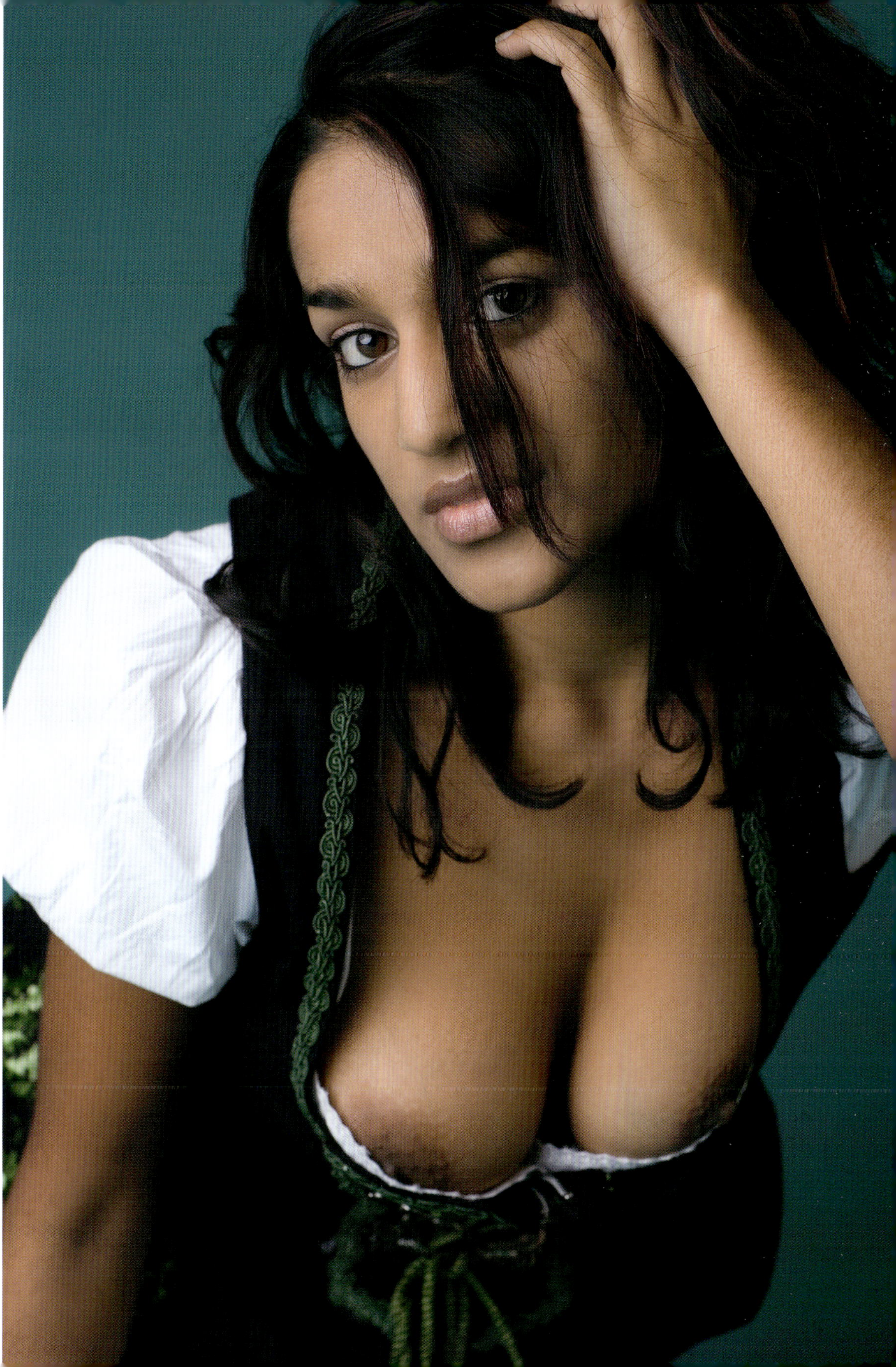

p.15 Sujatha (47°39'54.32"N, 9°26'40.18"E)

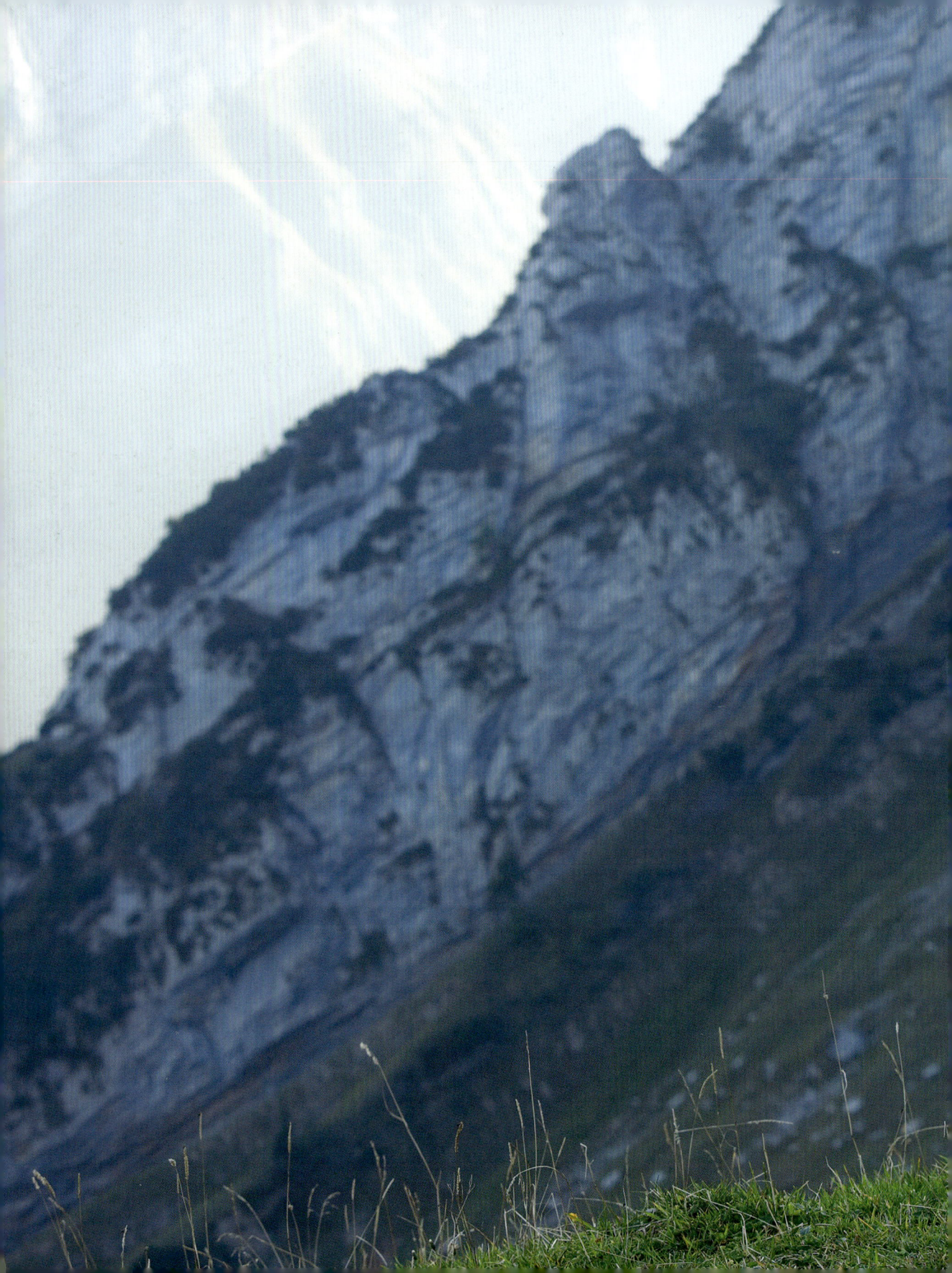

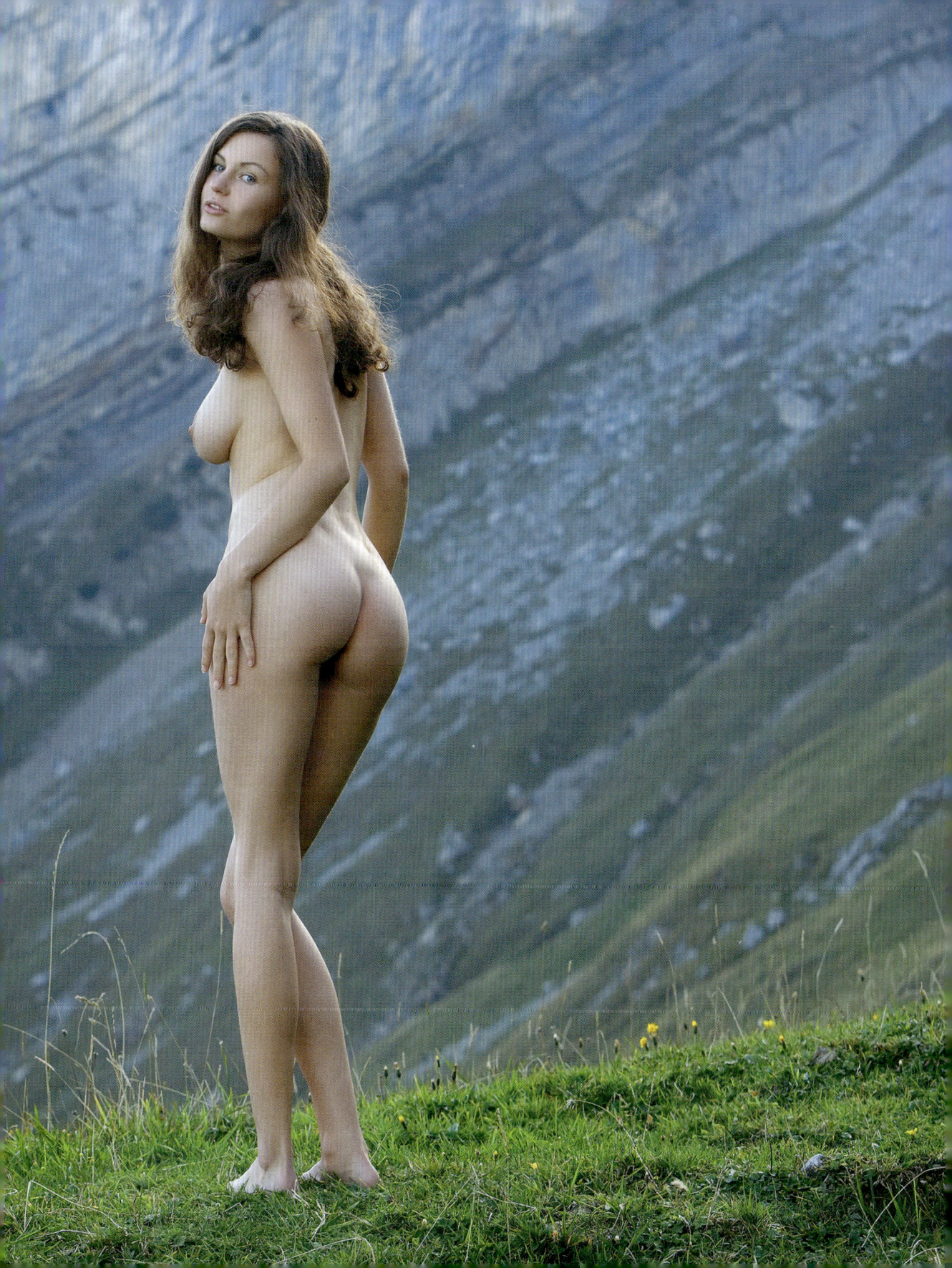

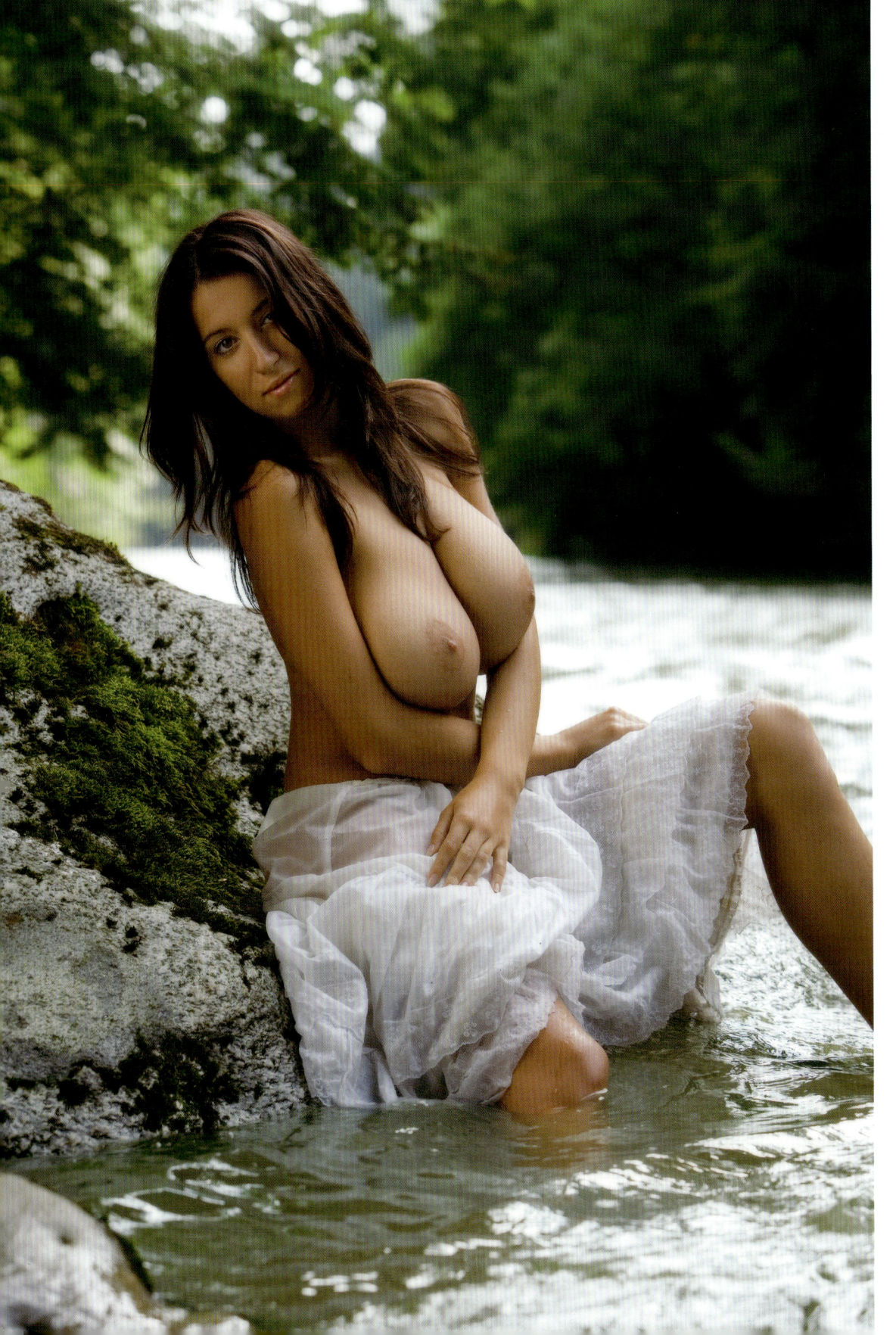

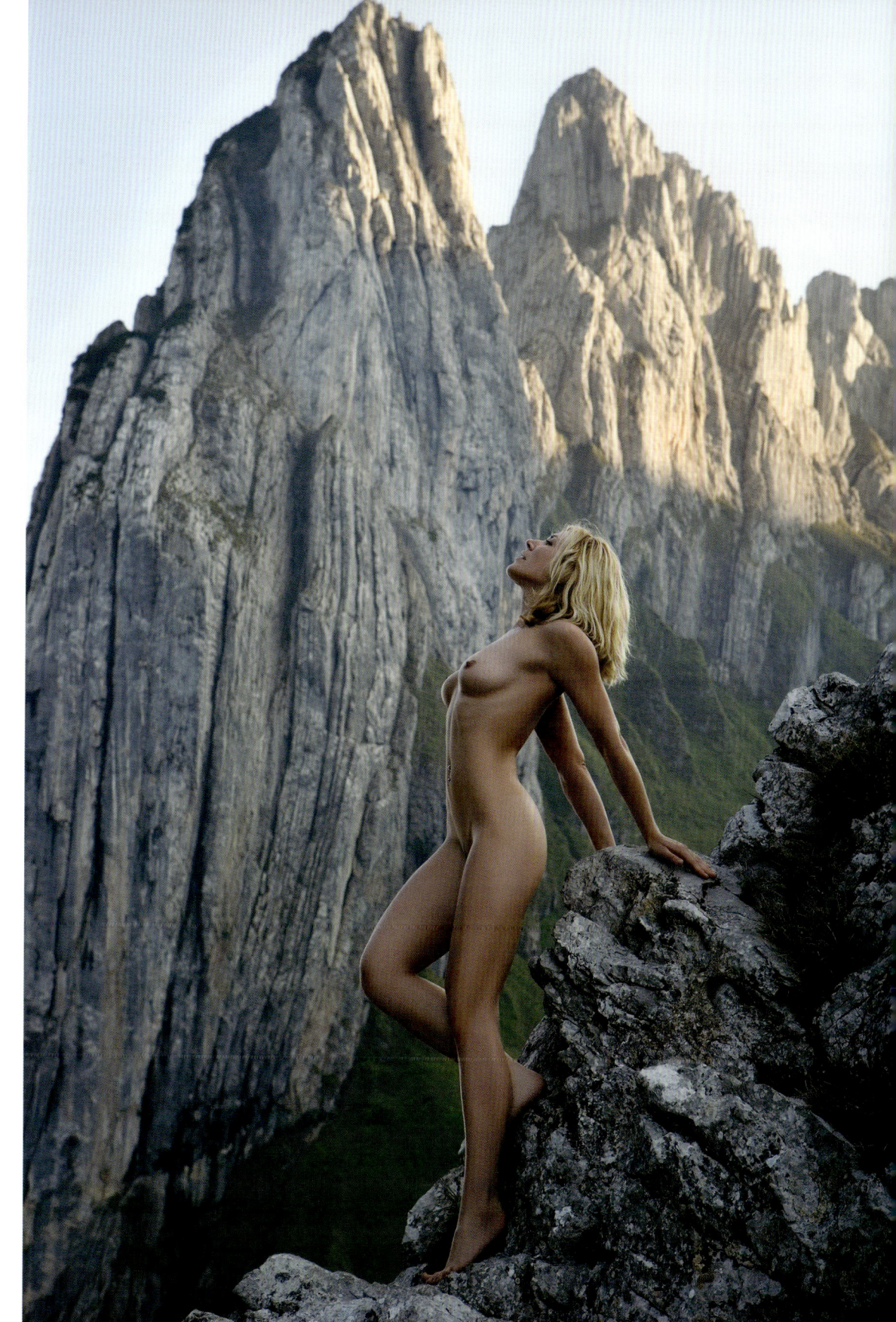

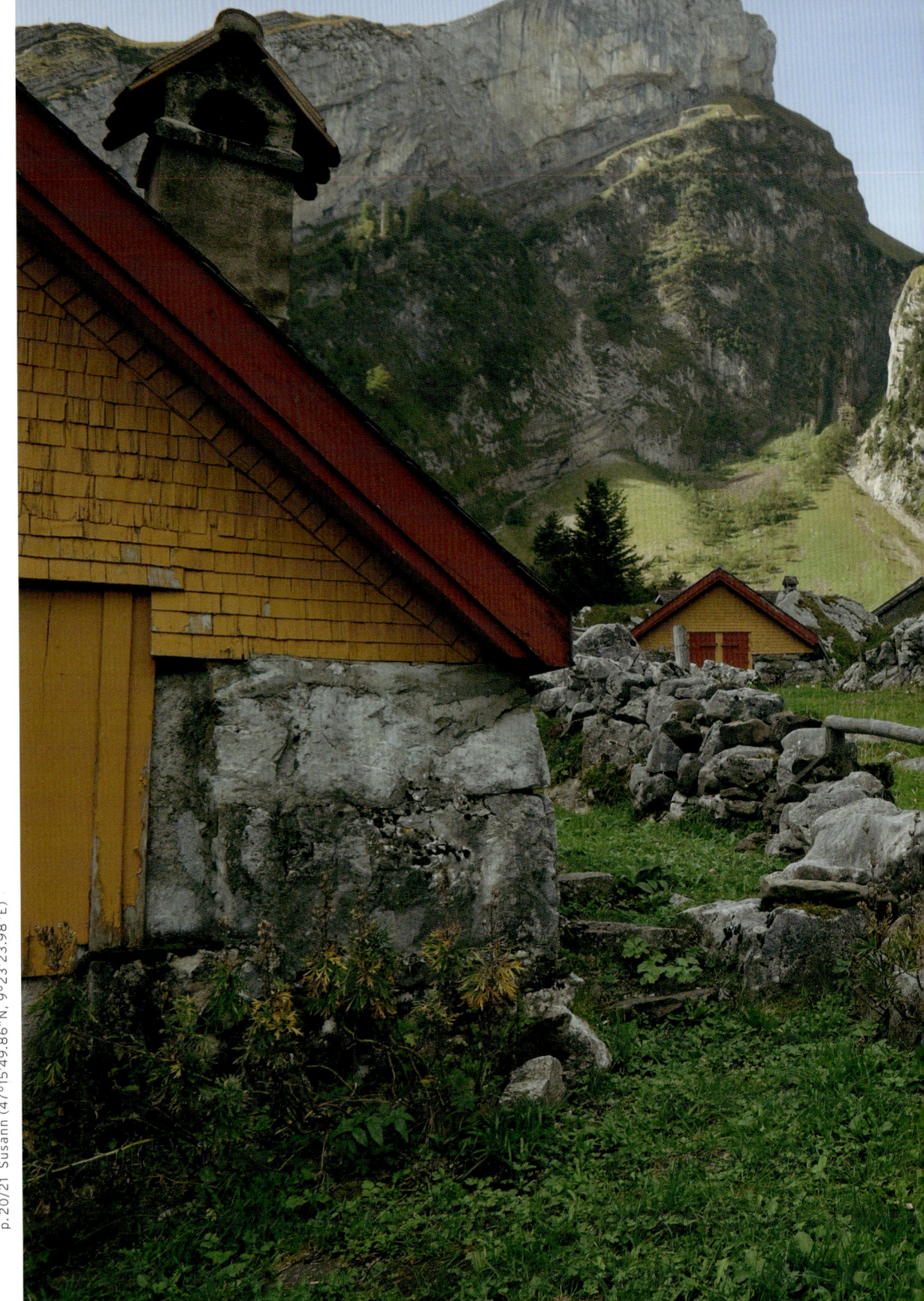

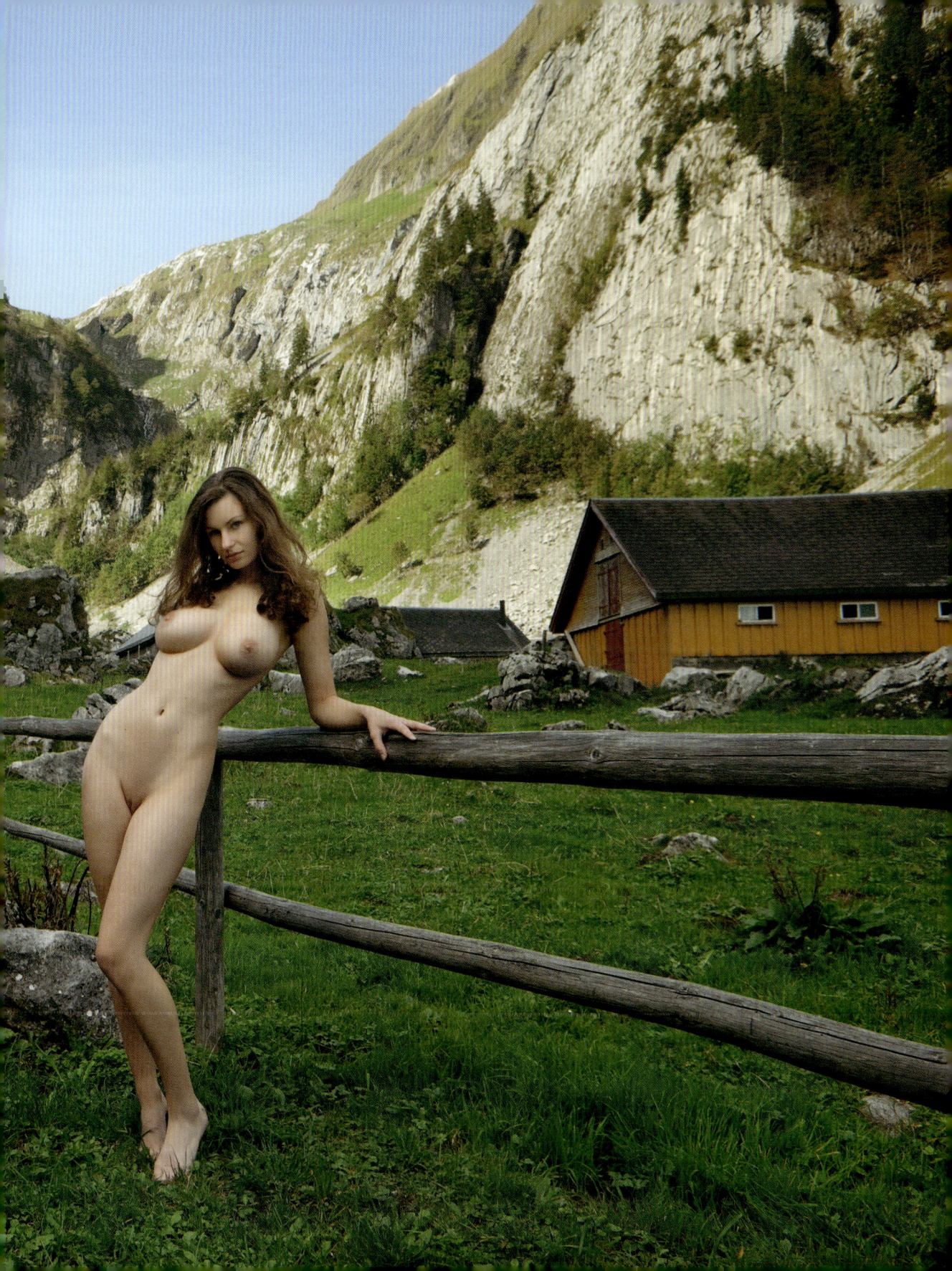

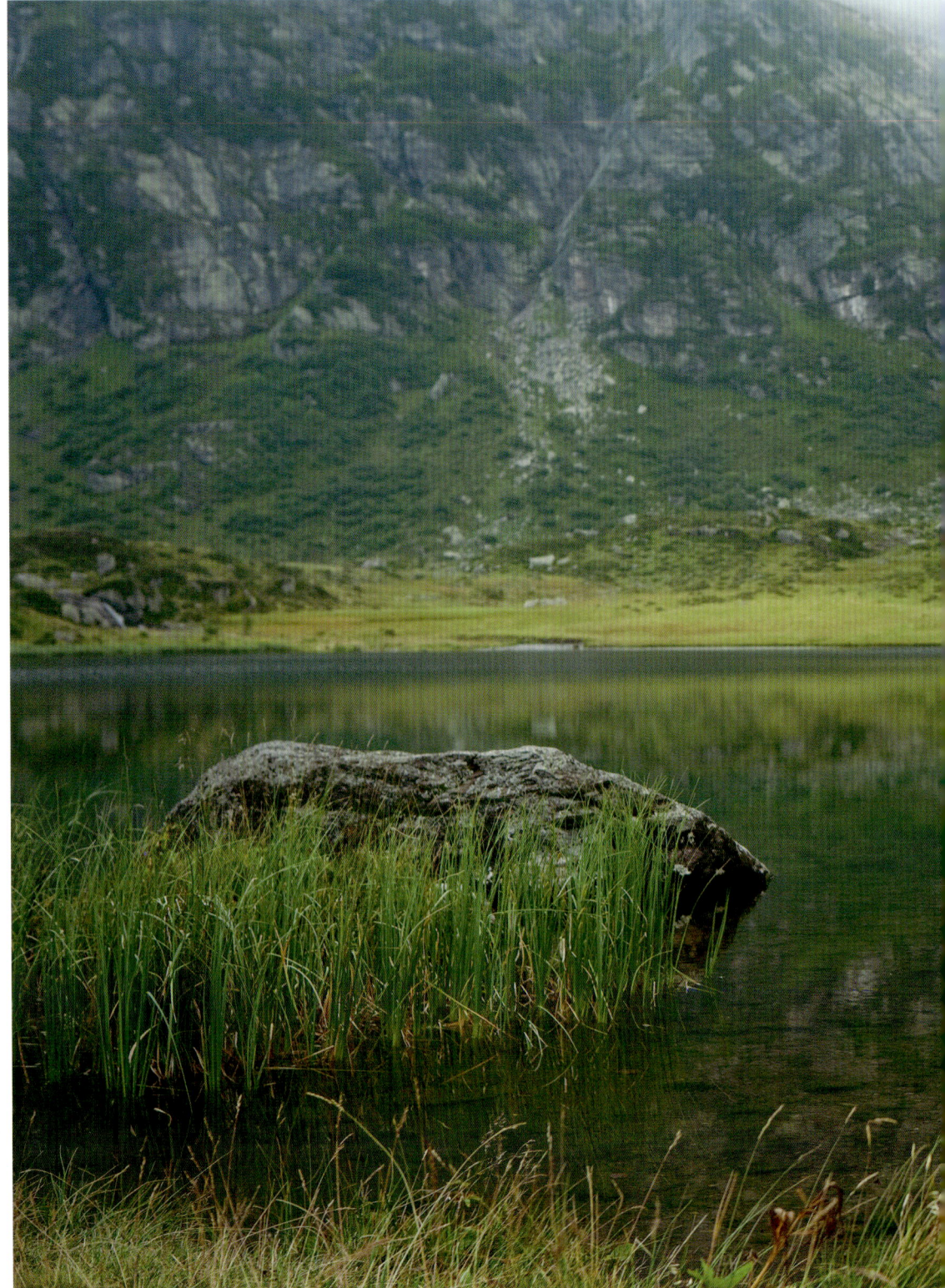

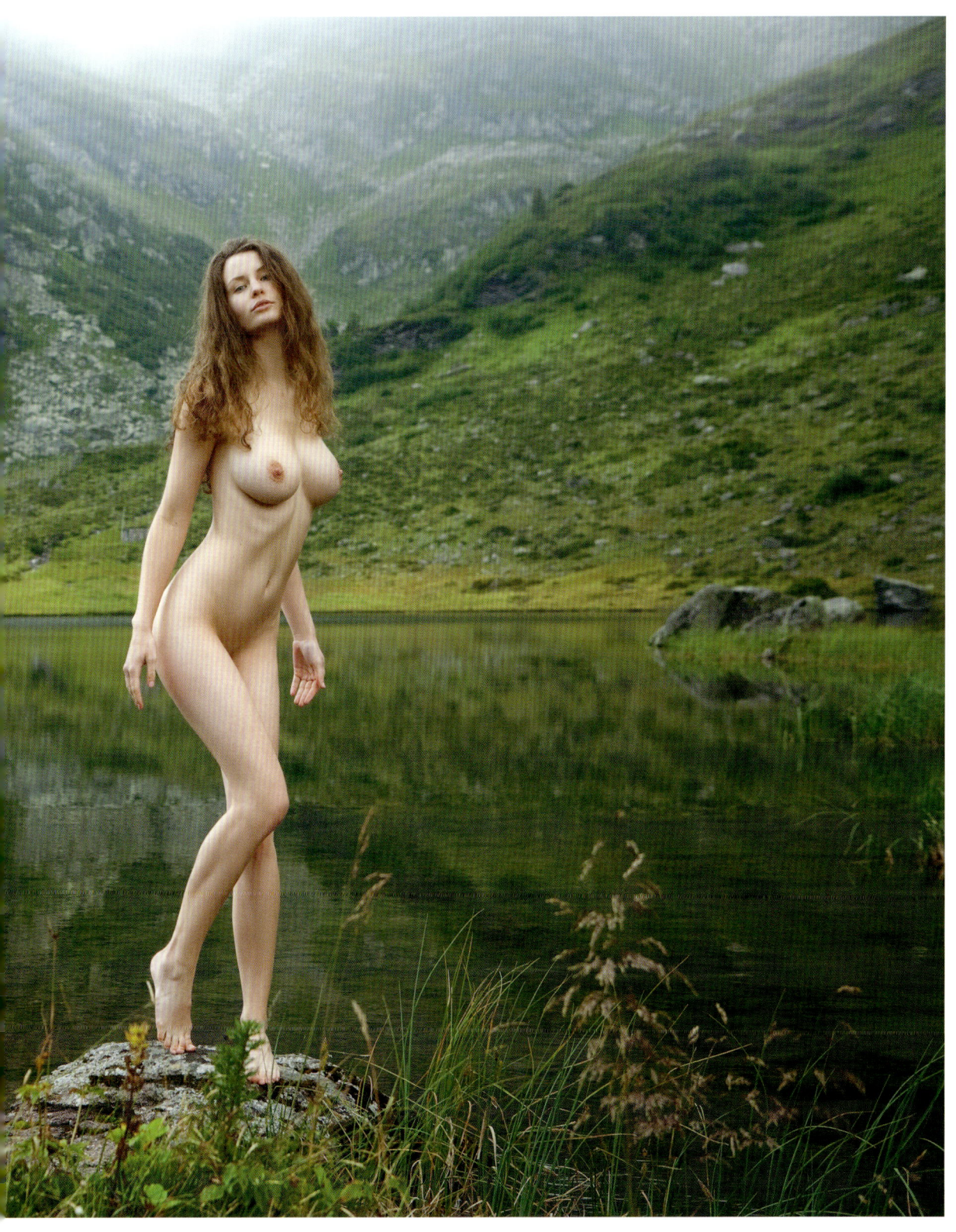

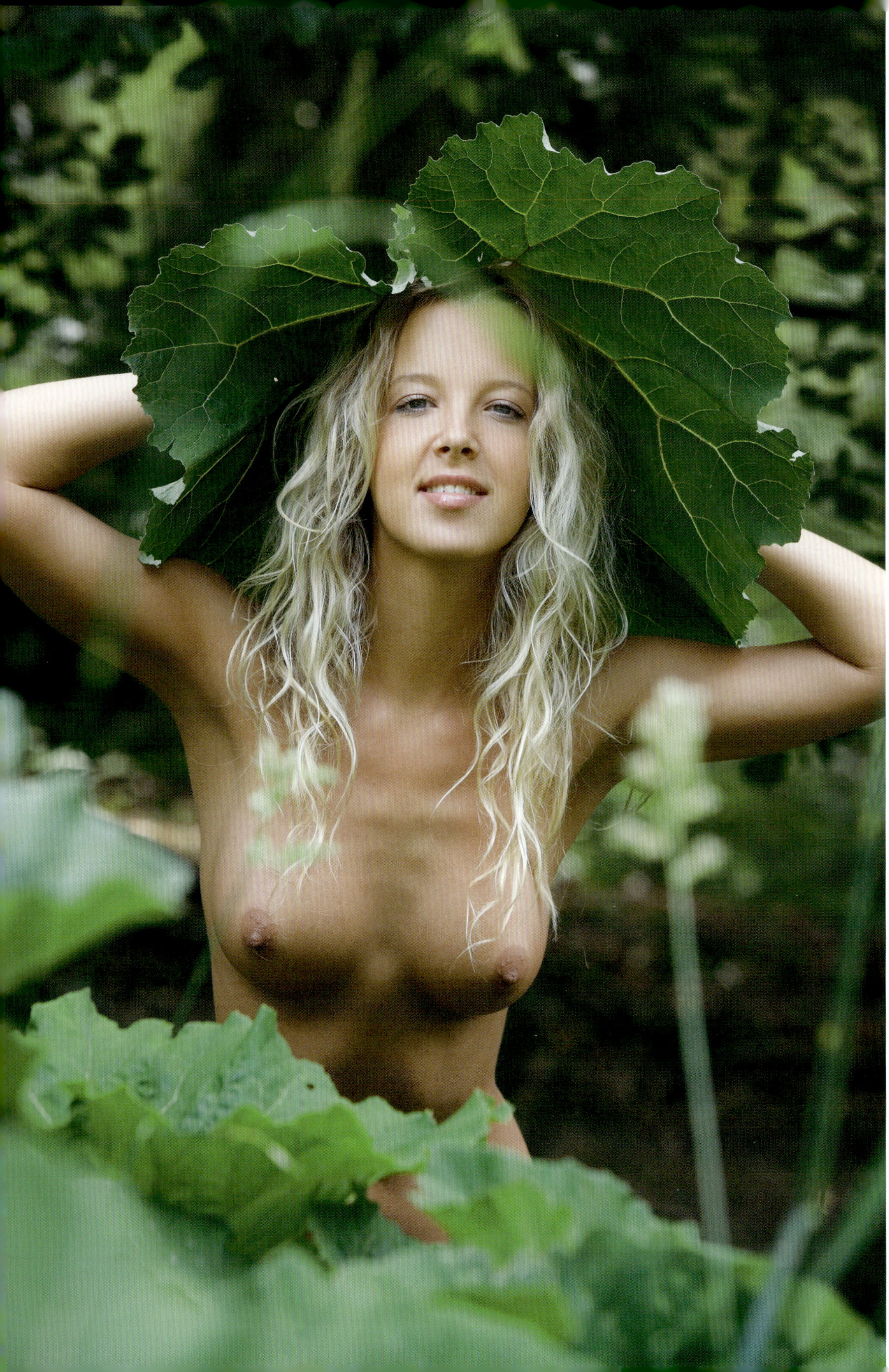

p.24 Anke (47°38'11.99"N, 9°42'58.37"E)

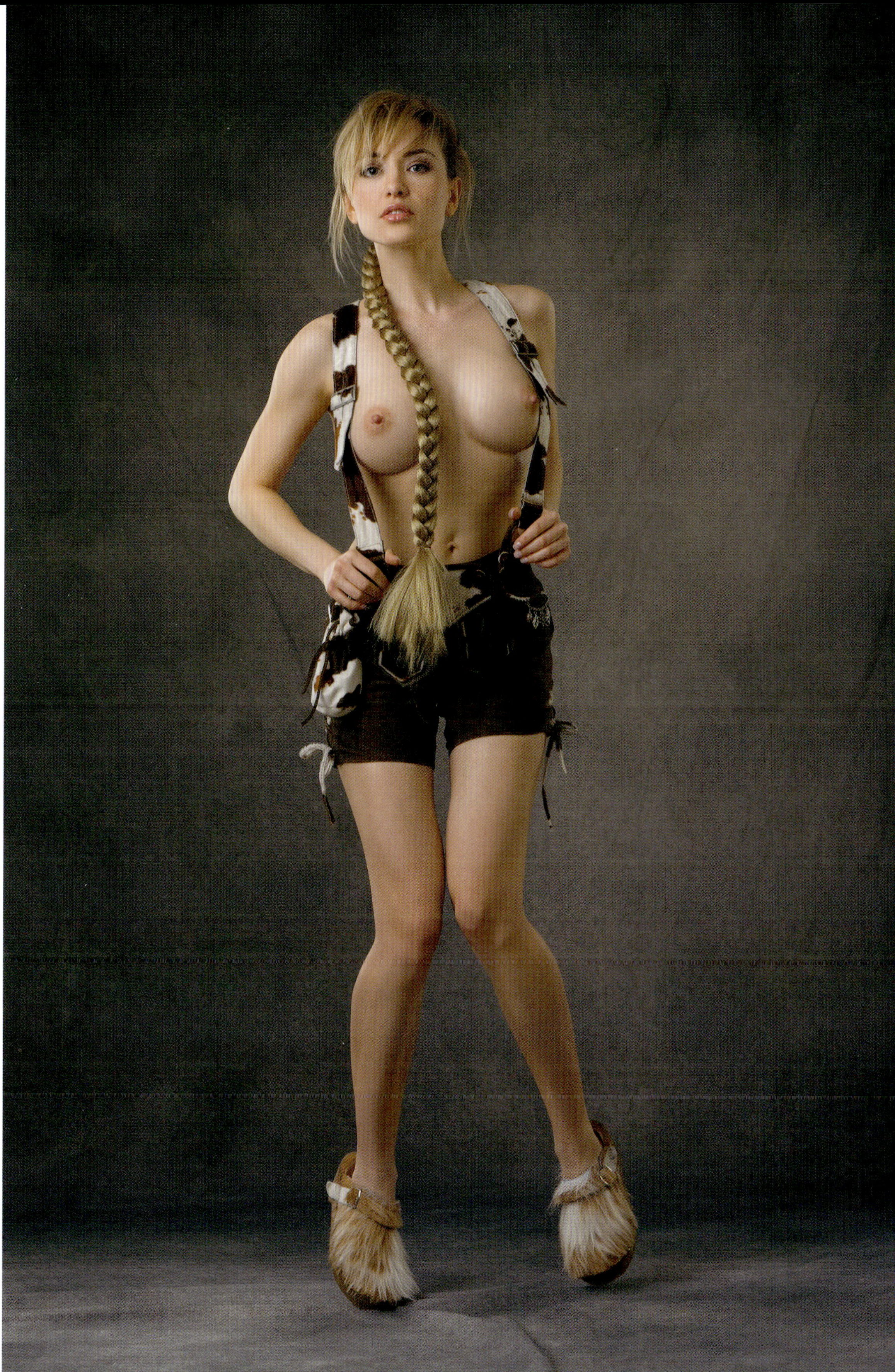

p. 25 Lia (47°39'54.32"N, 9°26'40.18"E)

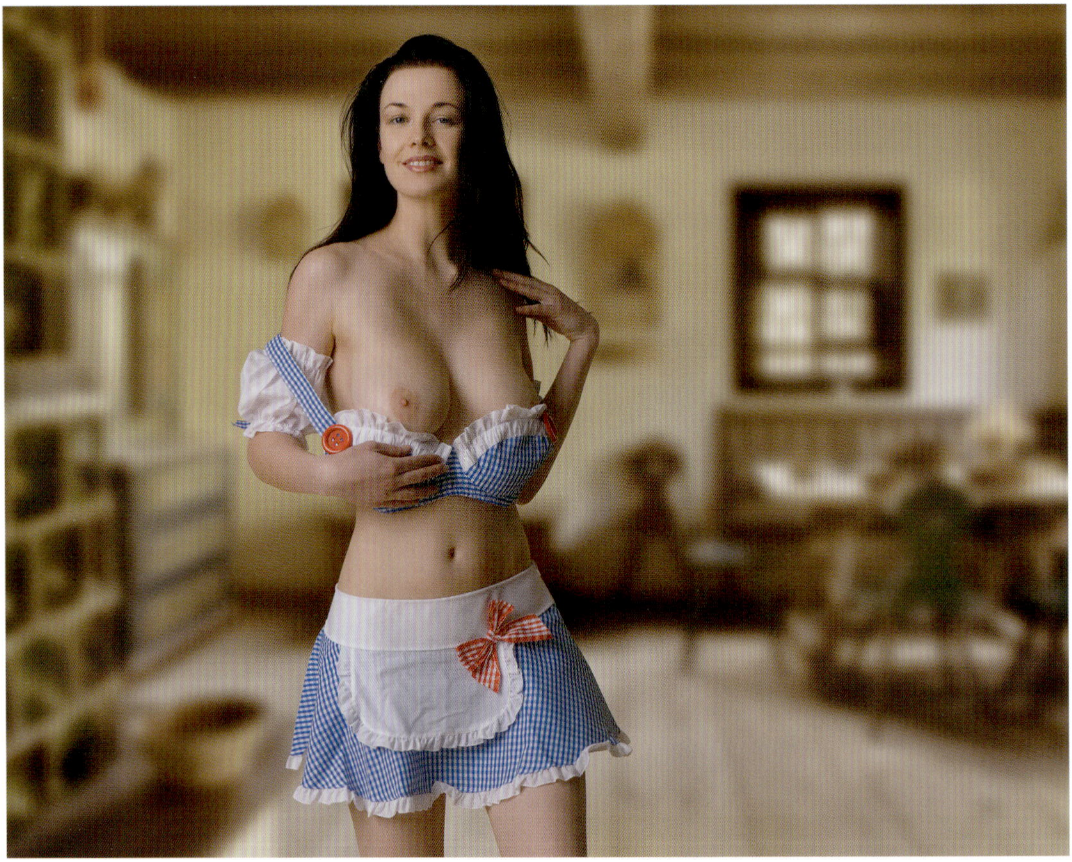

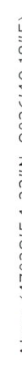

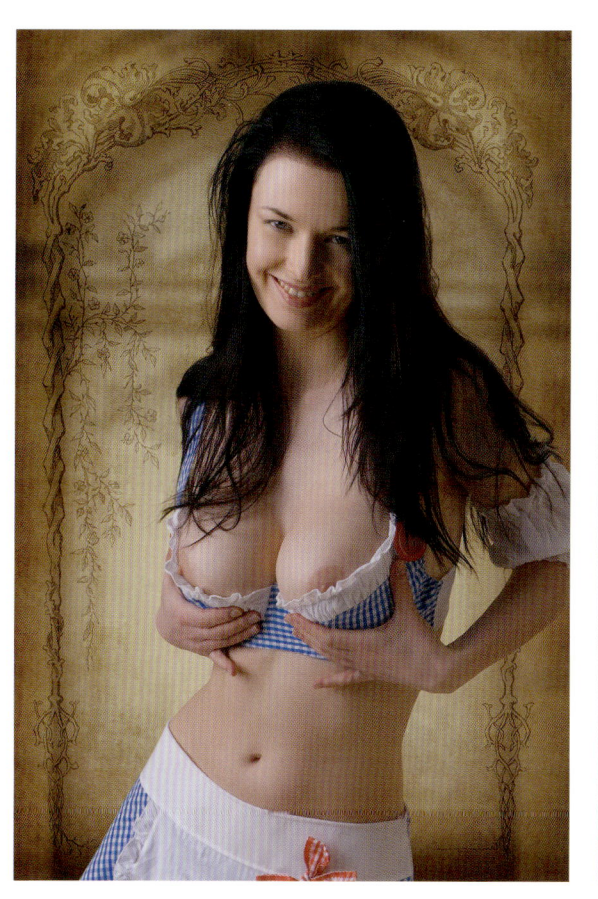 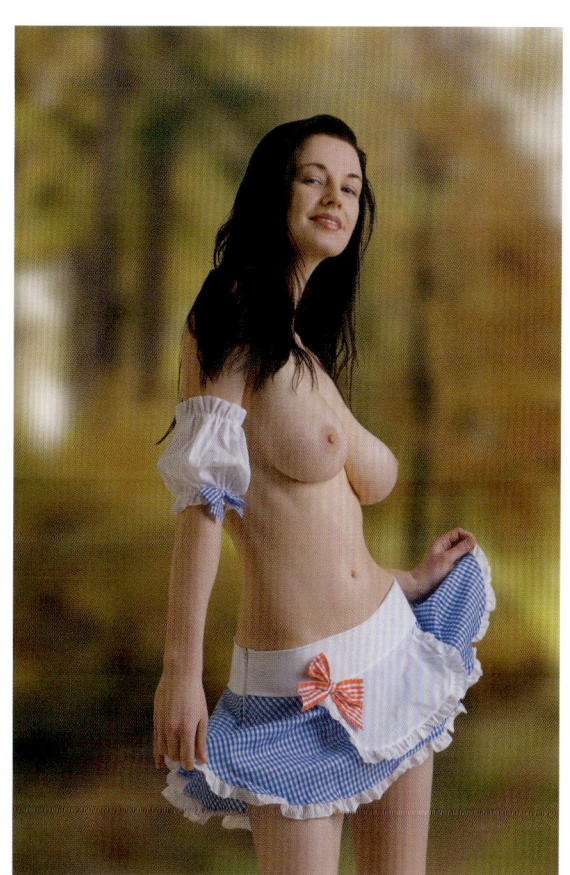

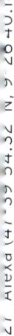

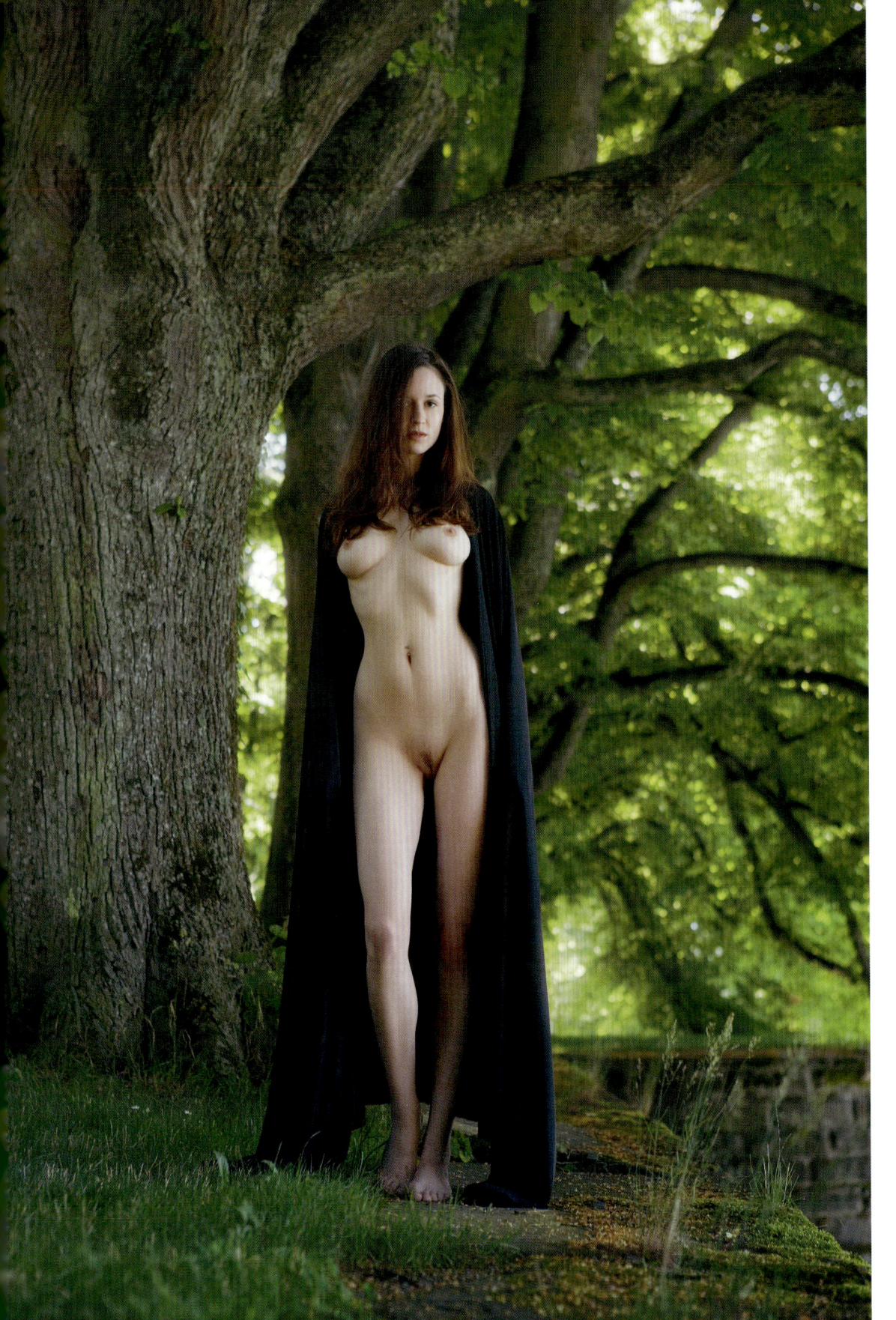

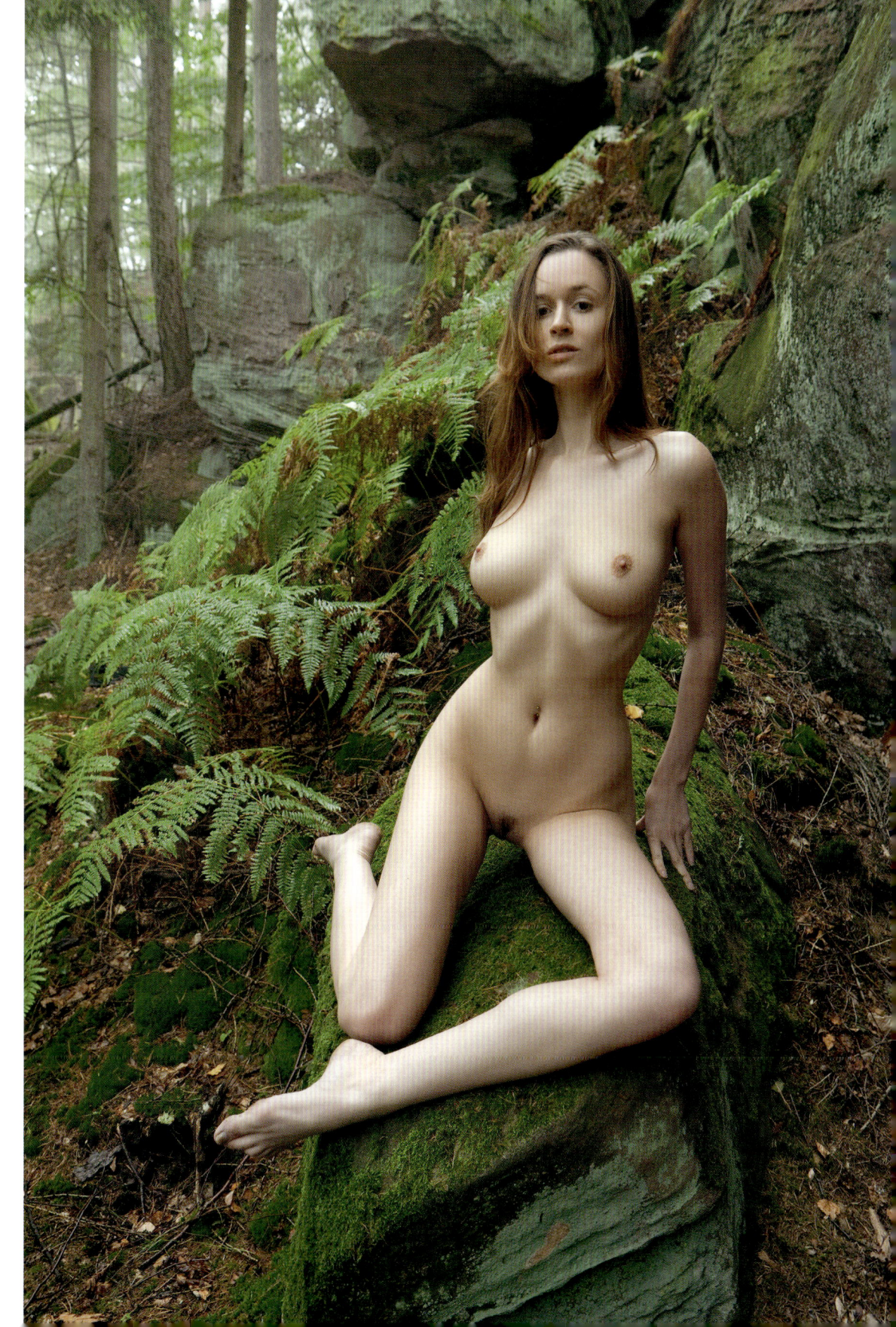

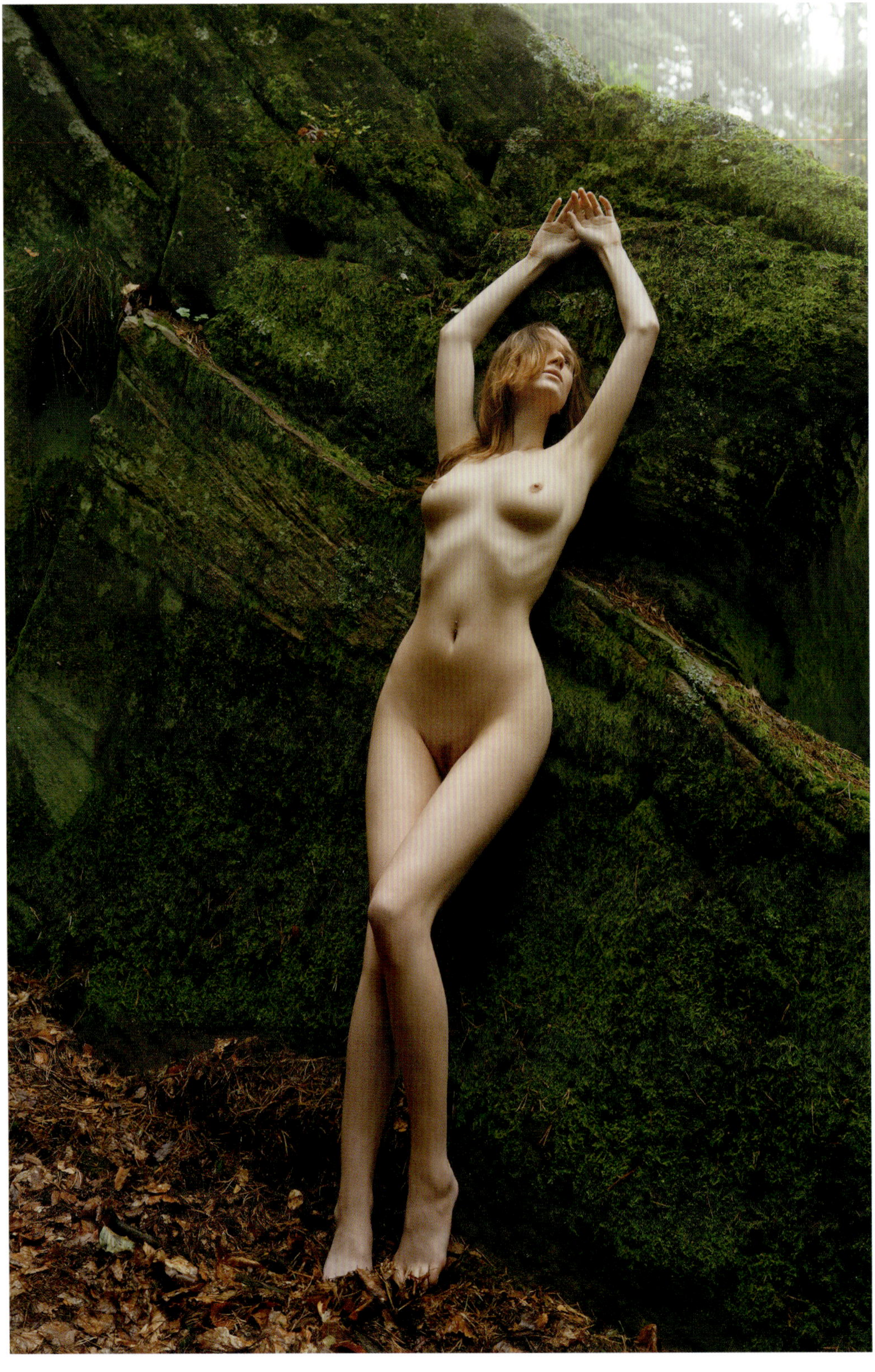

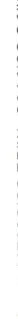

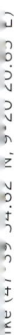

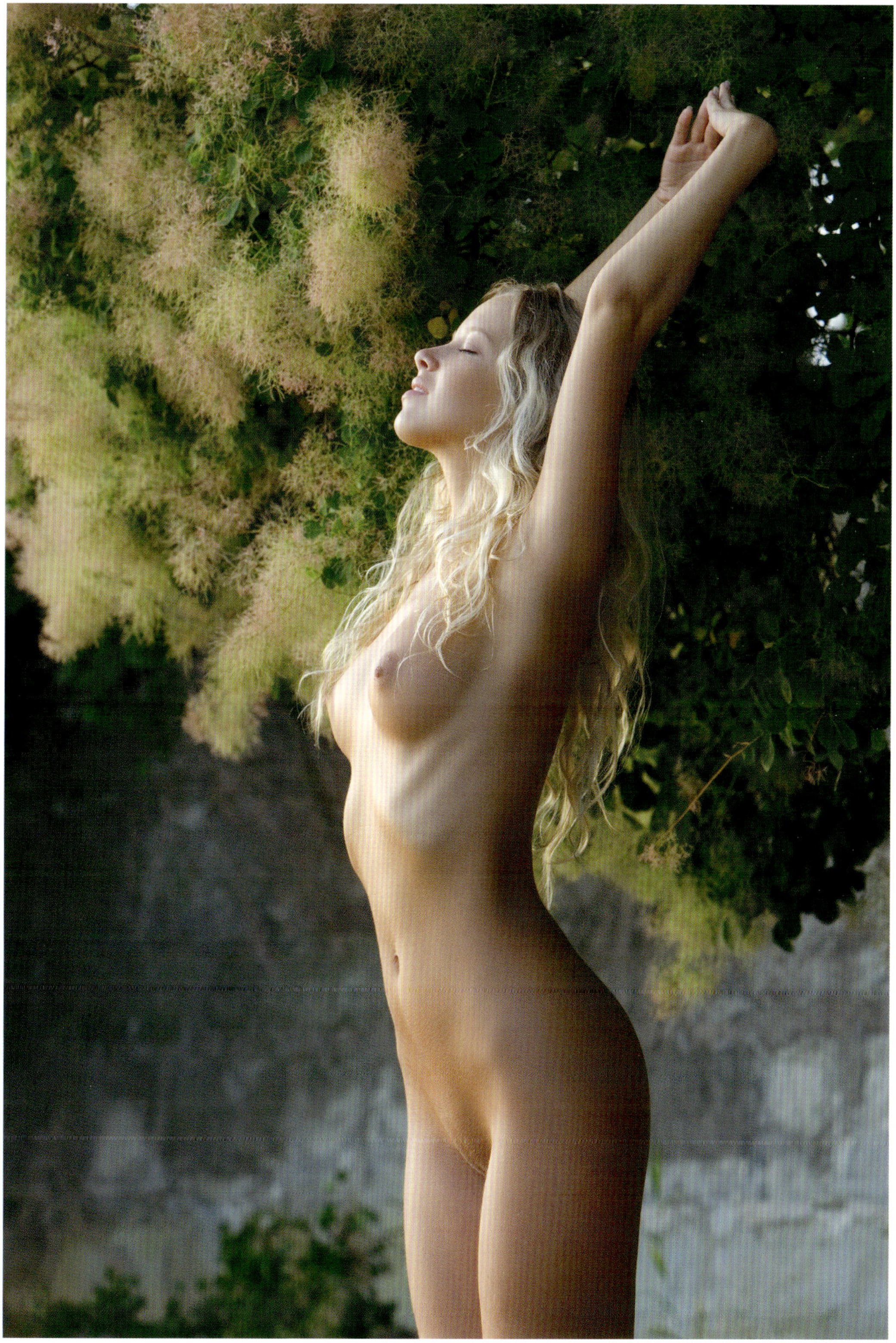

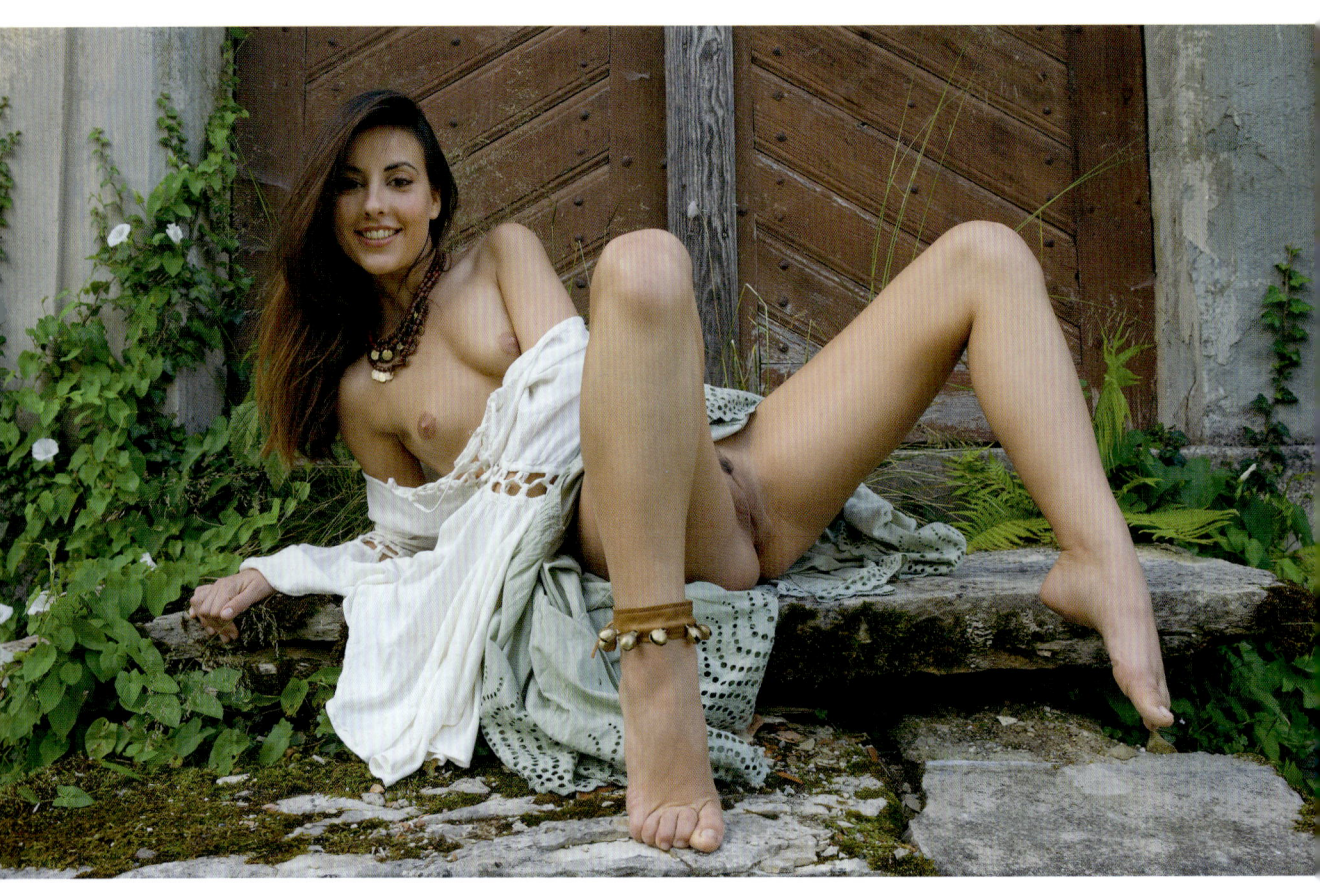

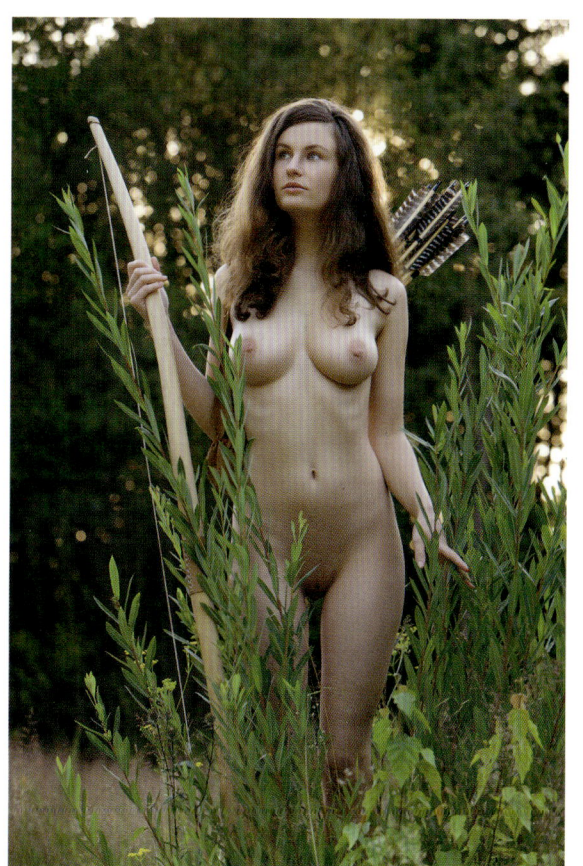
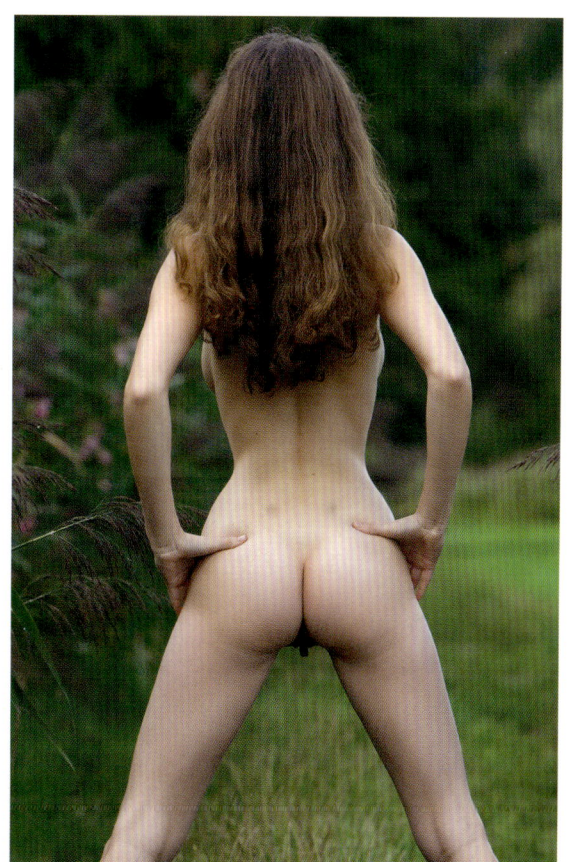

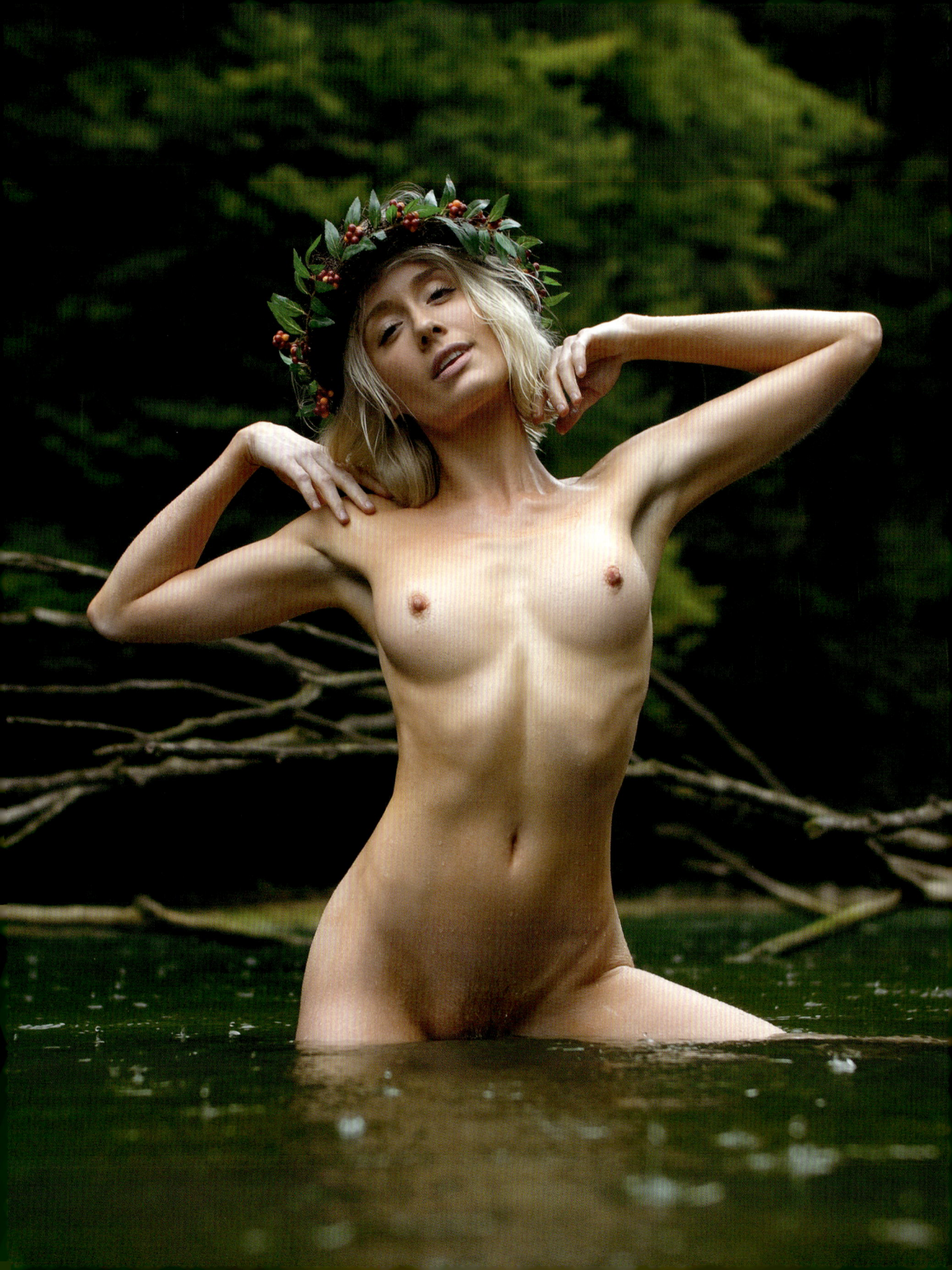

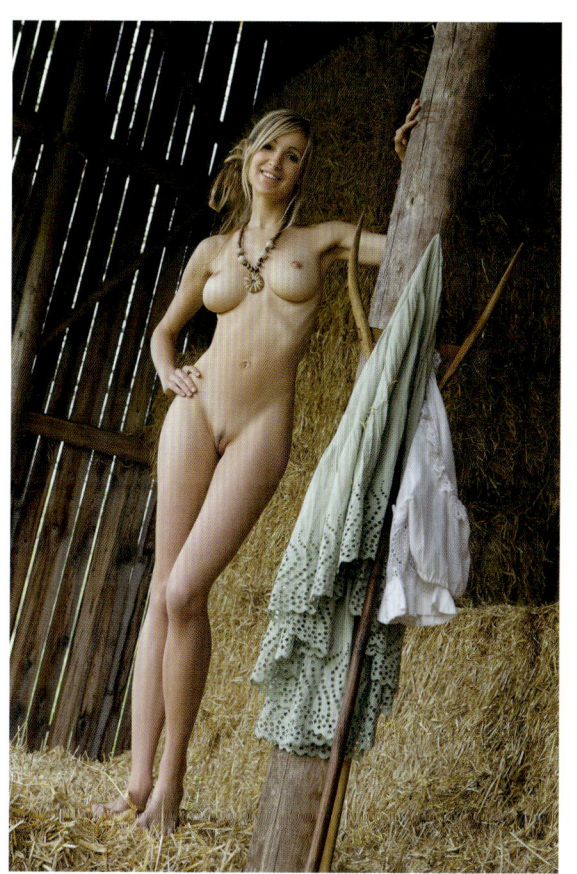
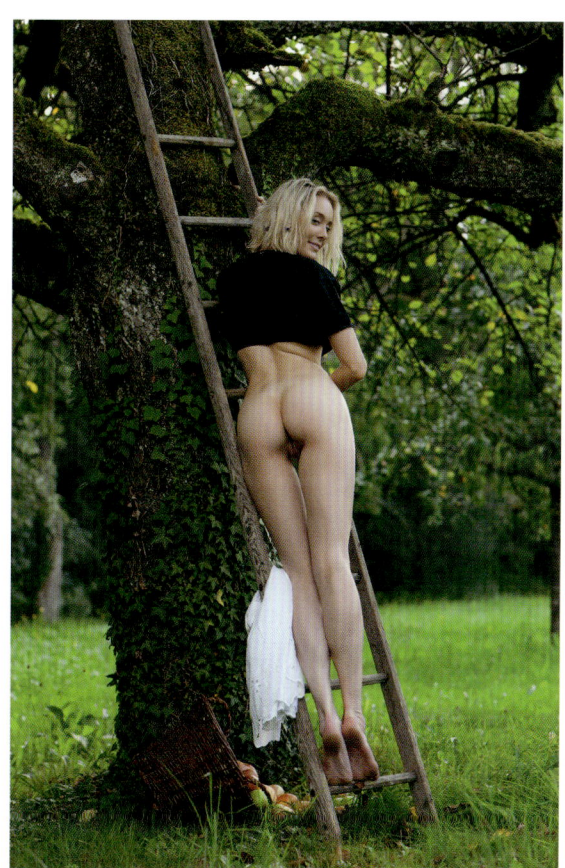

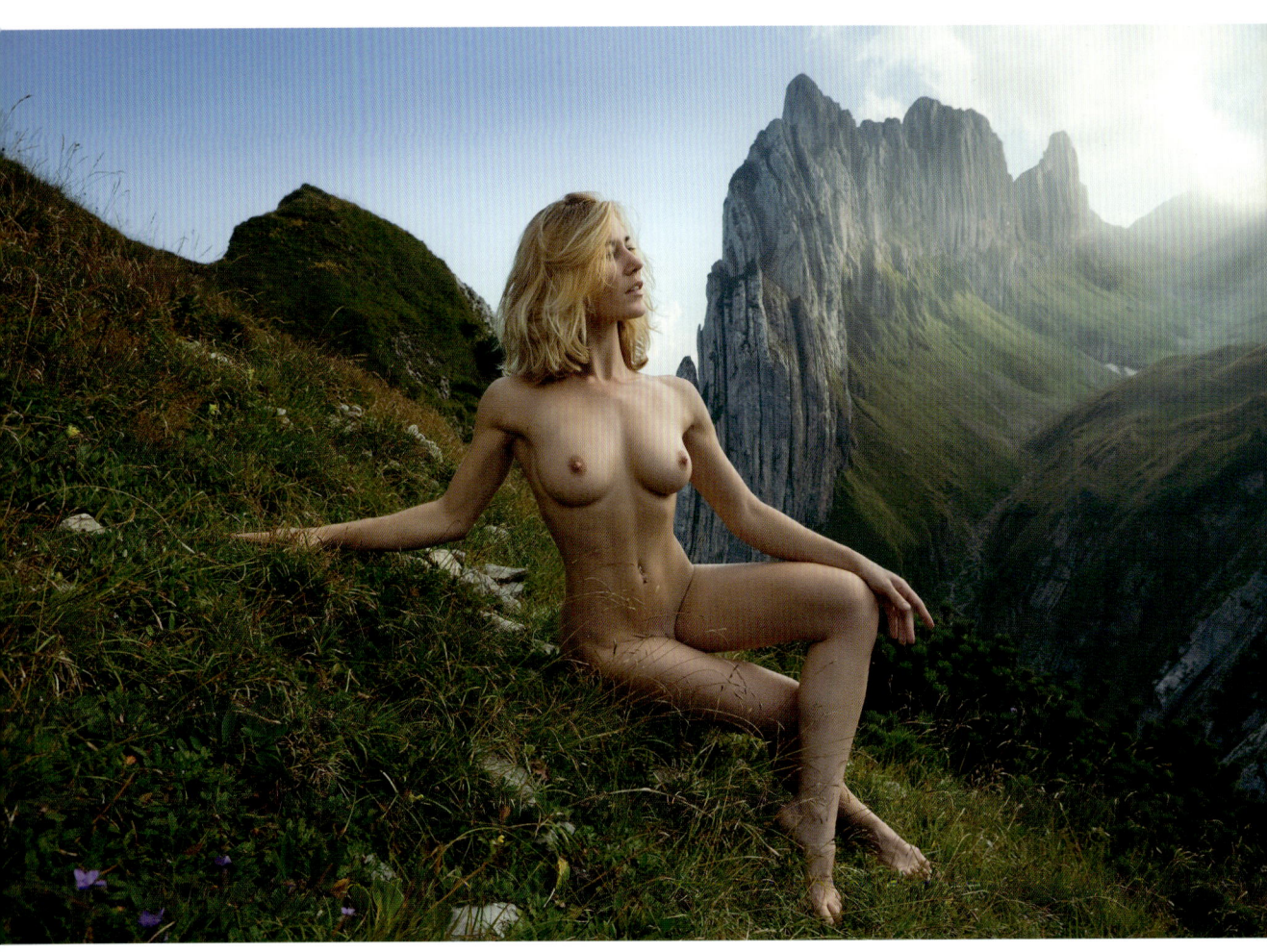

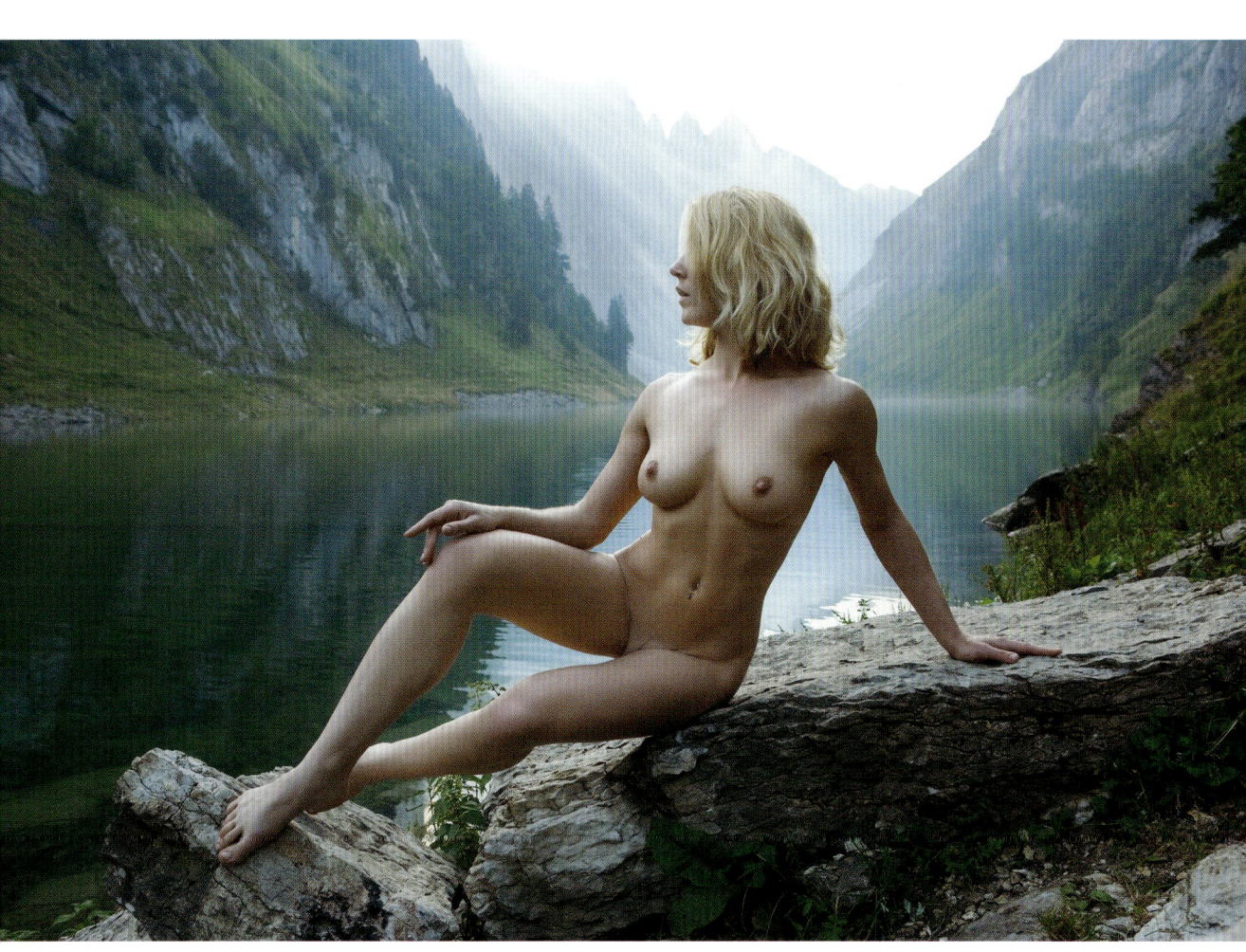

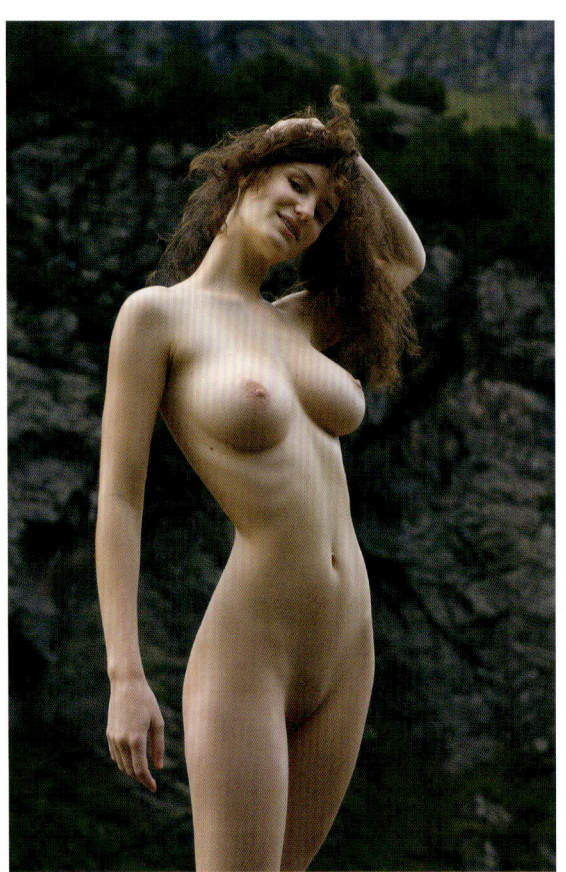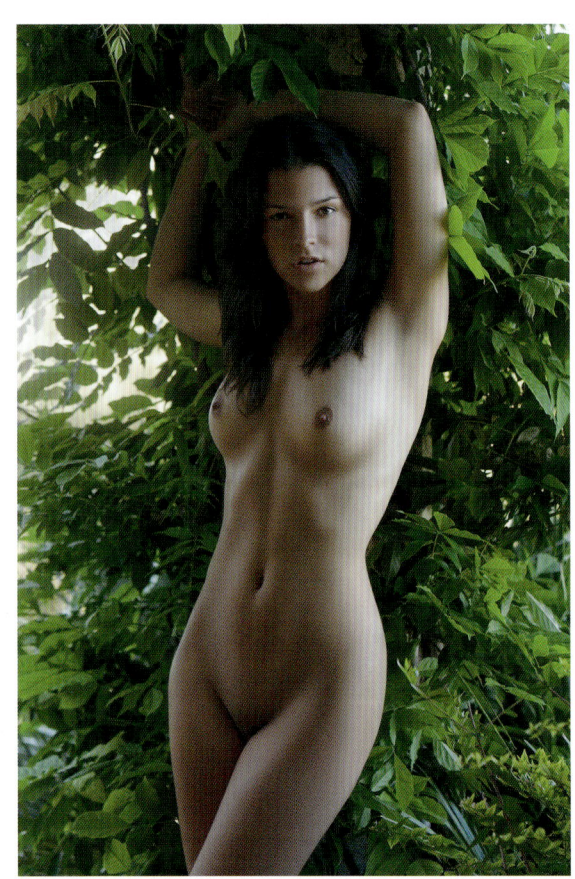

p. 38 Susann (47°2'28.60"N, 9°10'30.35"E);
Iva (47°47'40.63"N, 9°2'39.32"E)

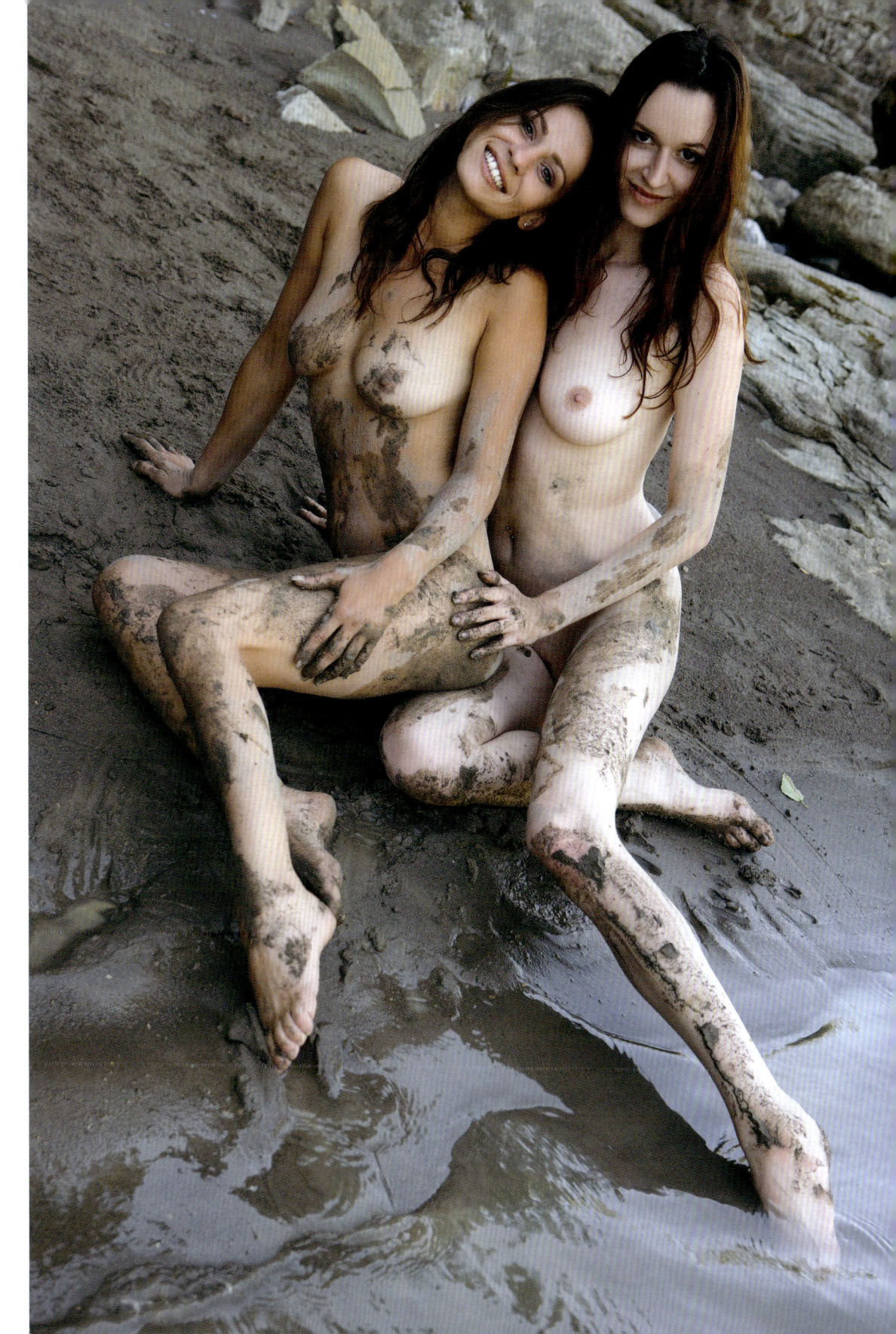

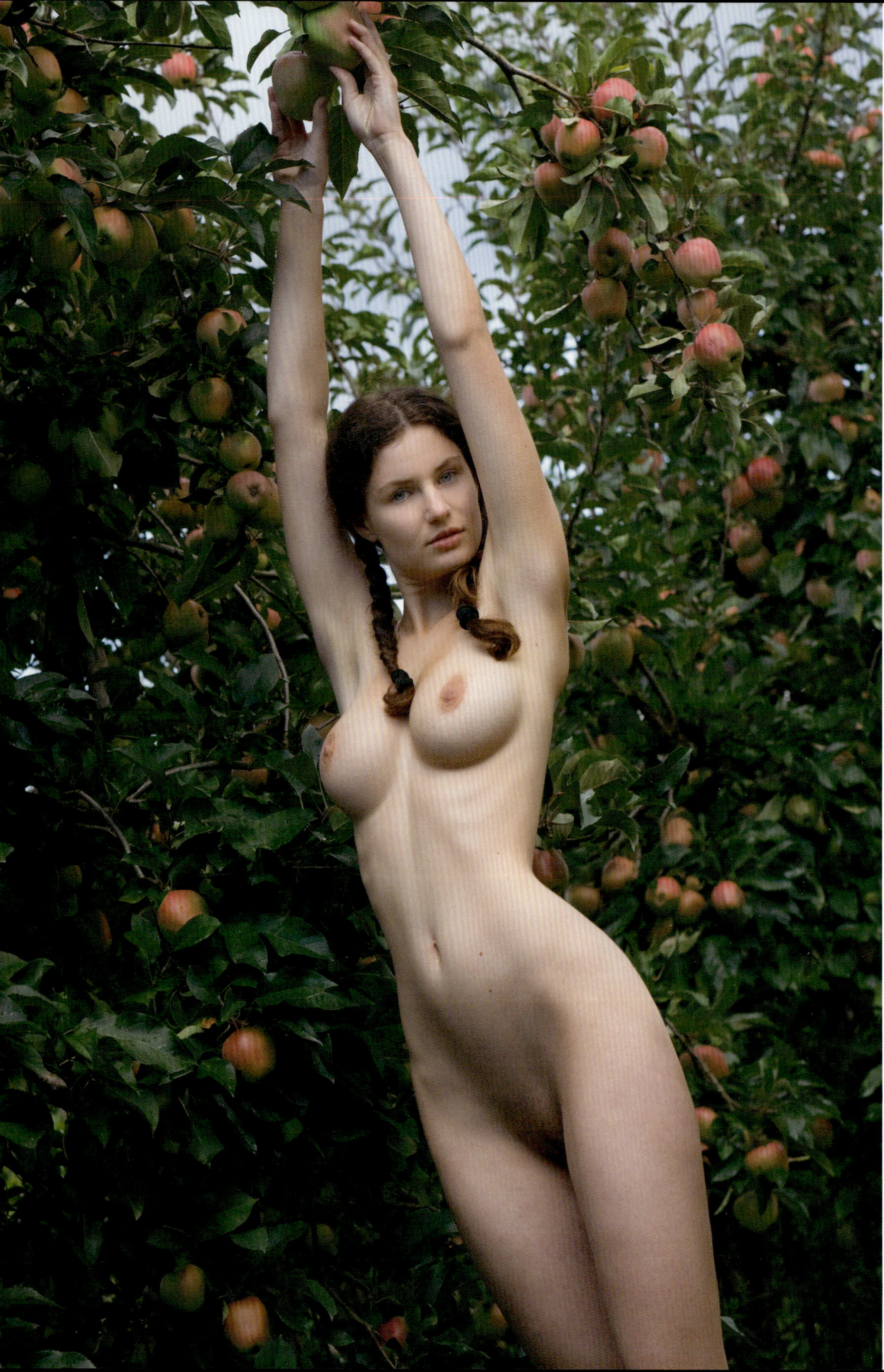

p. 40 Susann (47°41'41.98"N, 9°24'31.09"E)

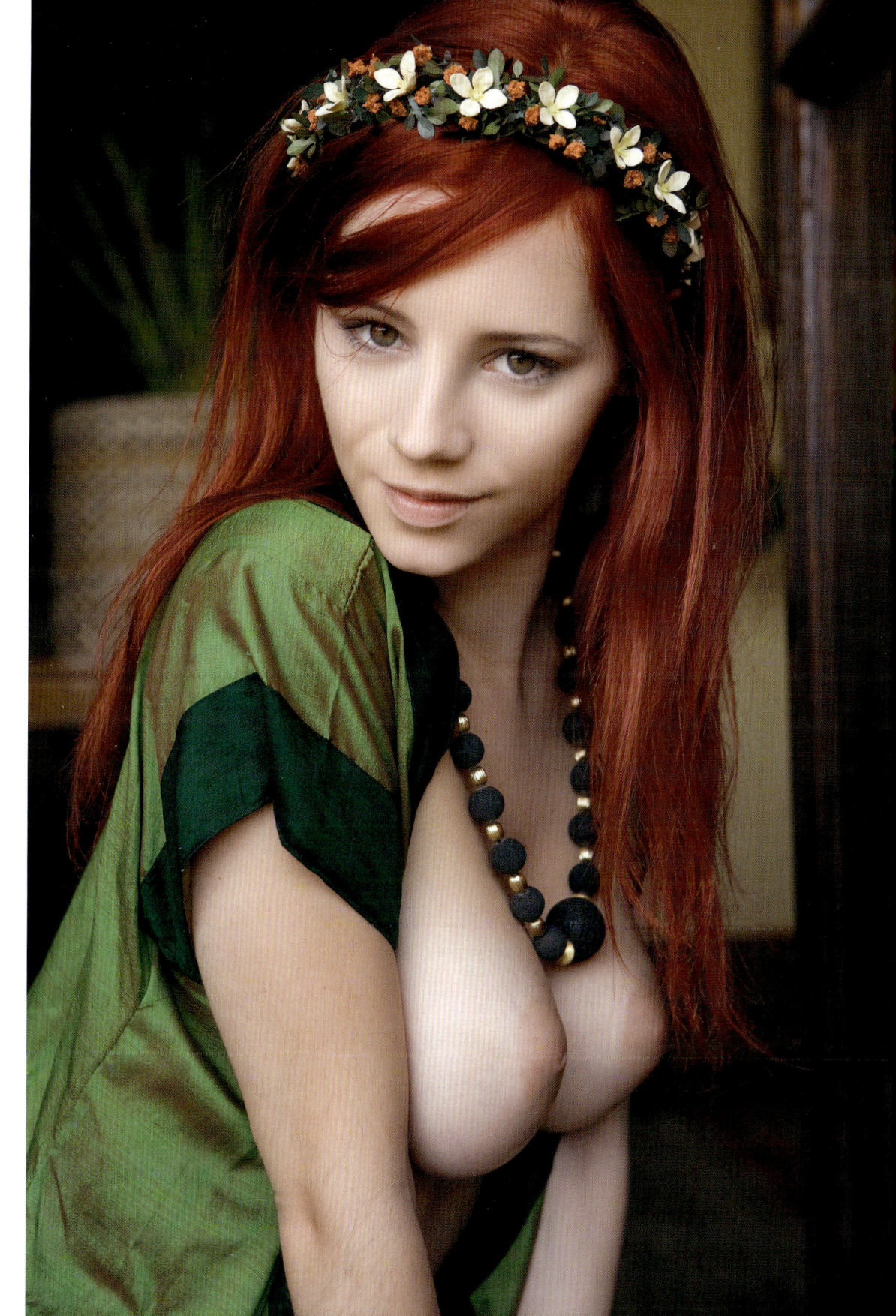

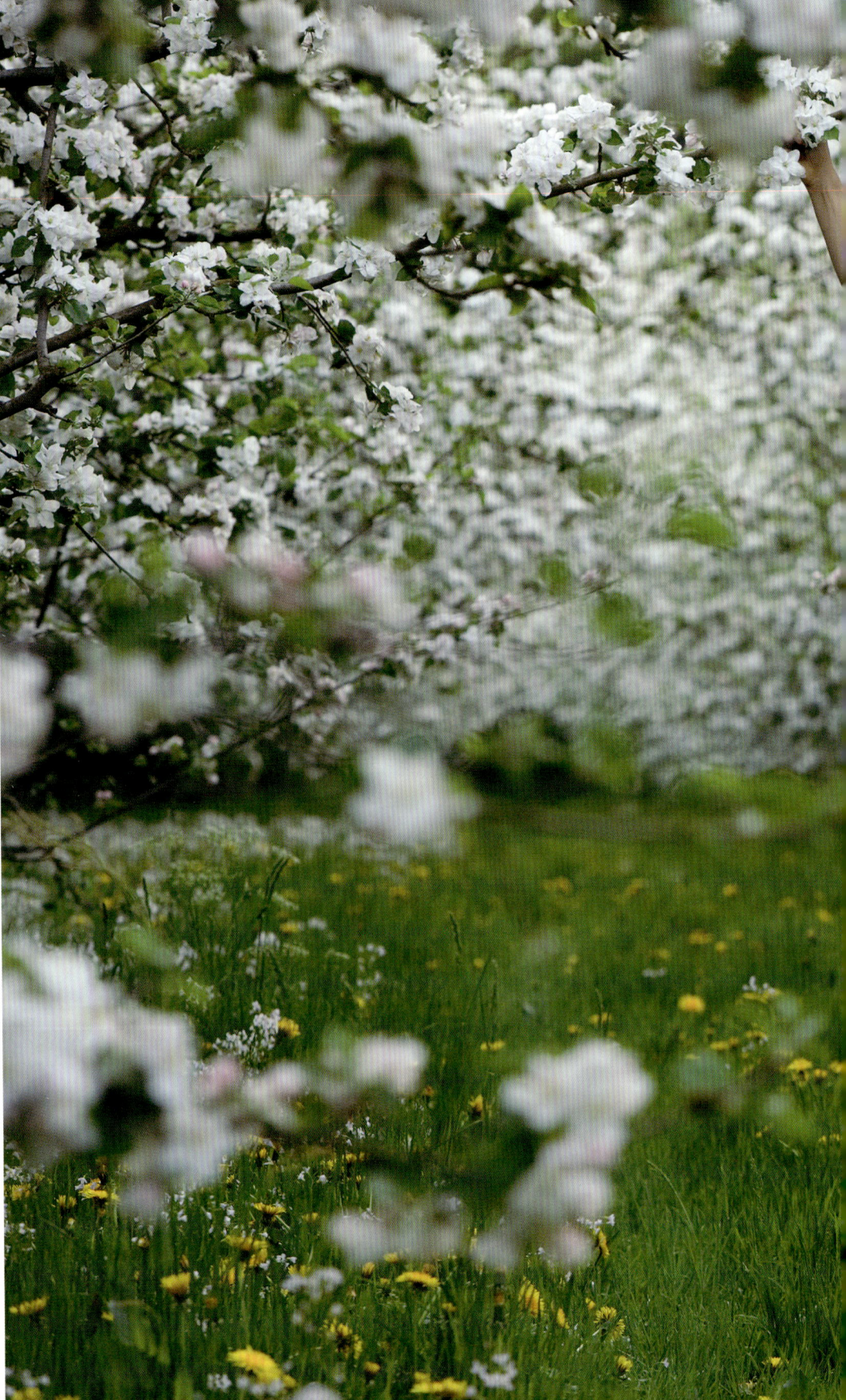

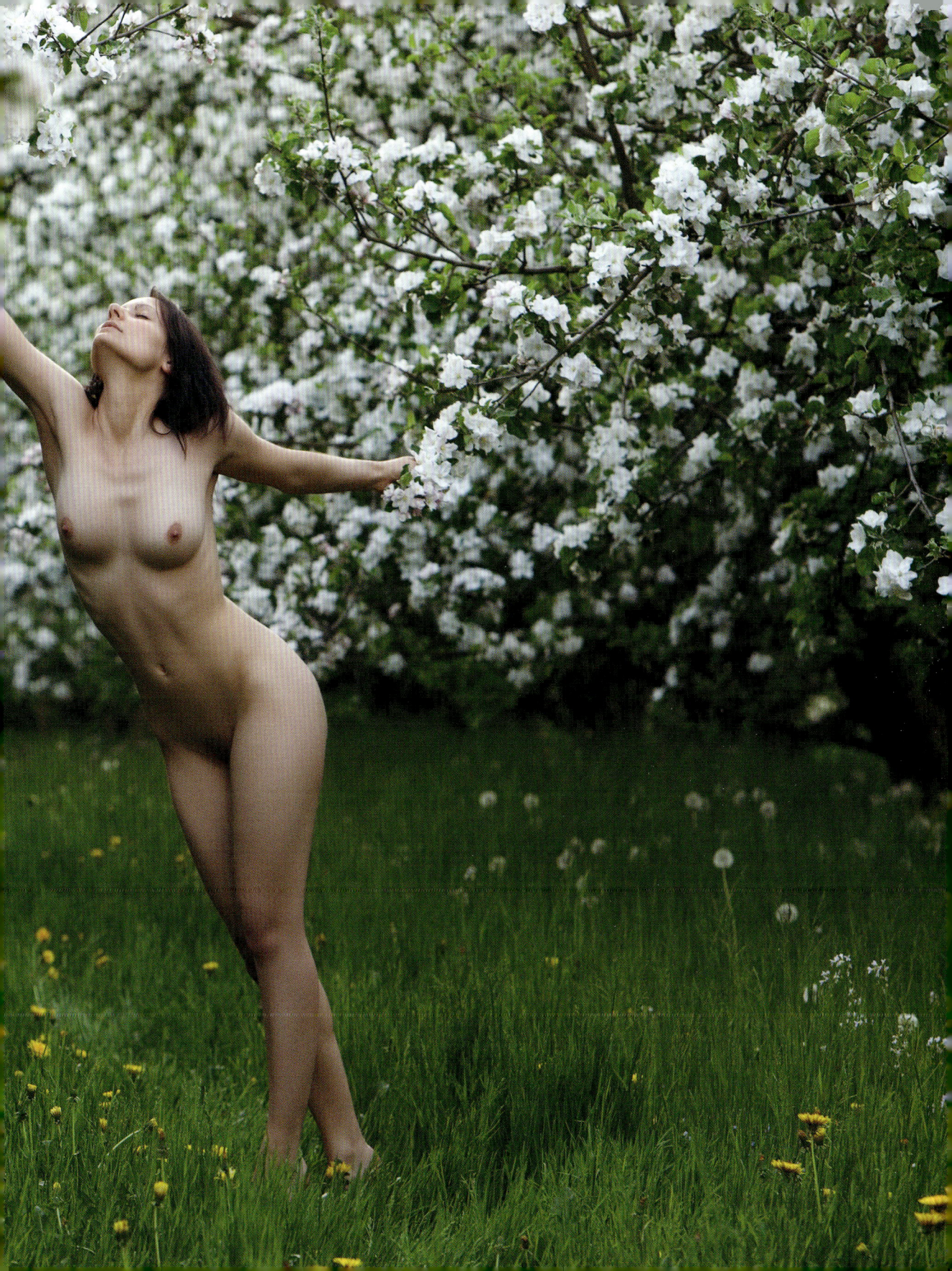

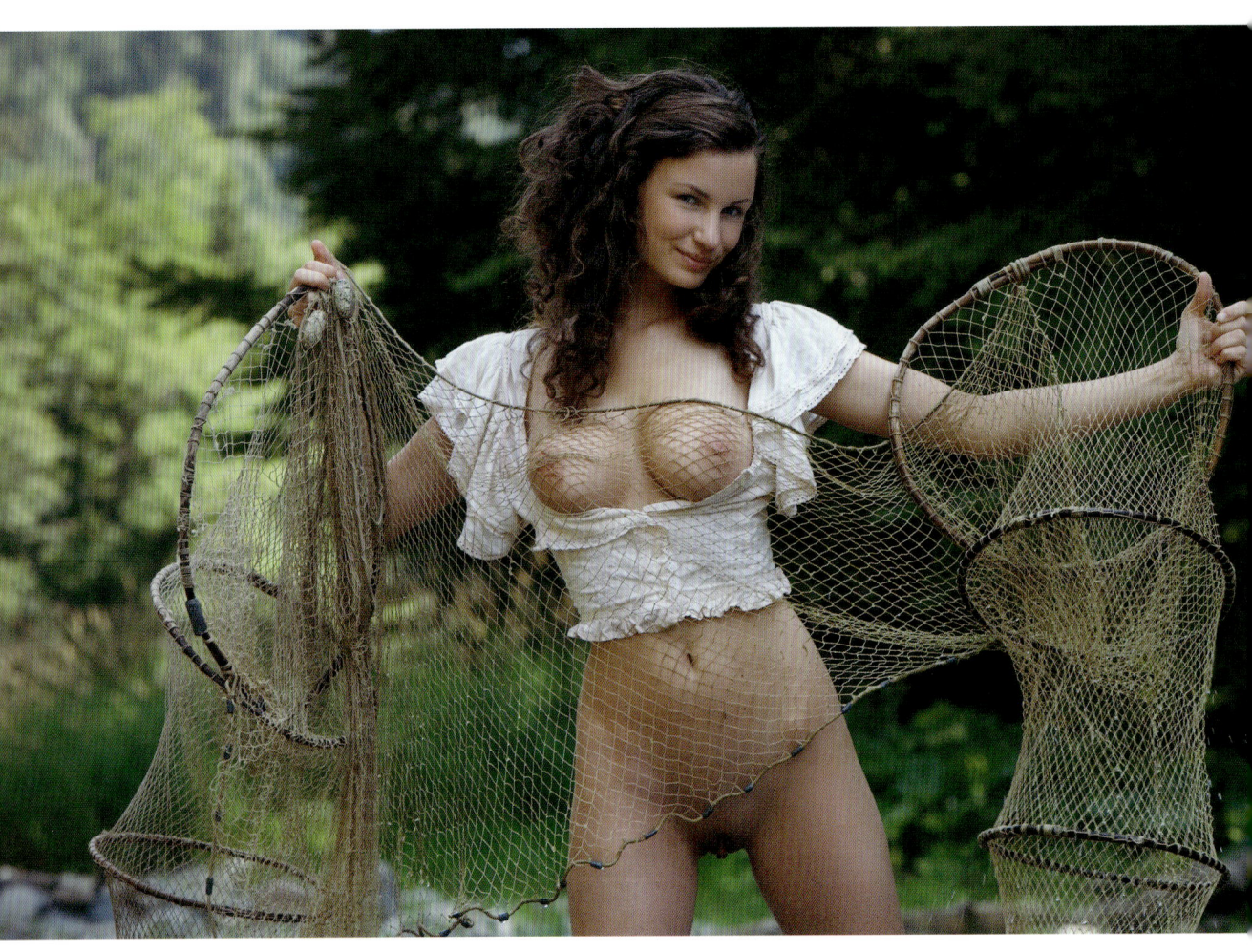

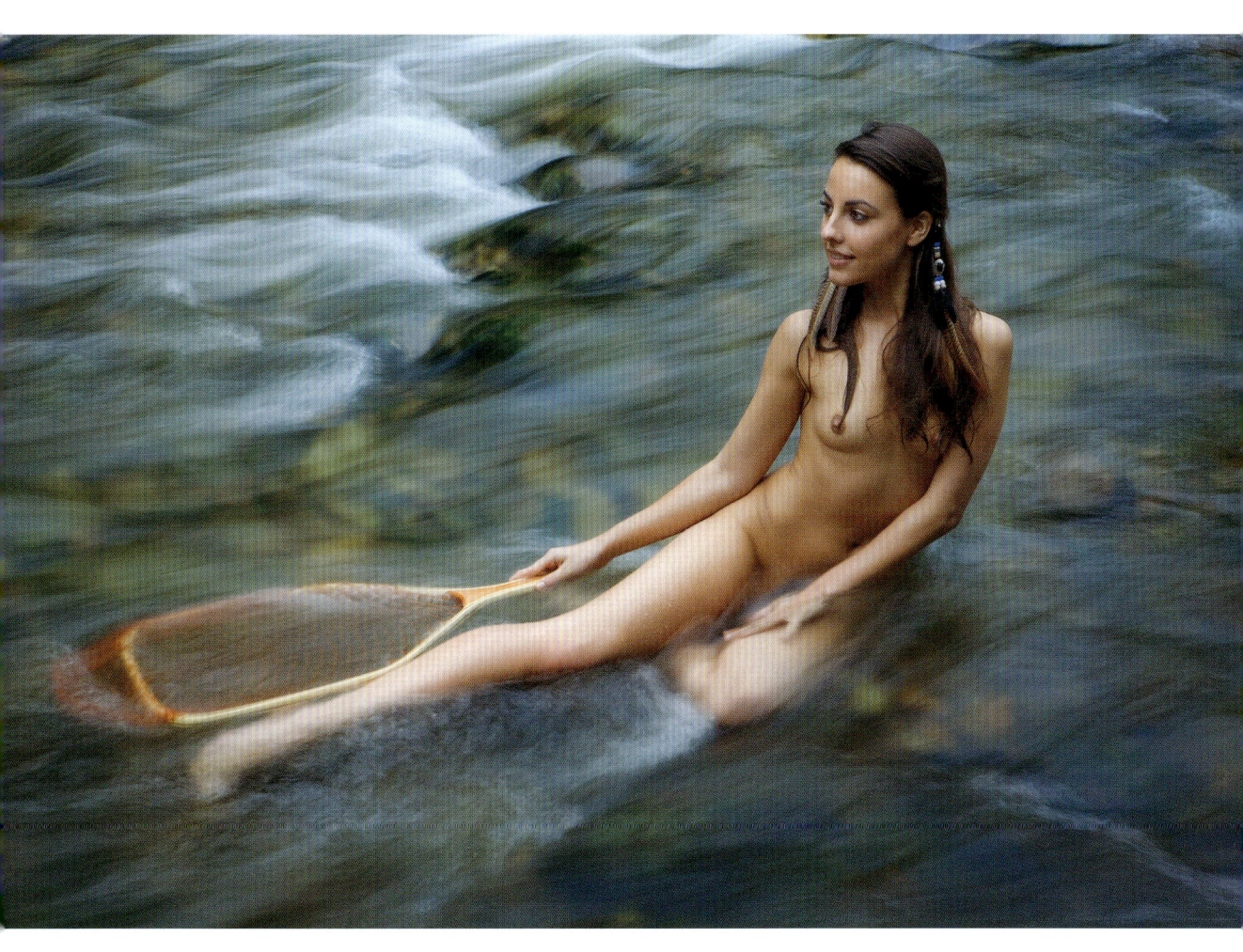

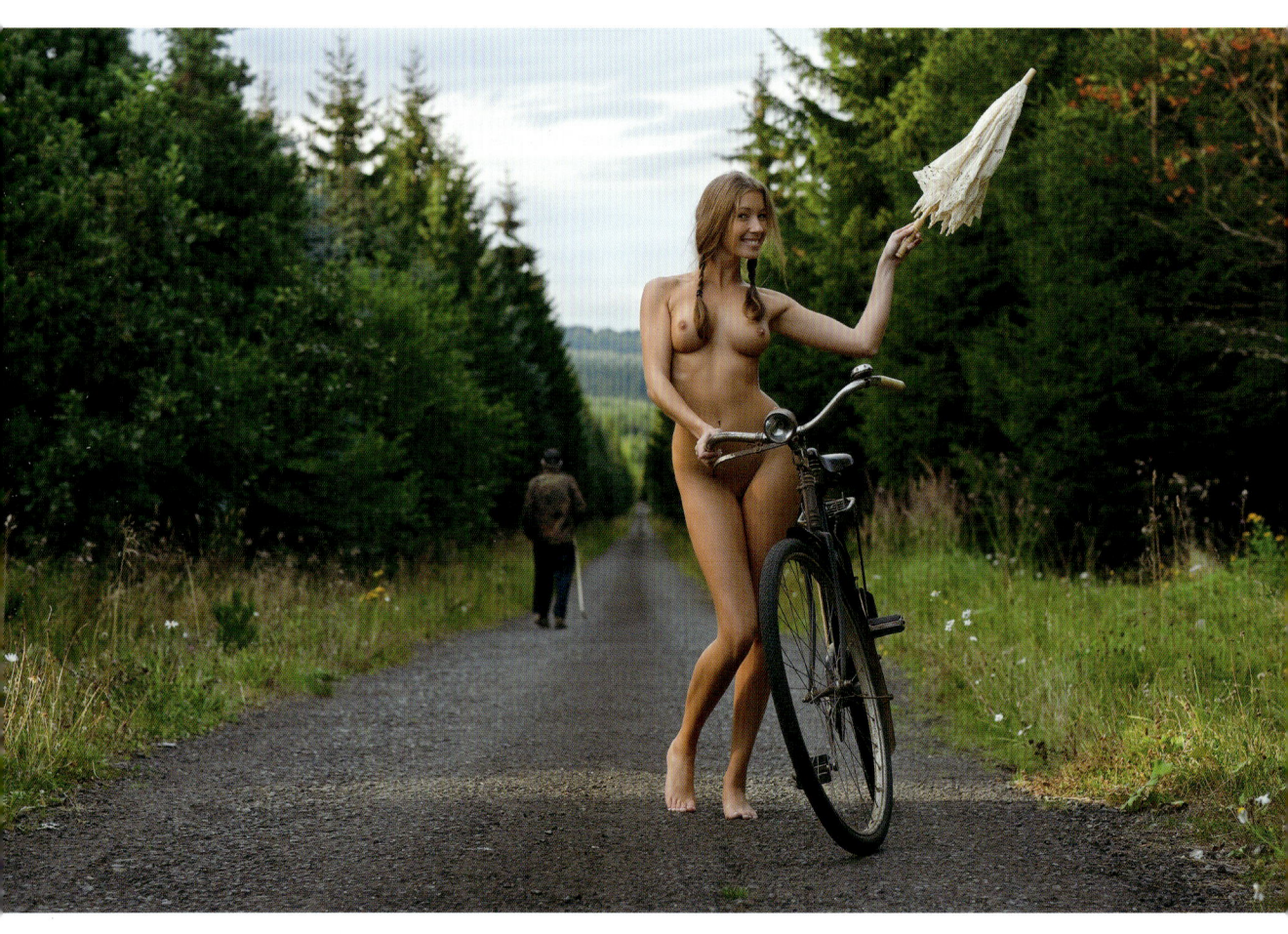

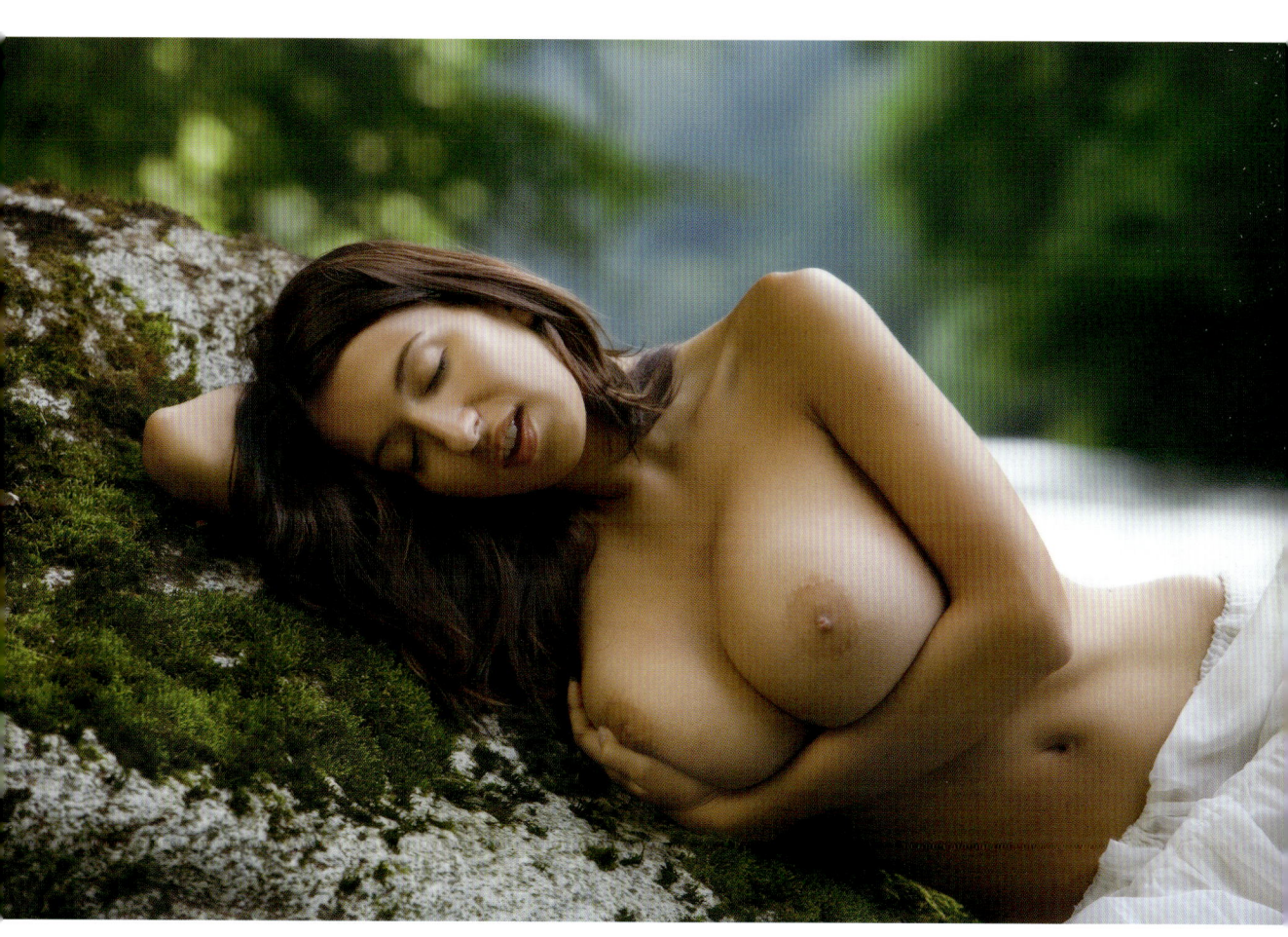

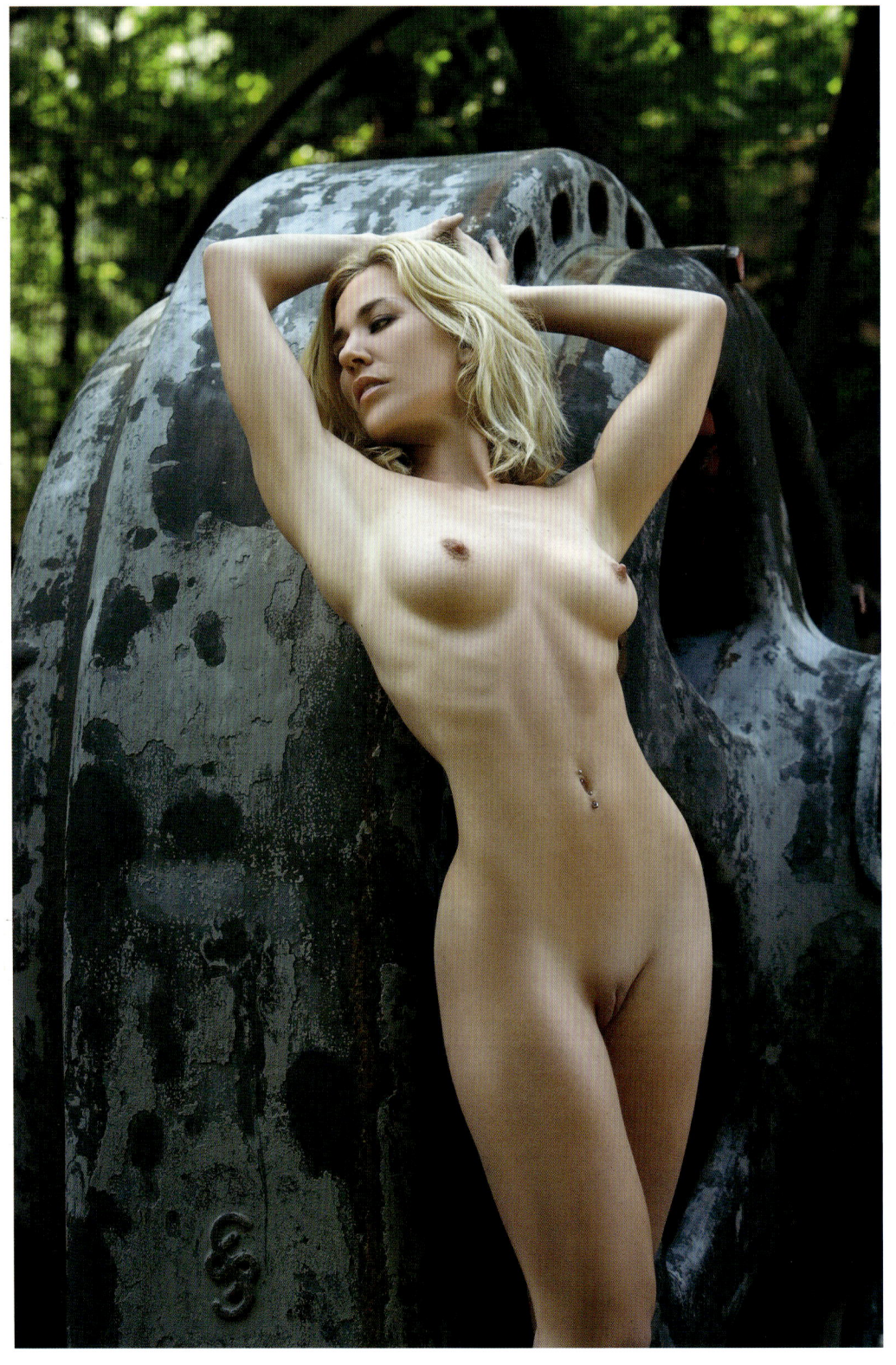

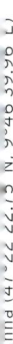

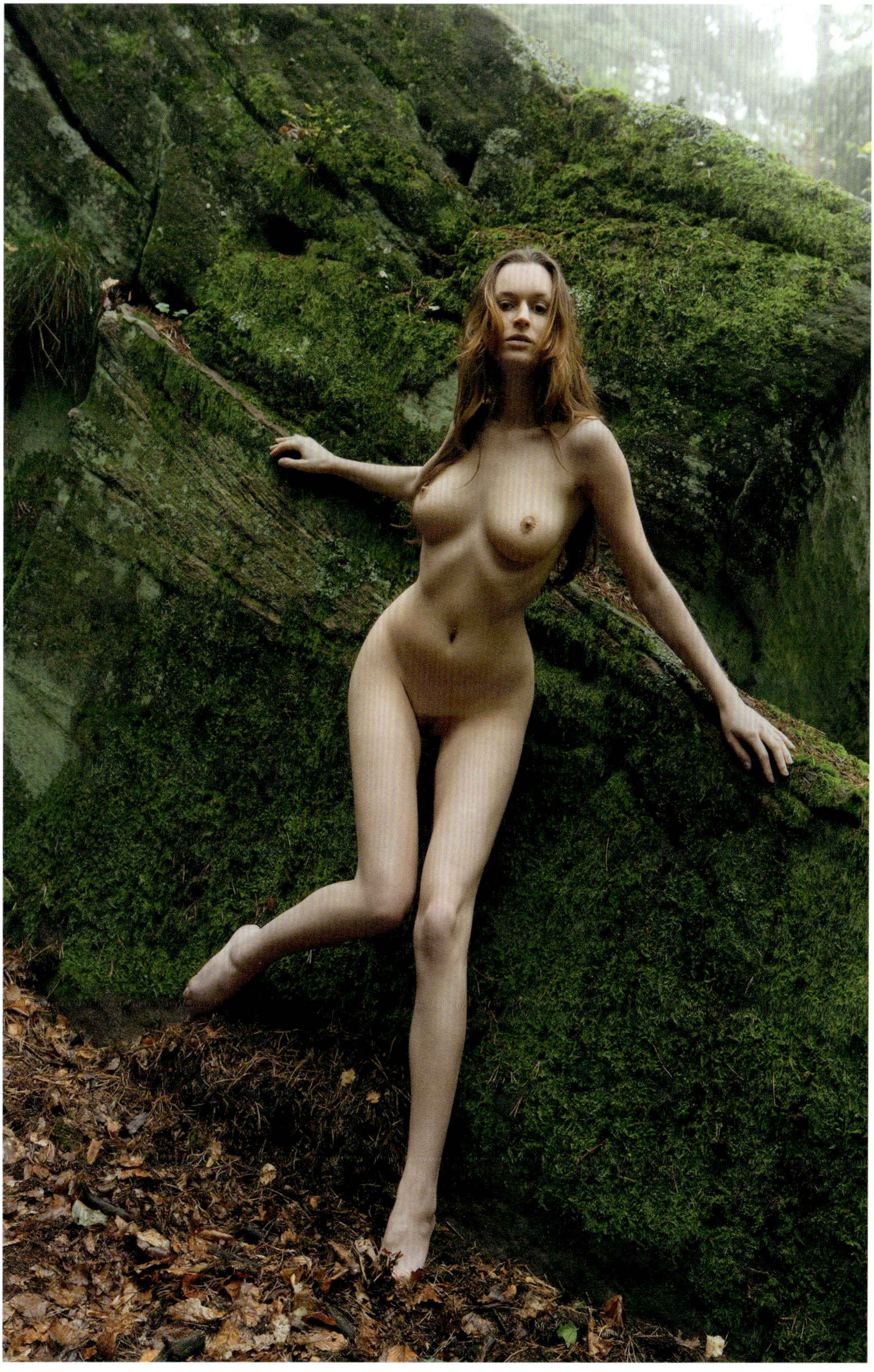

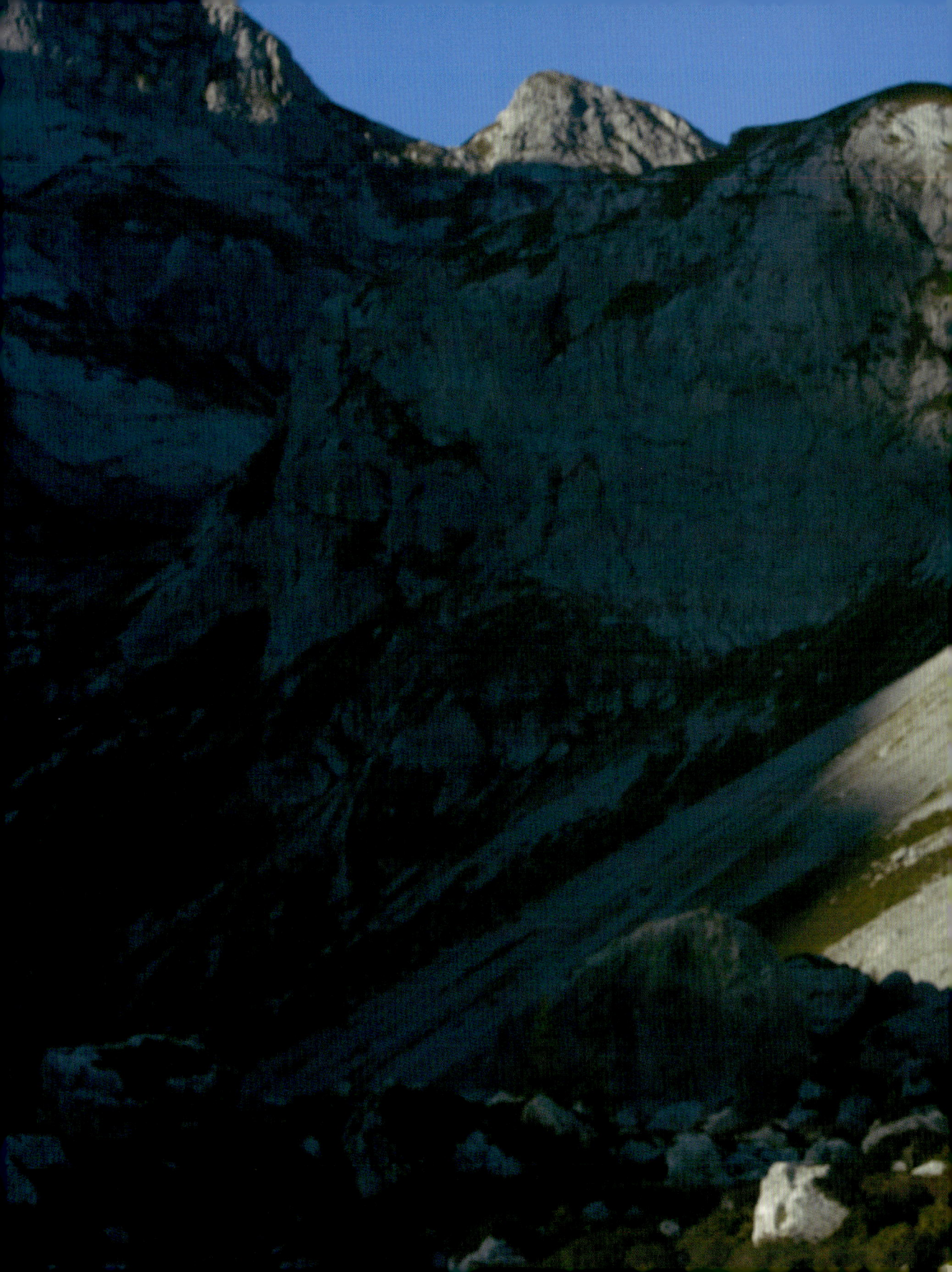

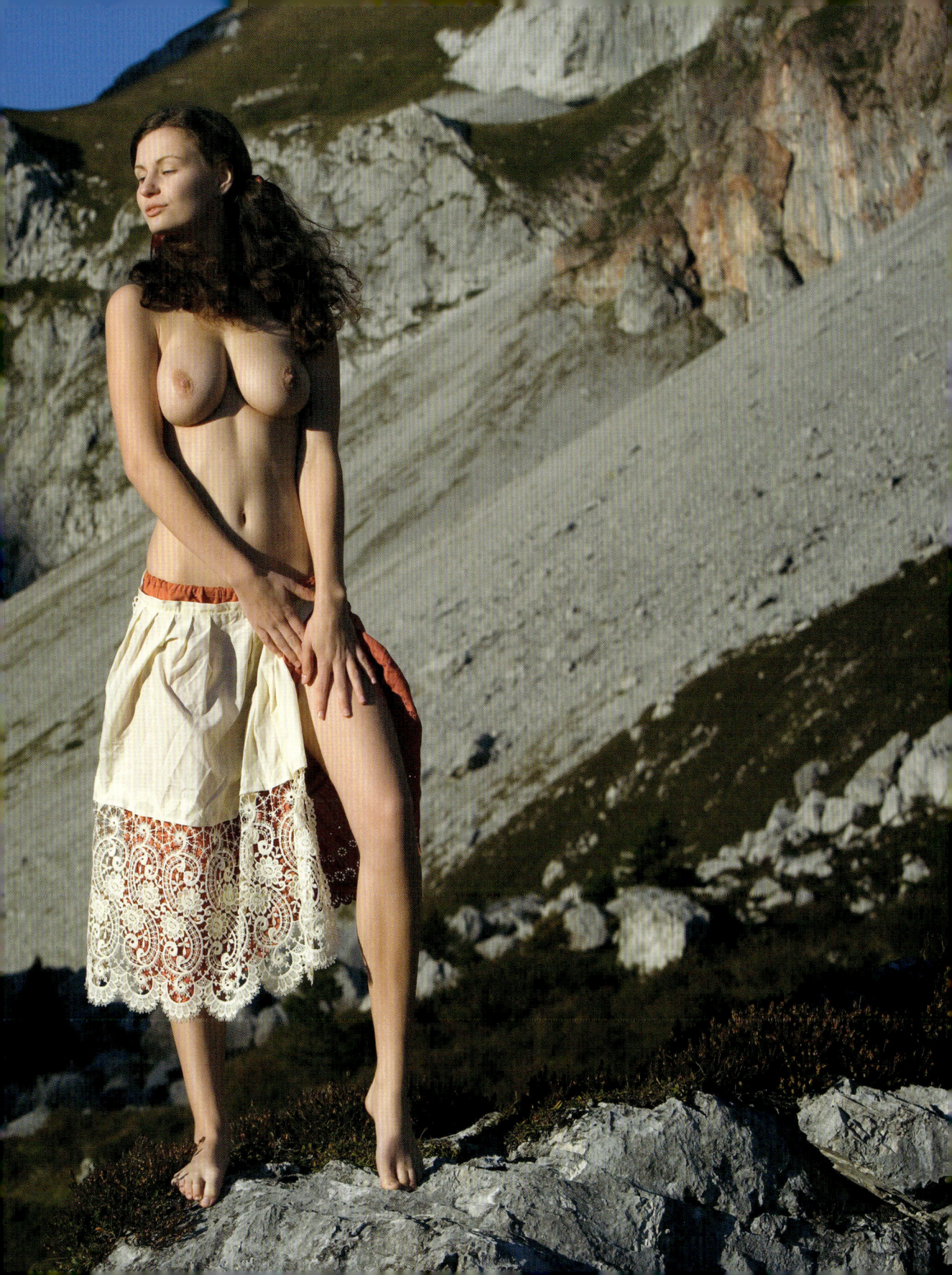

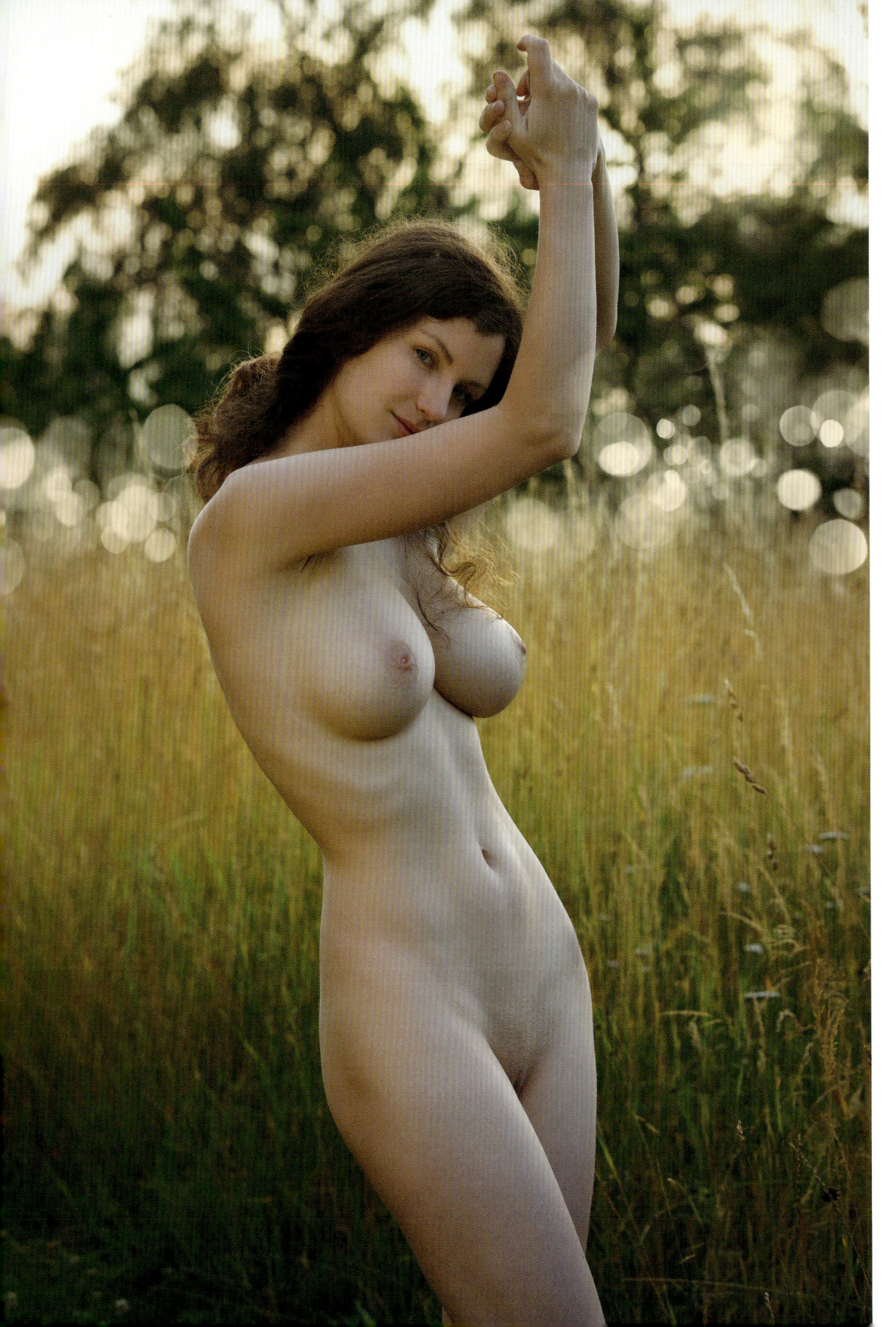

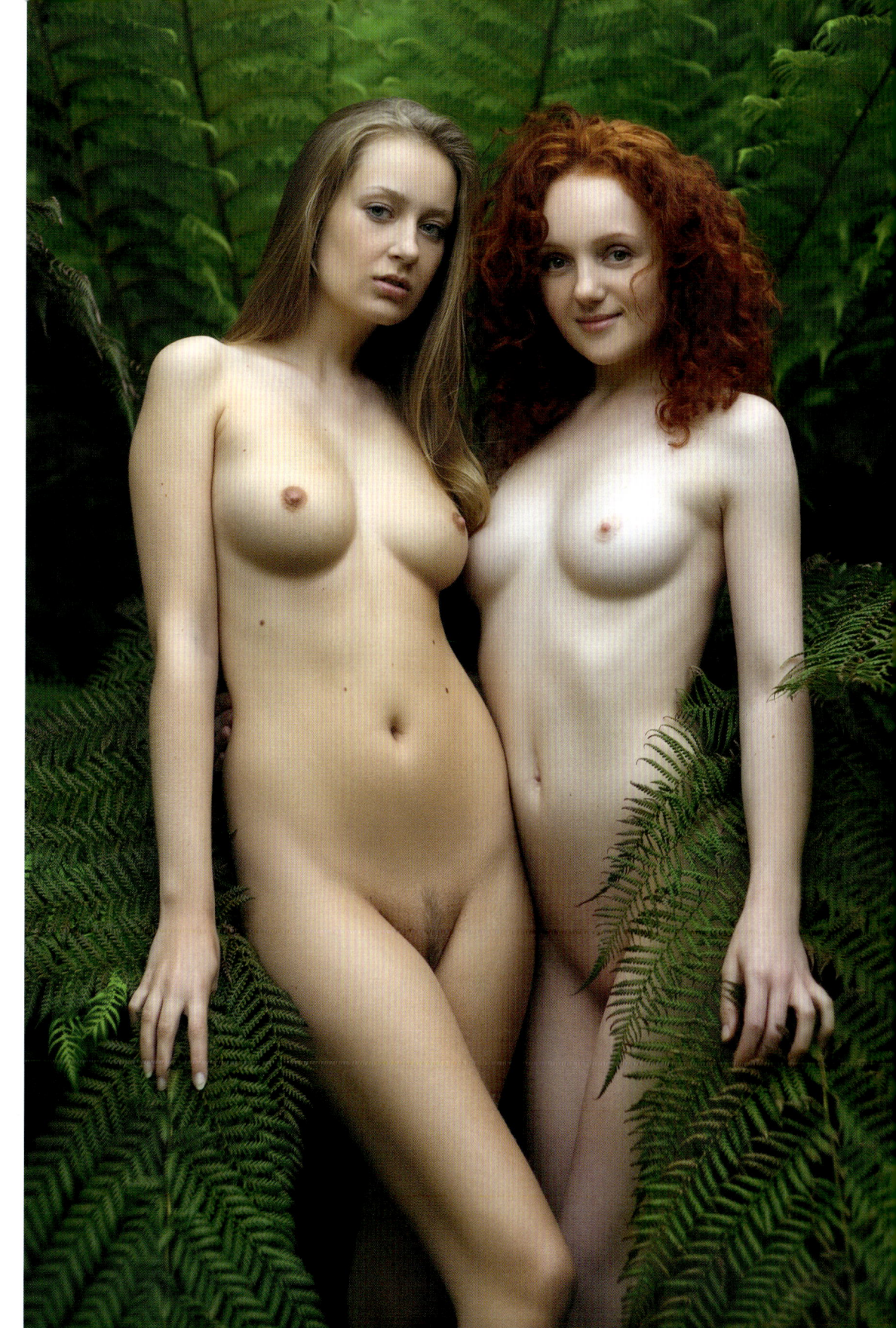

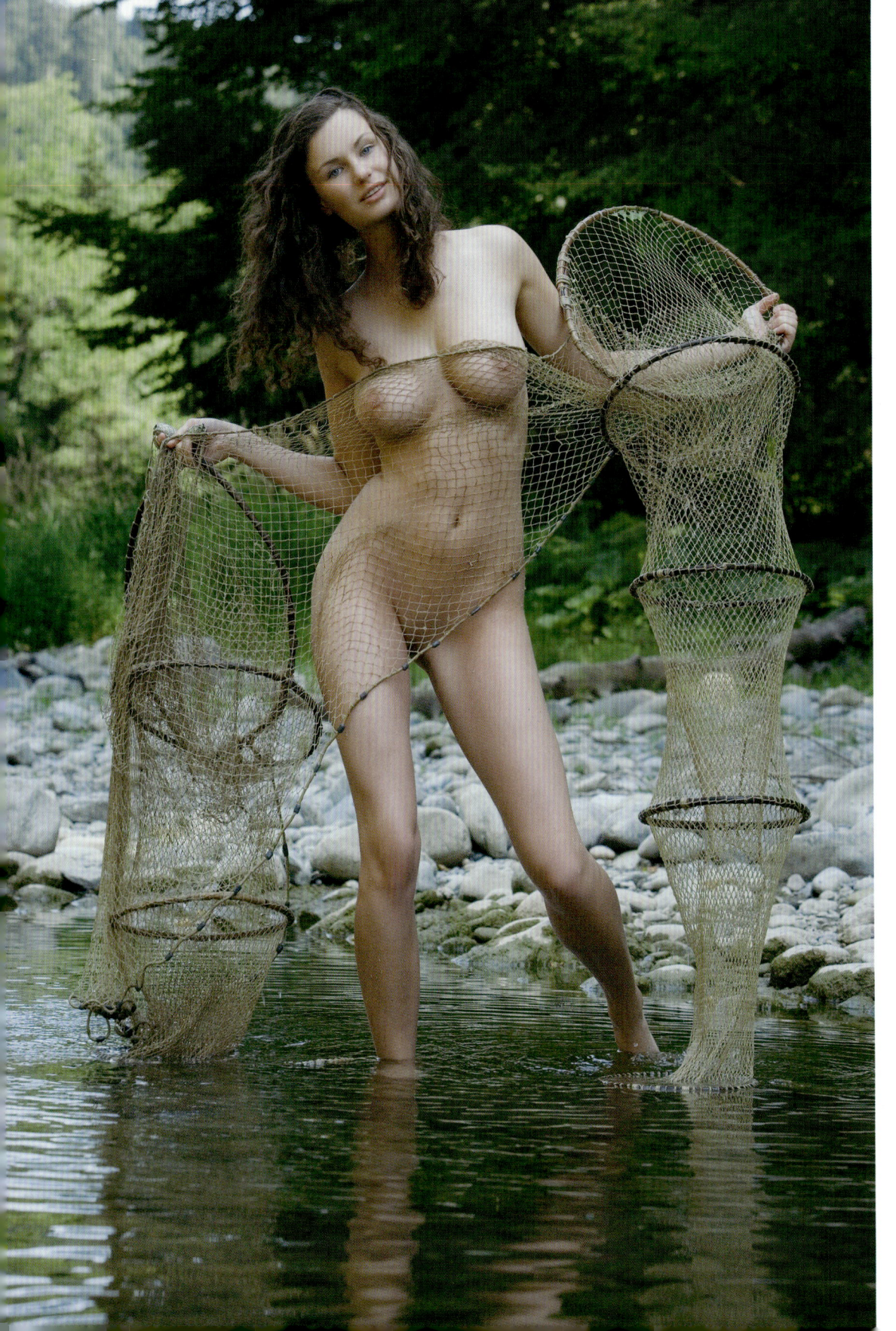

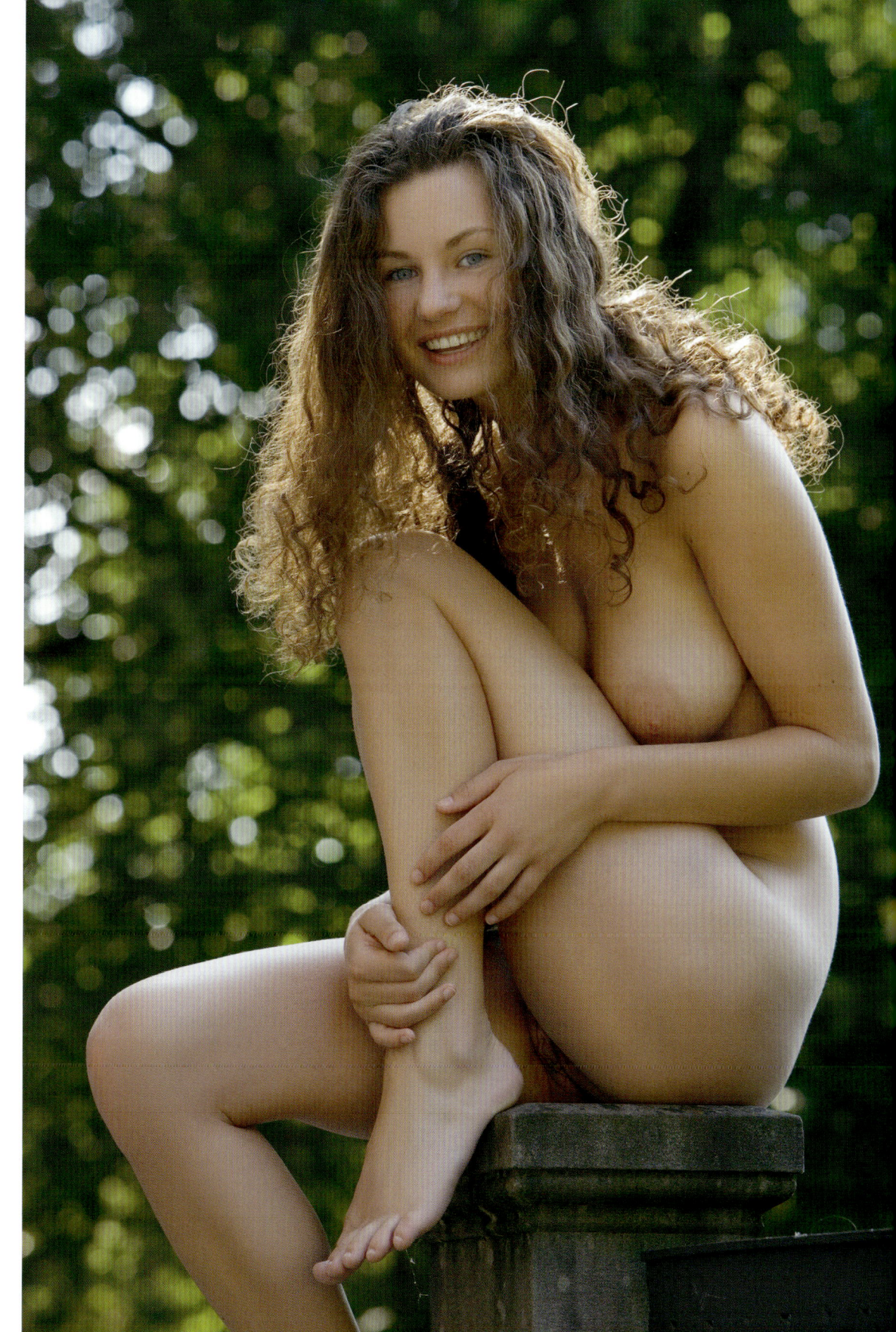

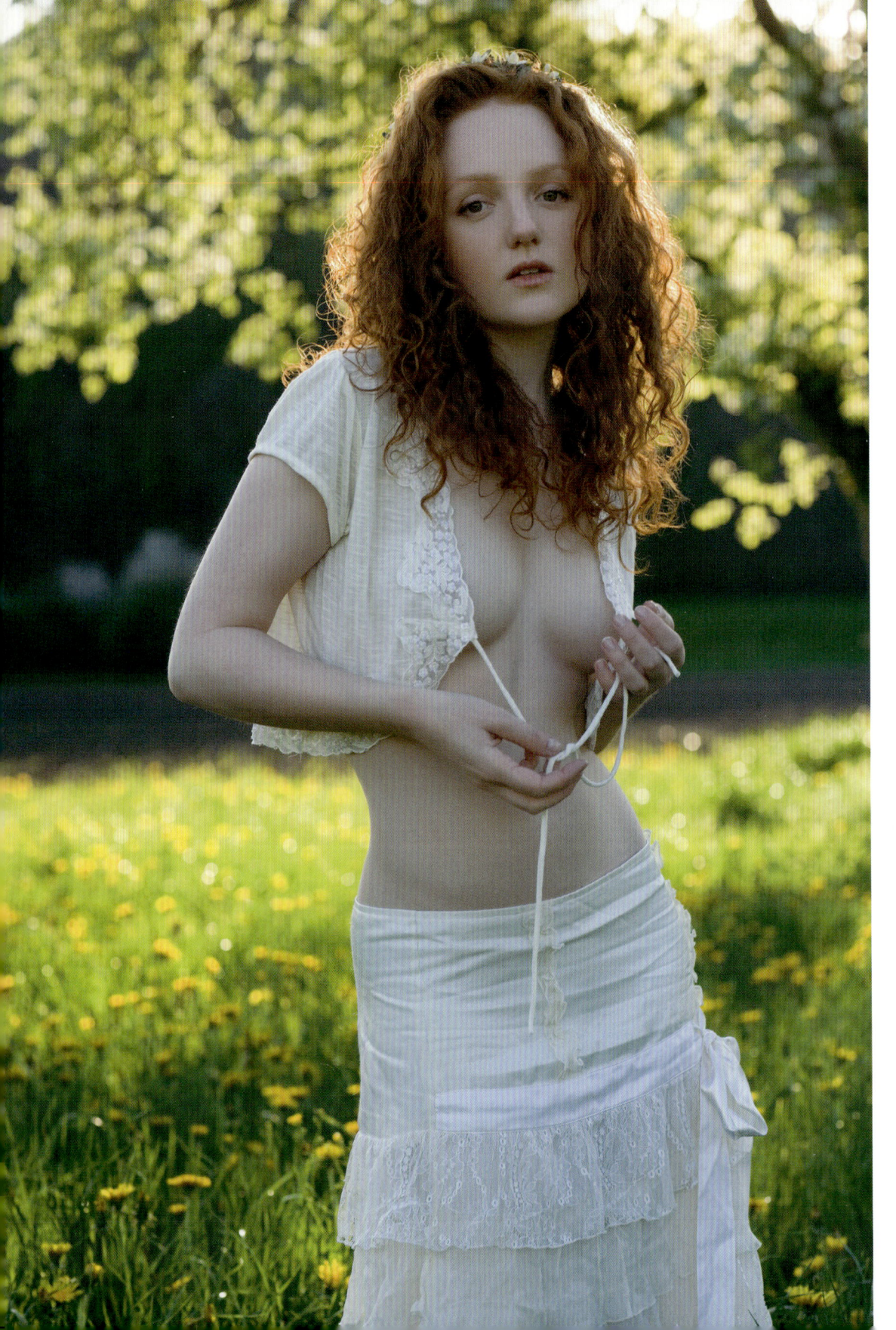

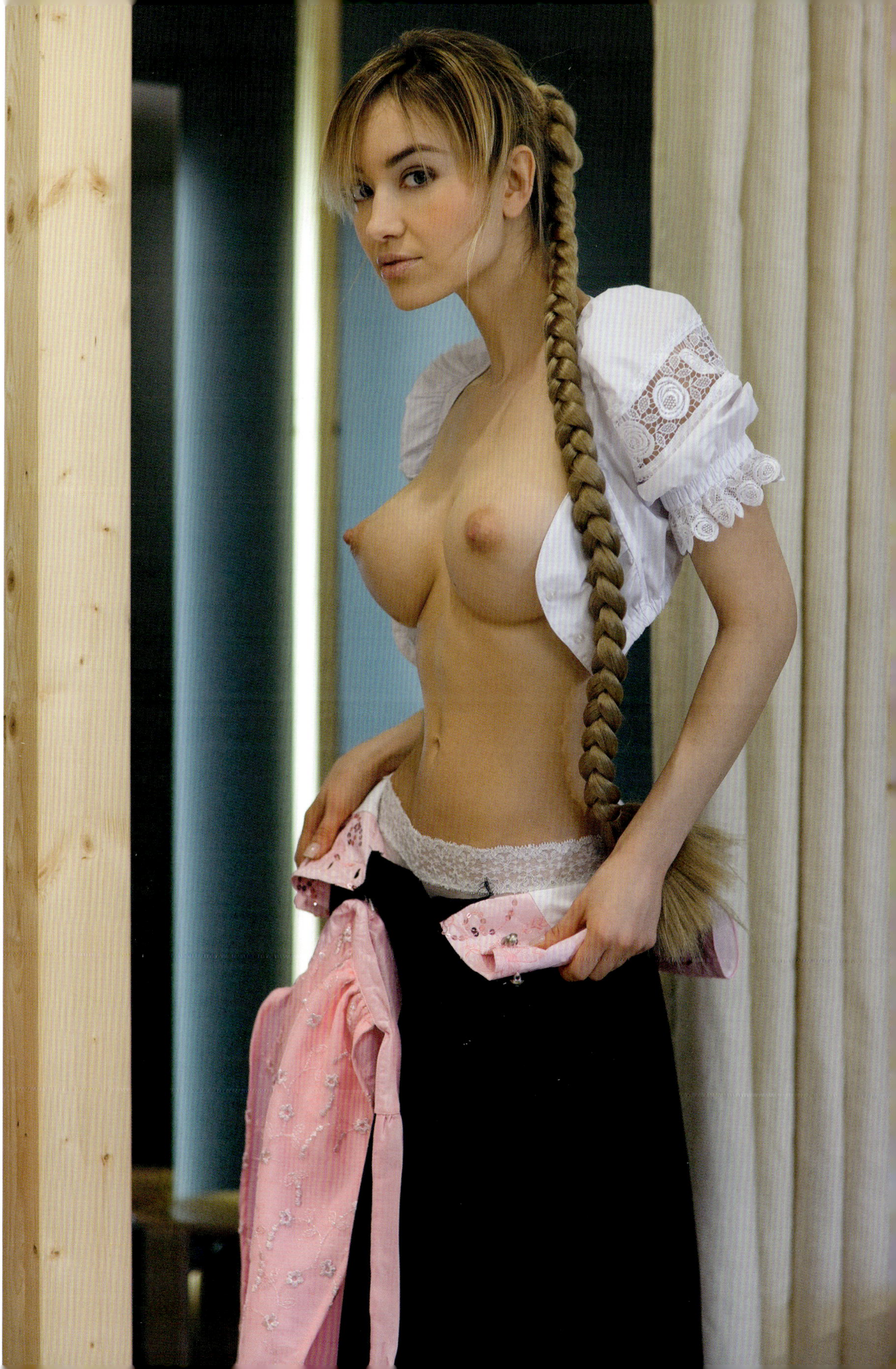

p. 57 Lia (47°39'44.02"N, 9°34'15.46"E)

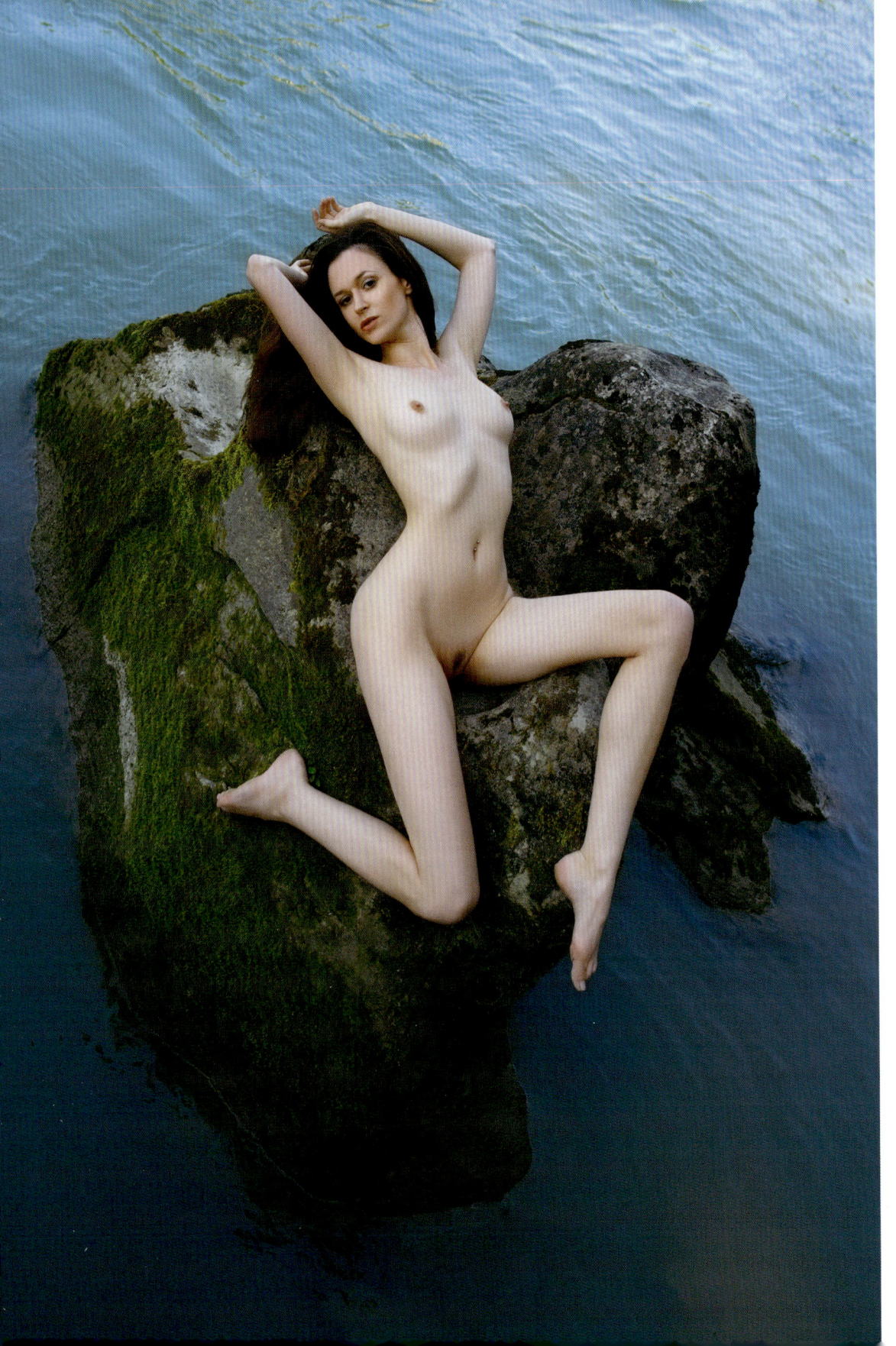

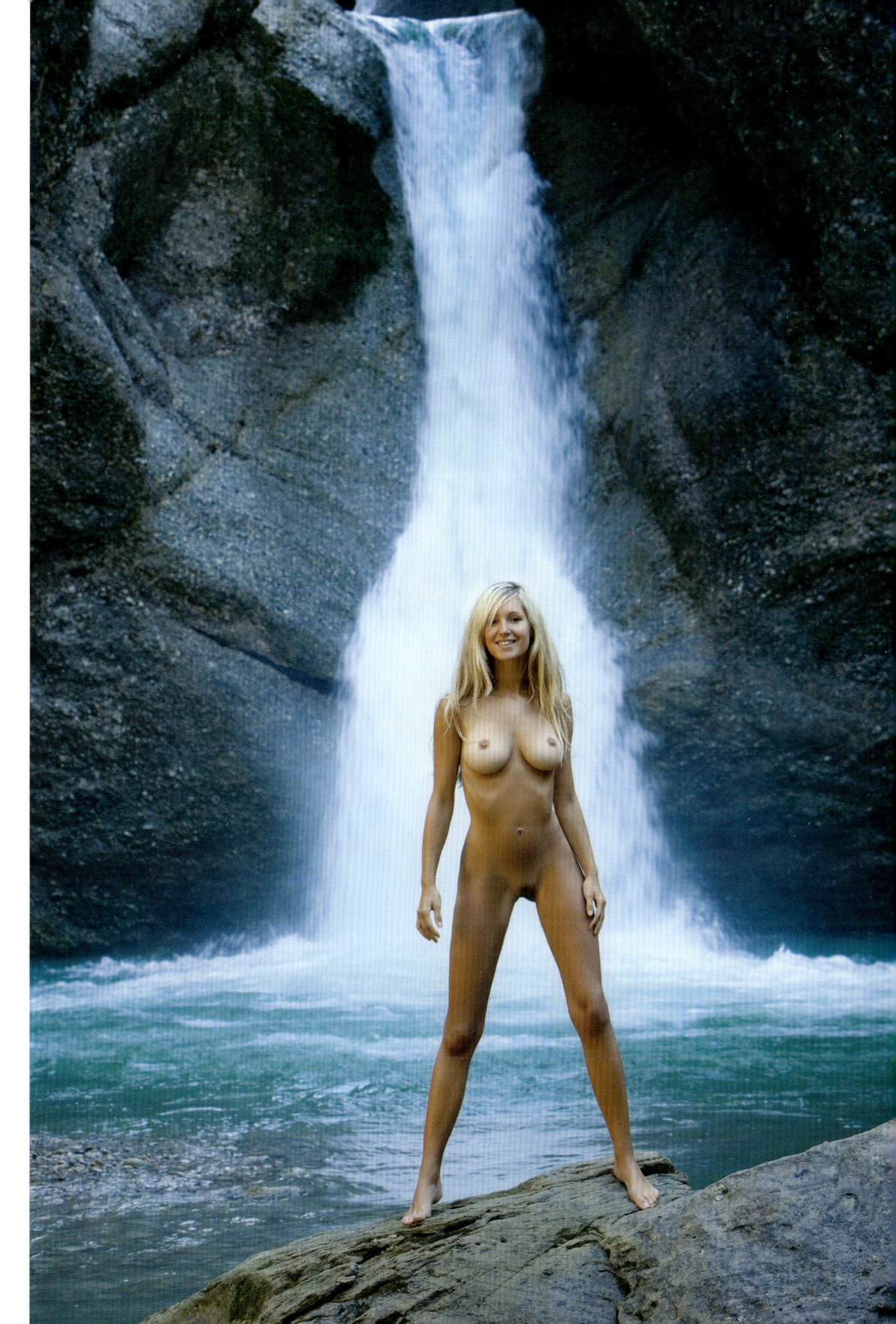

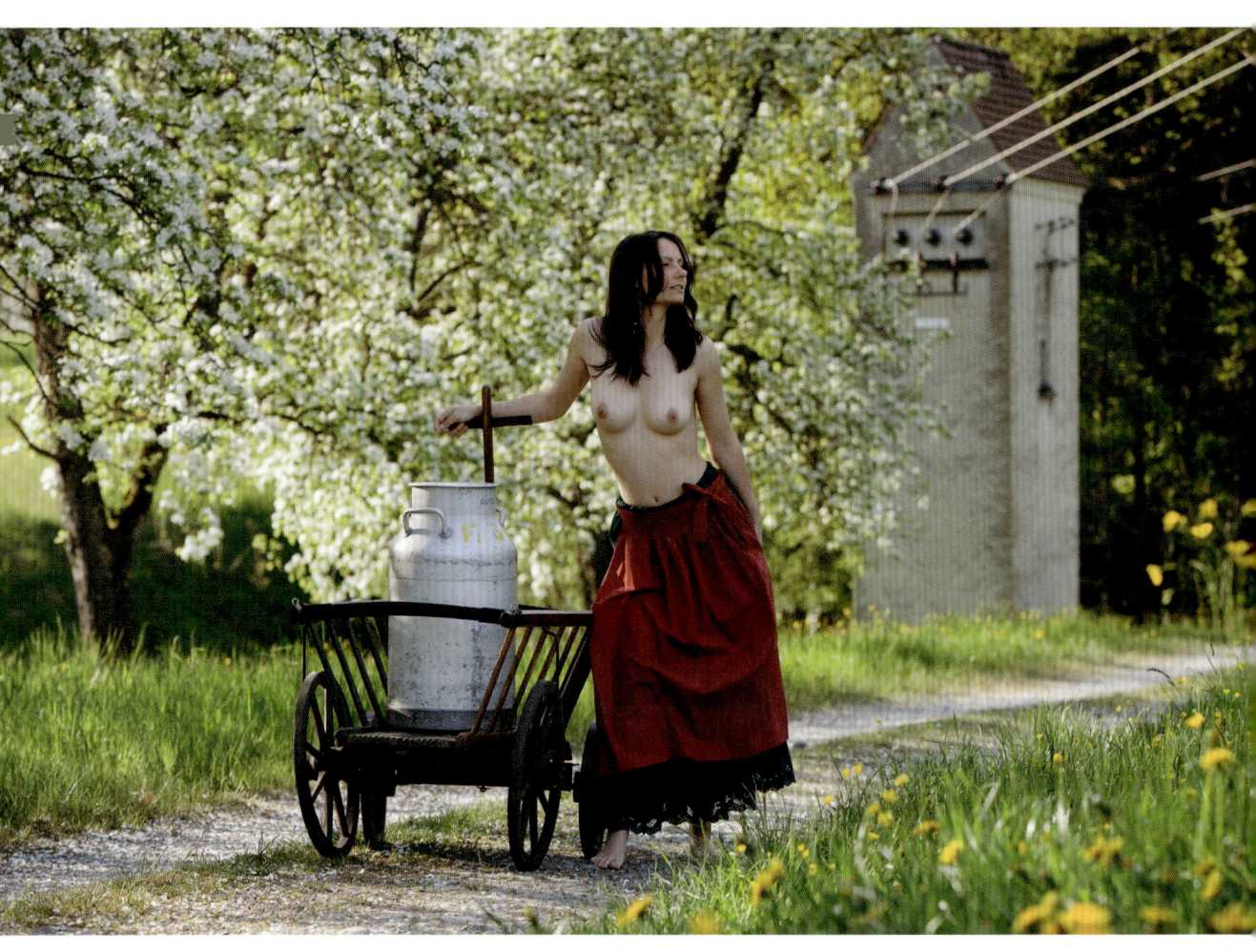

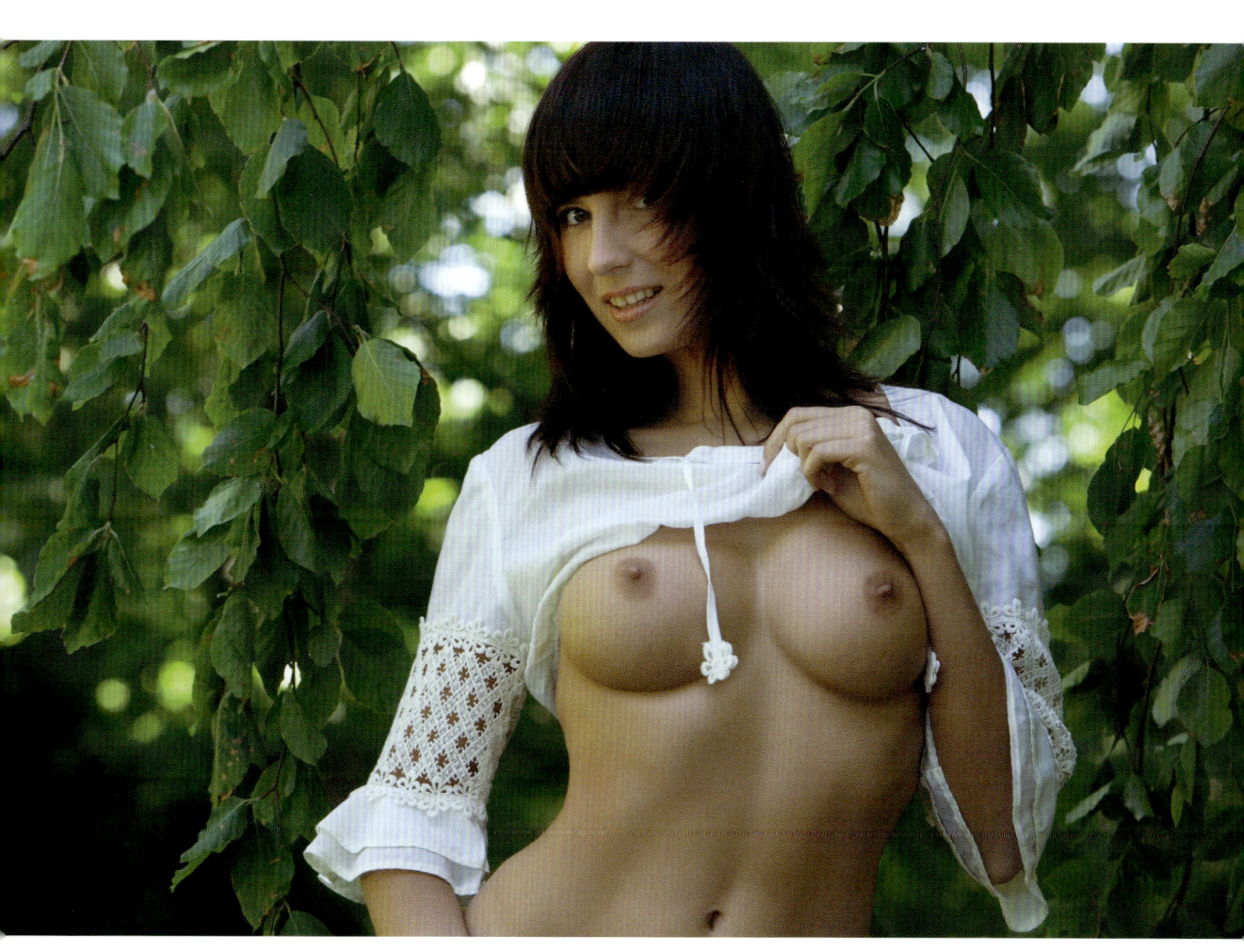

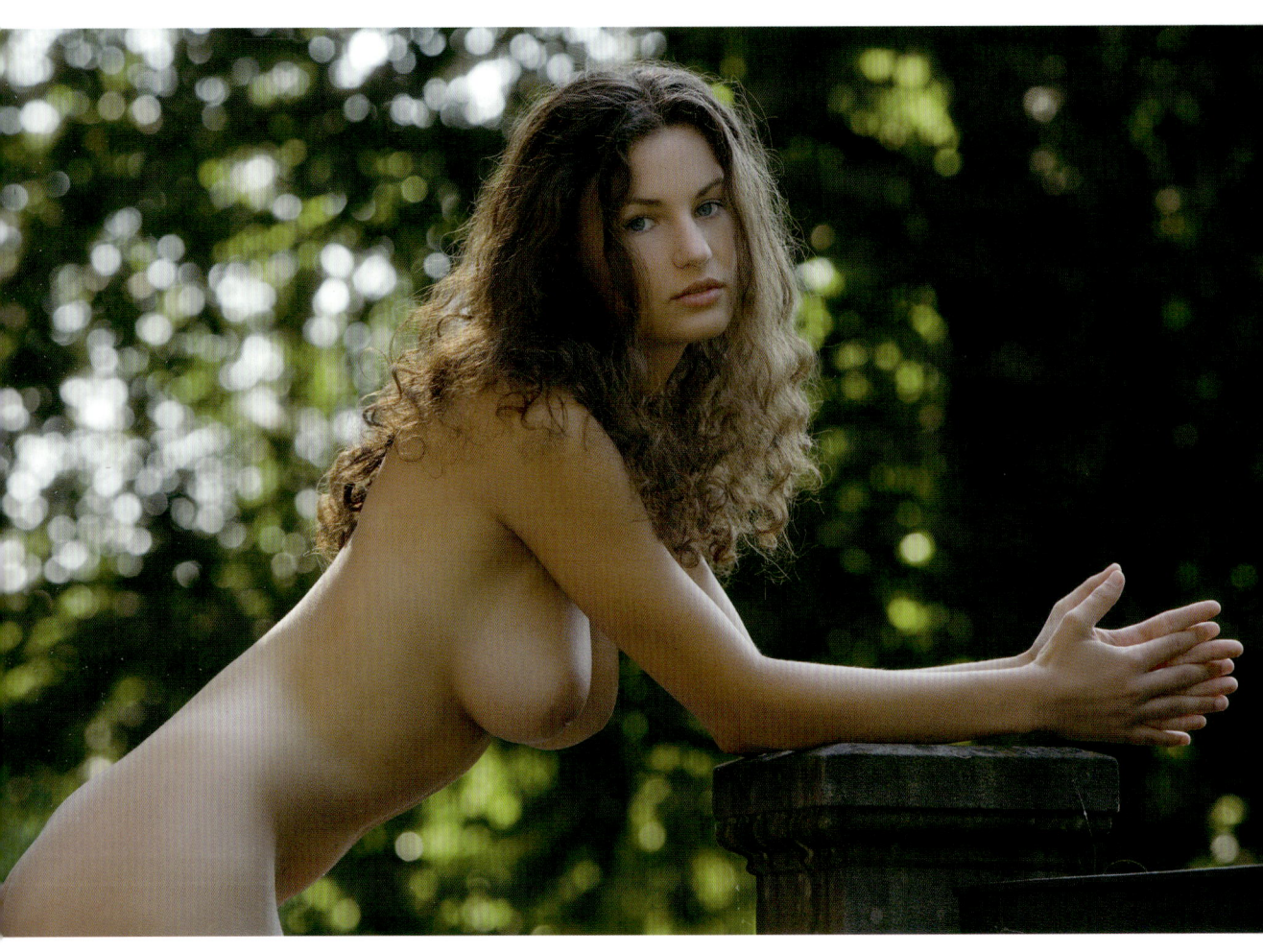

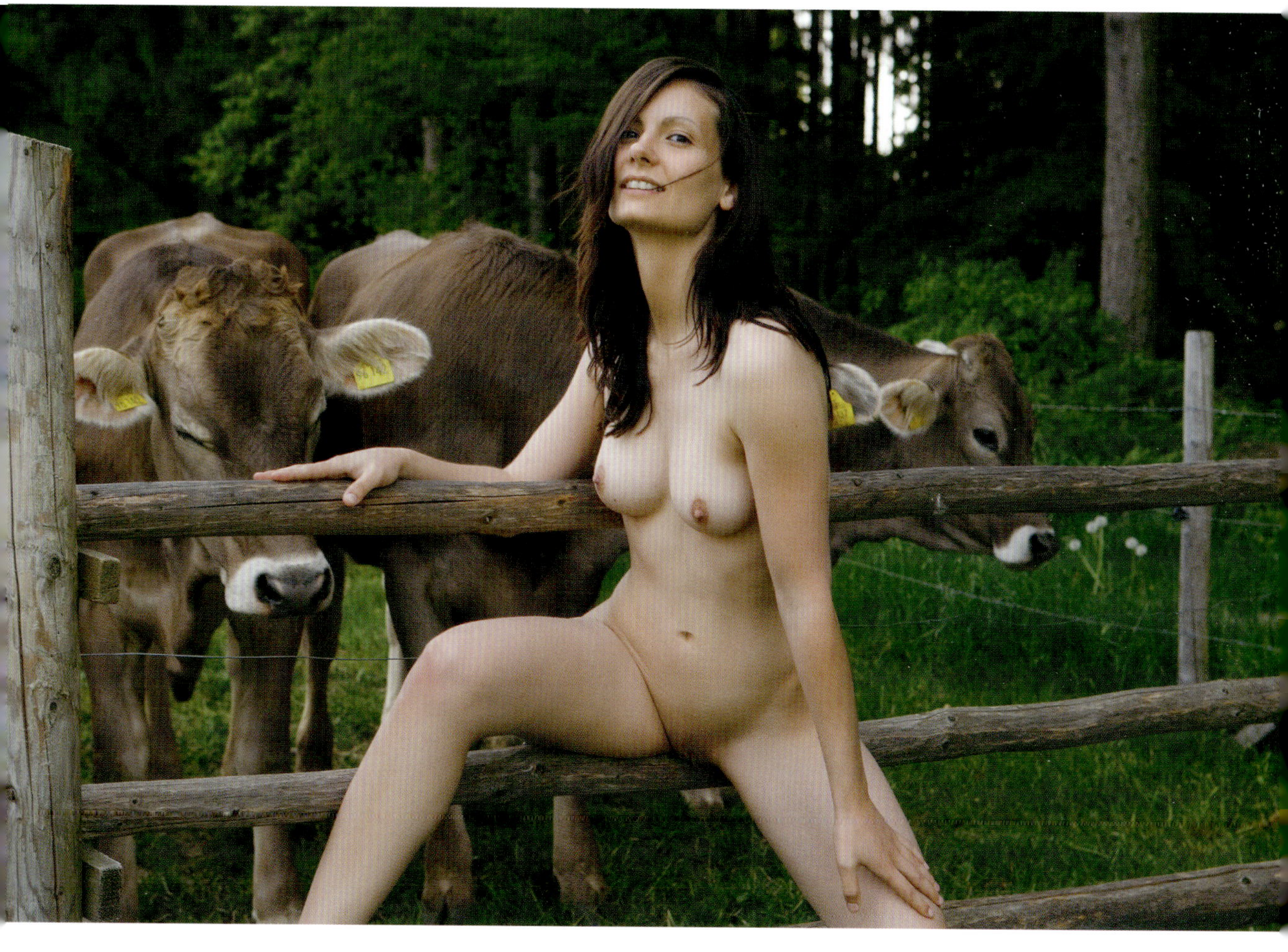

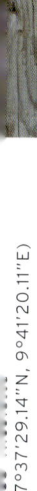

(47°37'29.14"N, 9°41'20.11"E)

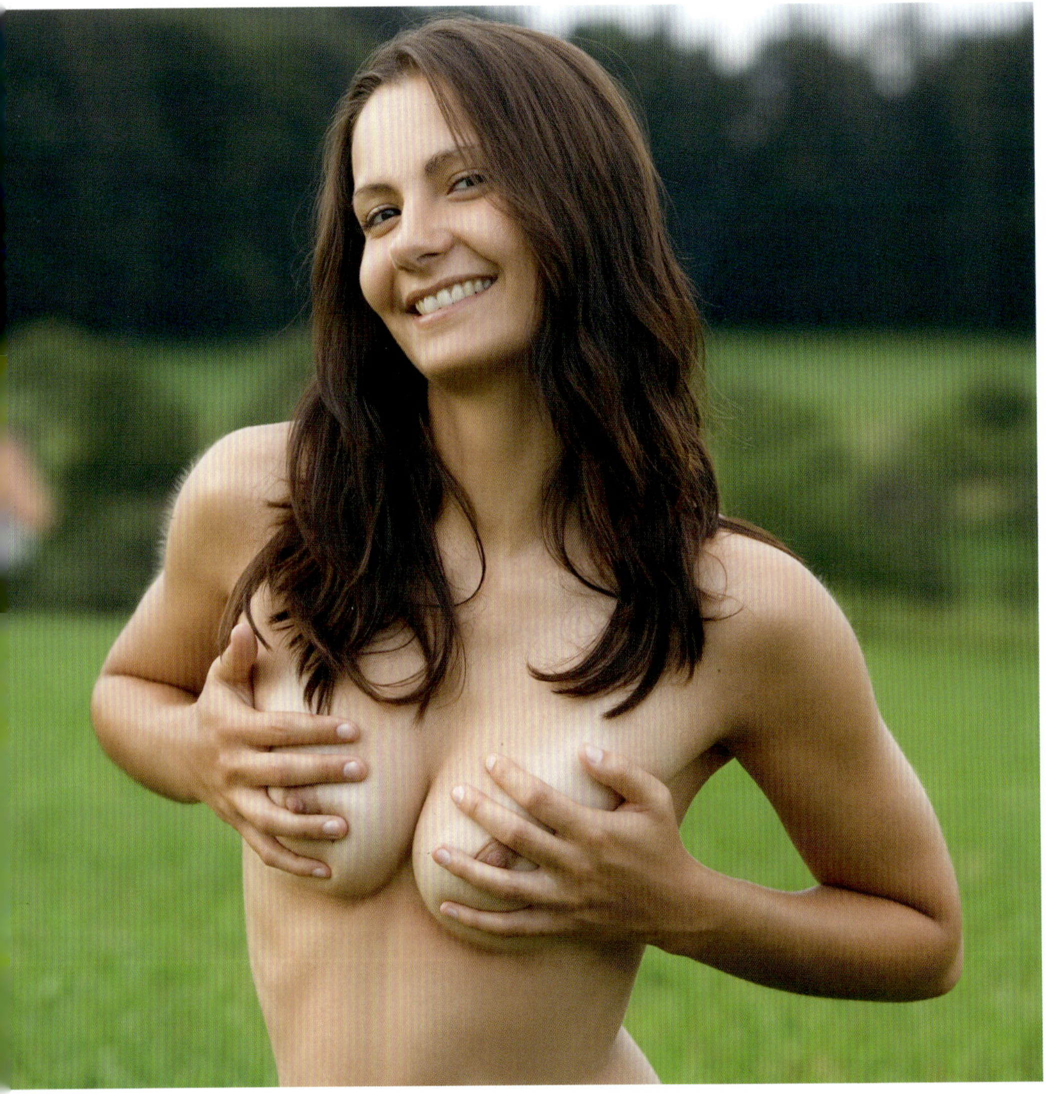

p. 64 Nicolette (47°37'31.24"N, 9°41'31.07"E)

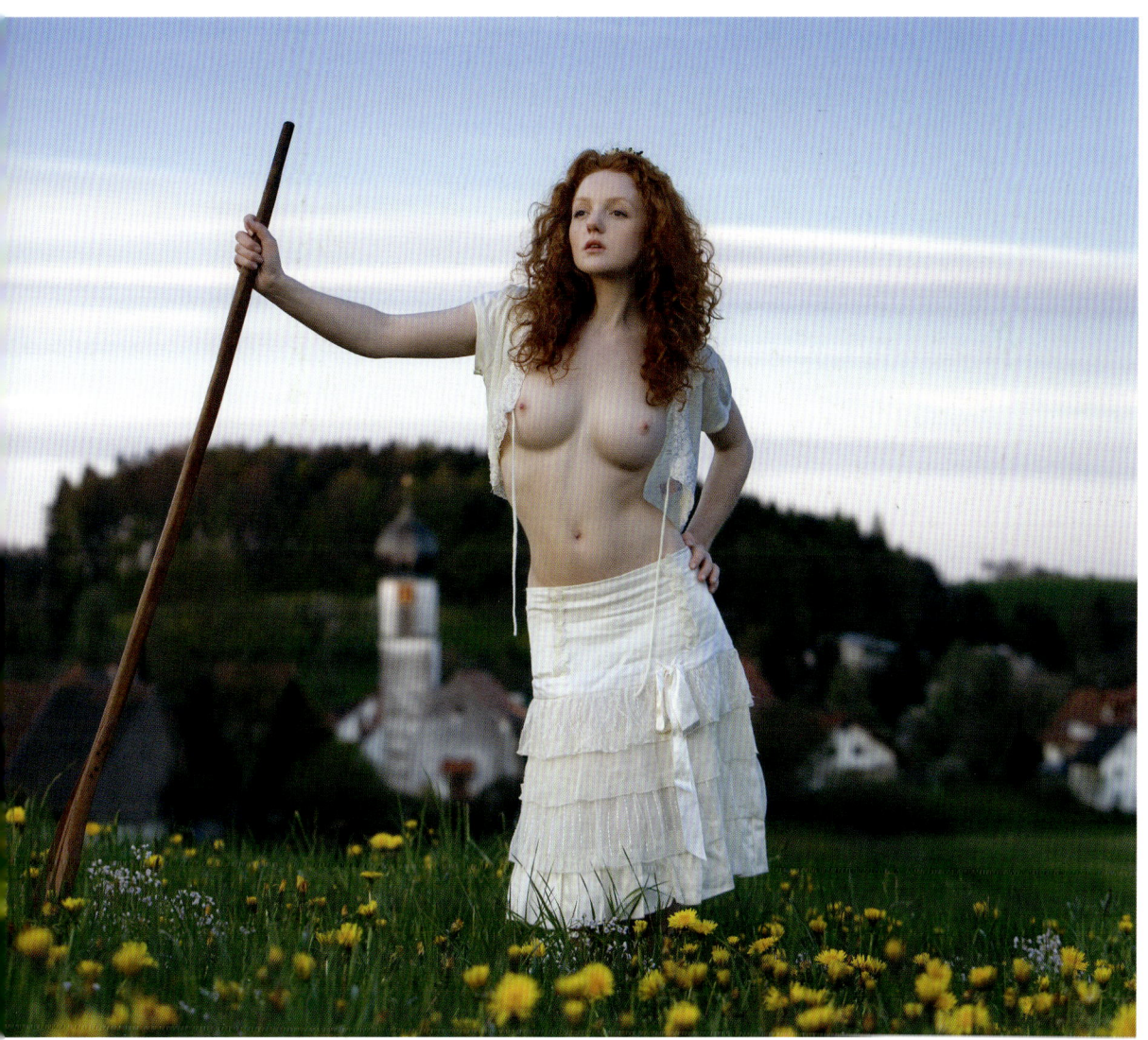

p. 65 Ivory Flame (47°37'29.13"N, 9°41'32.56"E)

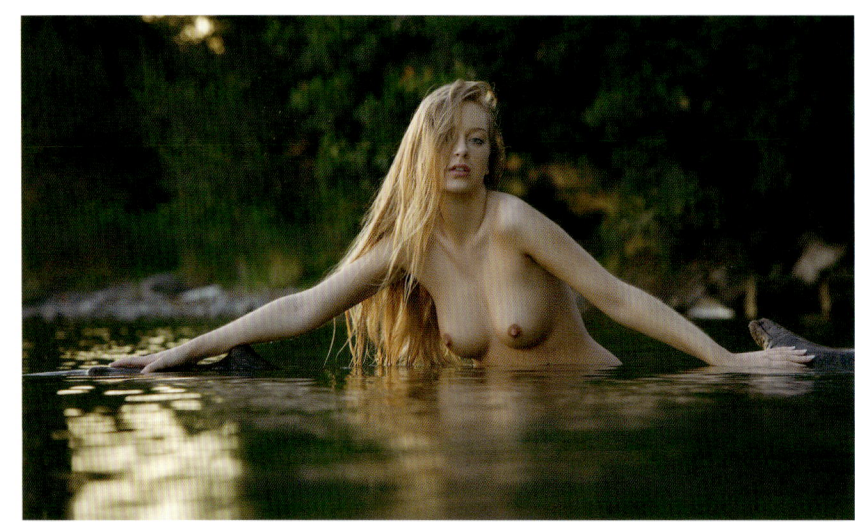

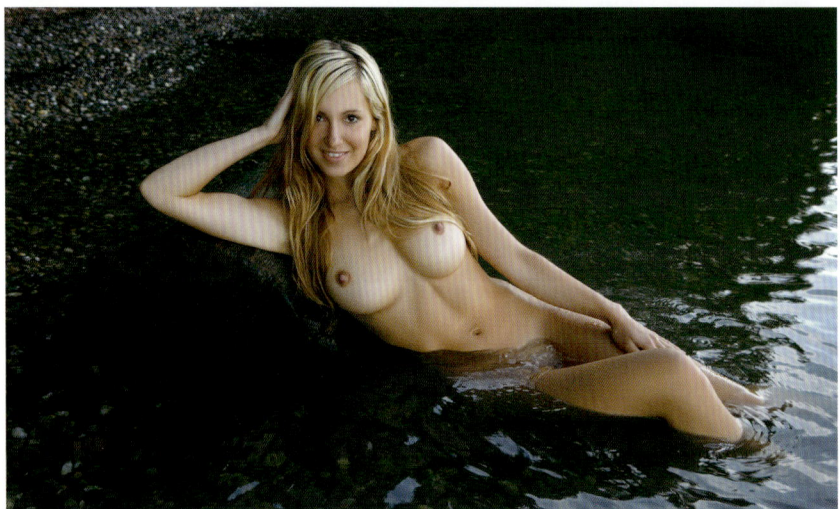

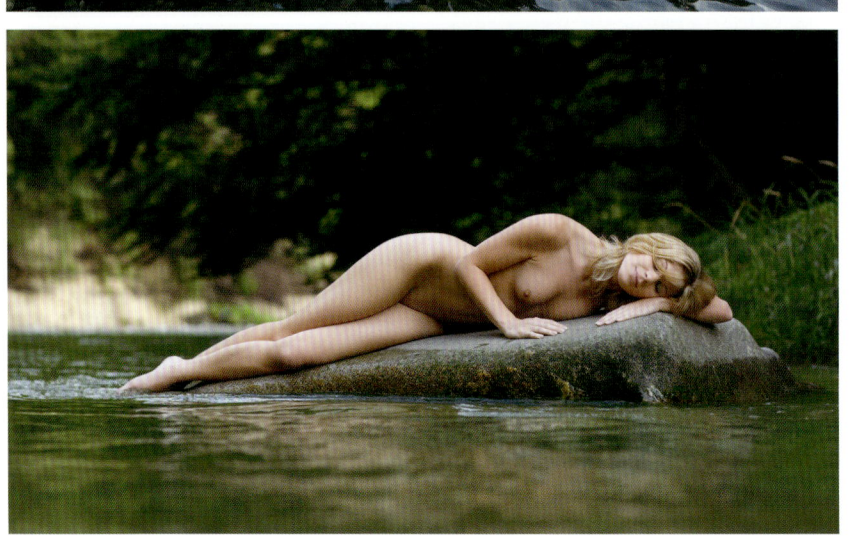

p. 66 Kinga (47°39'58.99"N, 9°20'14.16"E); Corinna (47°45'41.43"N, 9°6'40.54"E); Jade (47°38'0.95"N, 9°43'26.39"E)

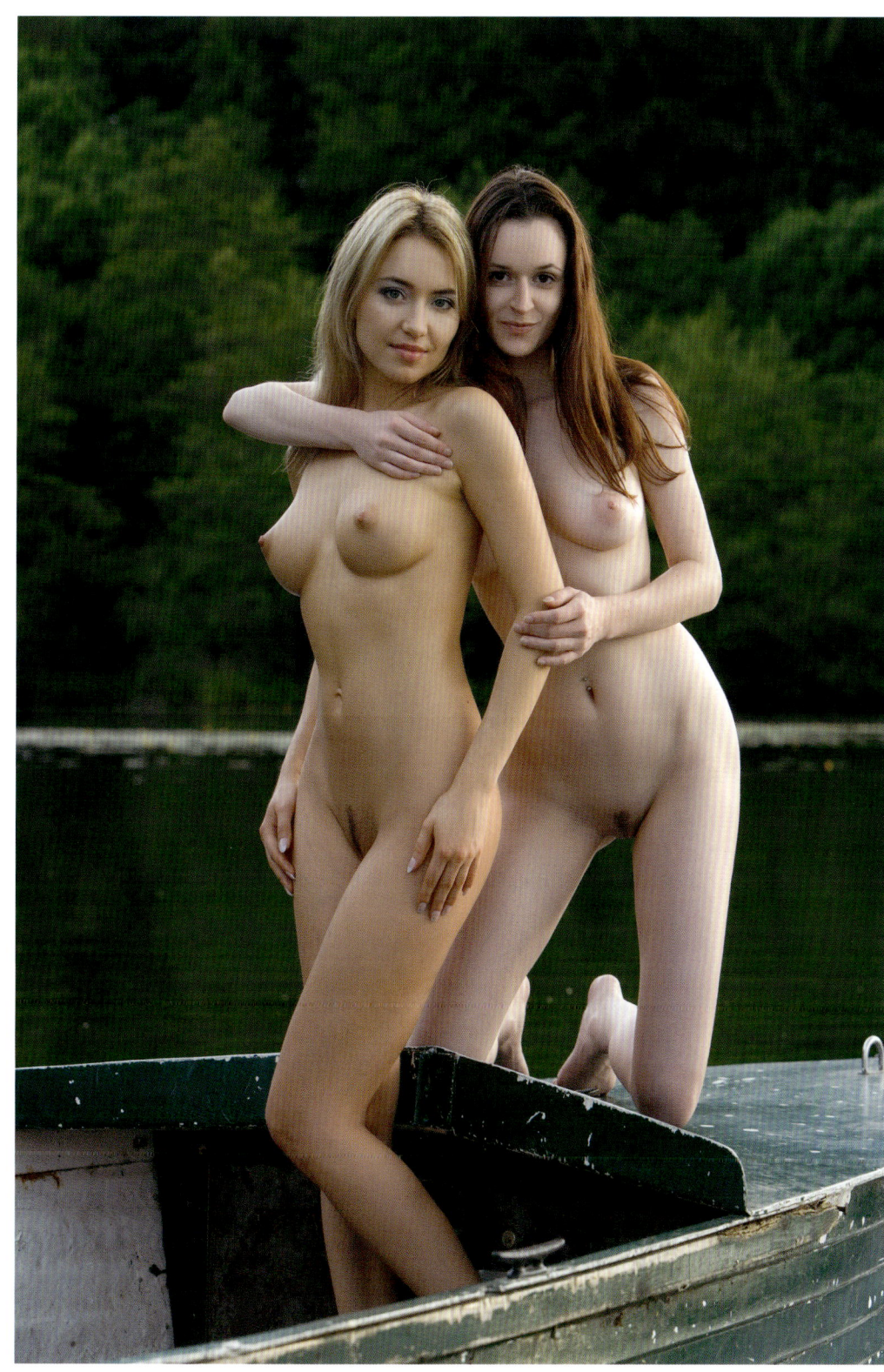

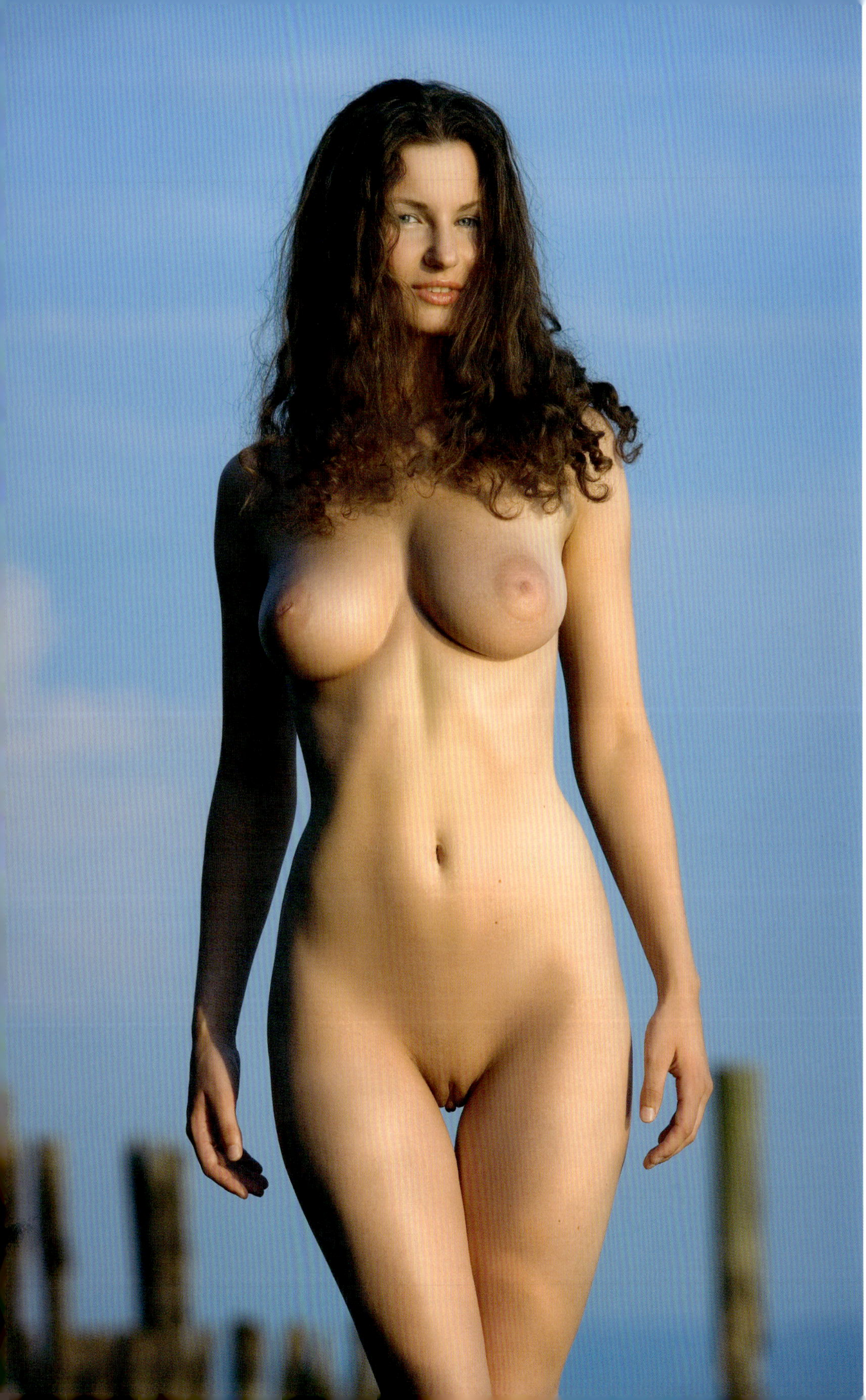

p. 68 Susann (47°39'53.06"N, 9°20'23.78"E)

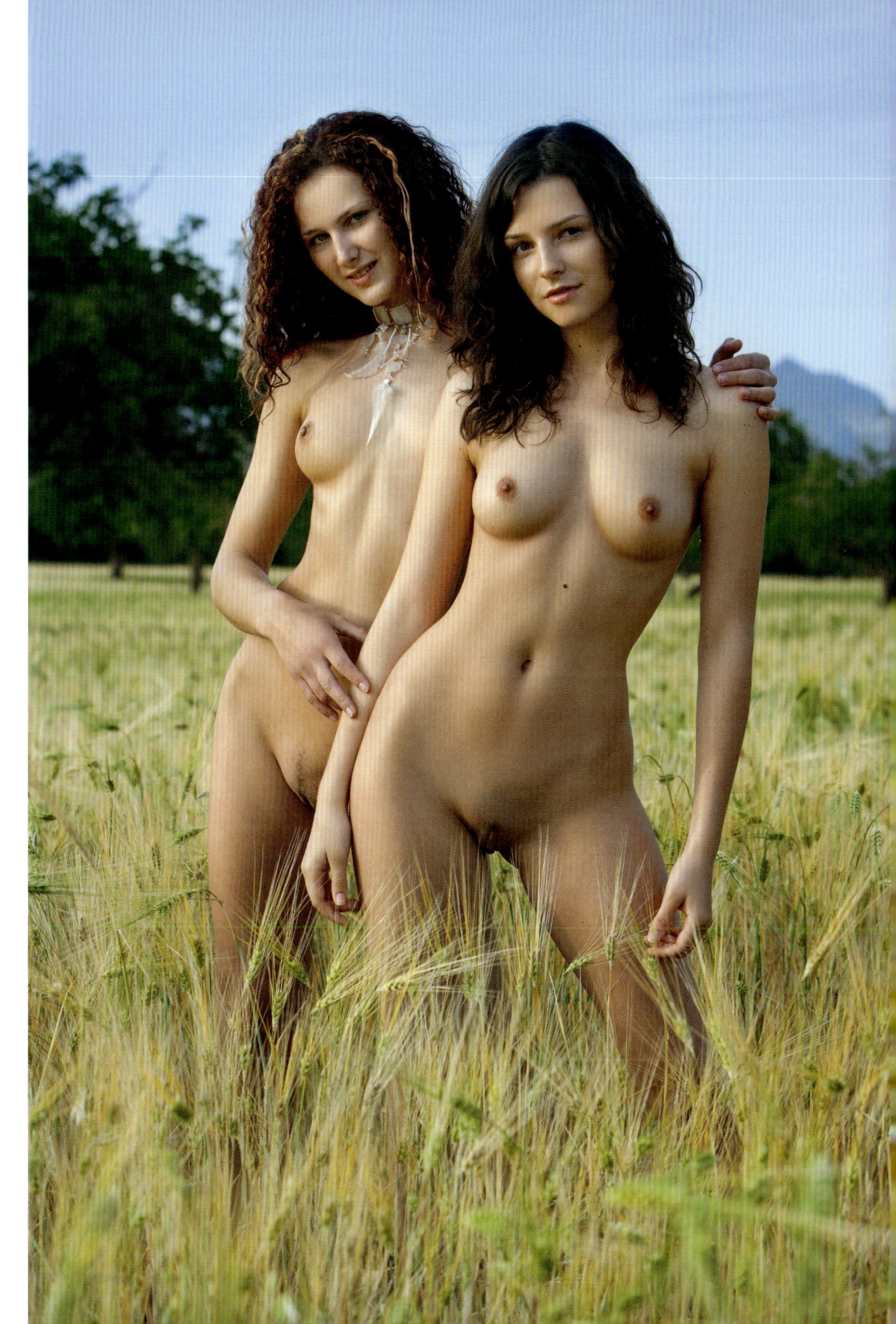

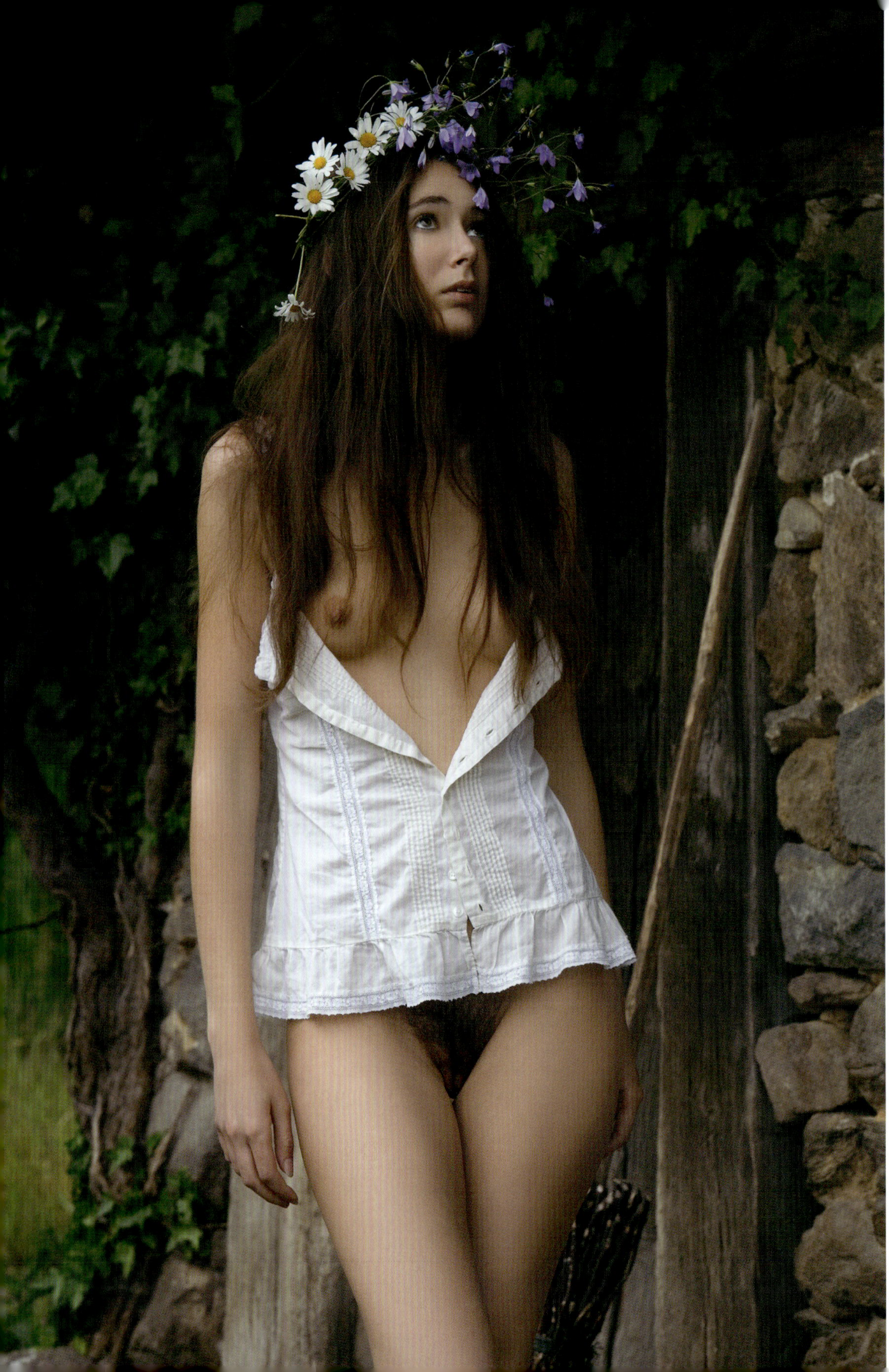

p. 70 Alison (48°18'9.02"N, 8°4'36.06"E)

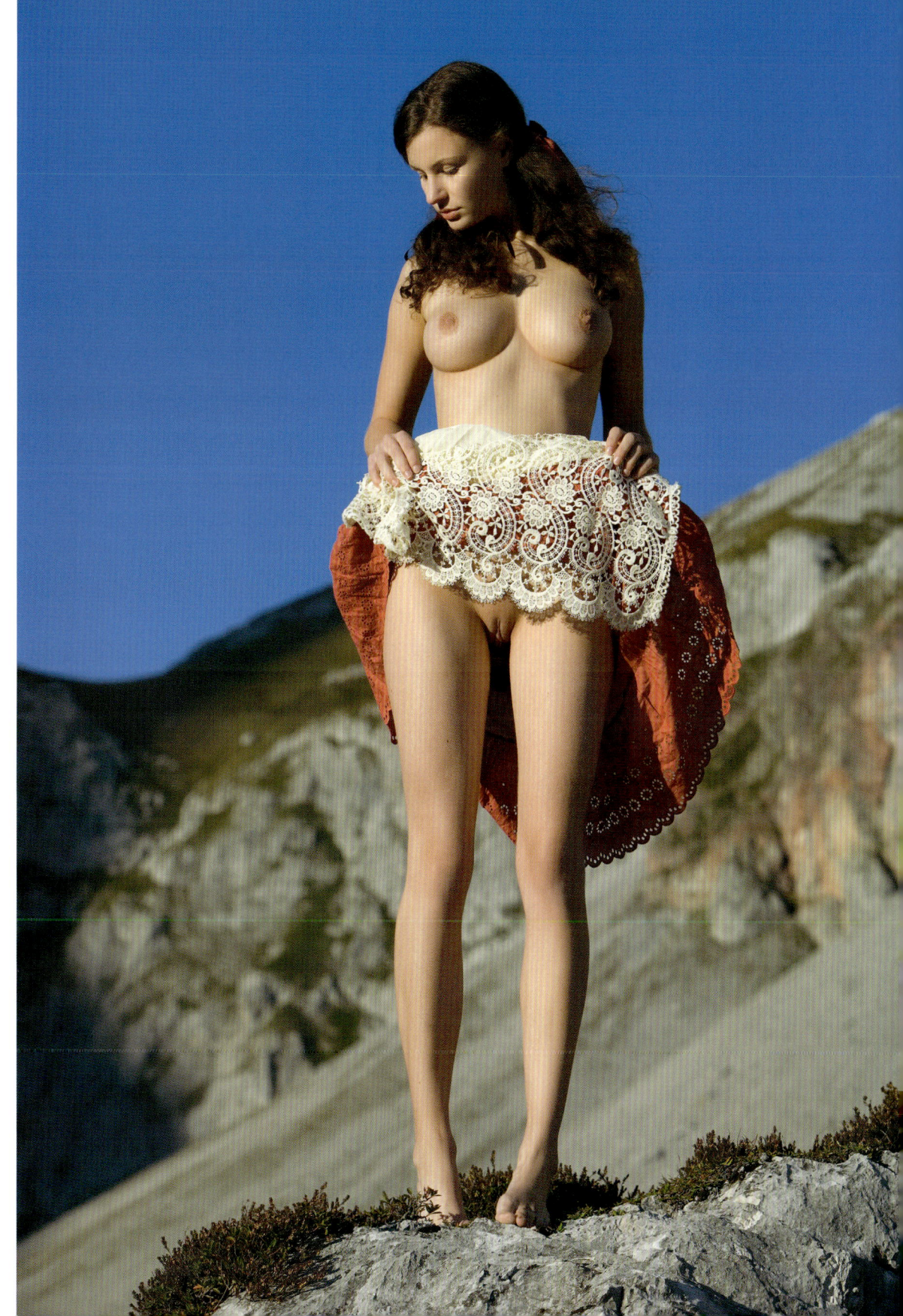

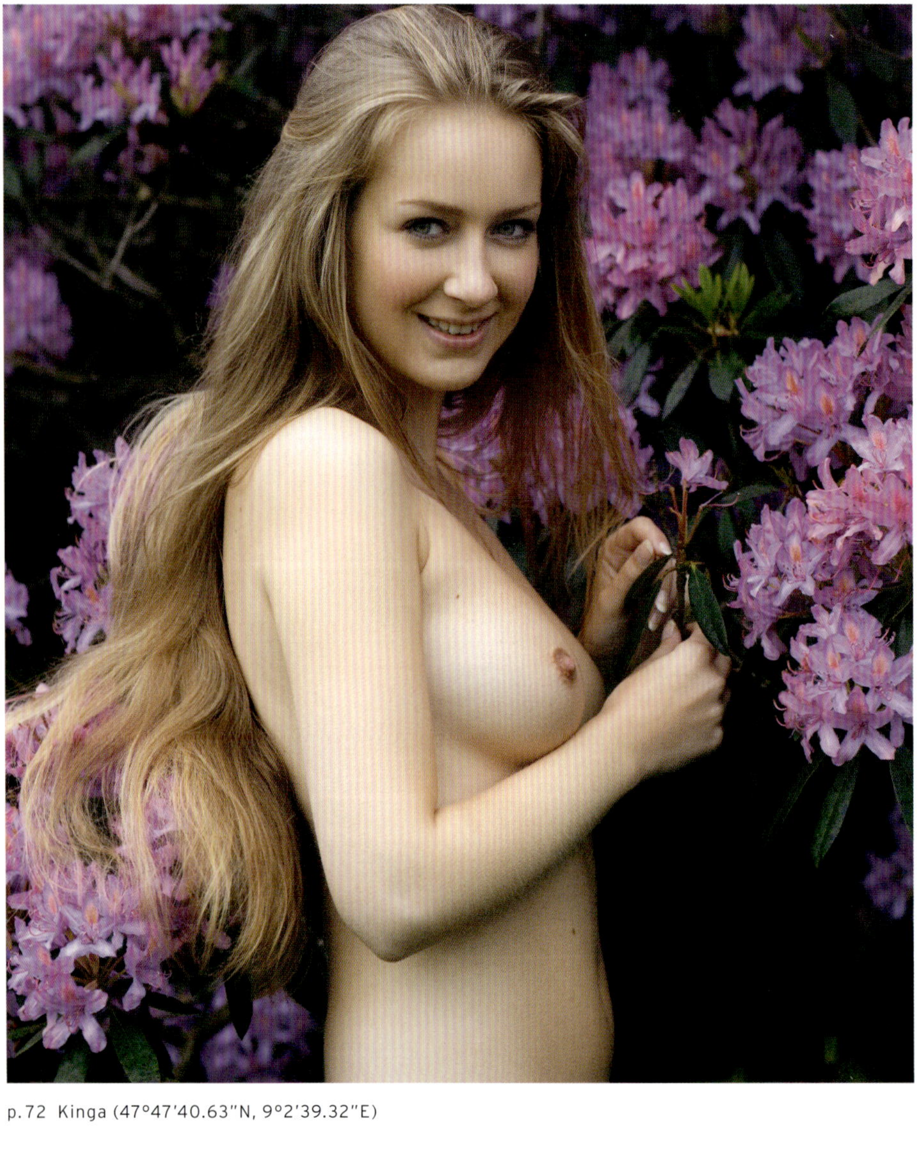

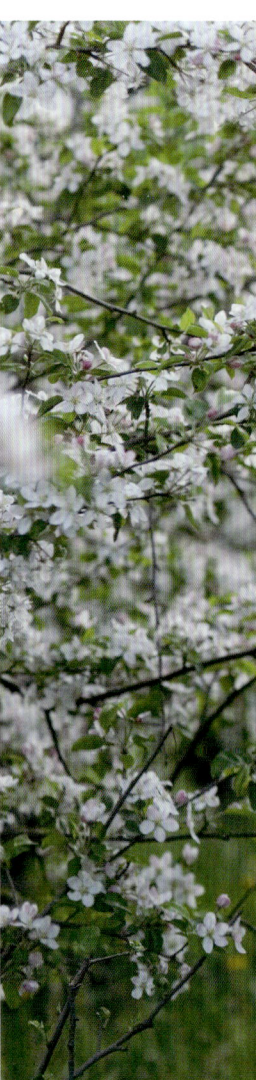

p.72 Kinga (47°47'40.63"N, 9°2'39.32"E)

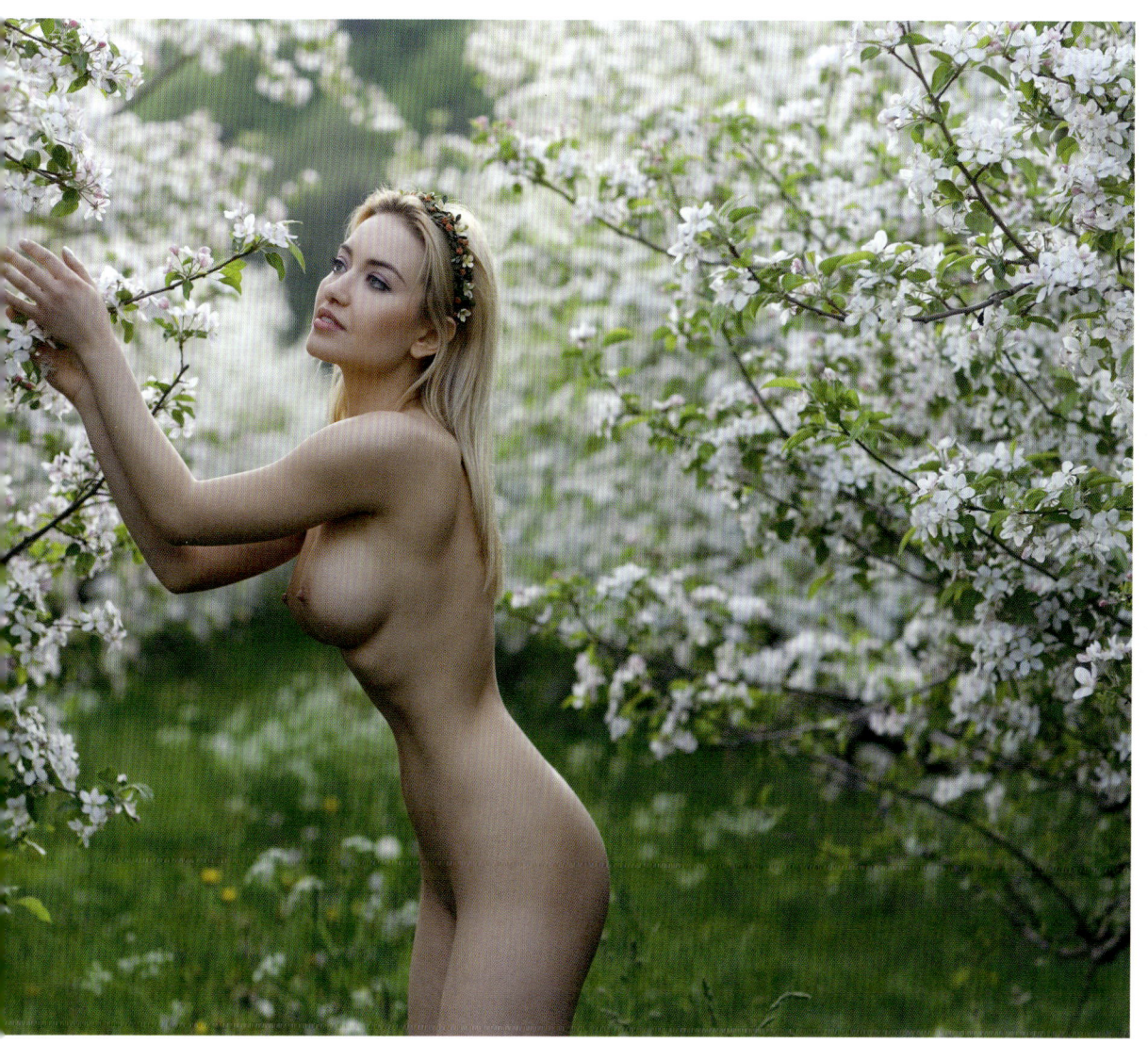

p. 73 Lia (47°37'59.01"N, 9°36'4.32"E)

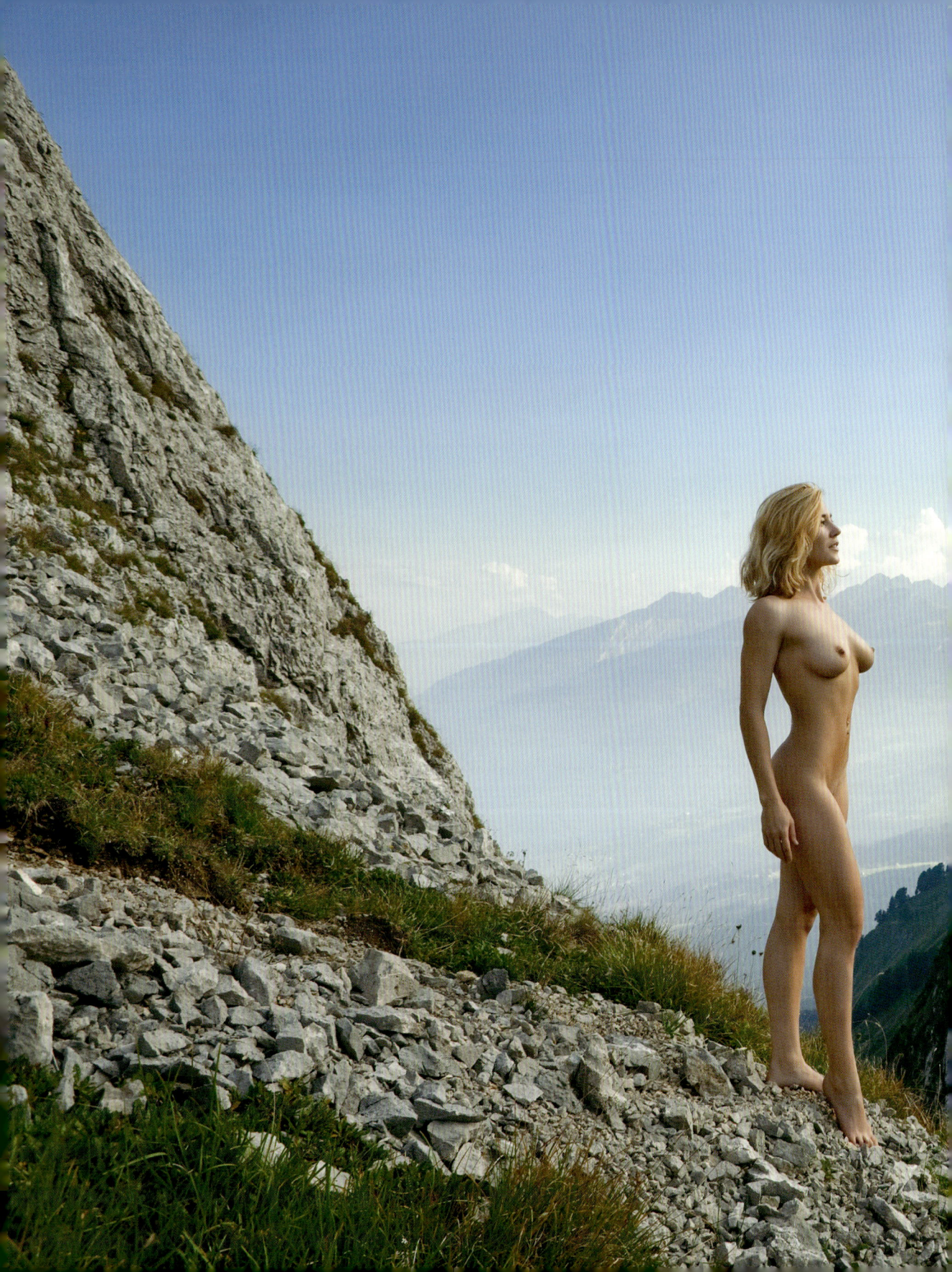

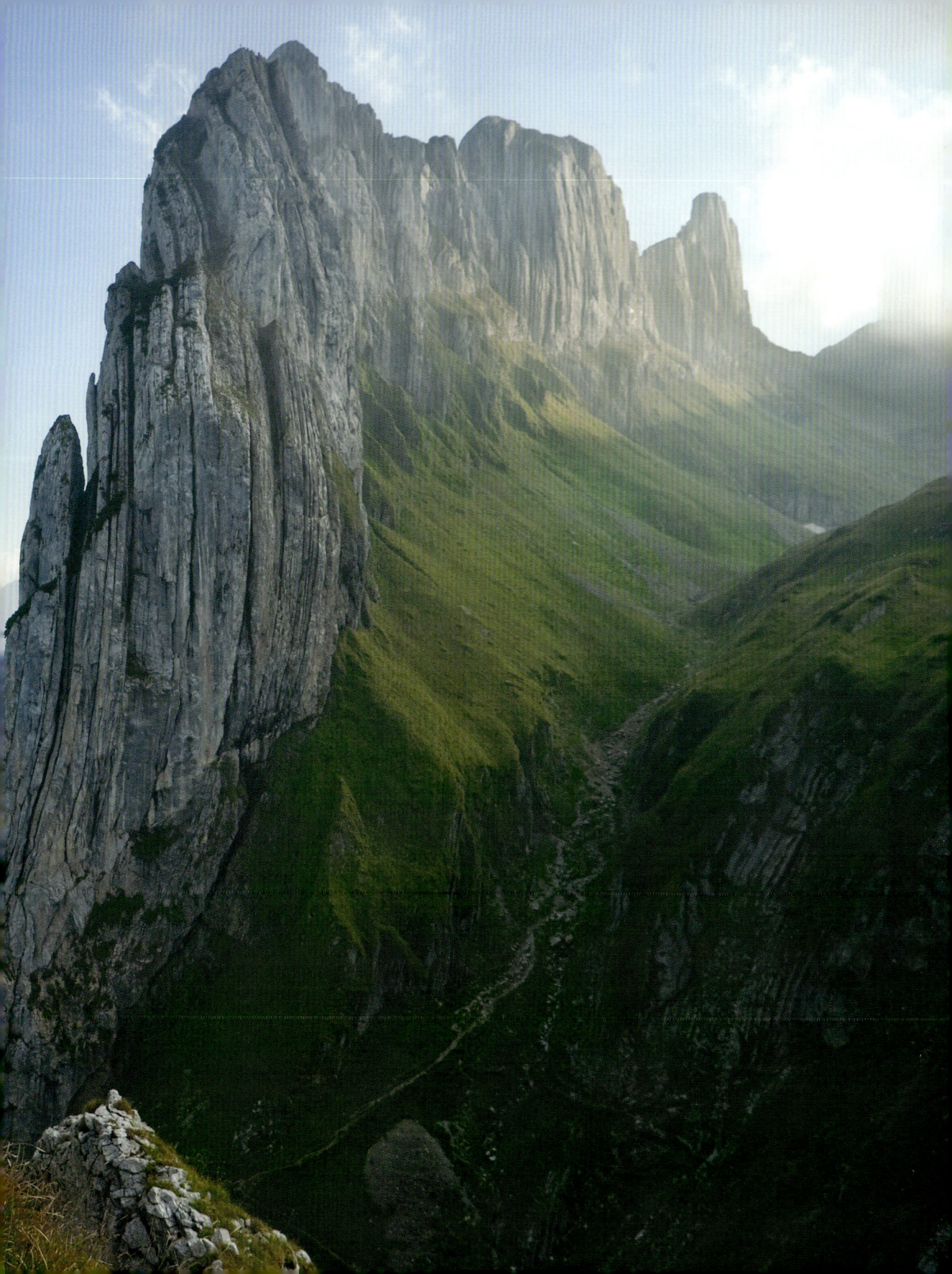

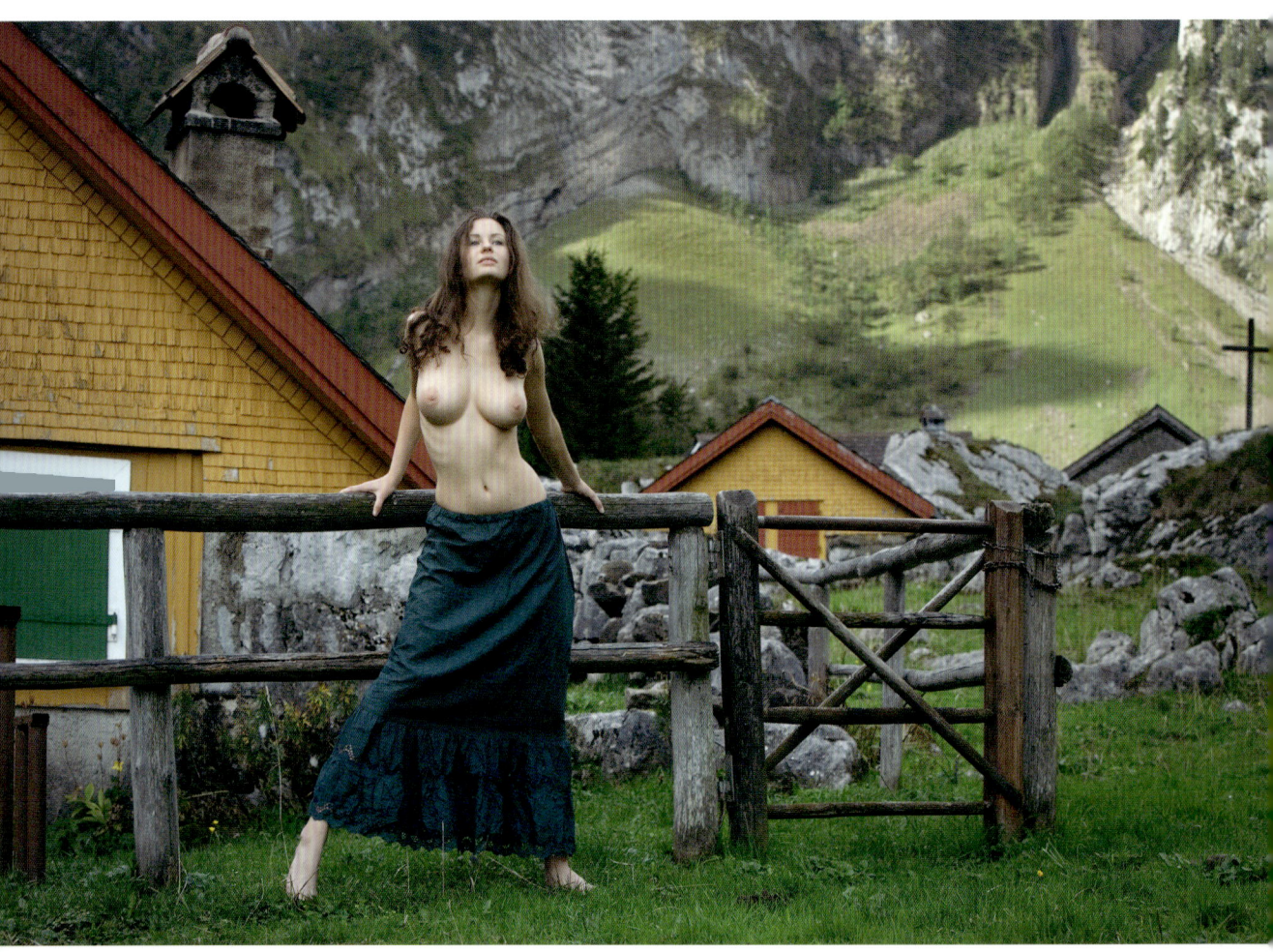

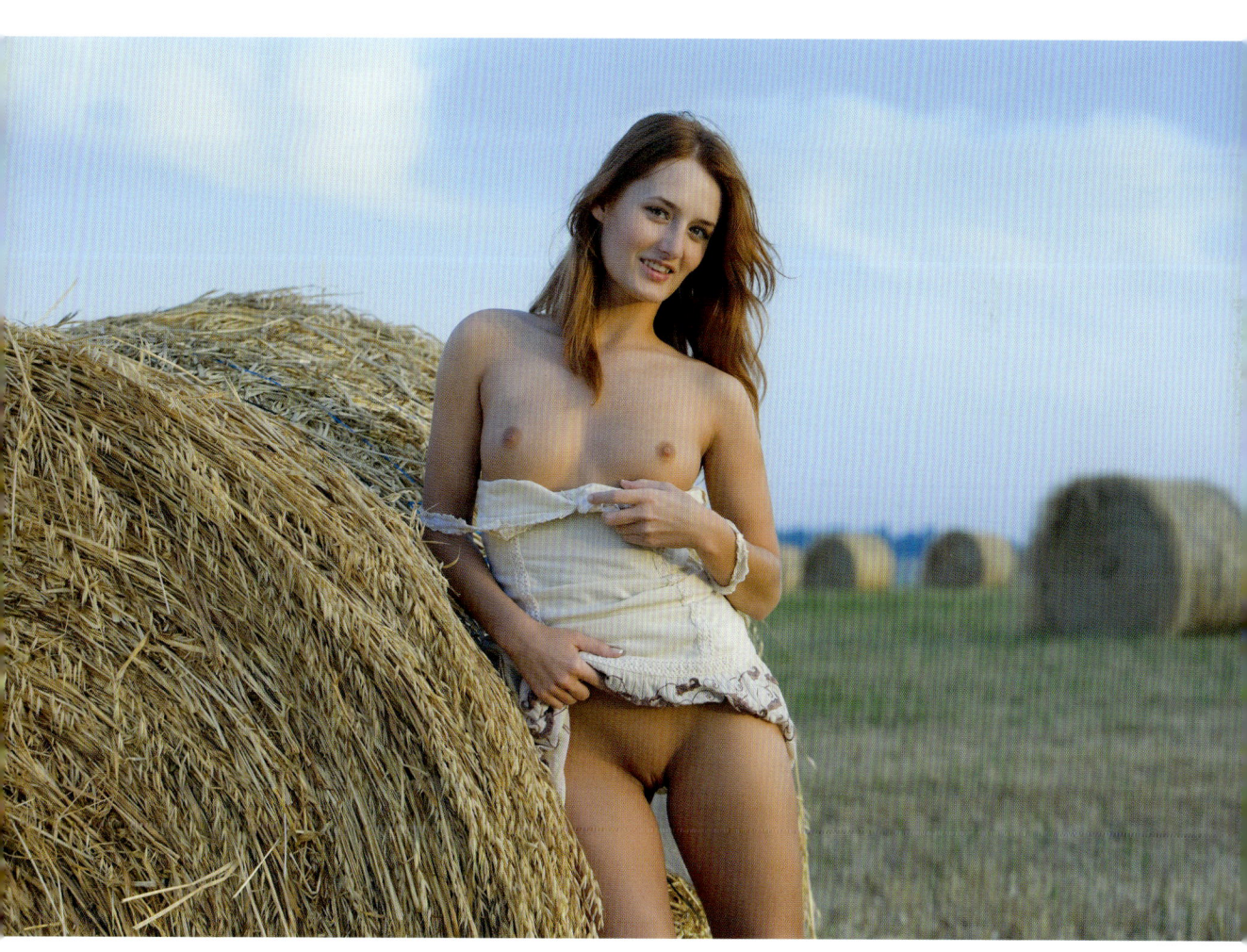

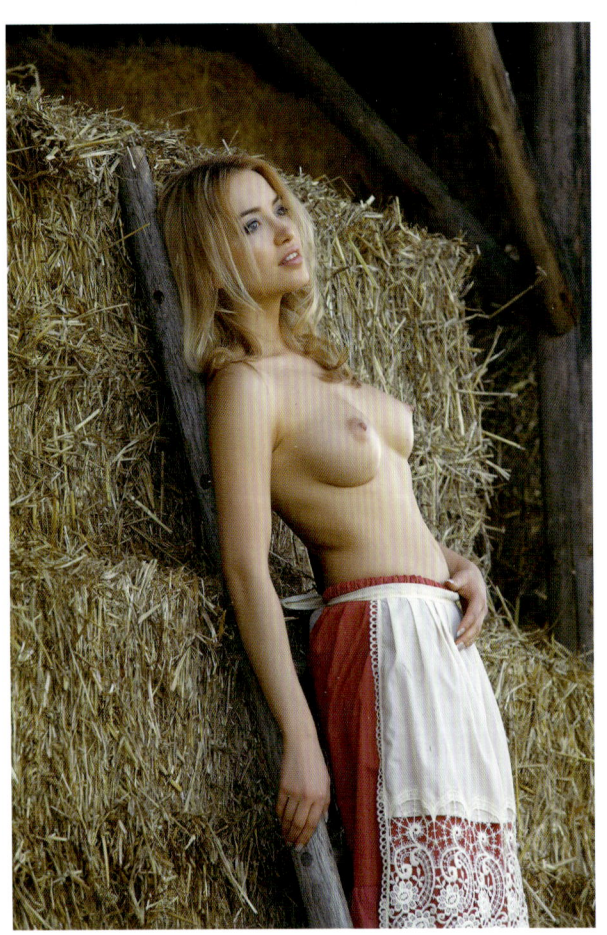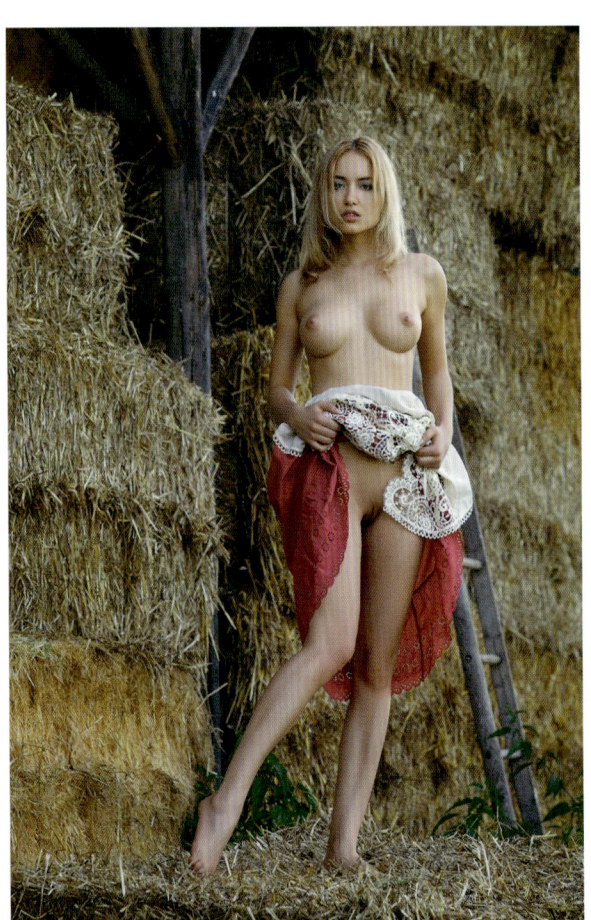

p.78 Lia (47°52'59.81"N, 9°25'25.43"E)

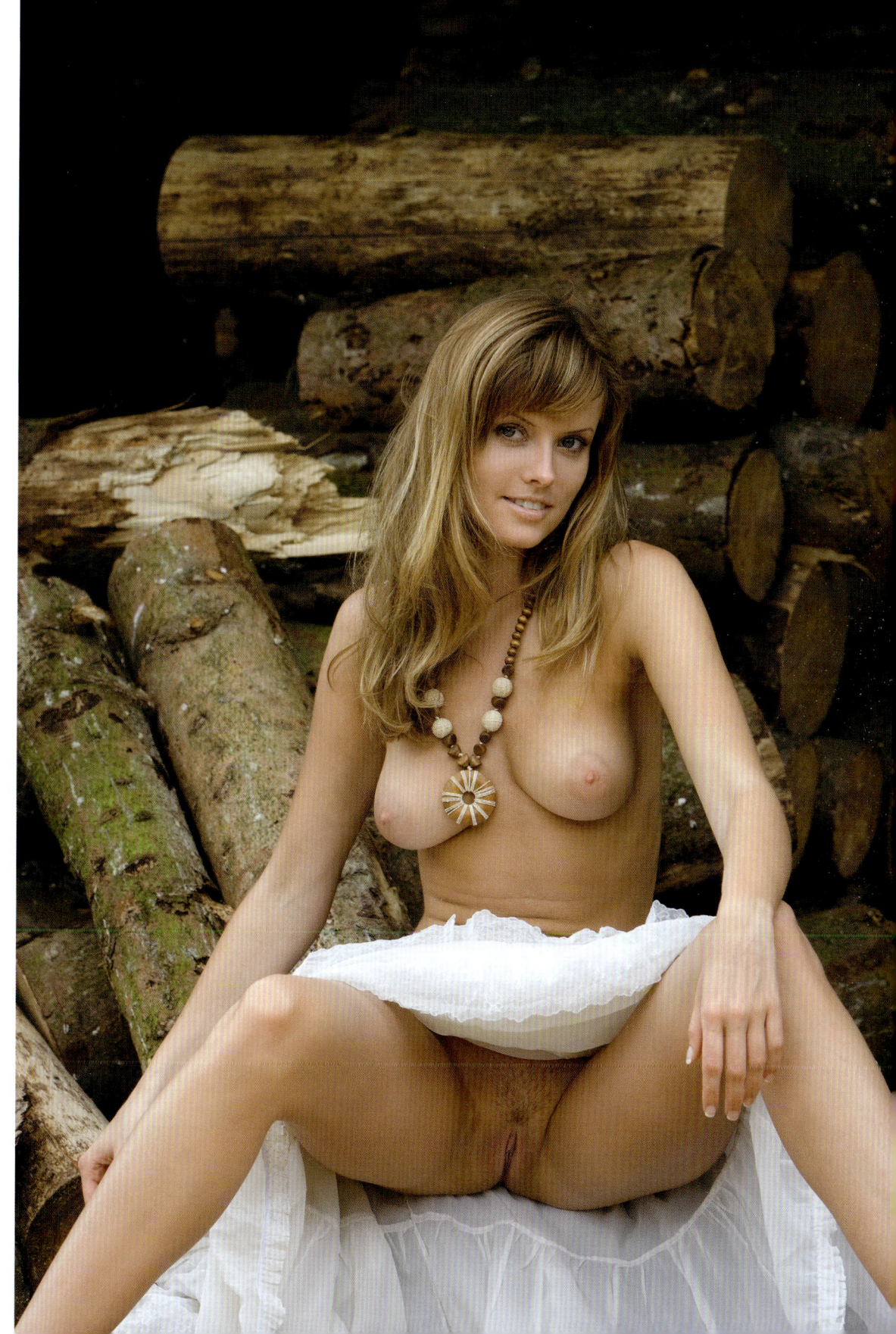

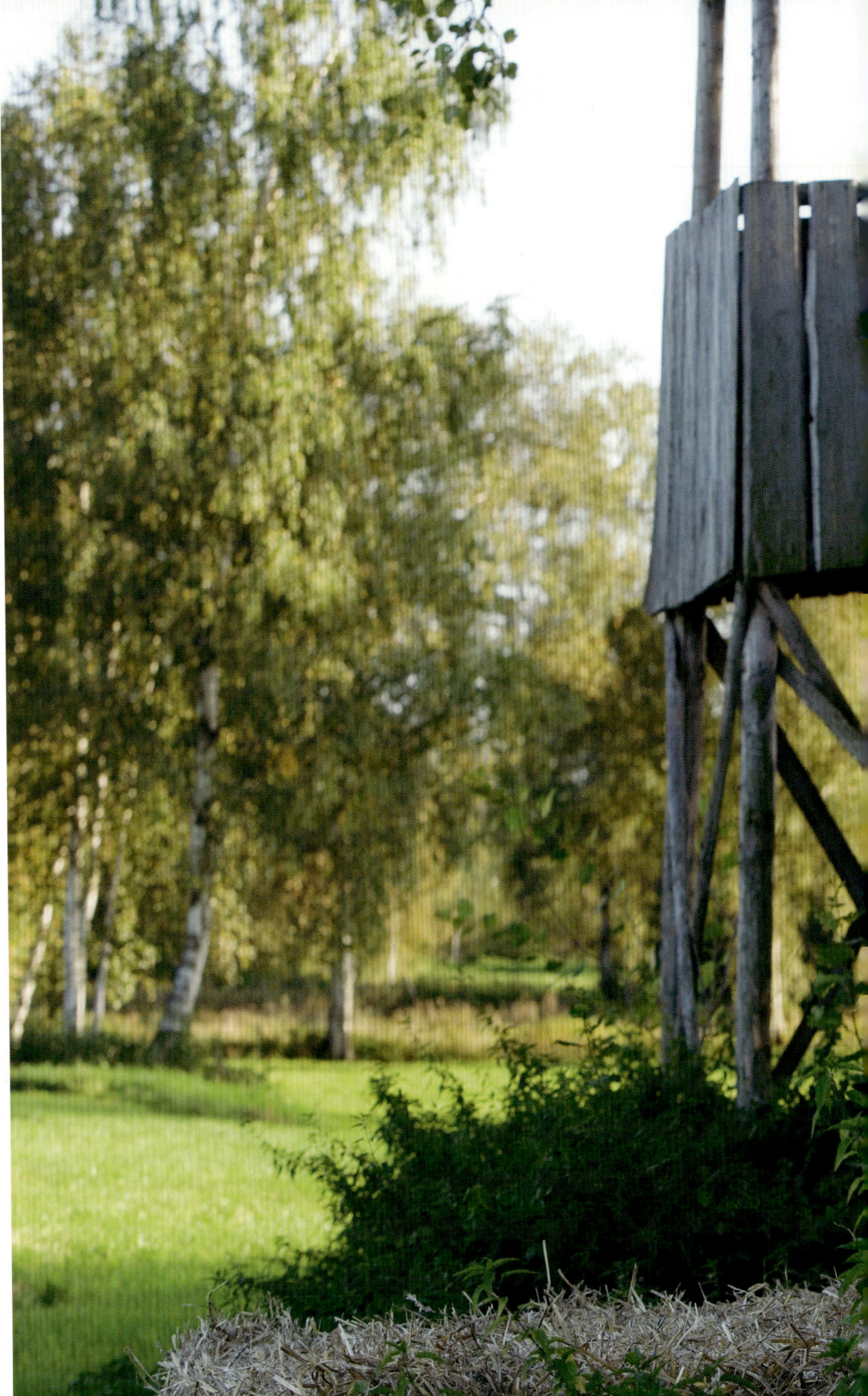

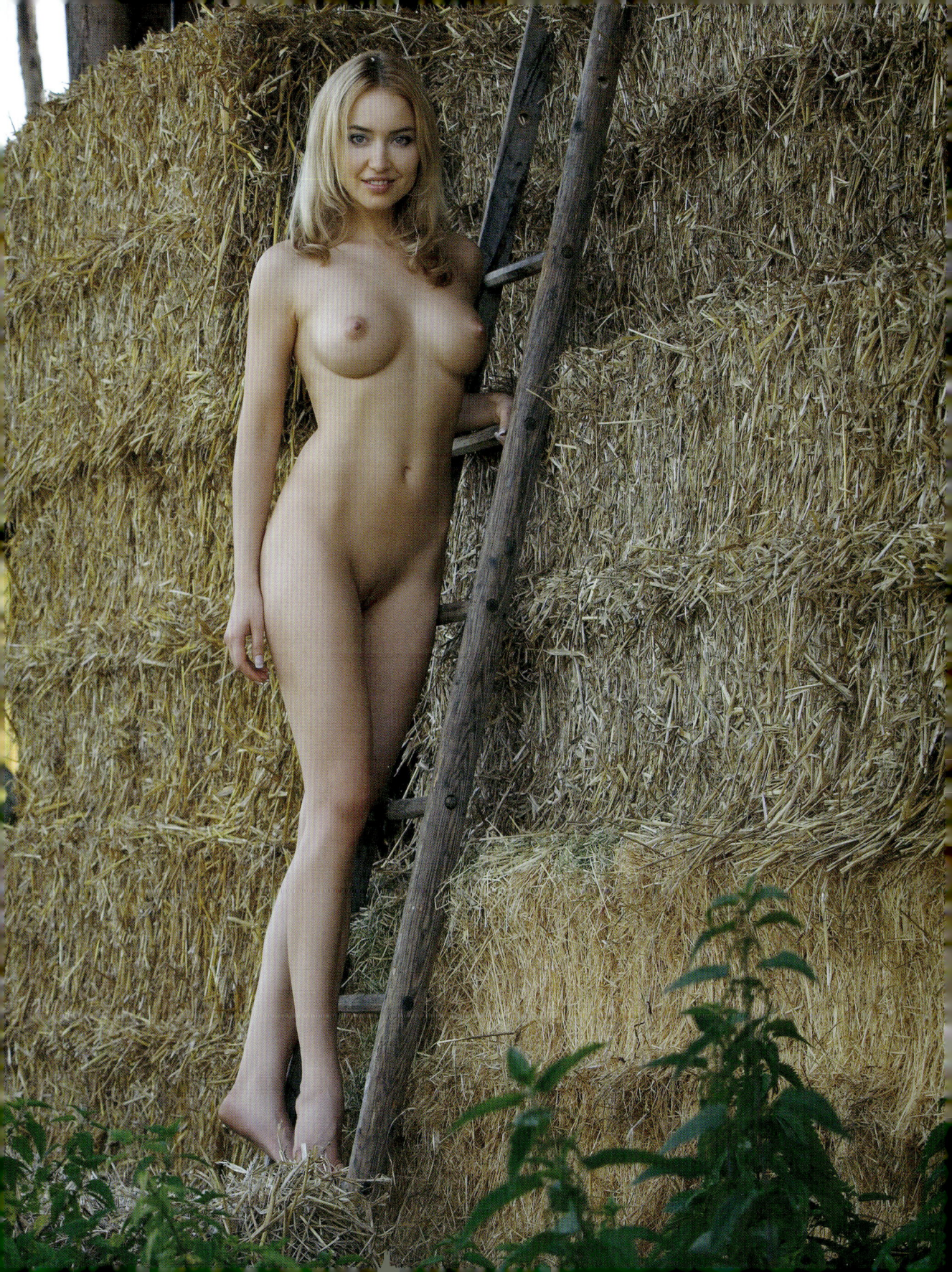

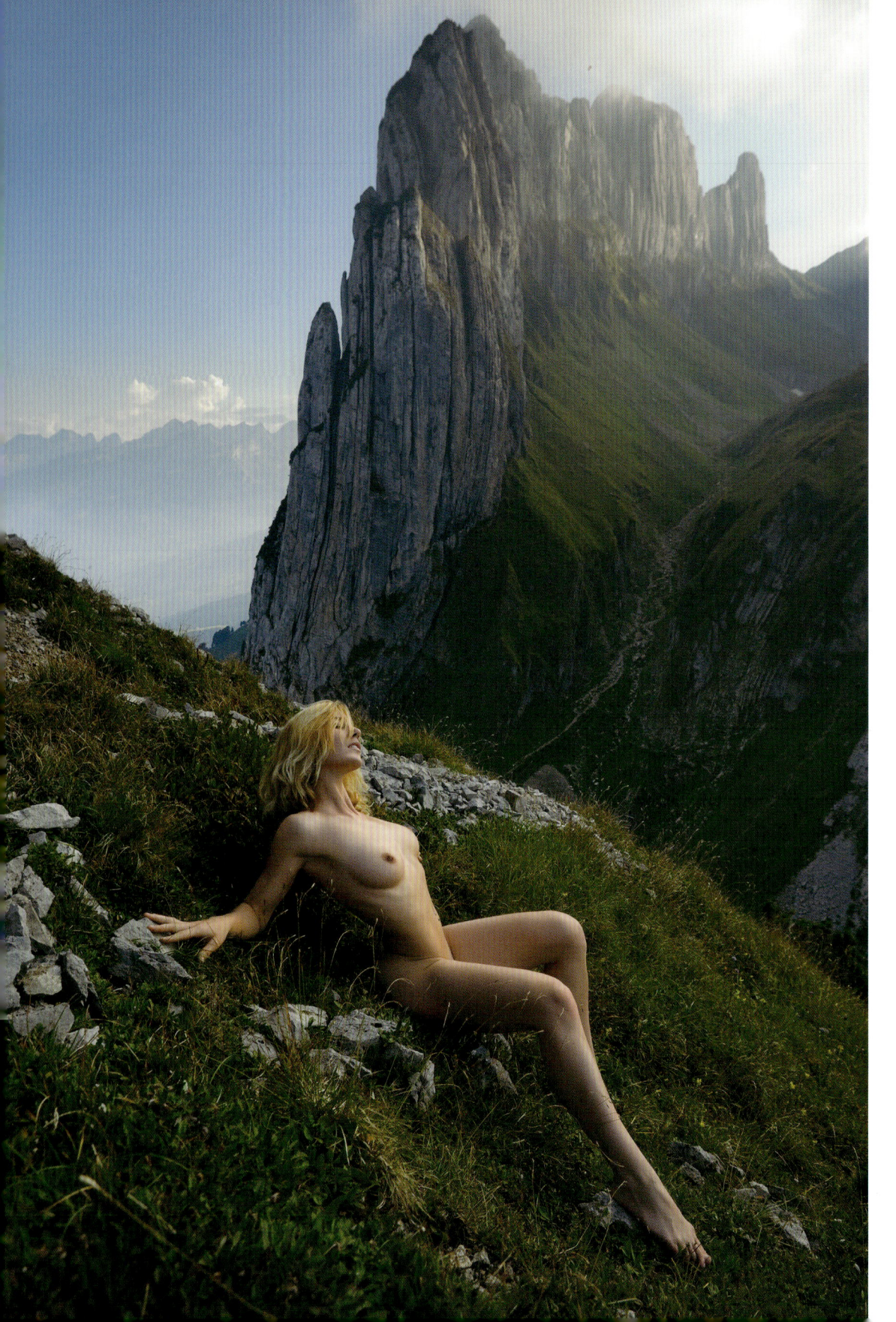

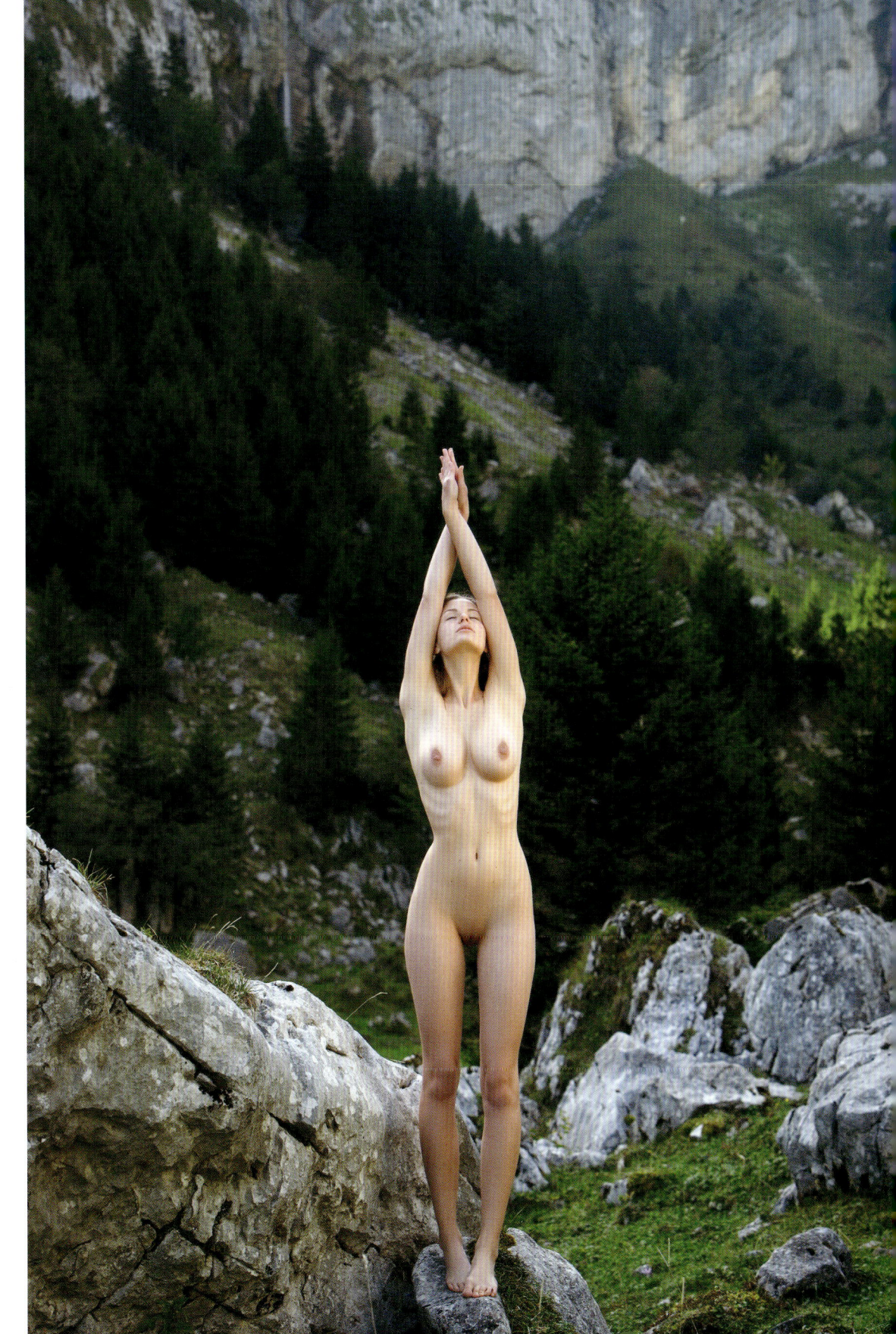

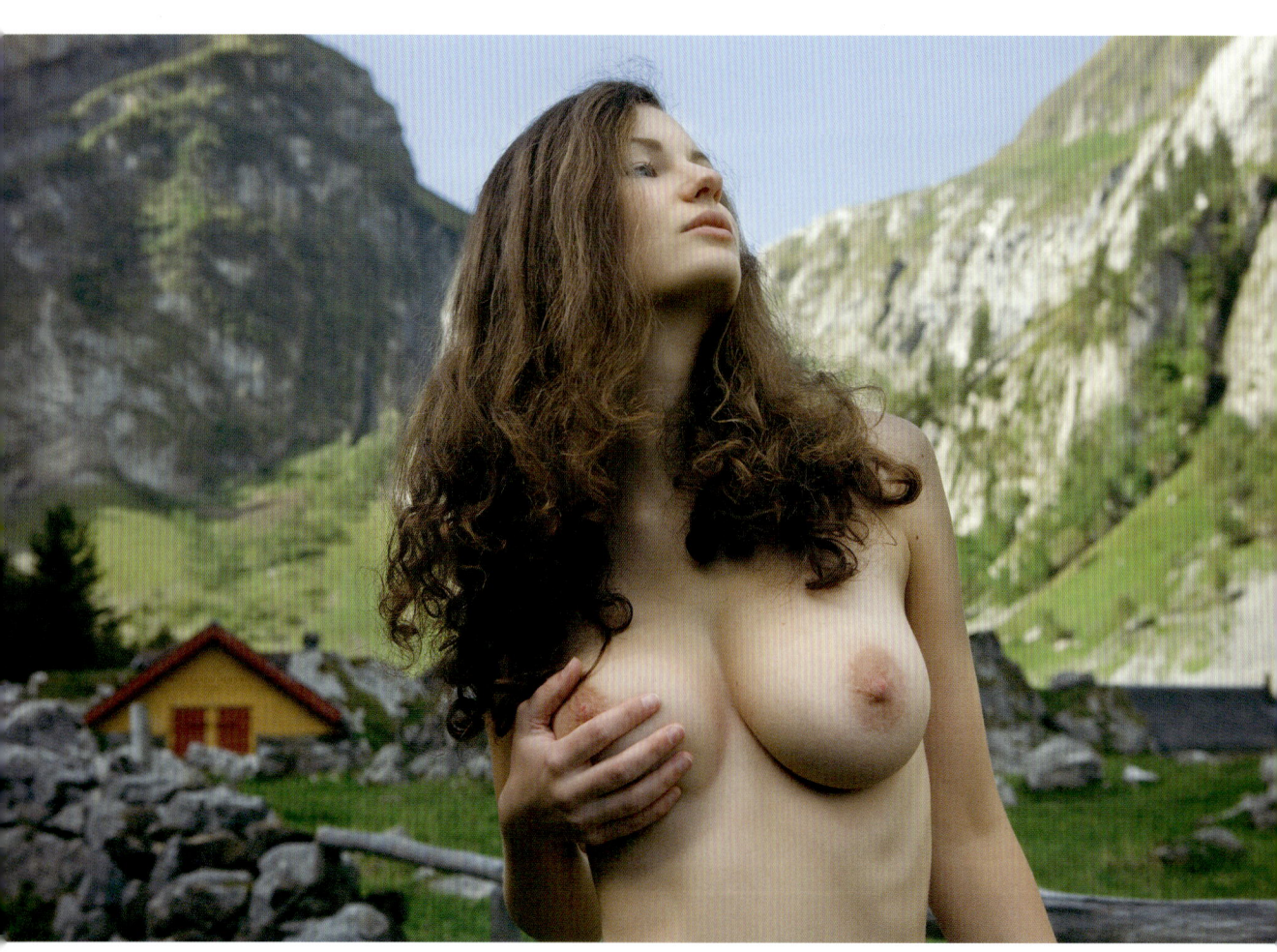

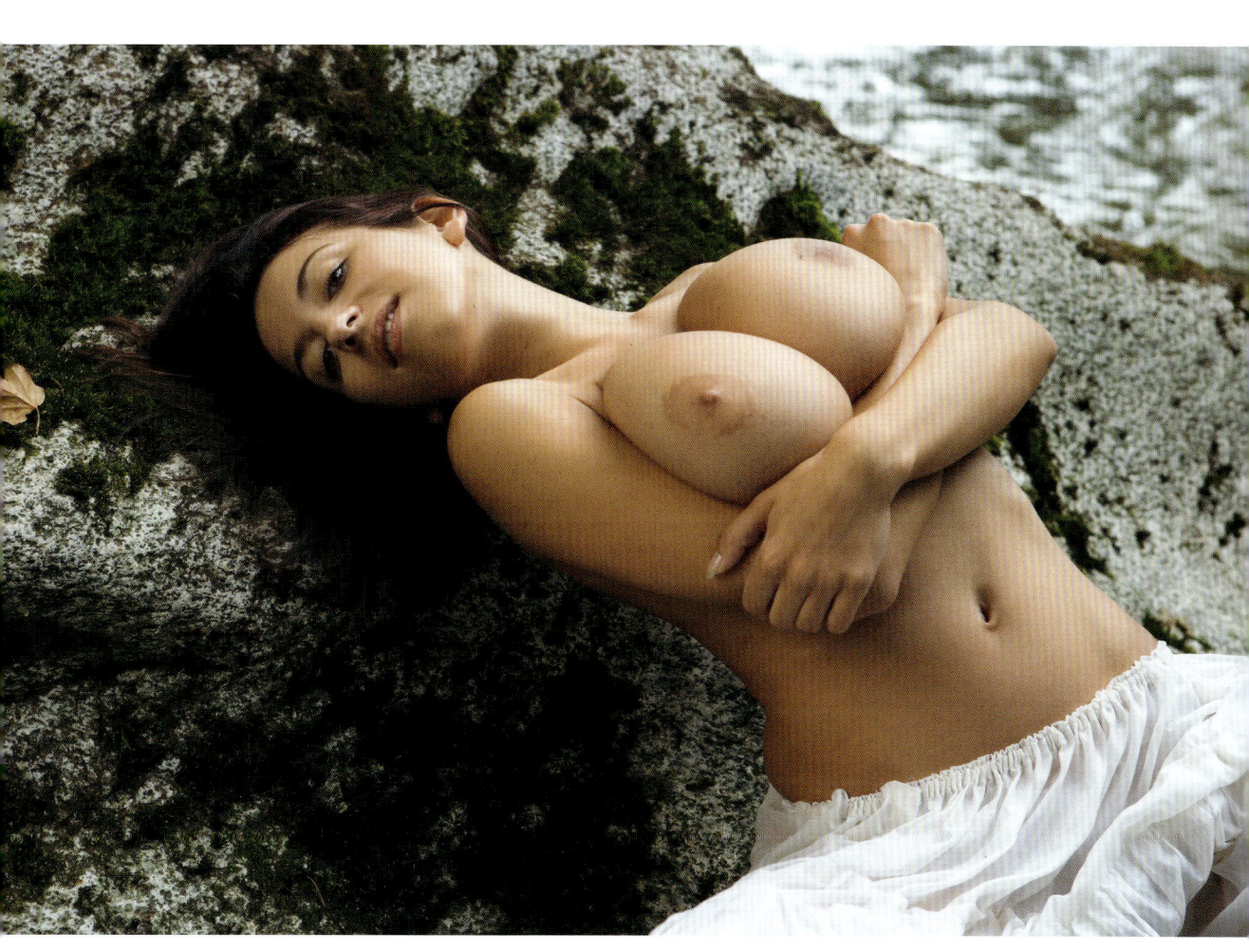

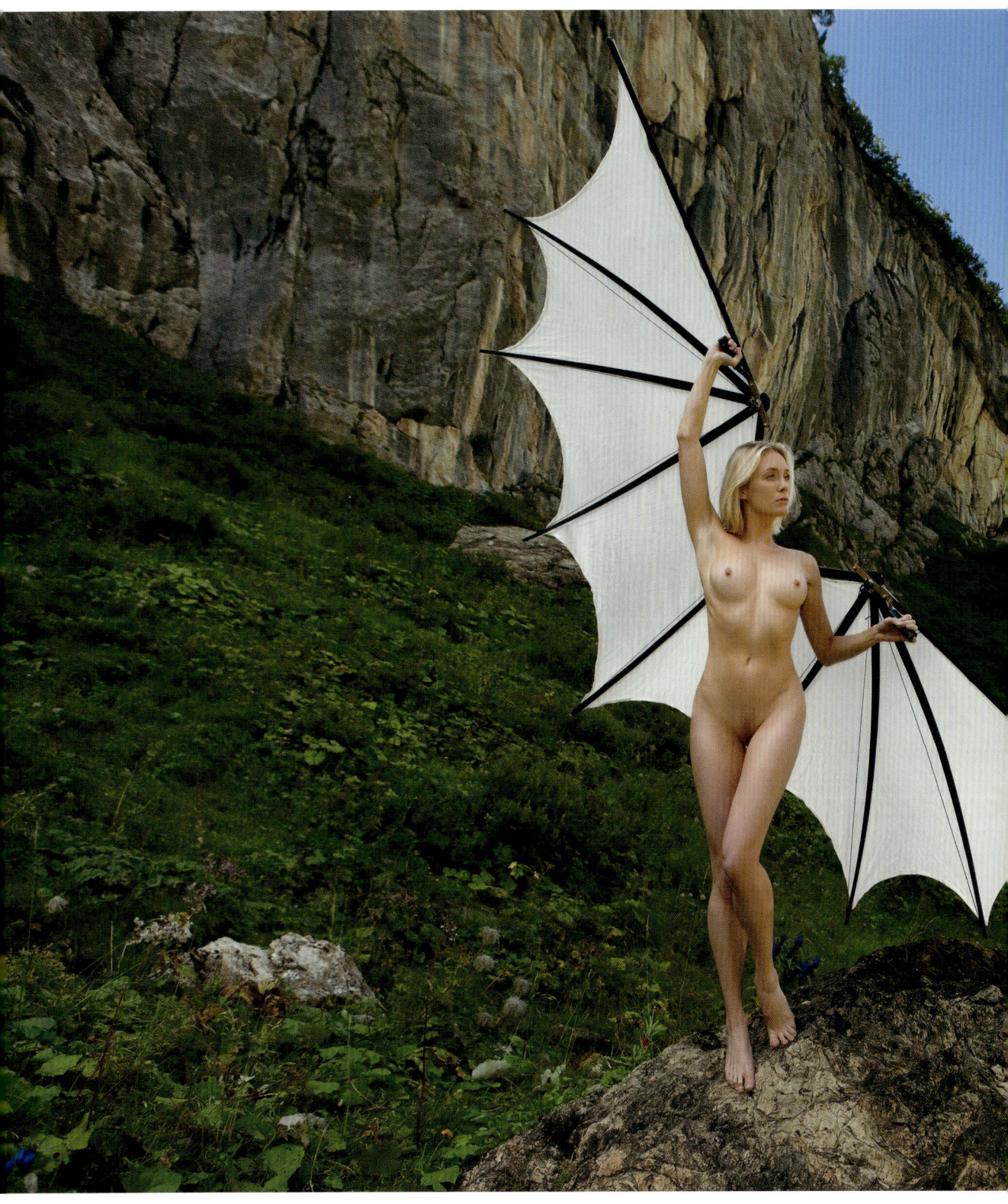

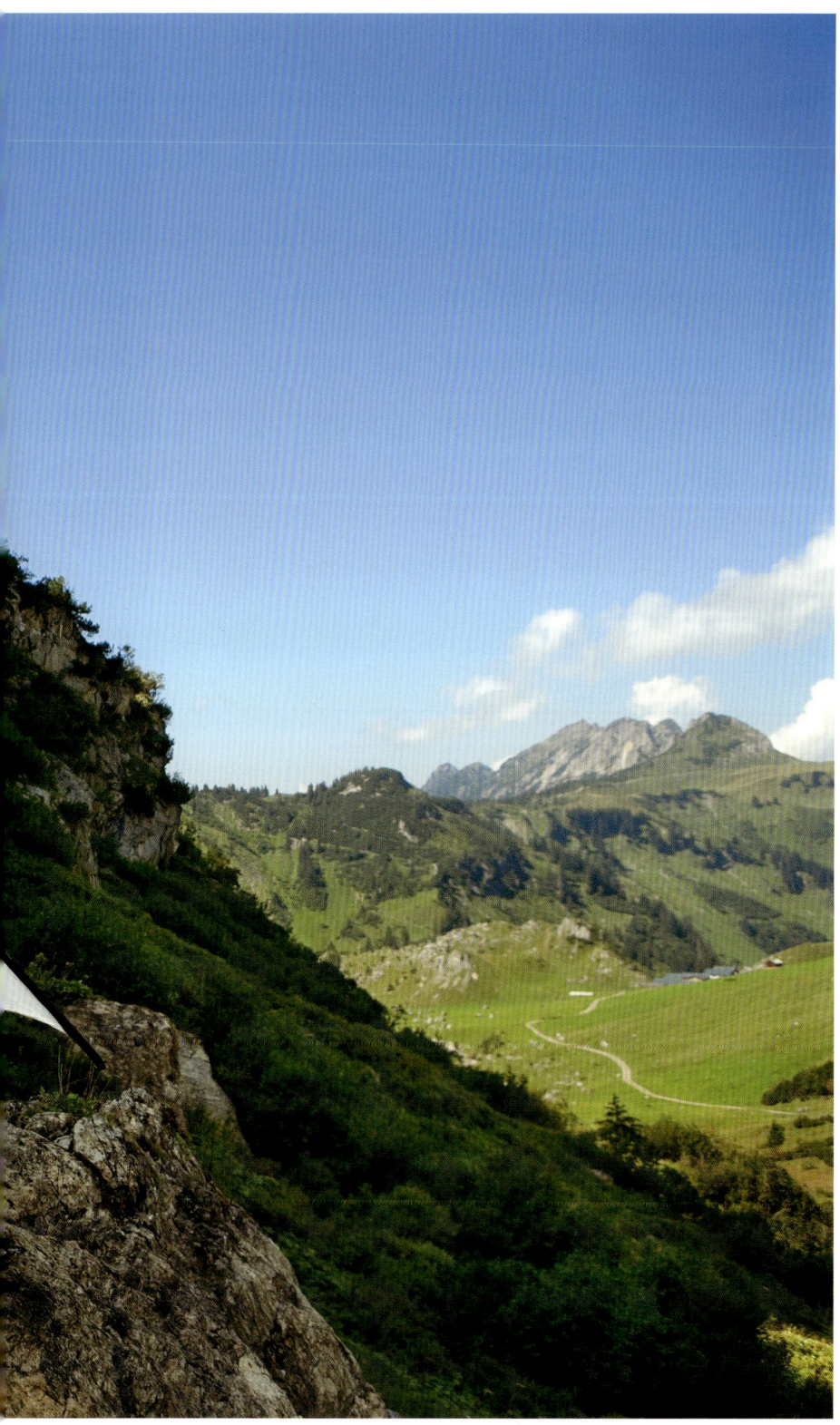

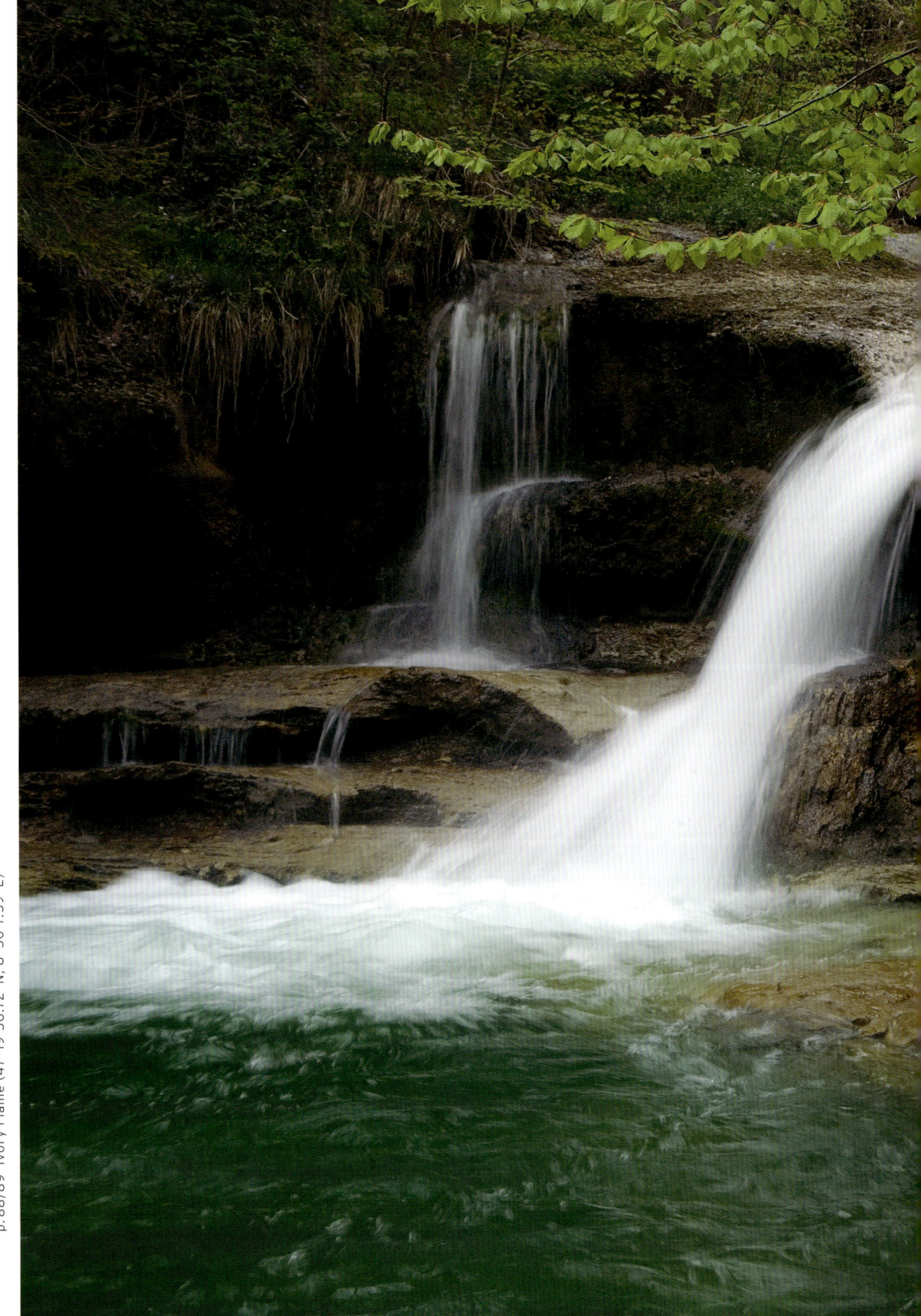

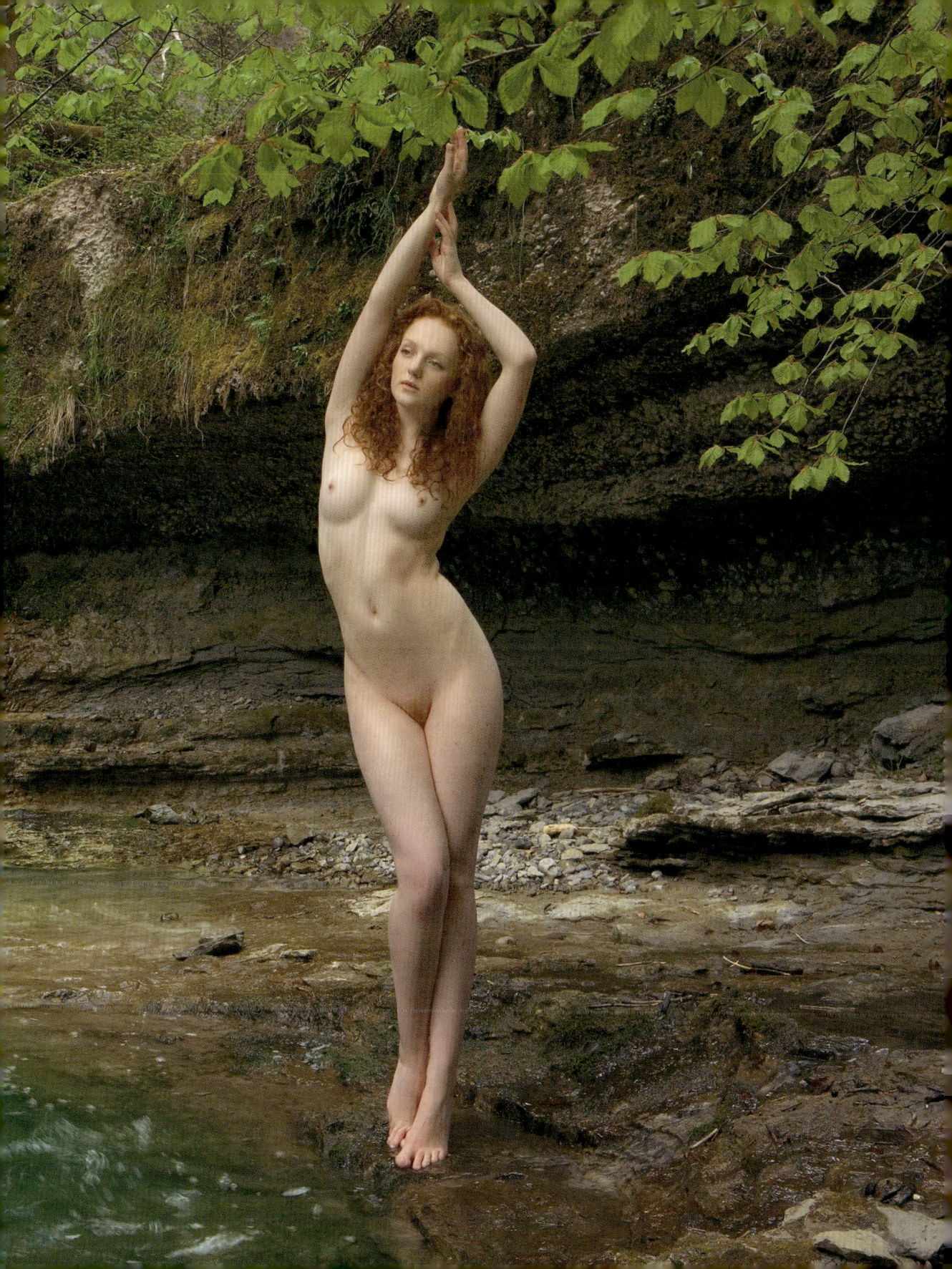

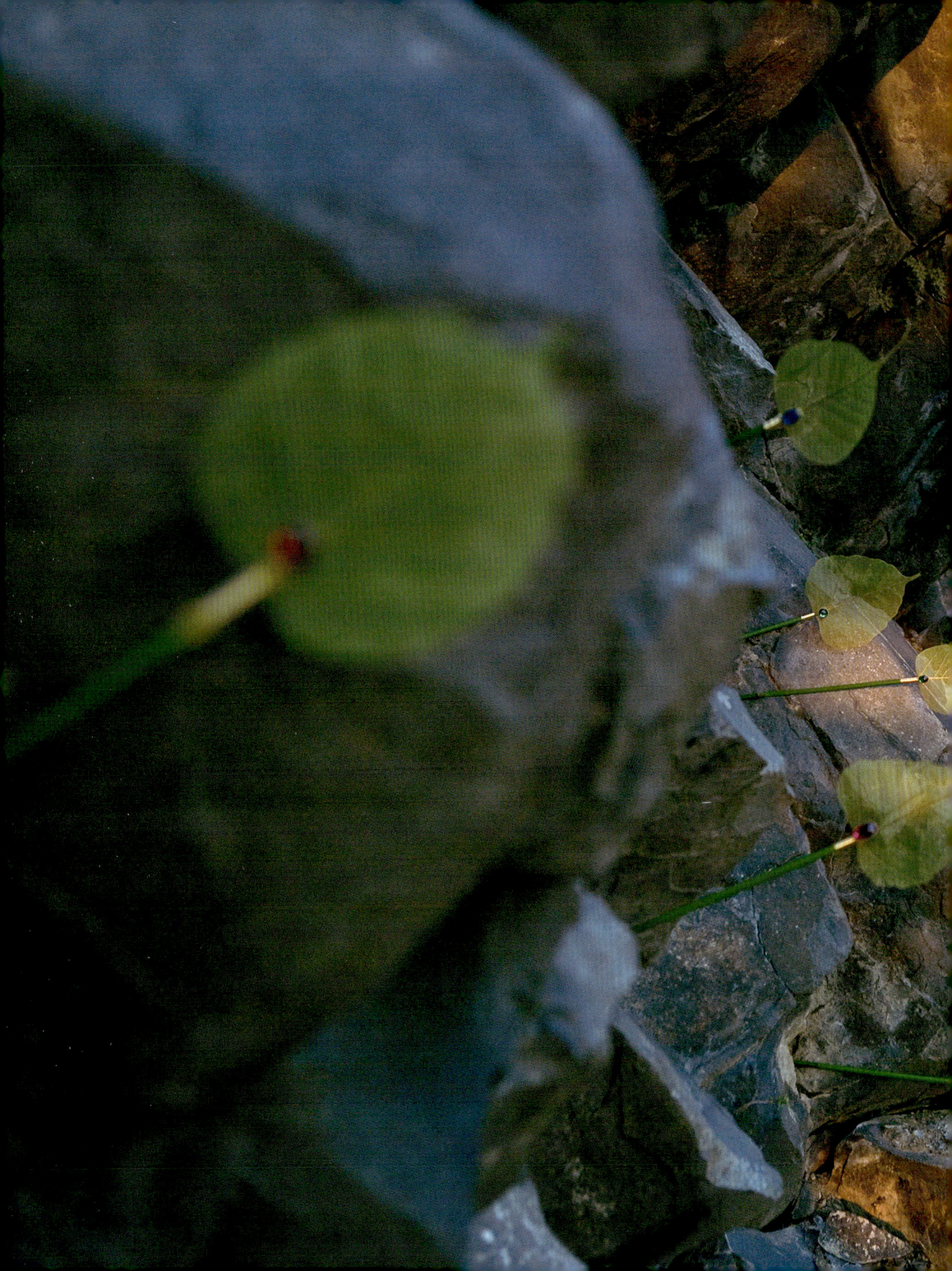

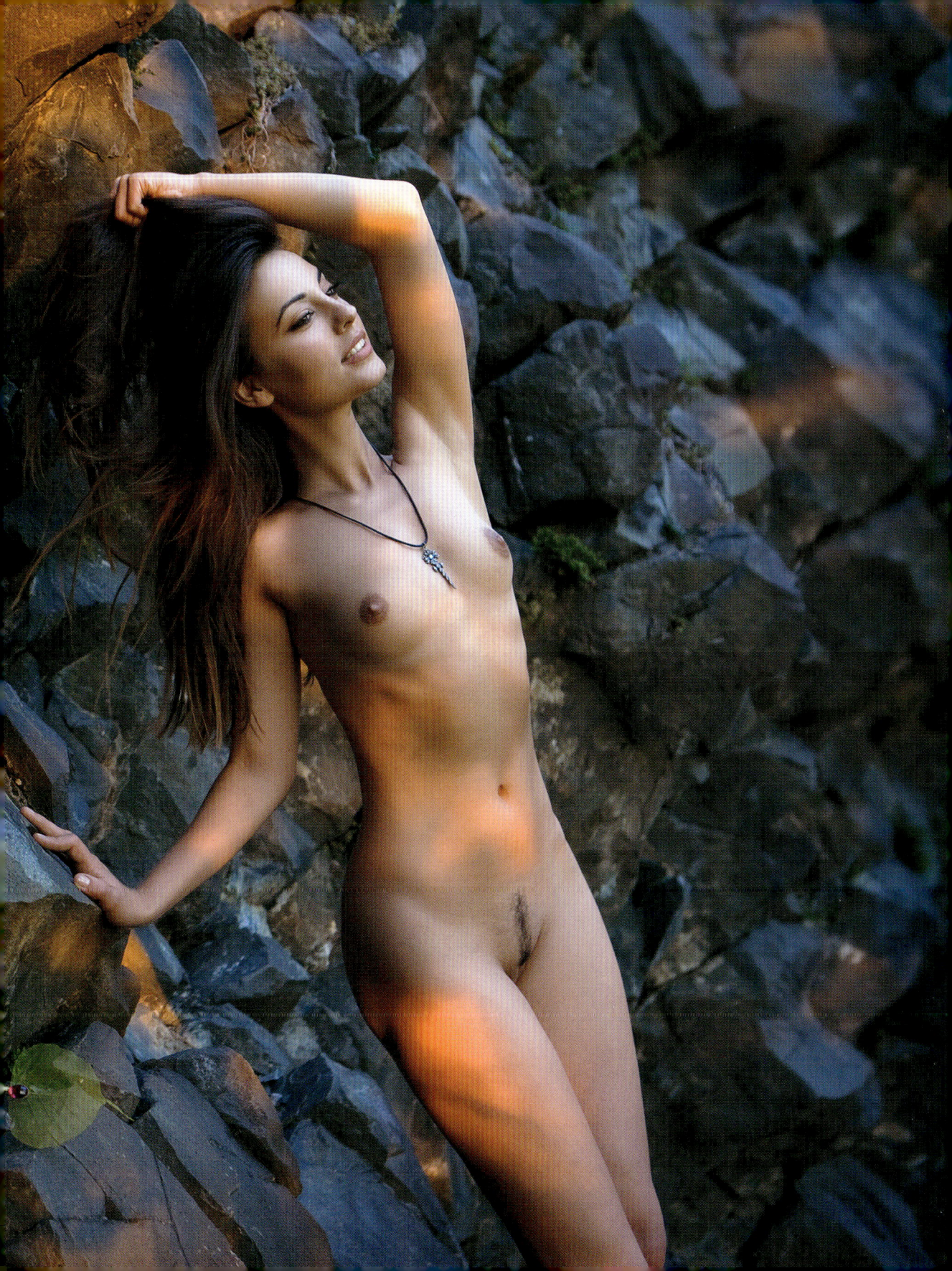

p. 92/93 Tess (47°33'27.99"N, 9°39'47.75"E) p. 90/91 Lorena (47°47'47.40"N, 8°45'2.31"E)

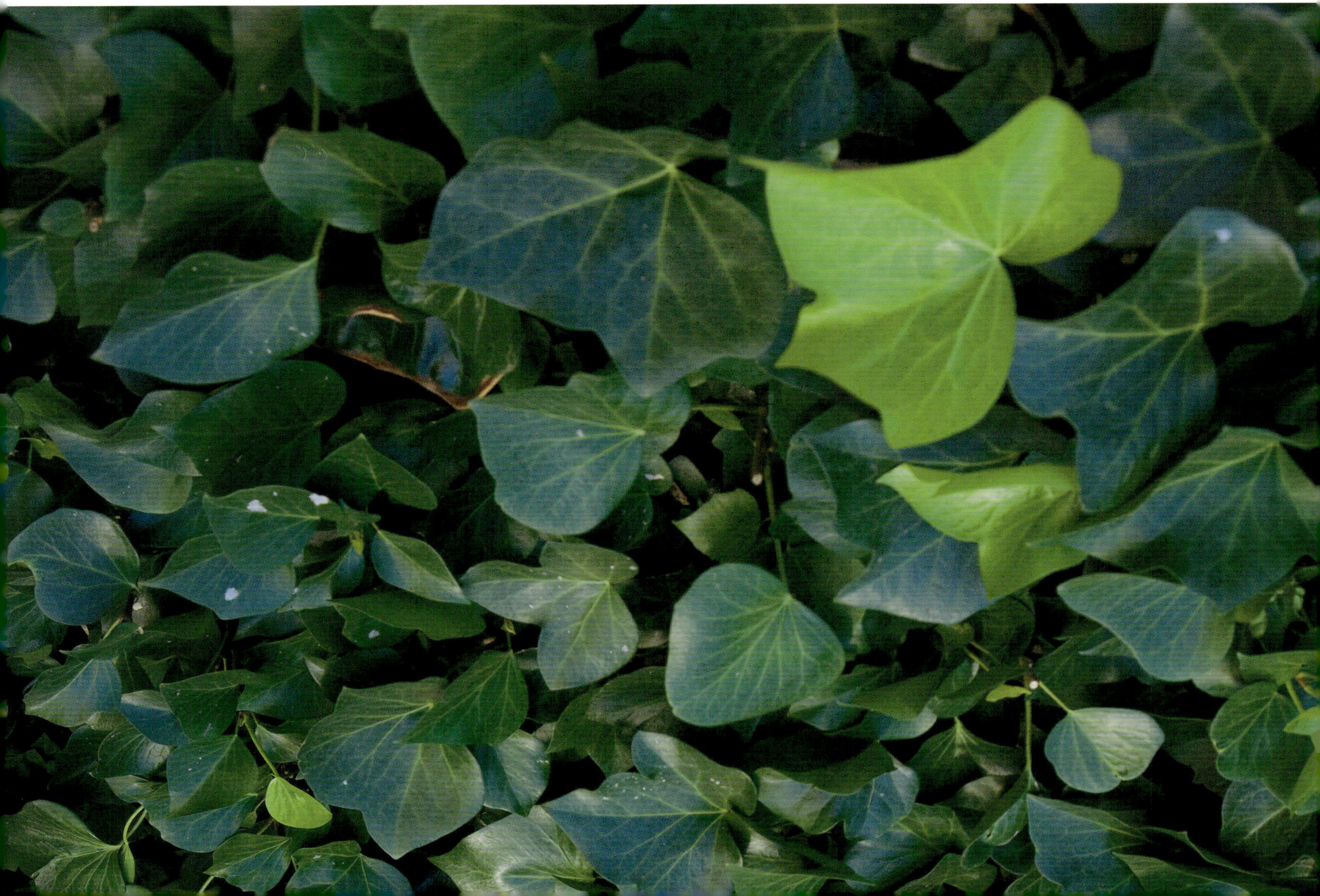

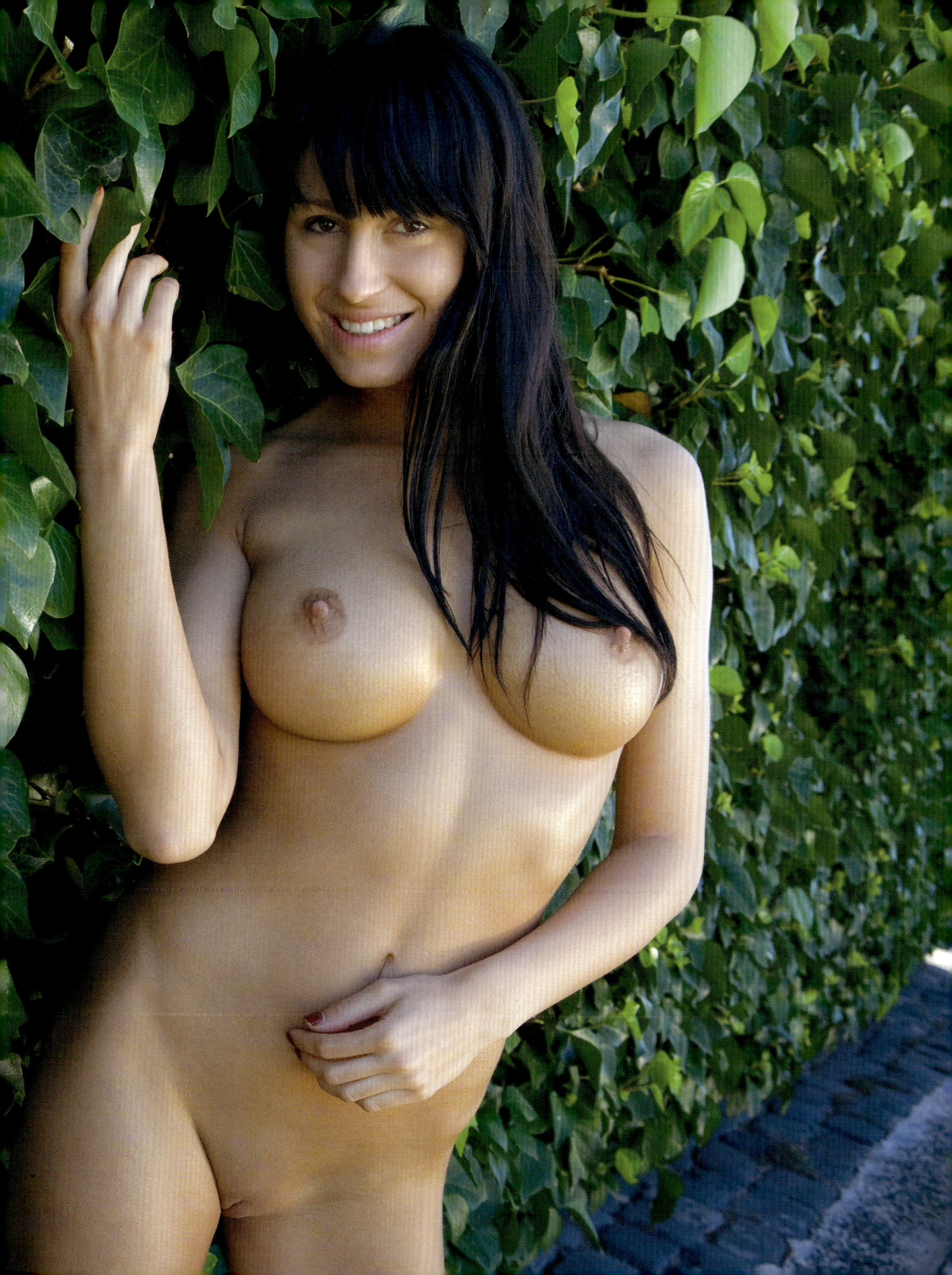

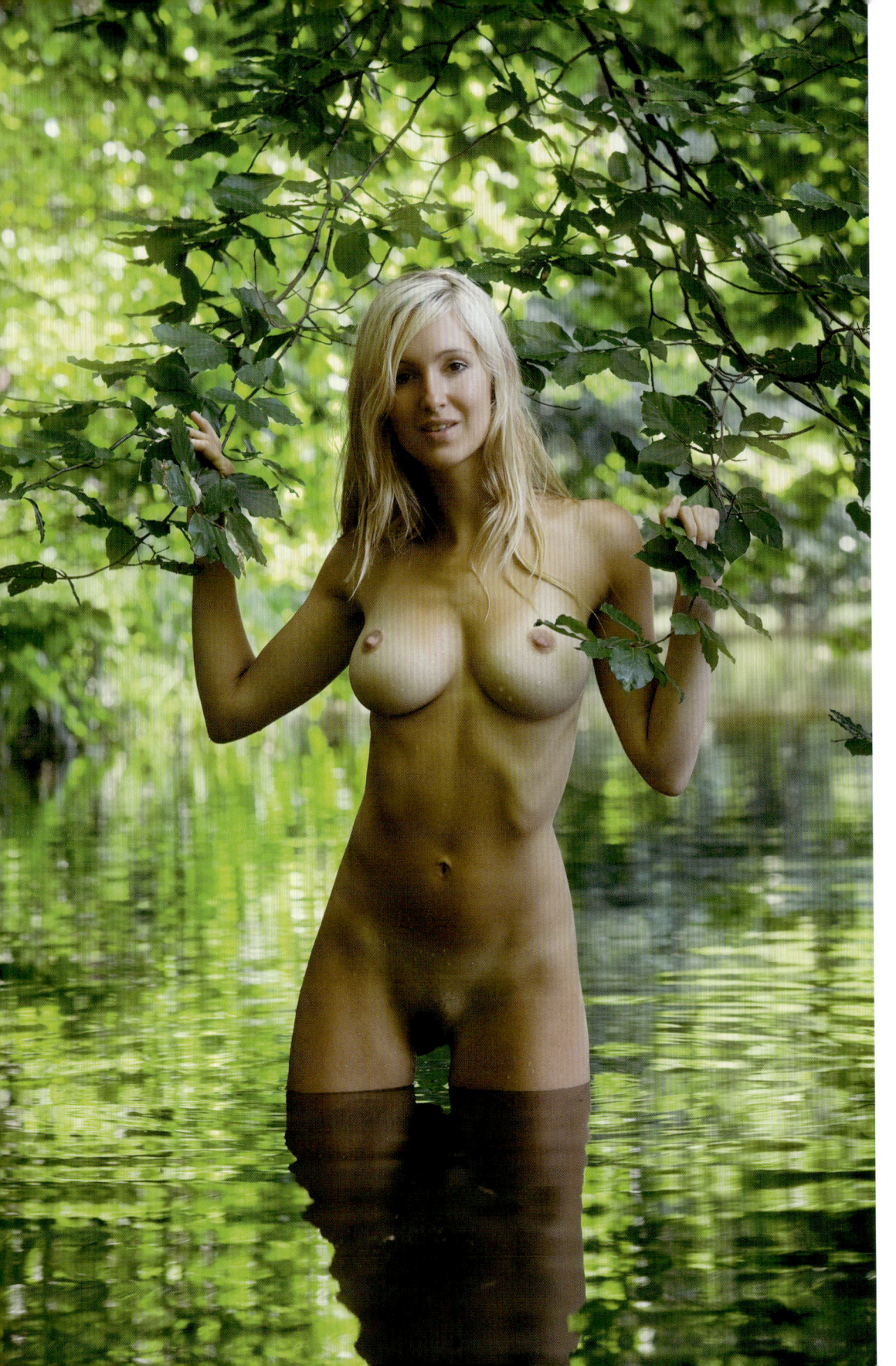

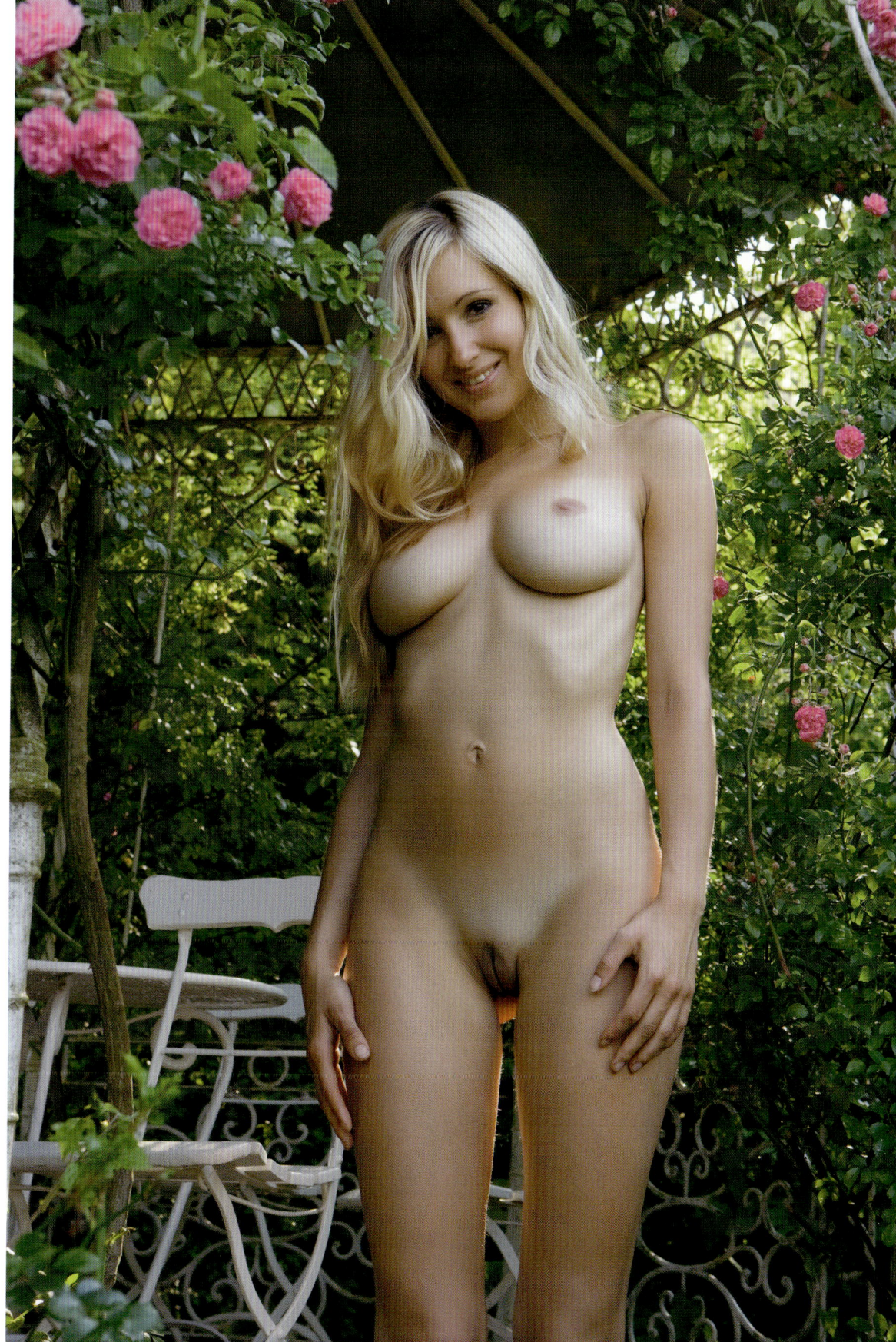

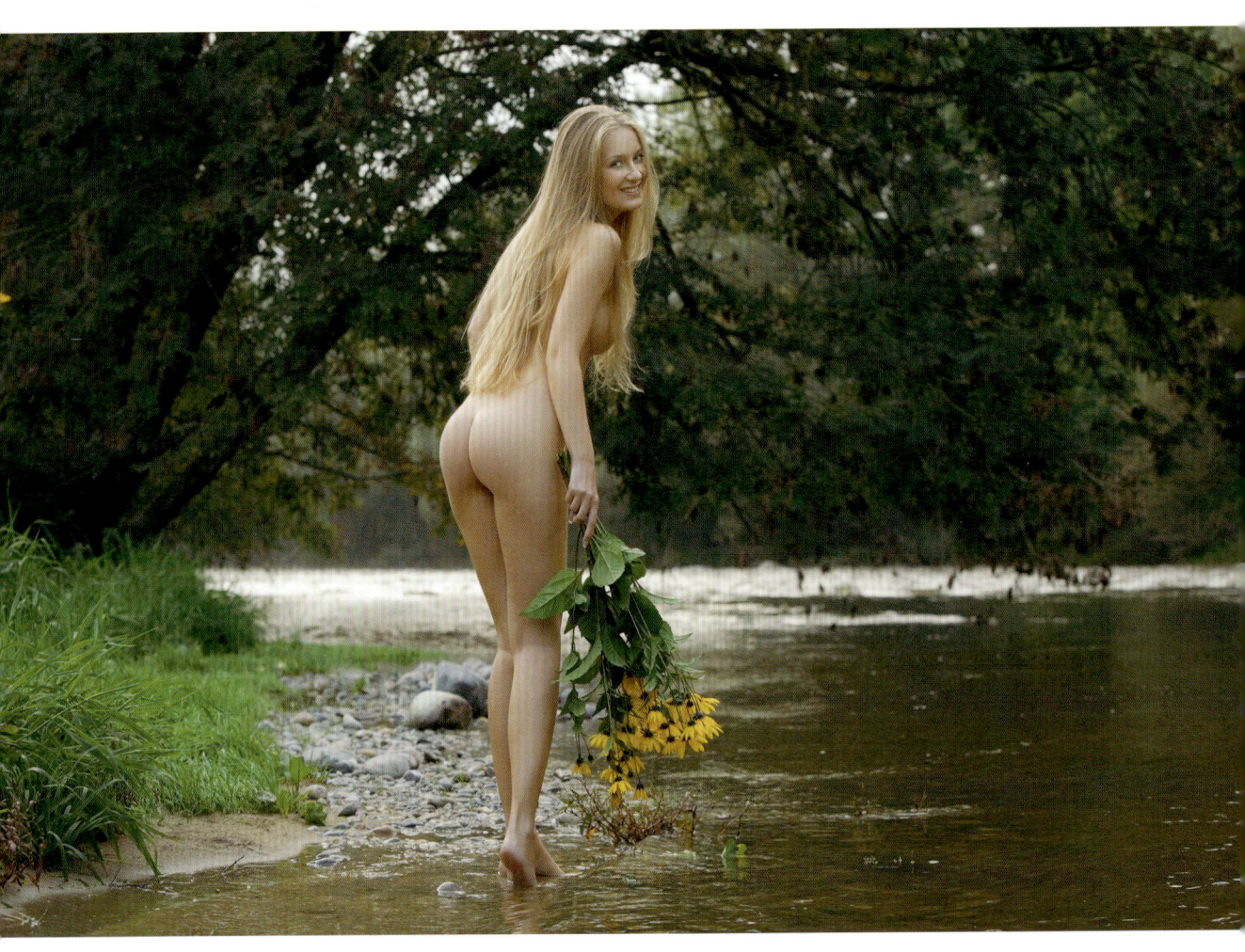

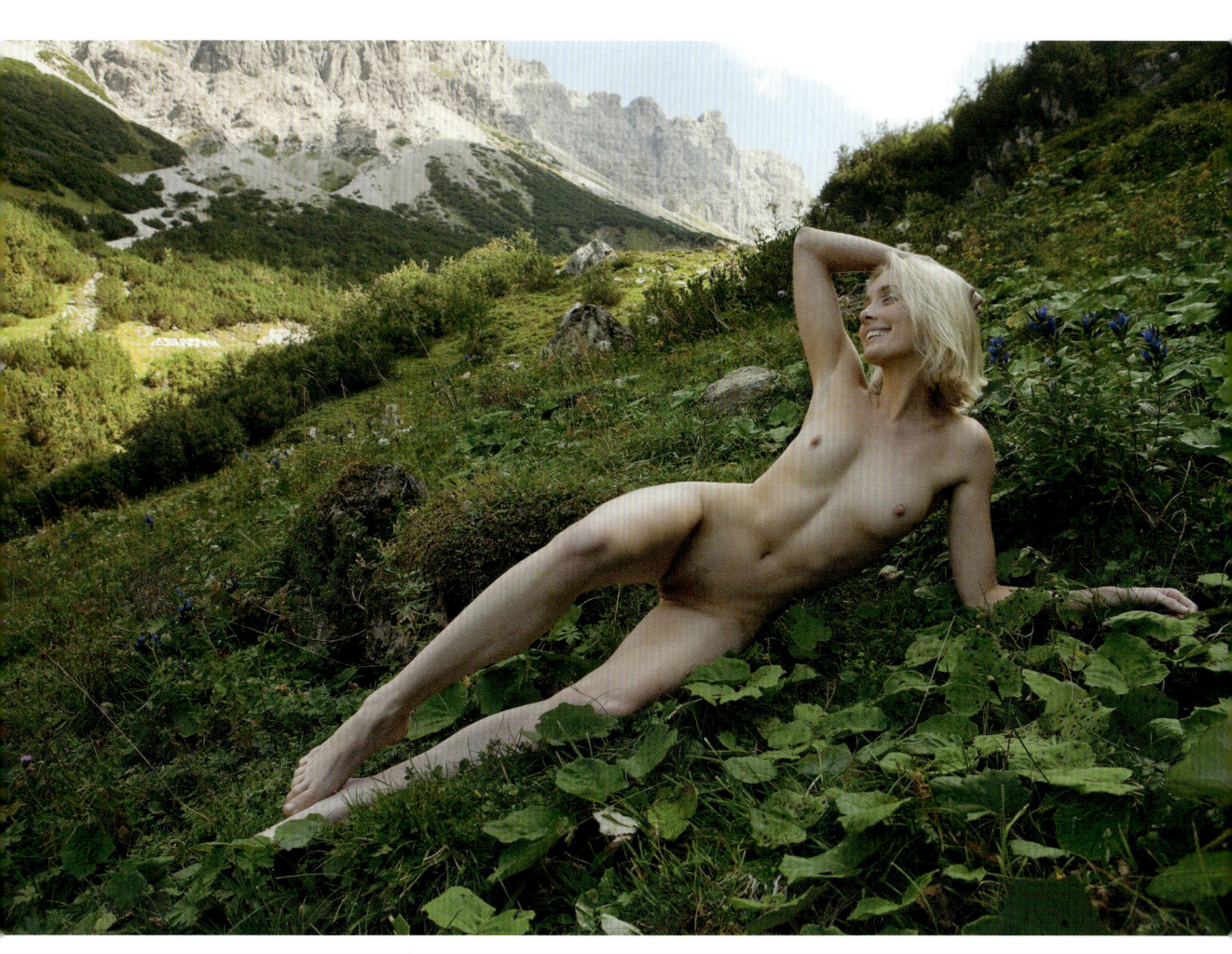

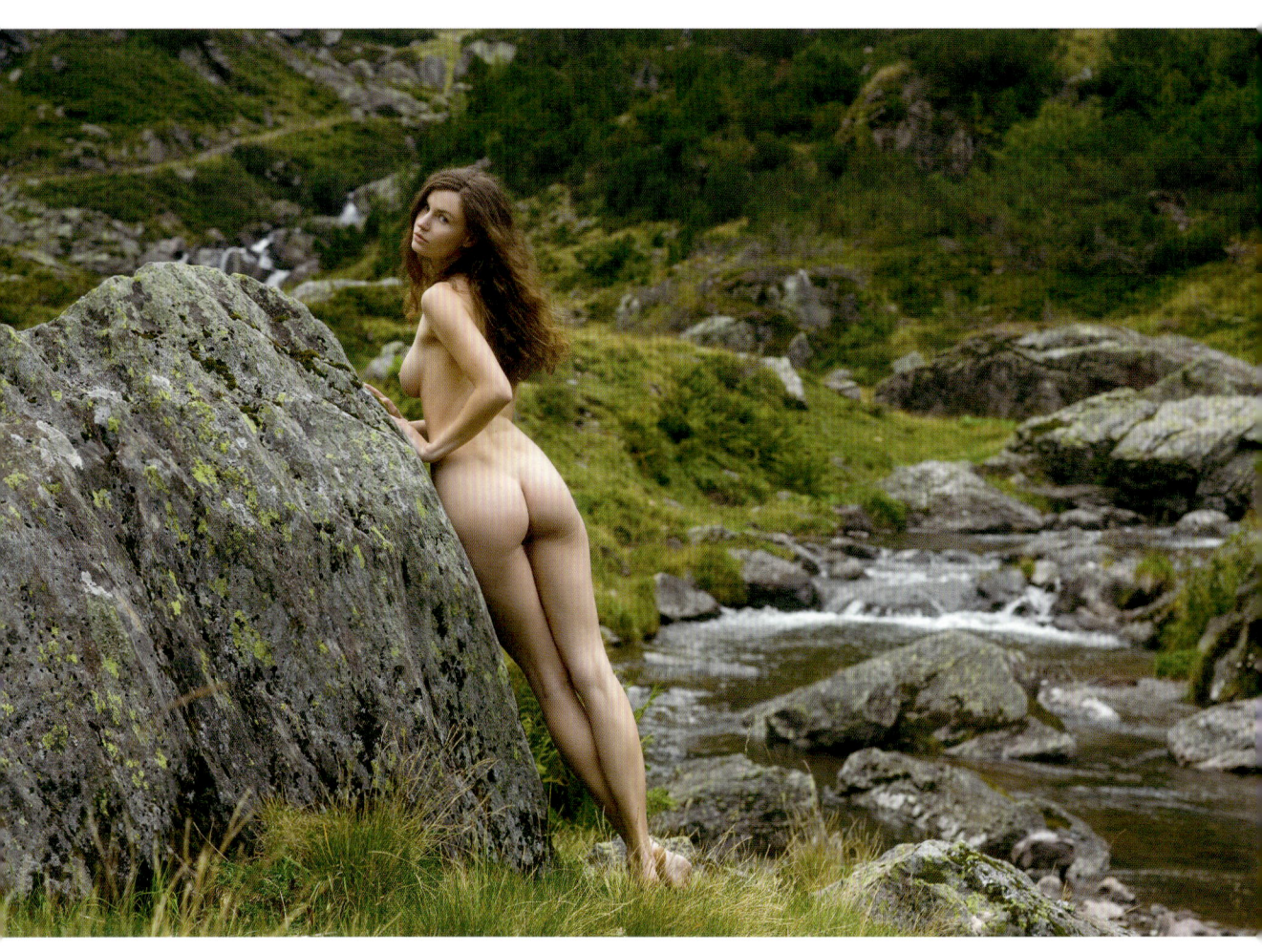

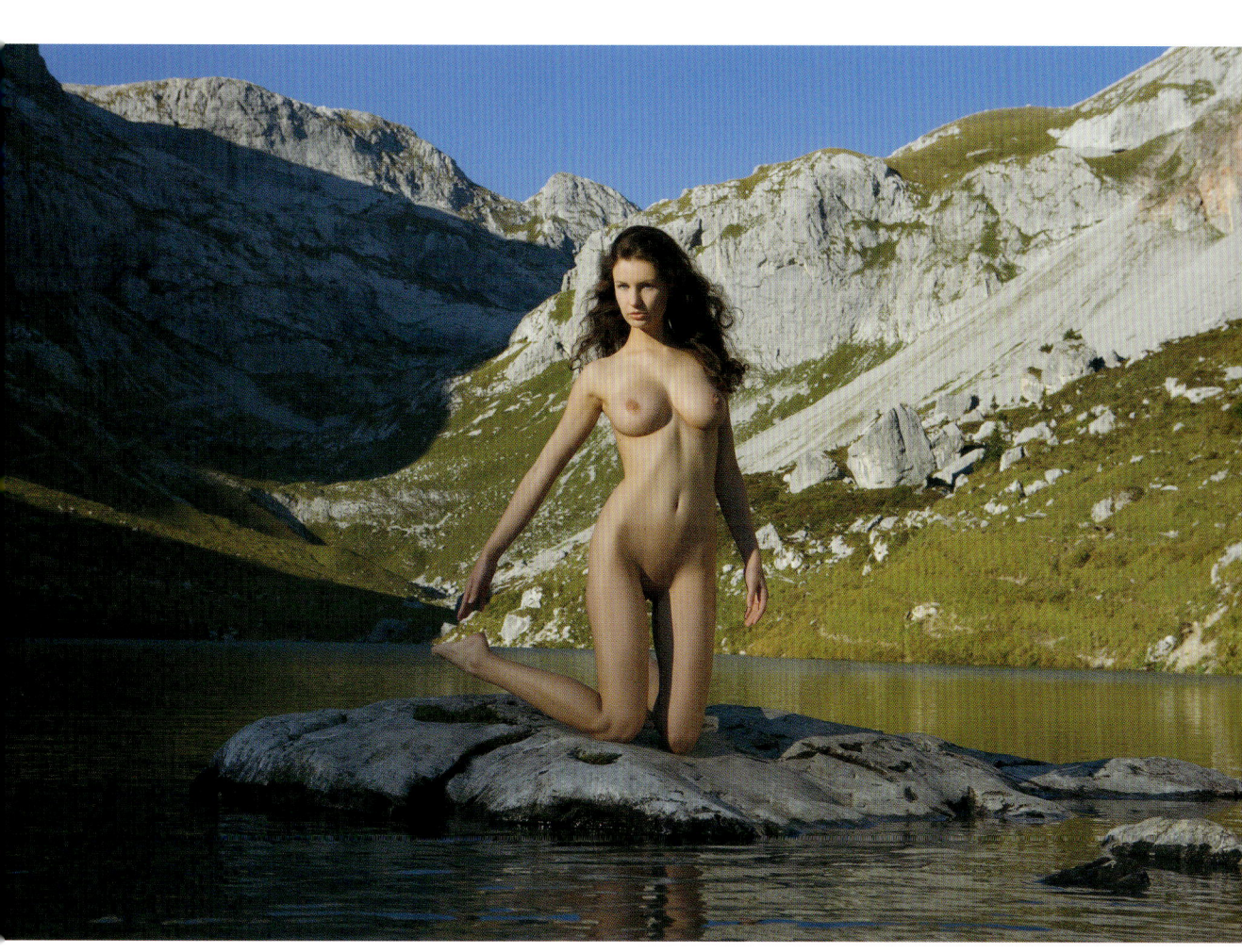

(47°0'19.32"N, 9°51'31.28"E)

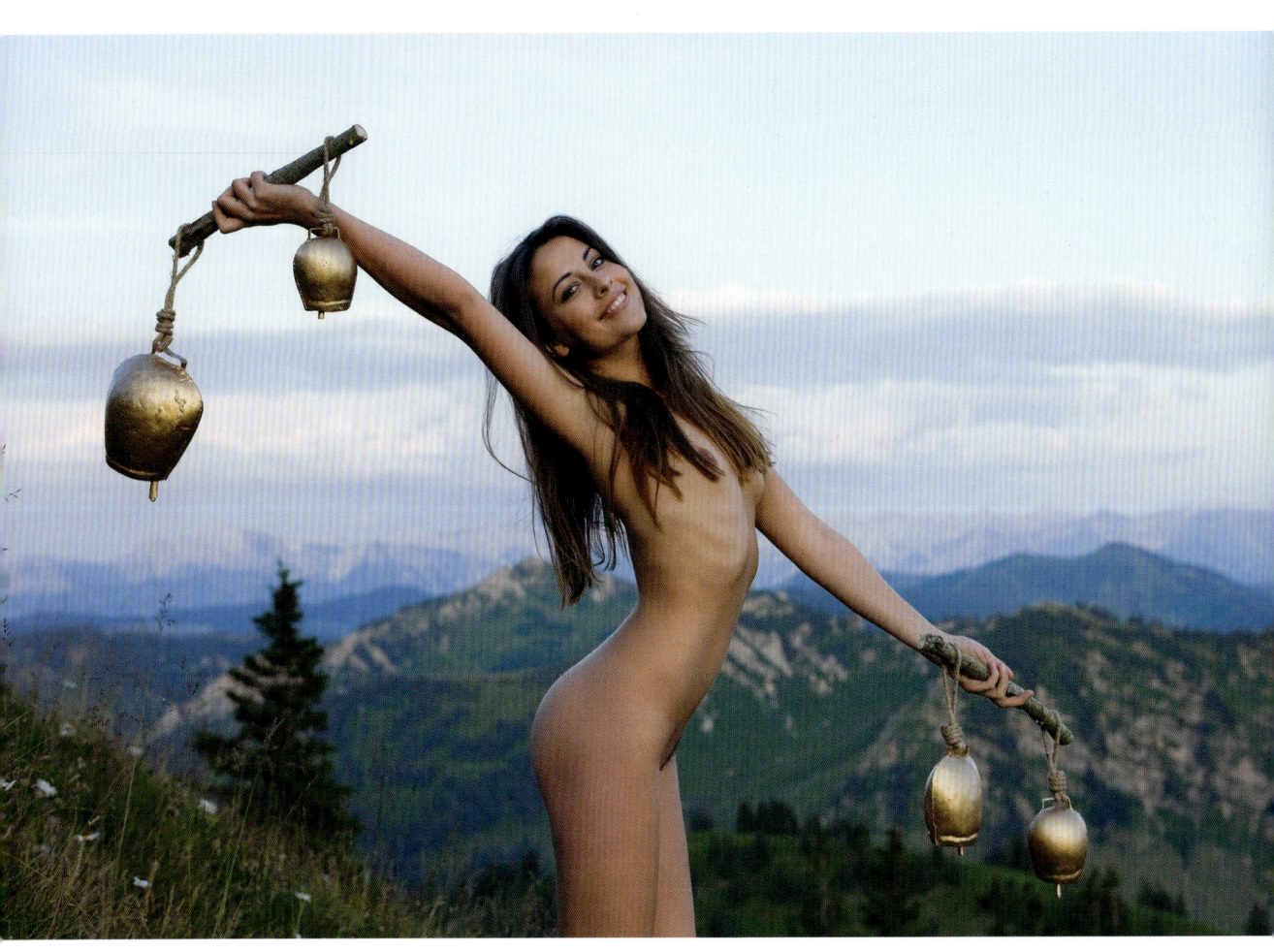

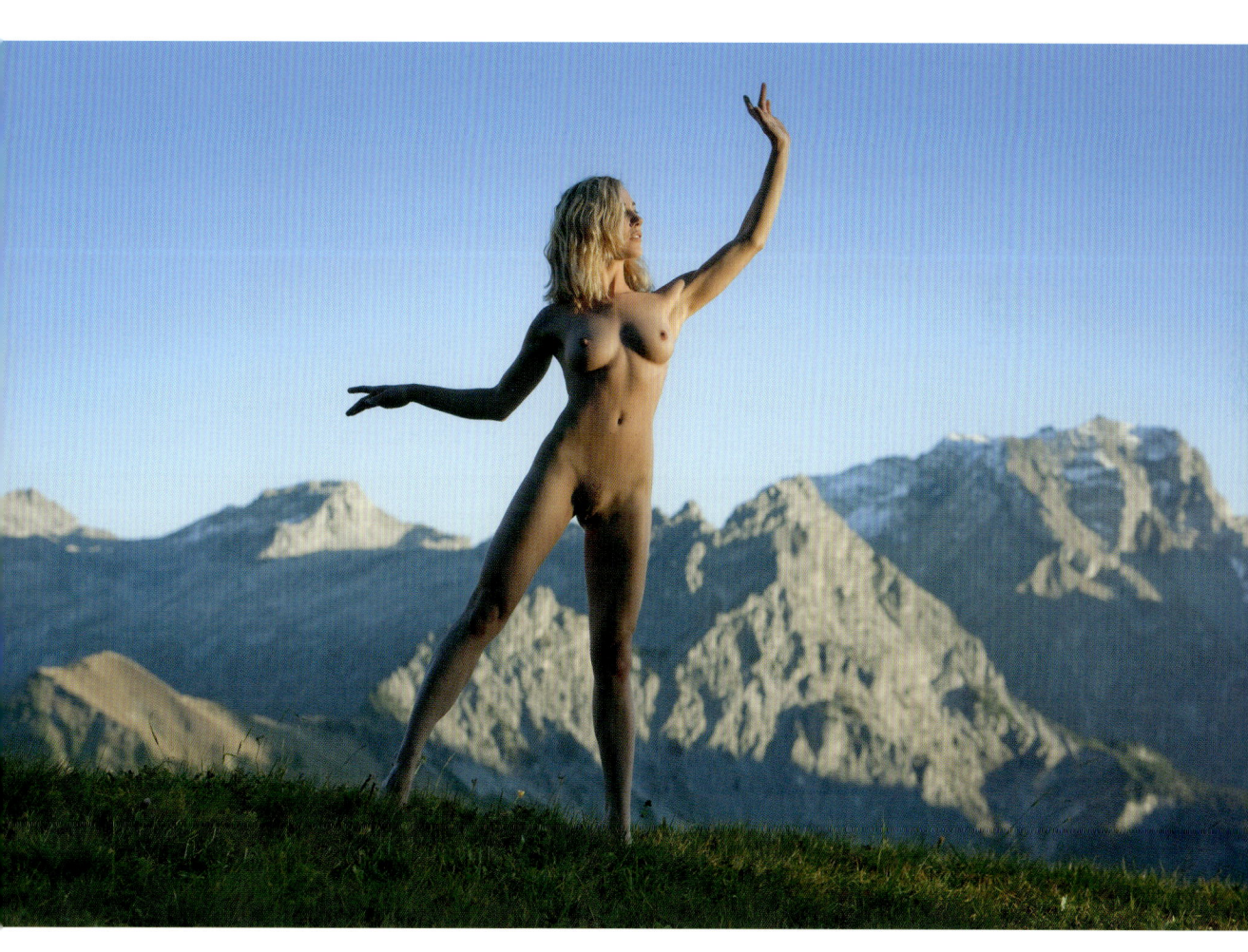

(47°15'40.90"N, 9°55'19.53"E)

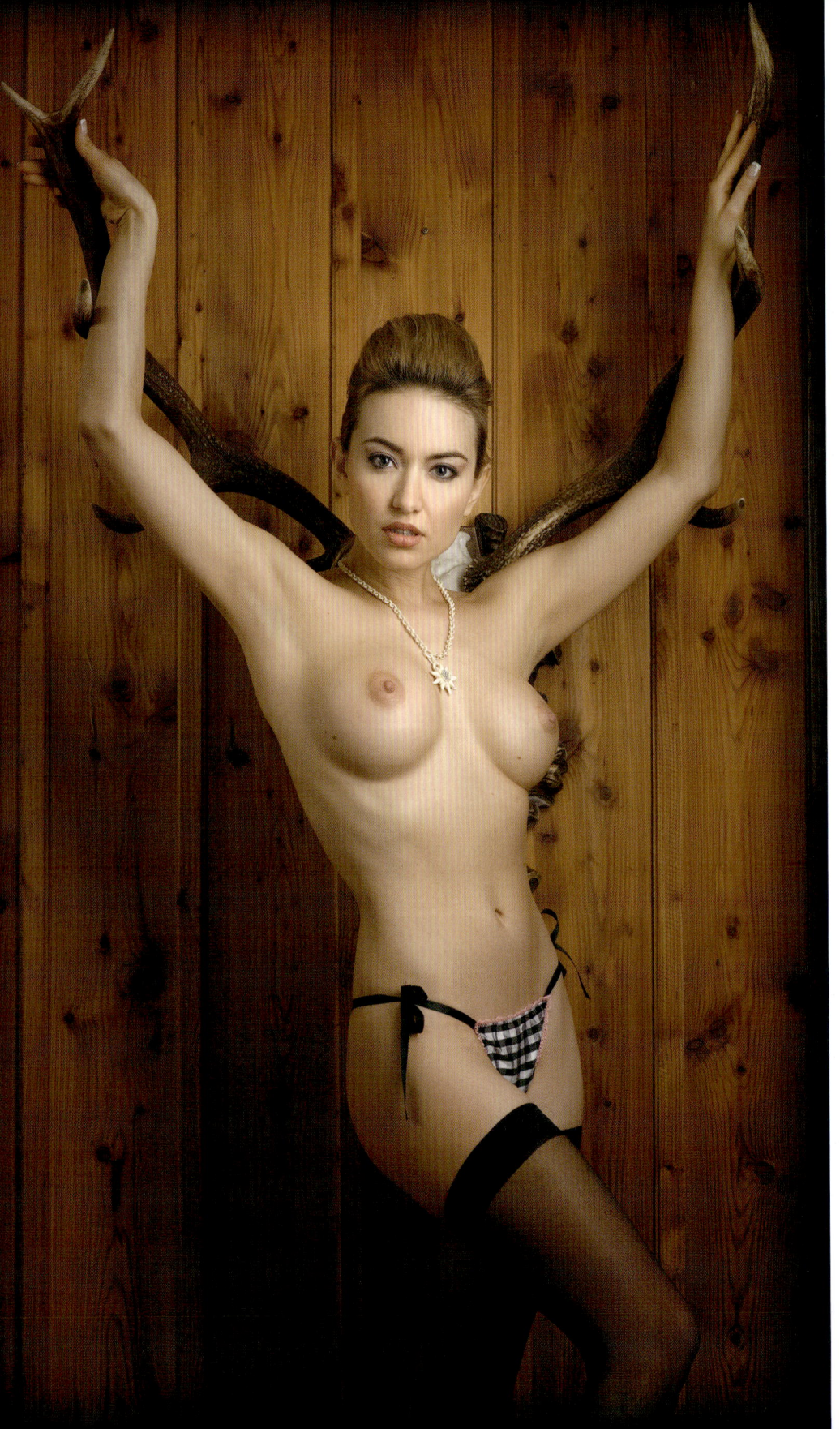

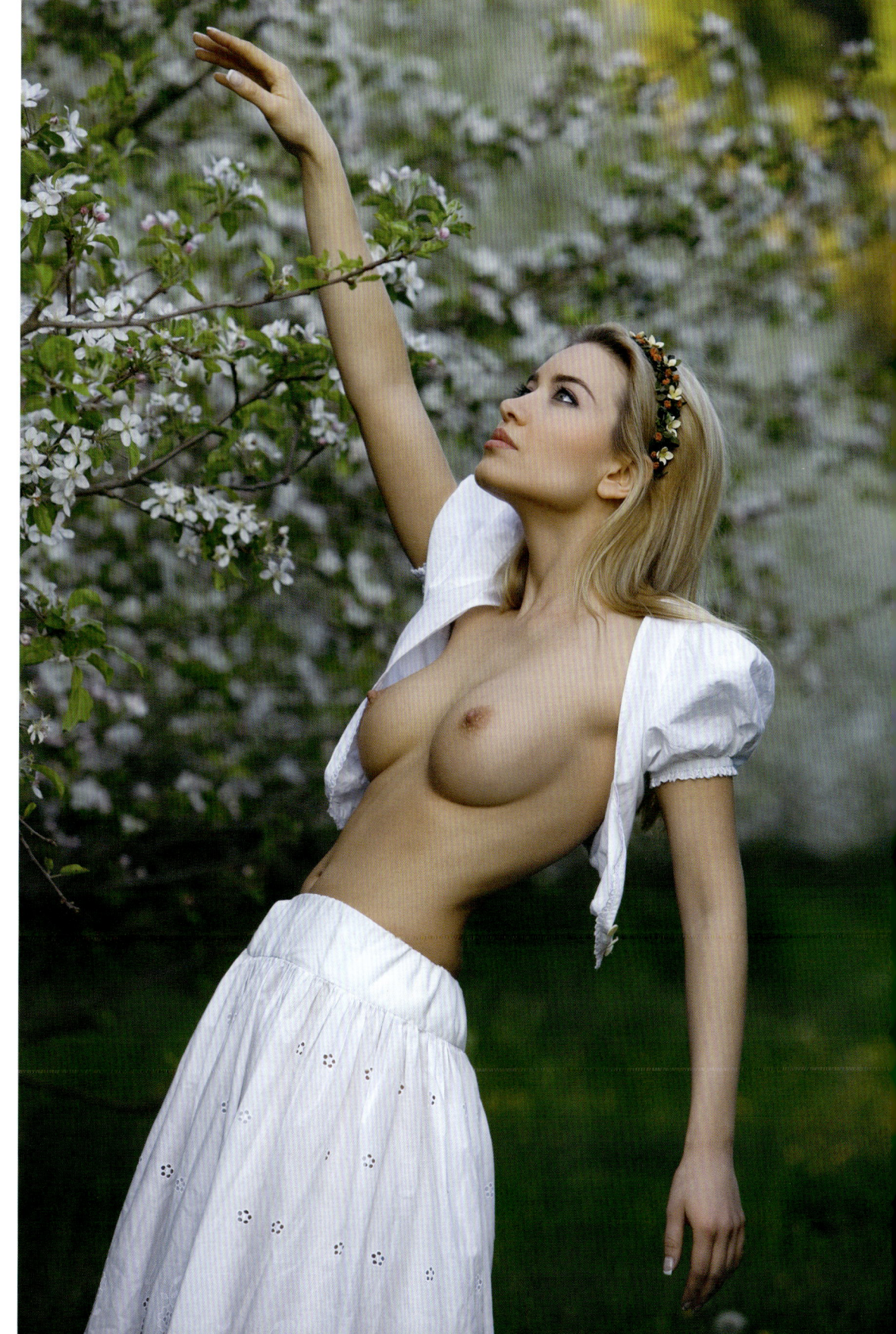

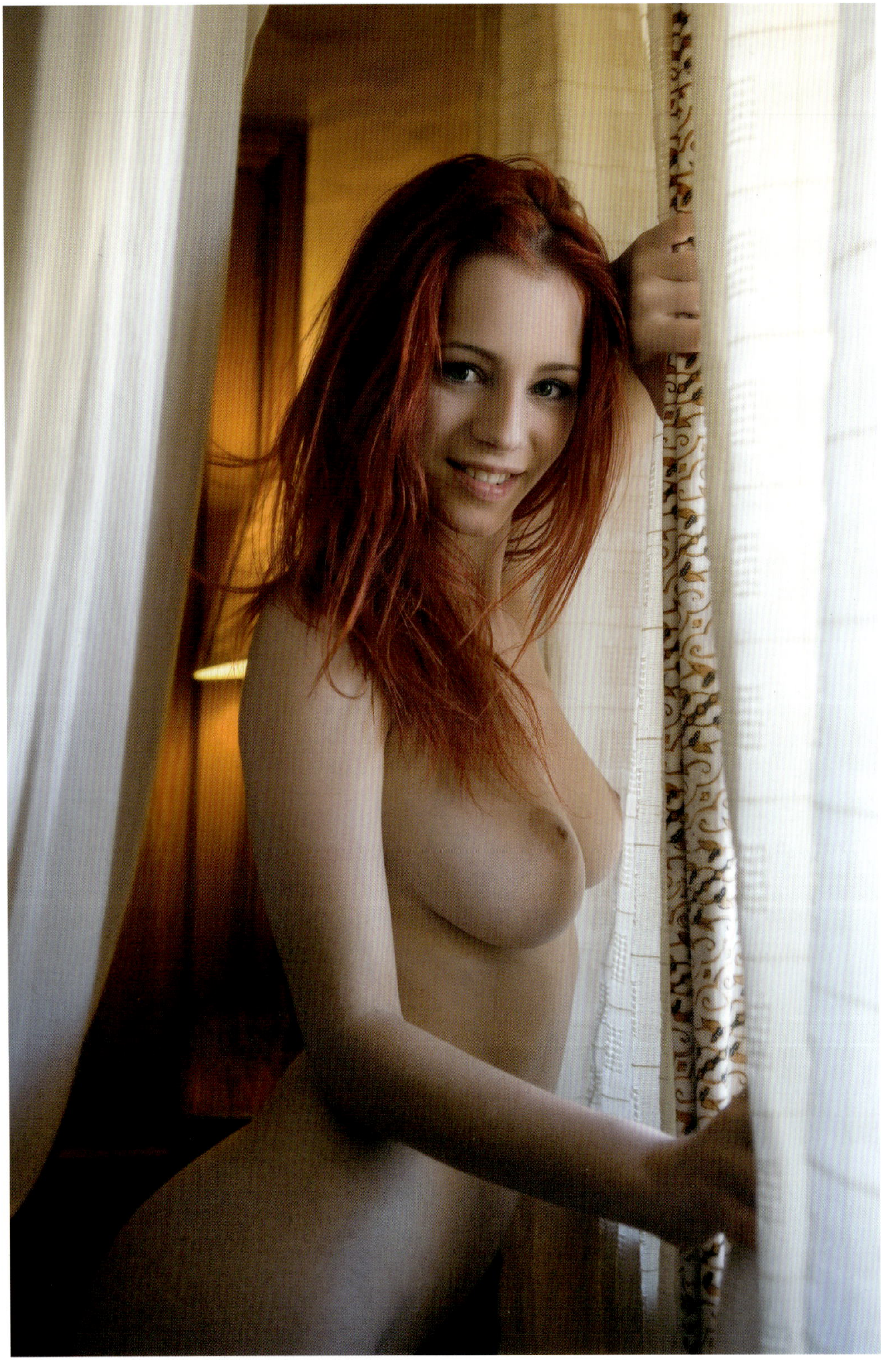

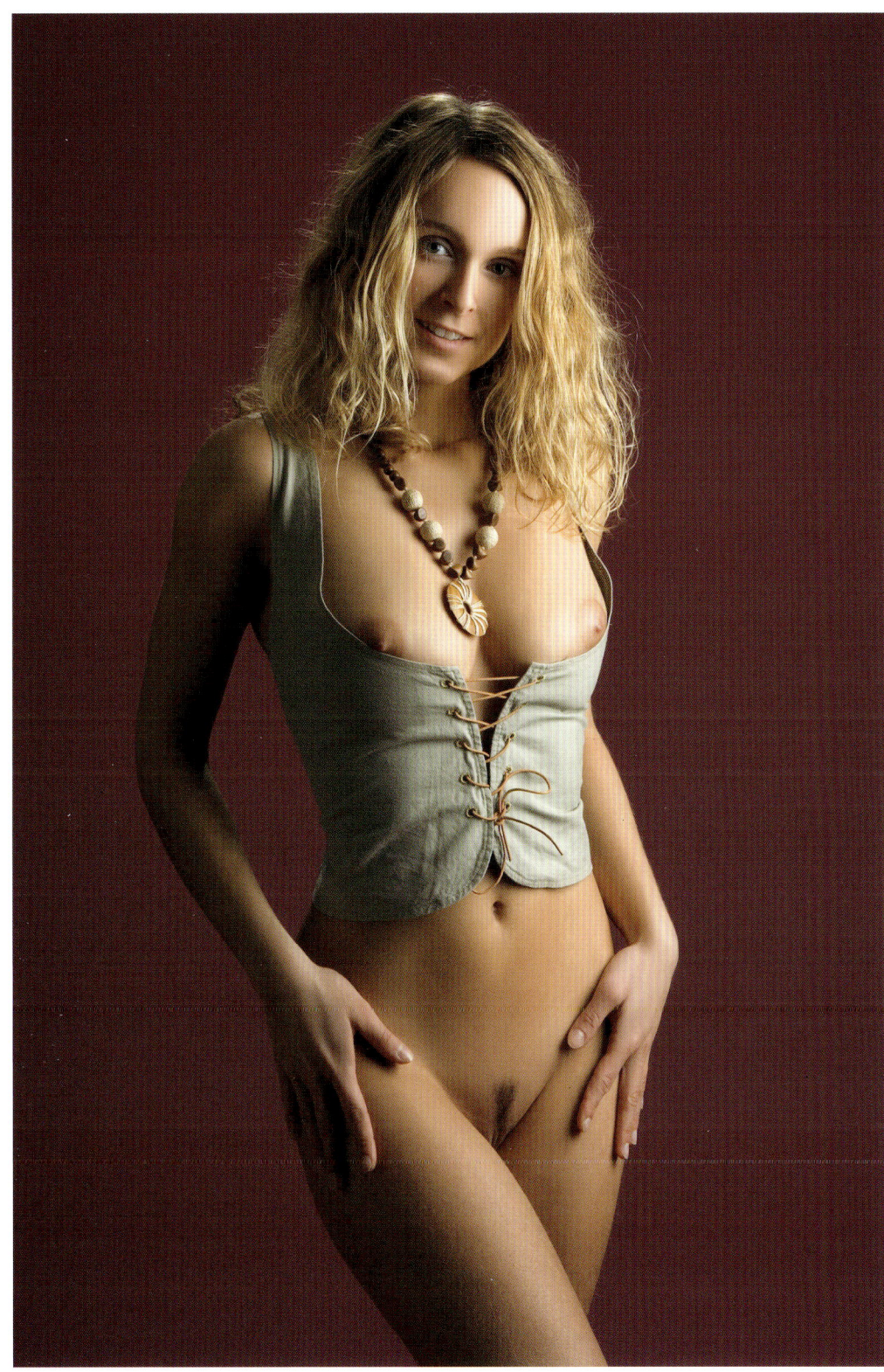

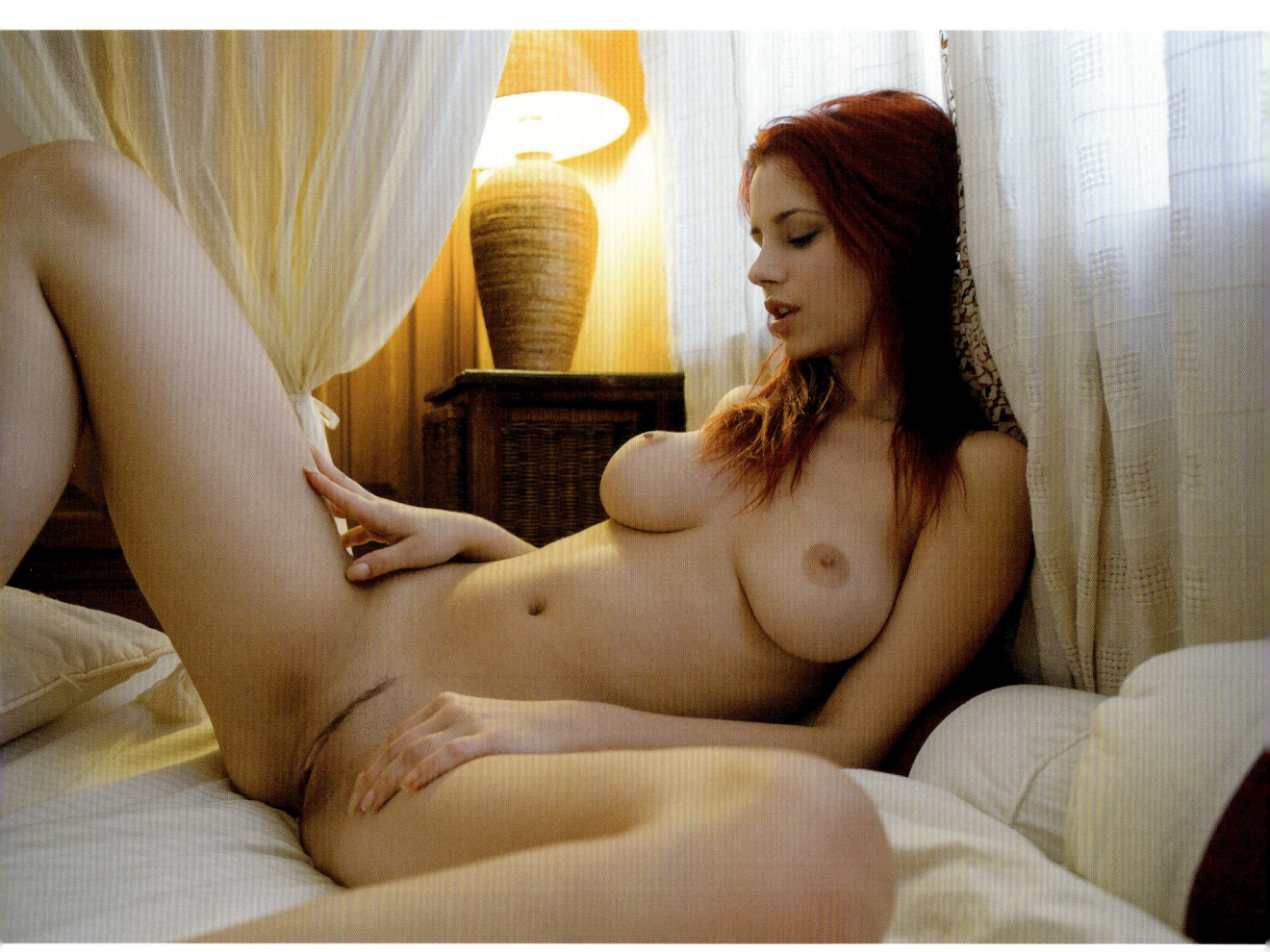

(47°45'31.42"N 9°42'43.84"E)

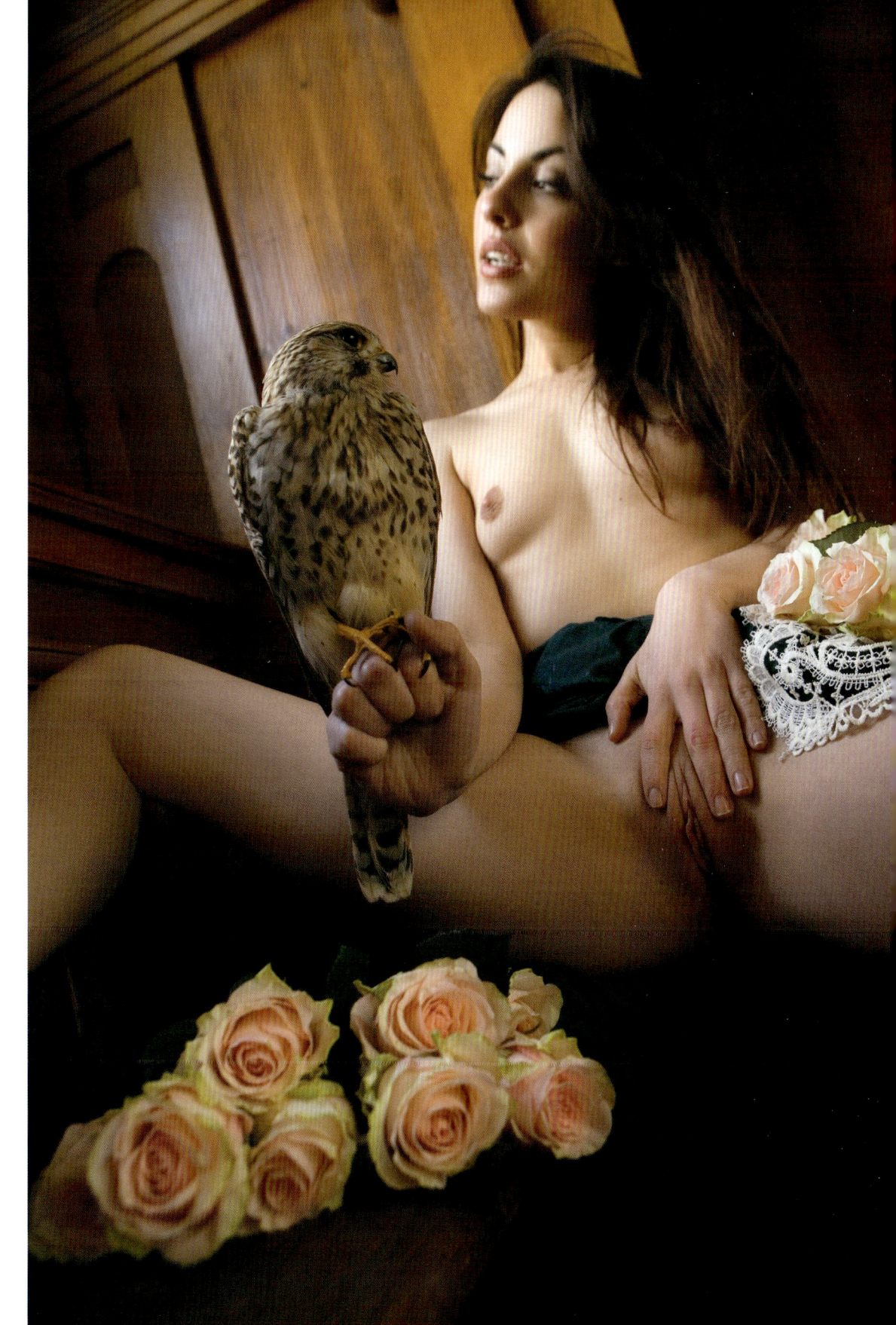

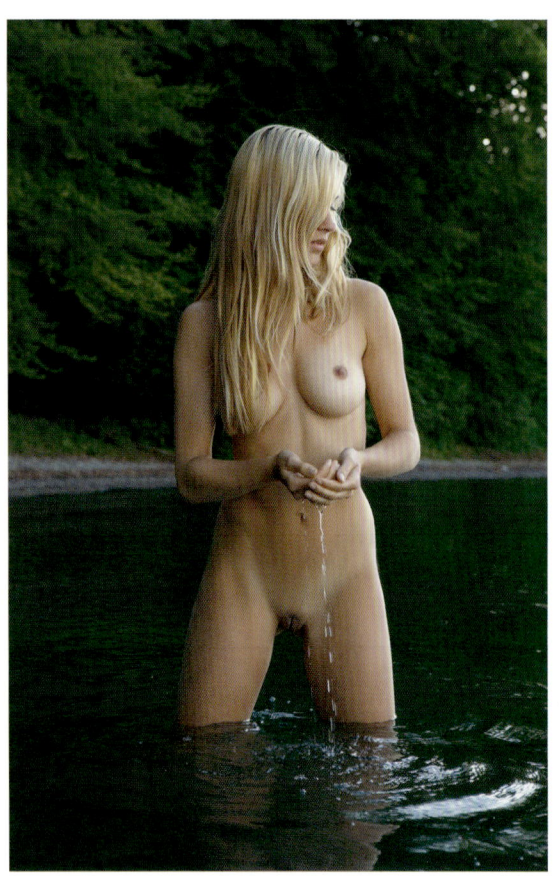
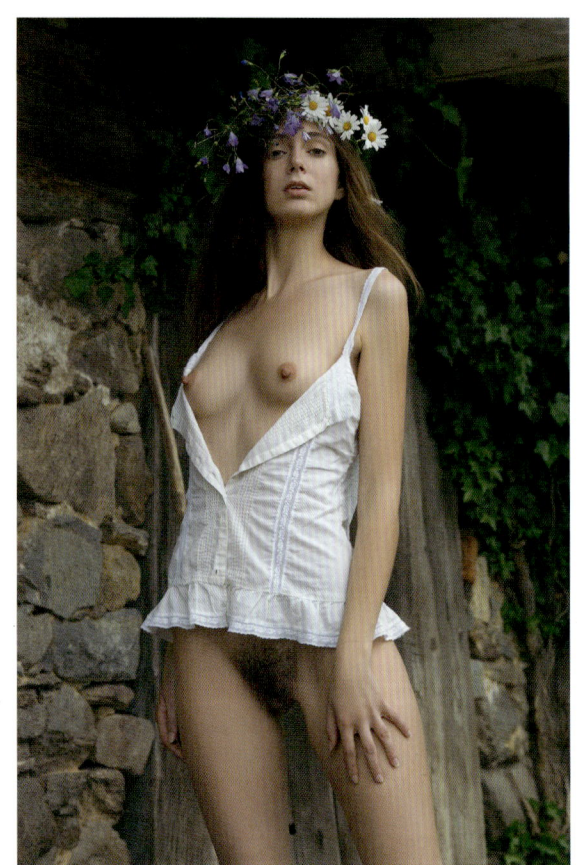

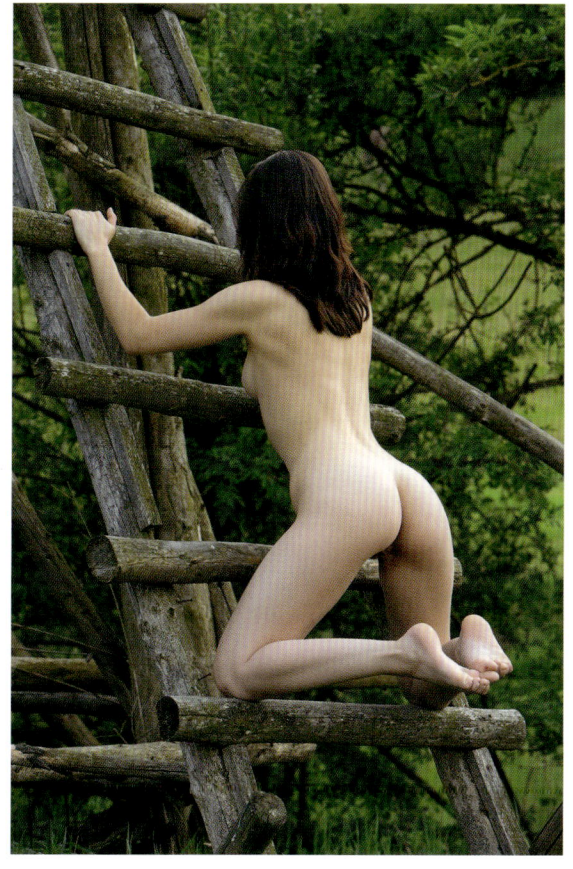 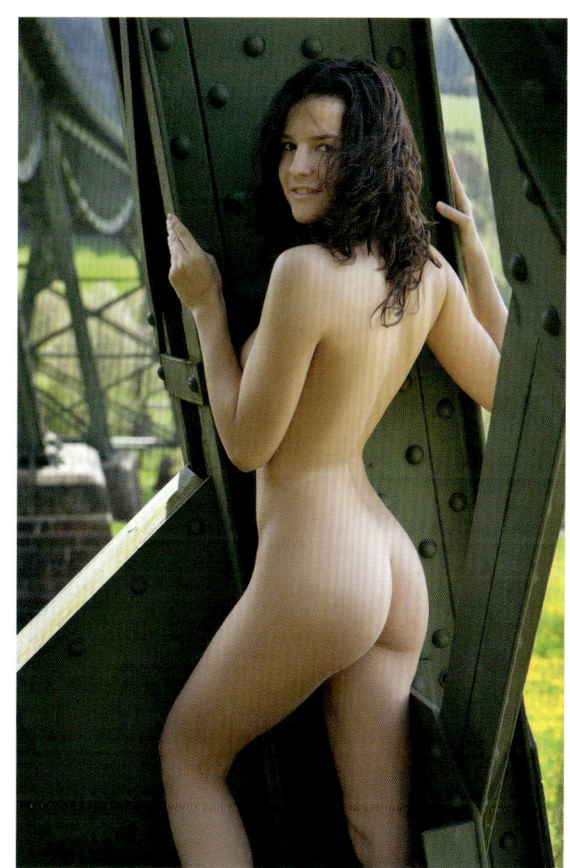

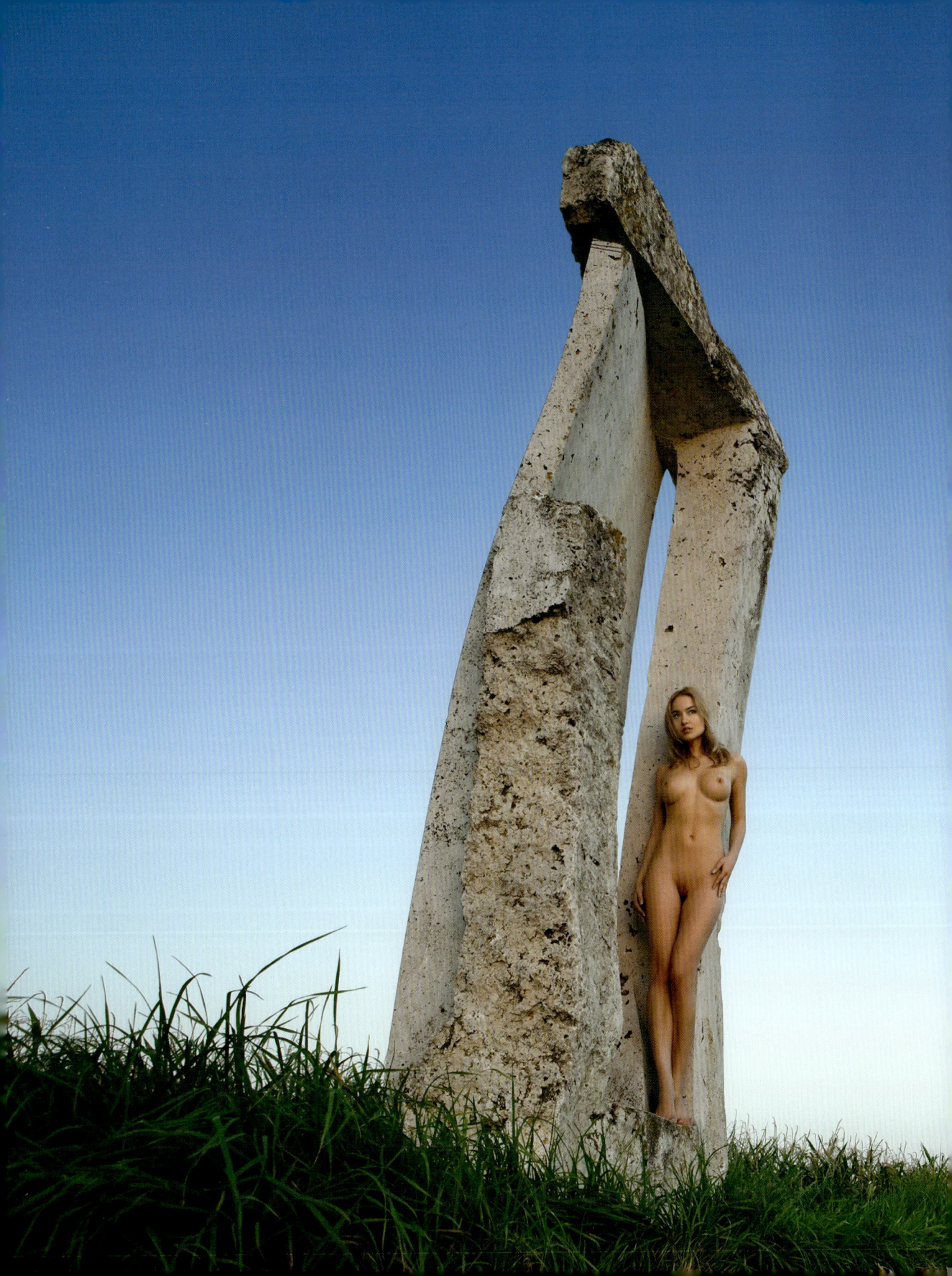

p. 112/113 Susann (47°33'1.43"N, 9°42'46.59"E)

p. 110/111 Lia (48°3'58.72"N, 9°39'26.87"E)

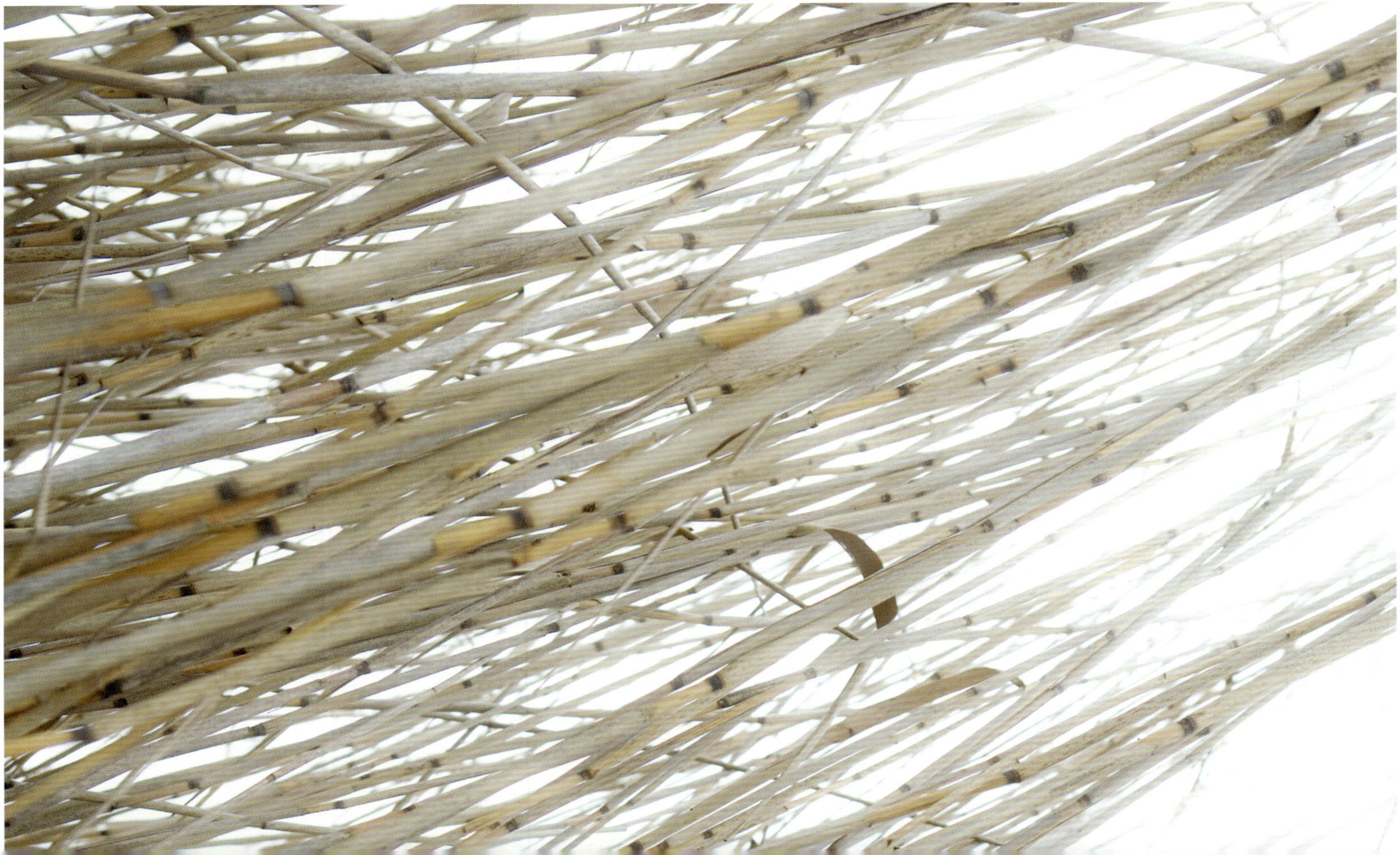

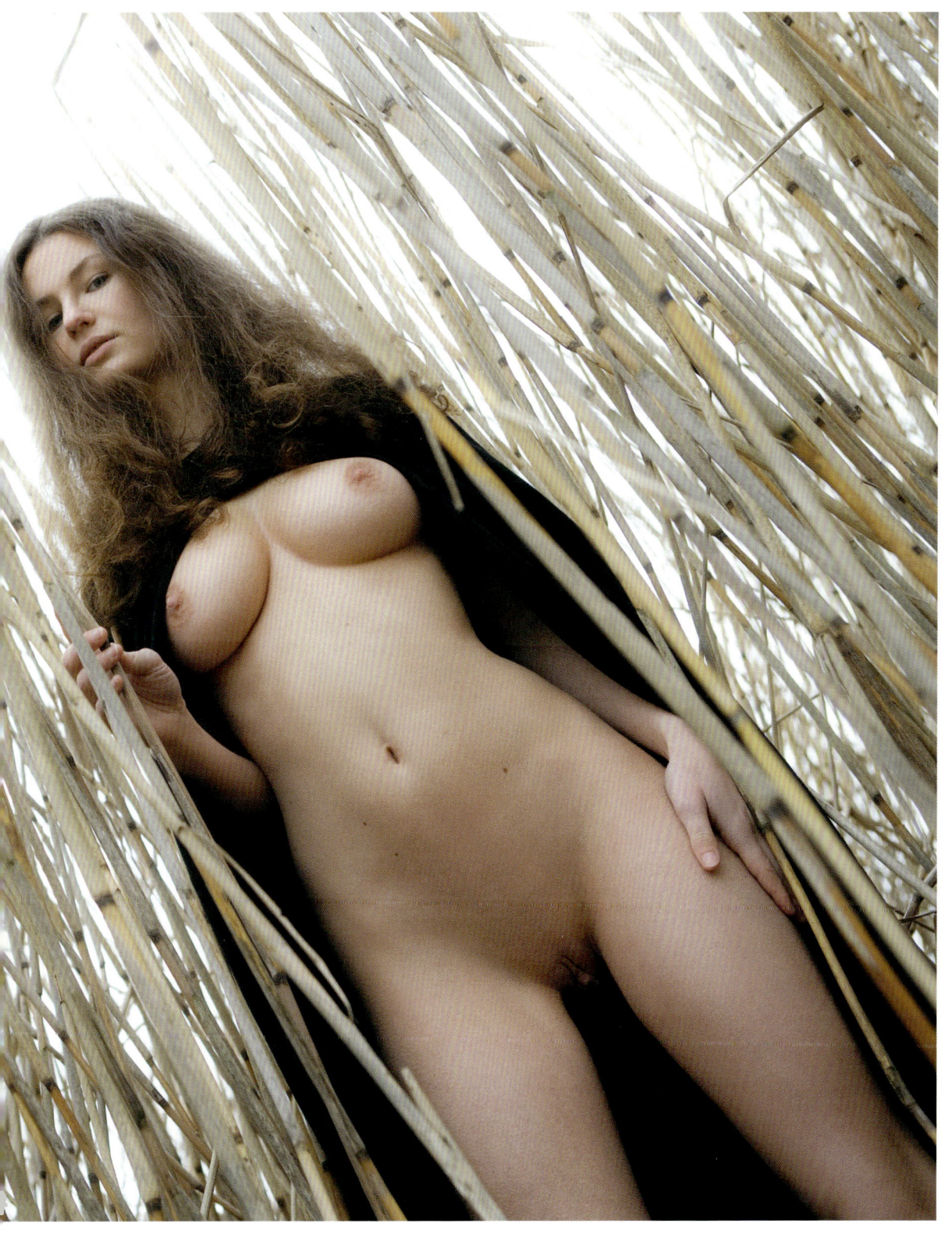

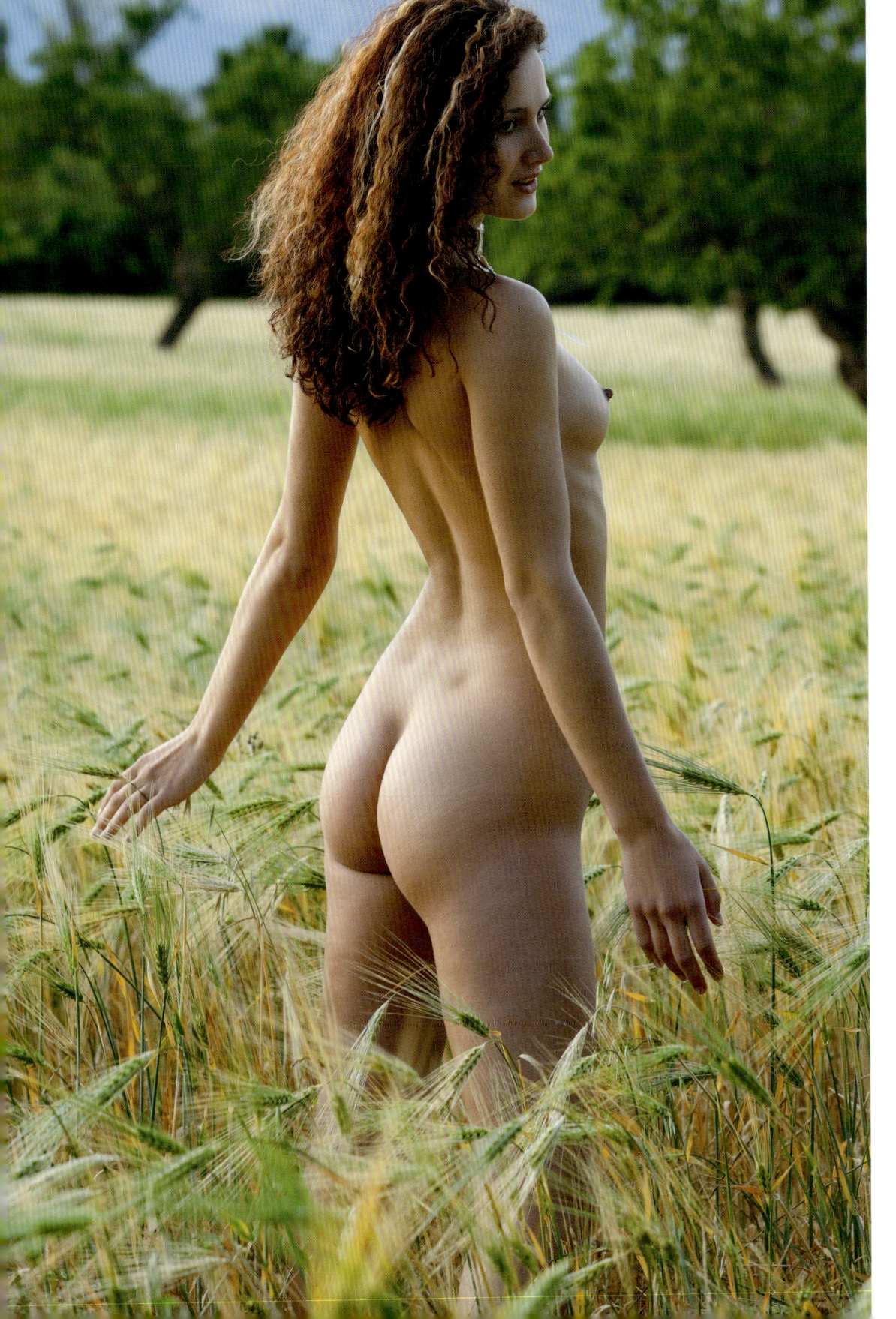

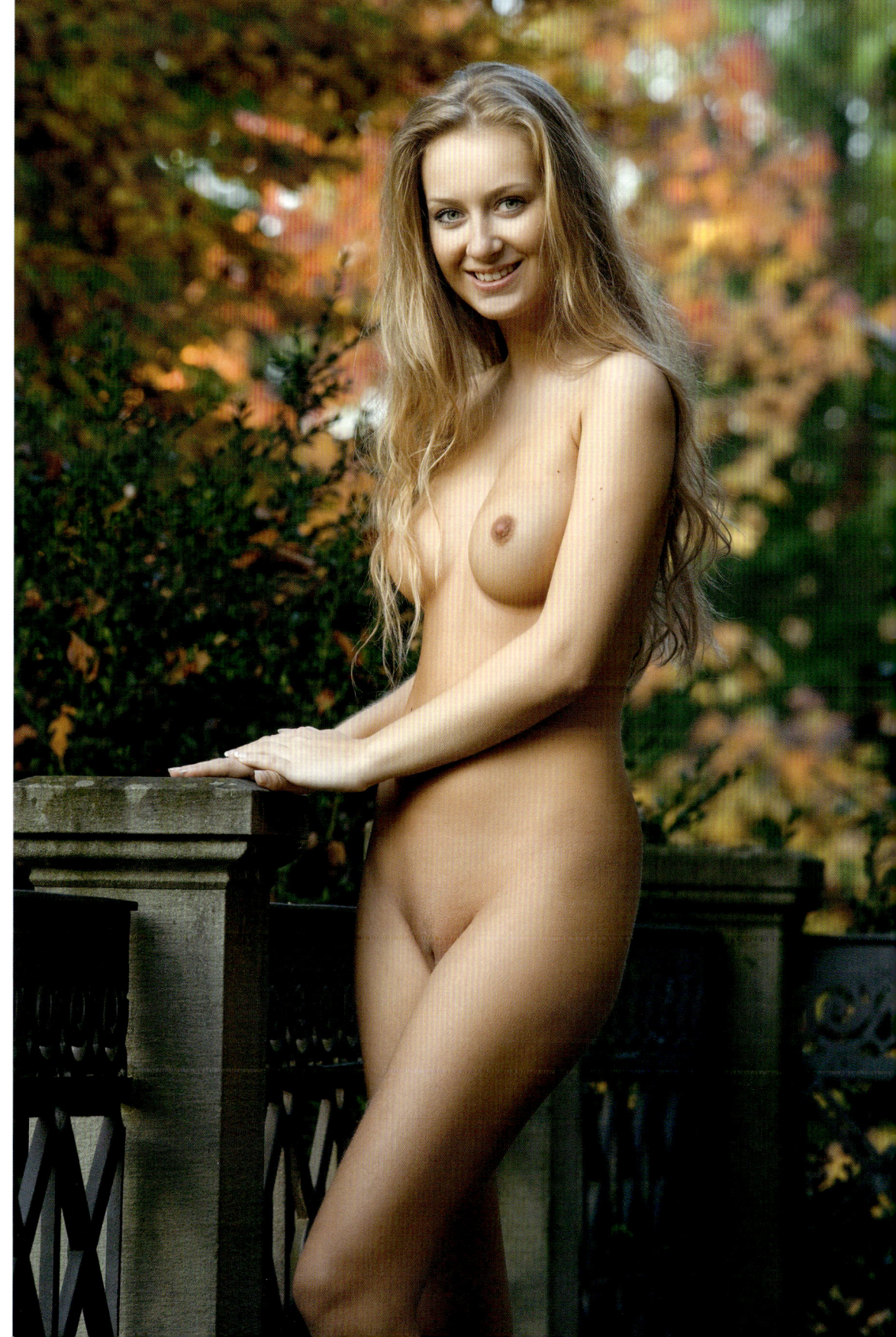

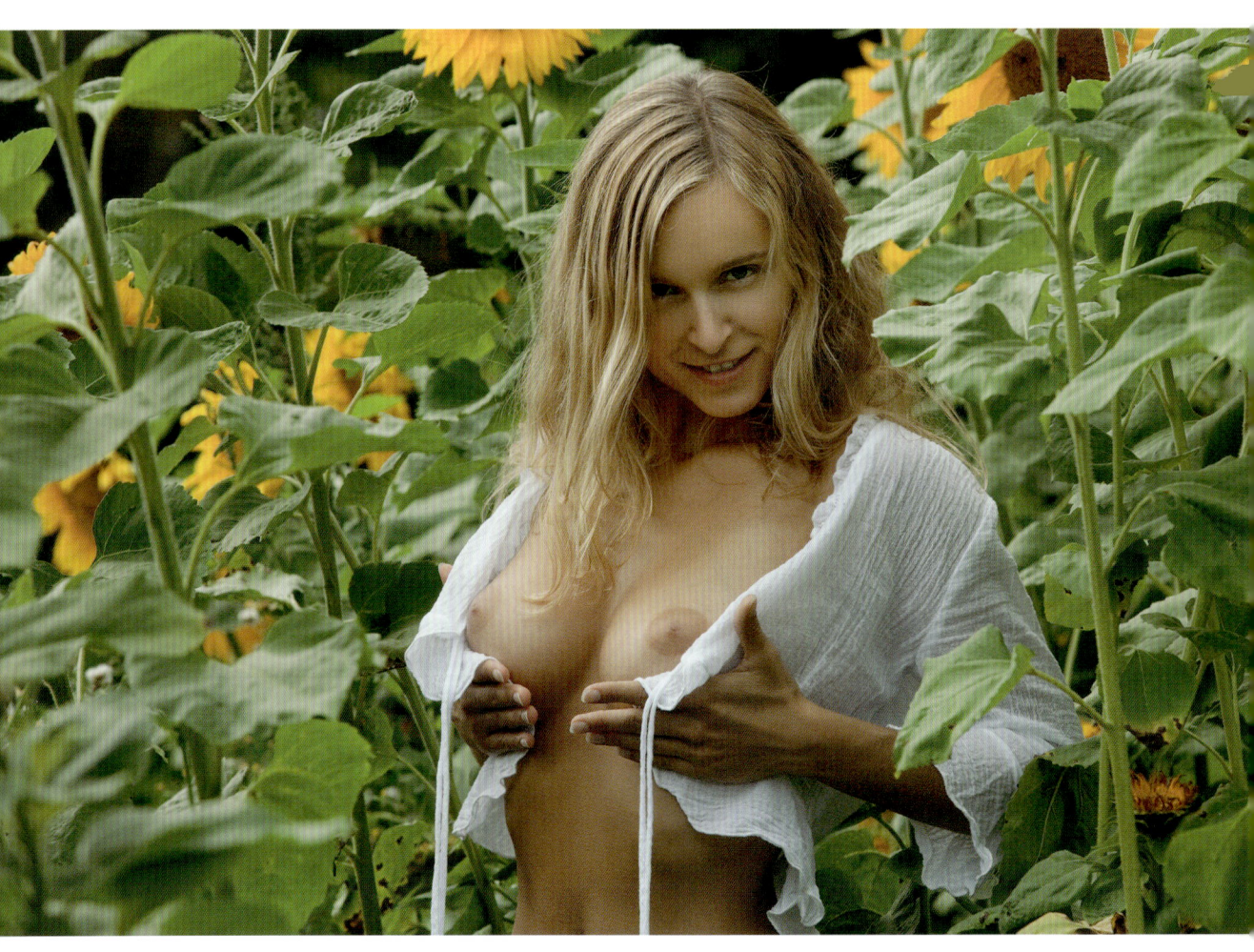

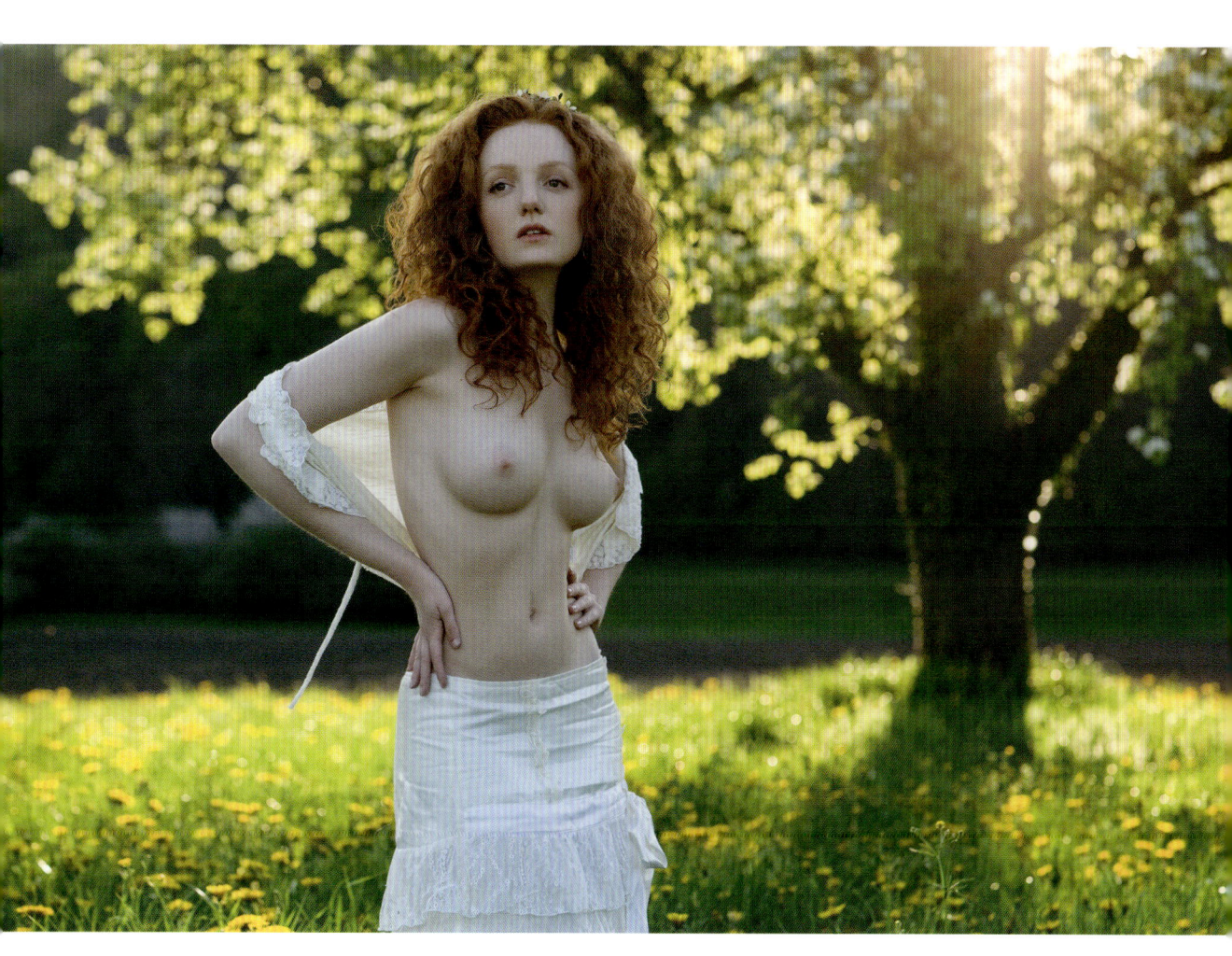

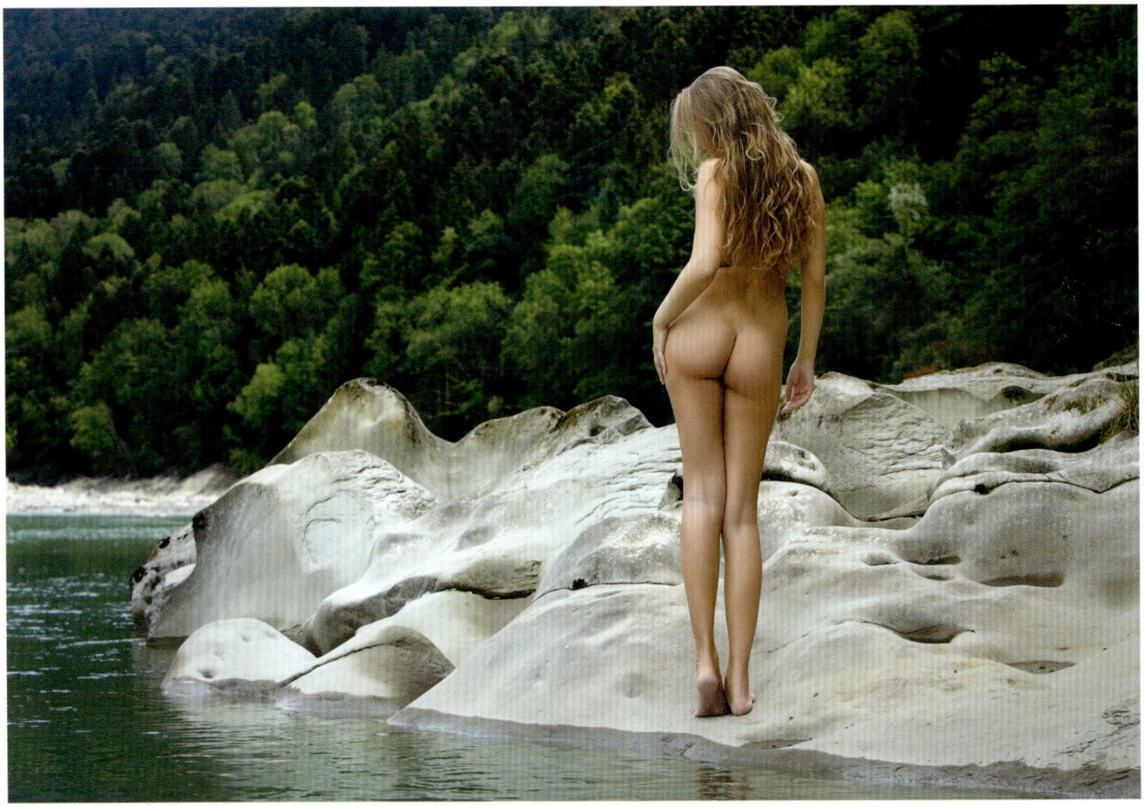

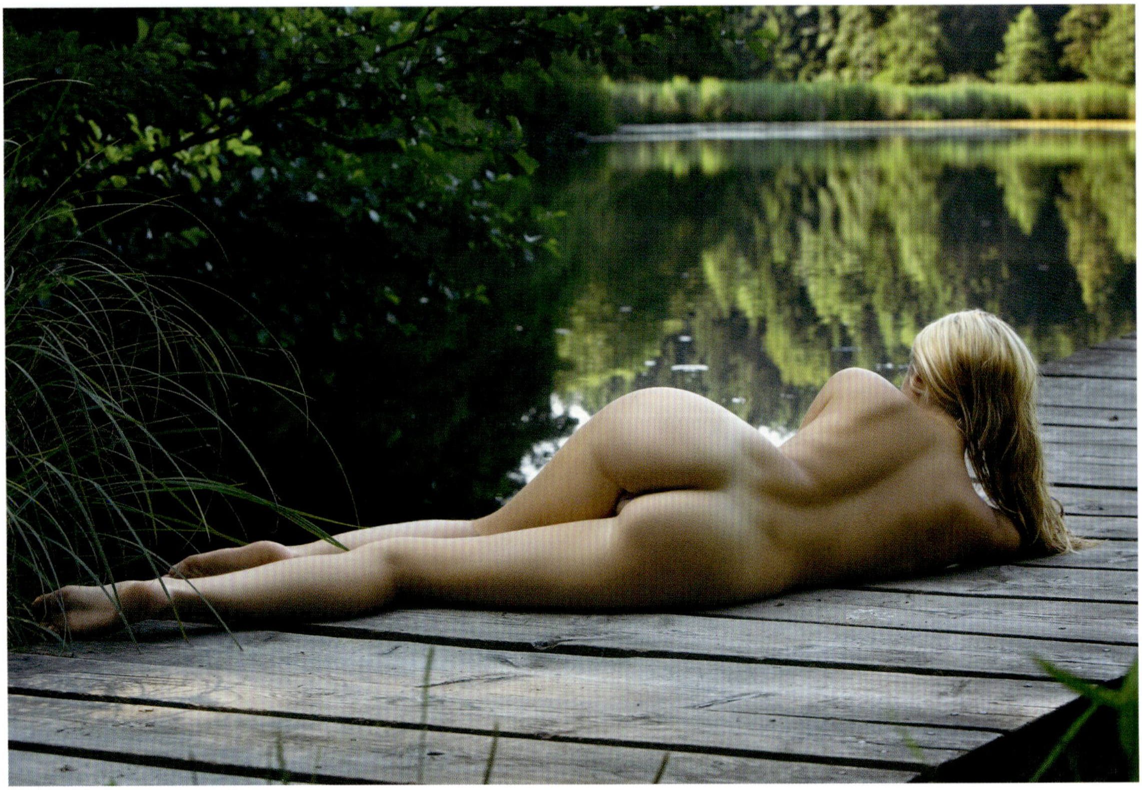

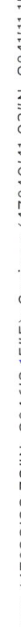

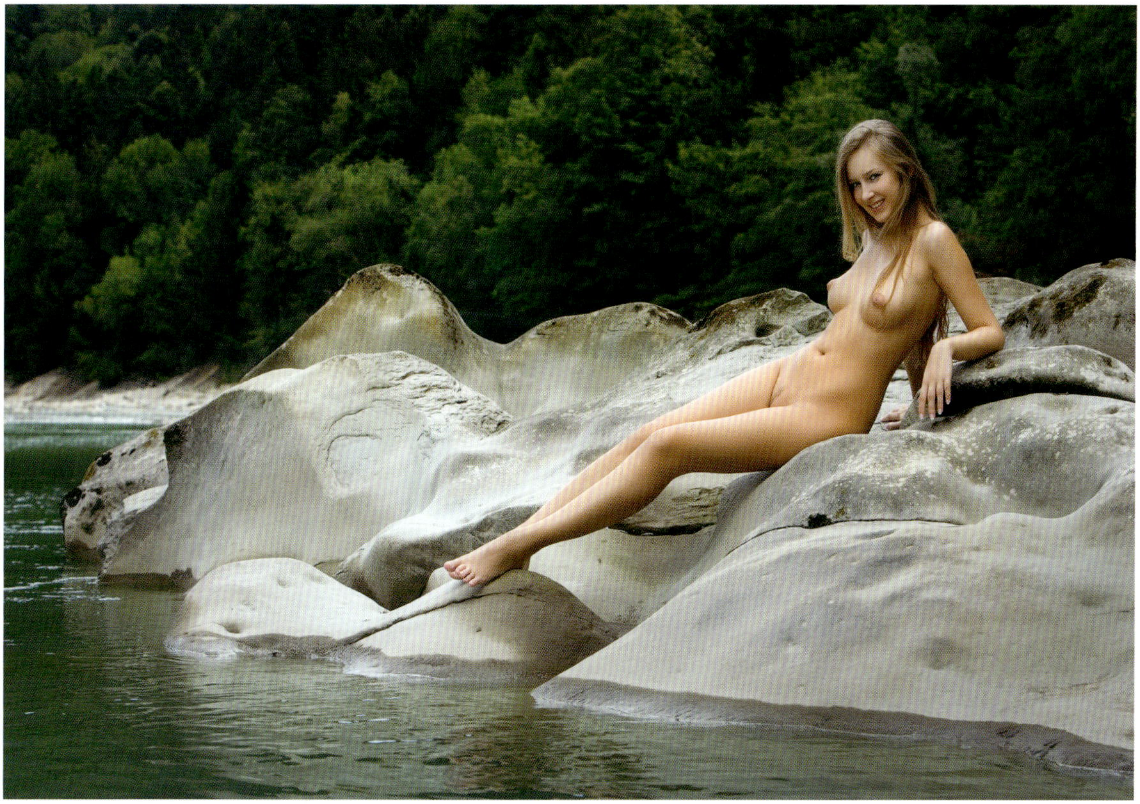

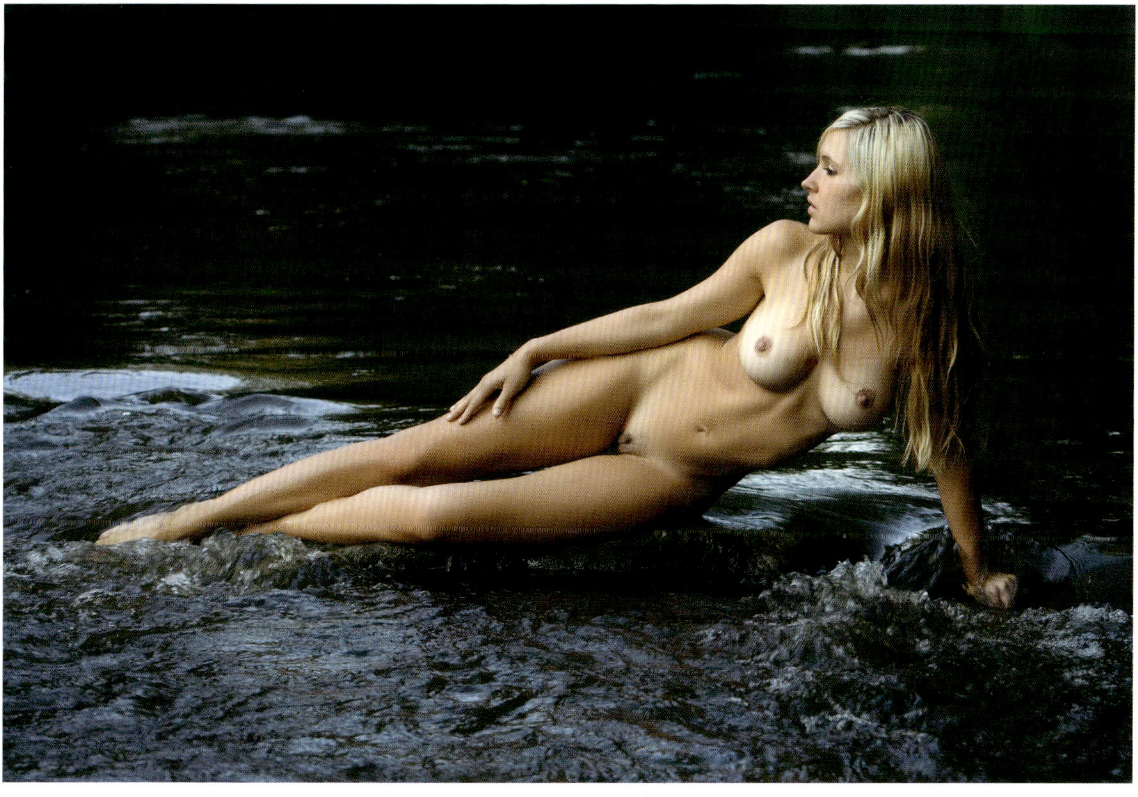

p. 119 Kinga (47°28'28.79"N, 9°46'2.15"E); Corinna (47°03'56.72"N, 9°42'40.45"E)

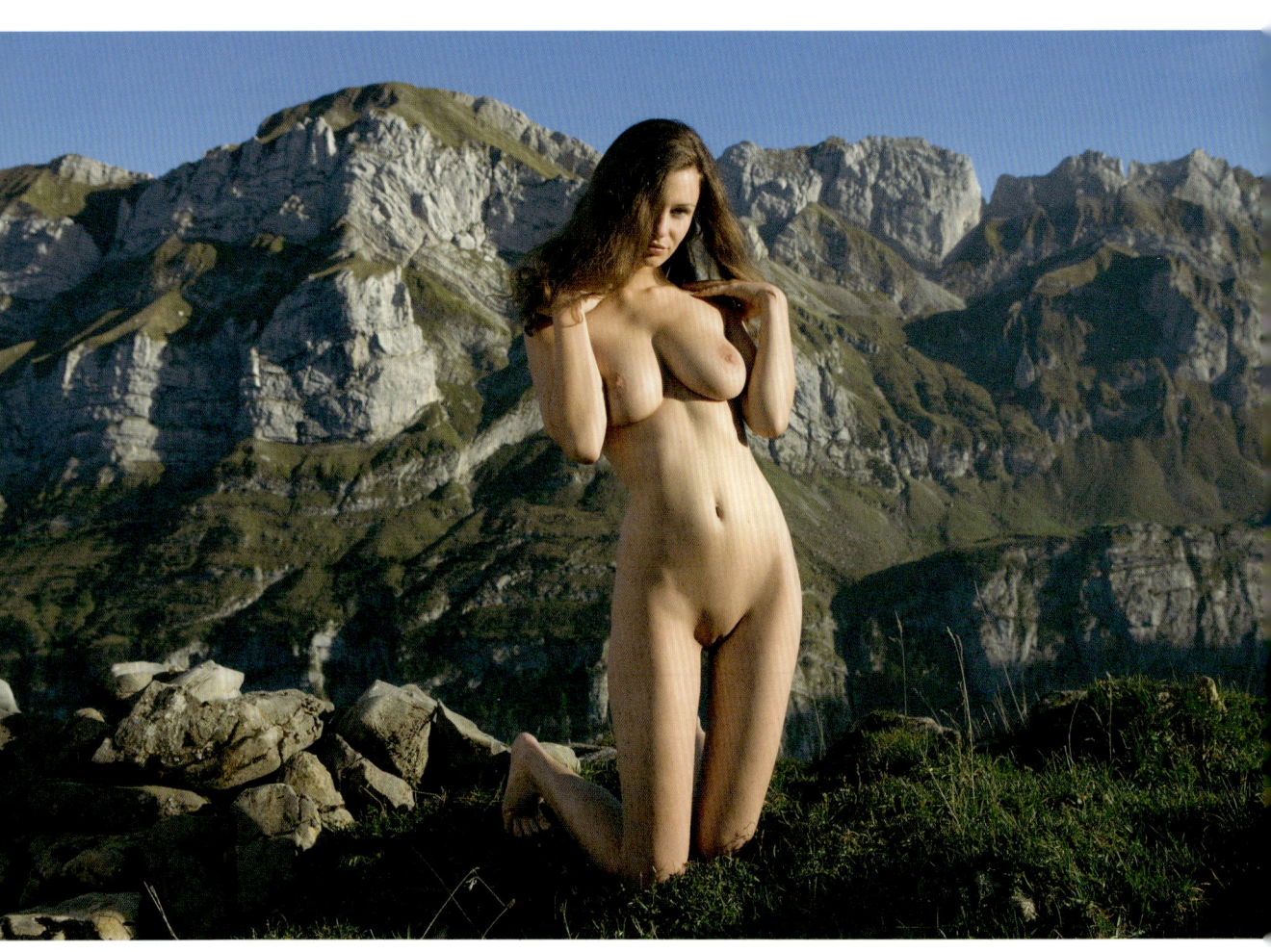

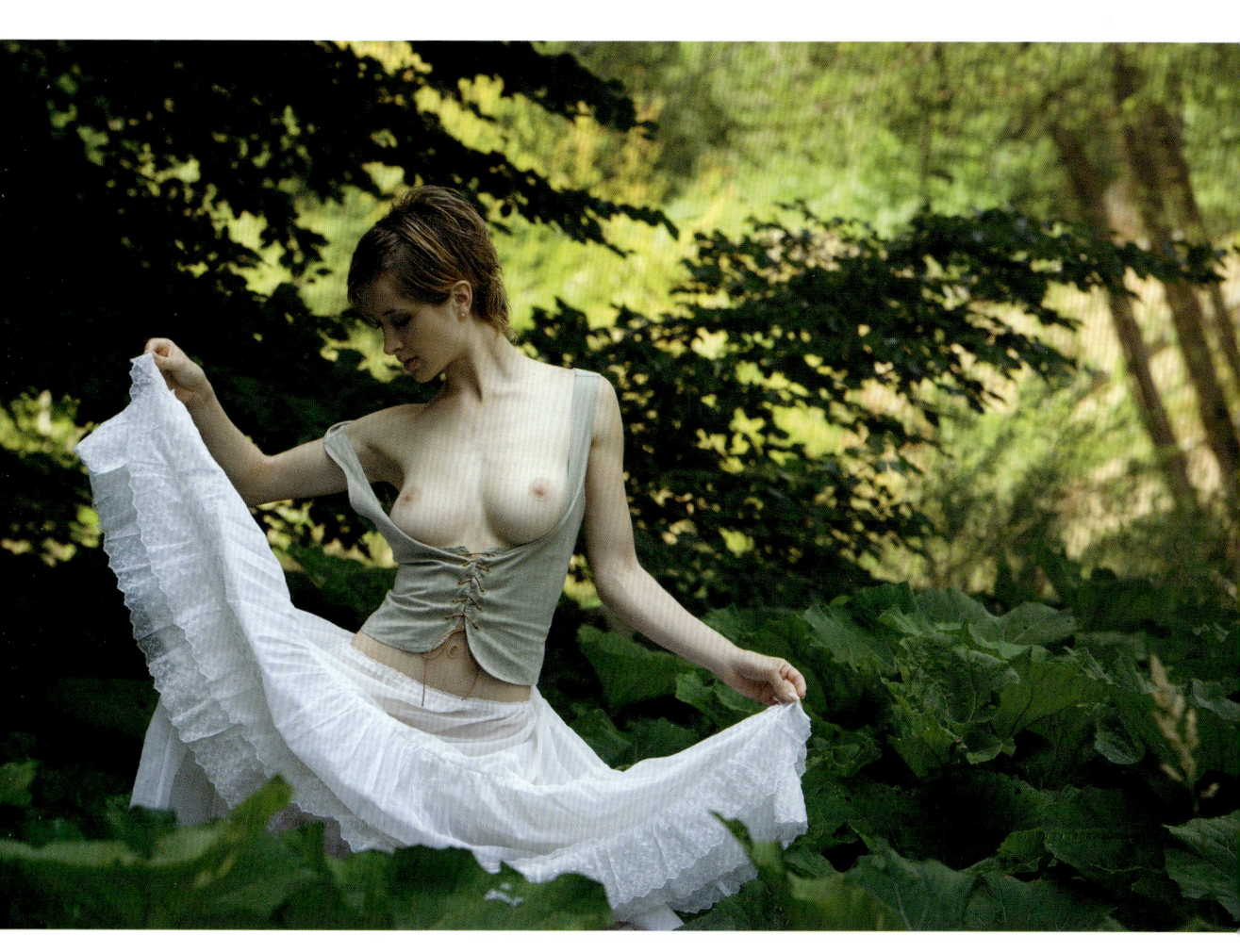

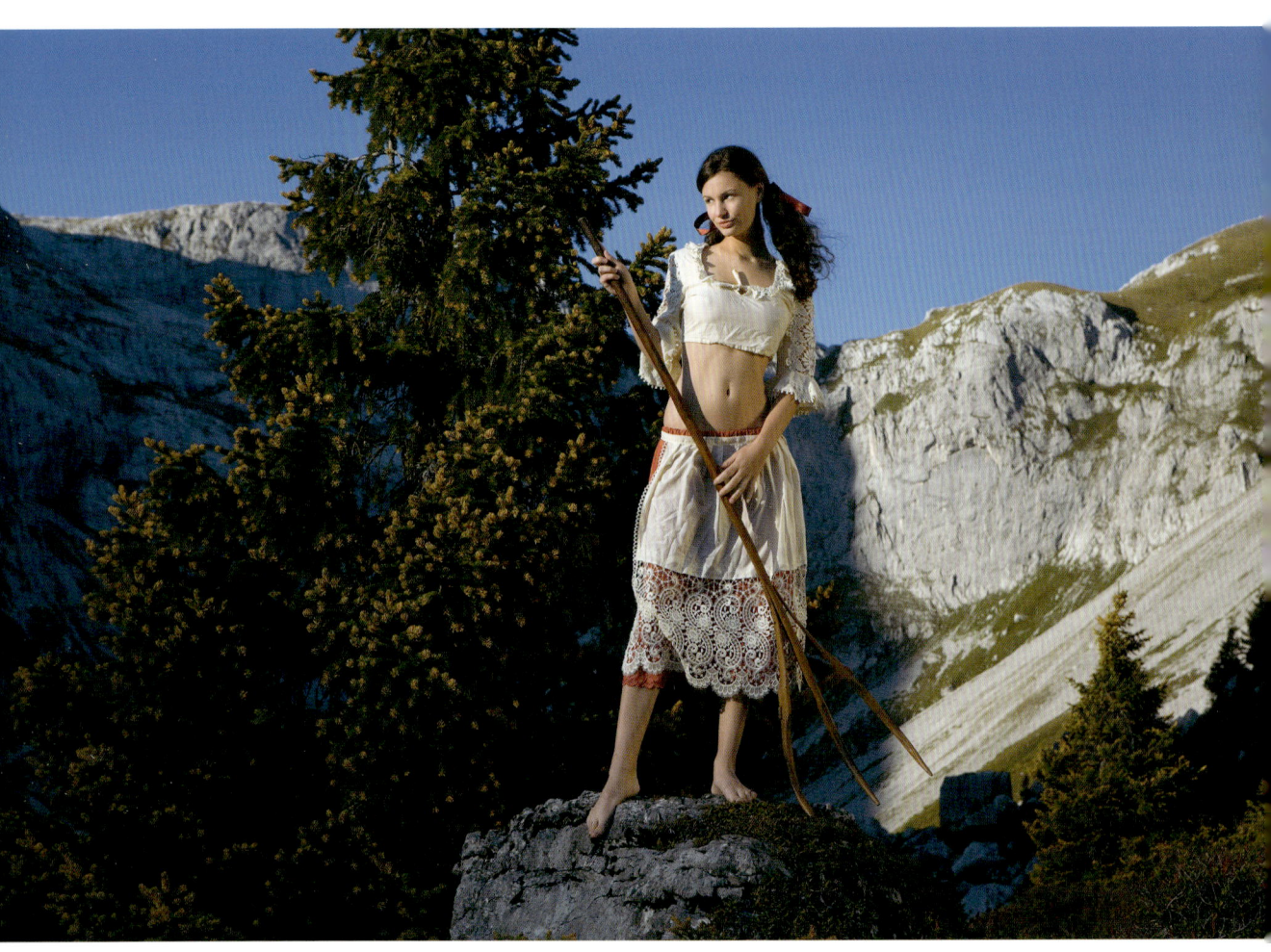

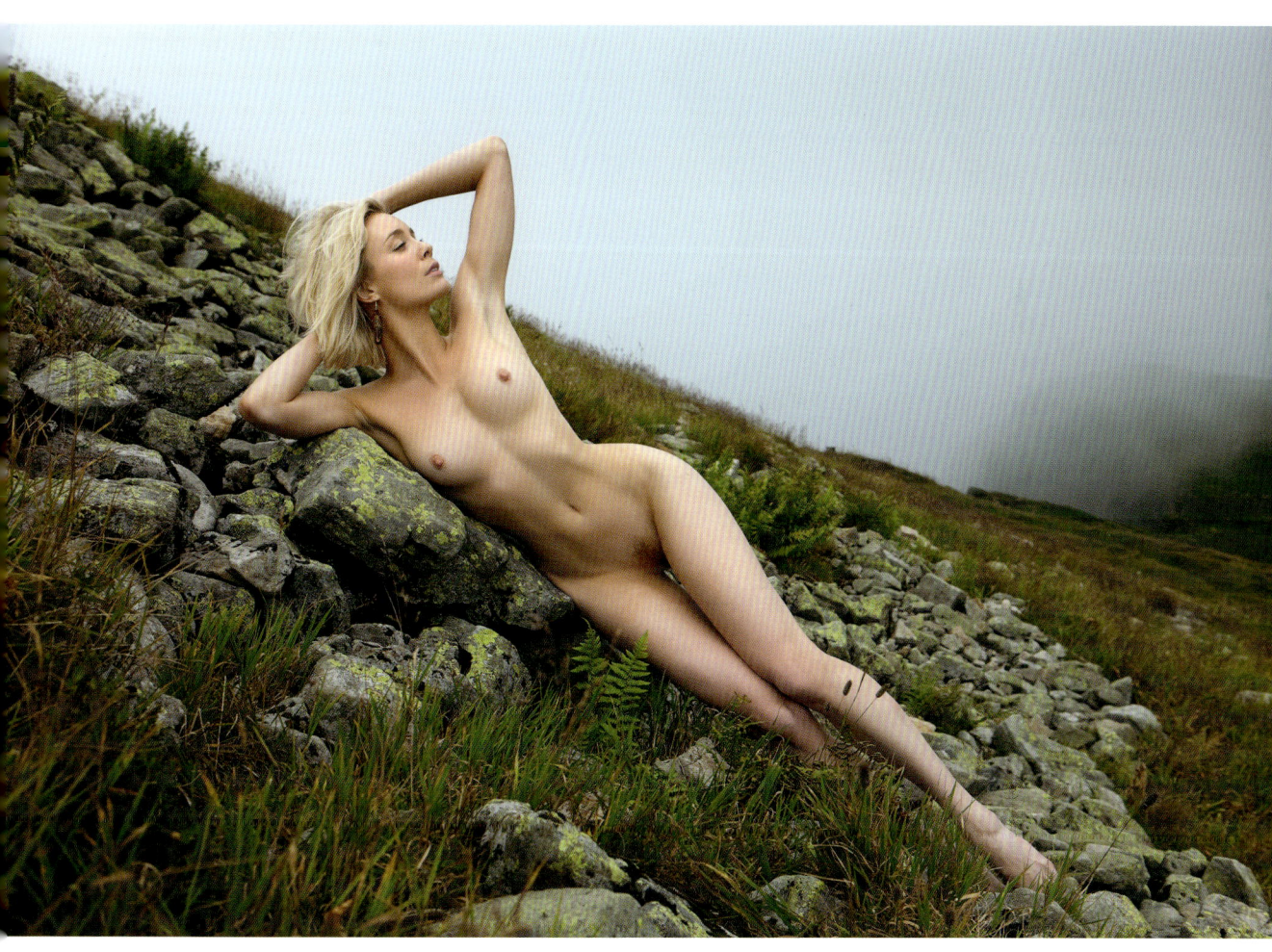

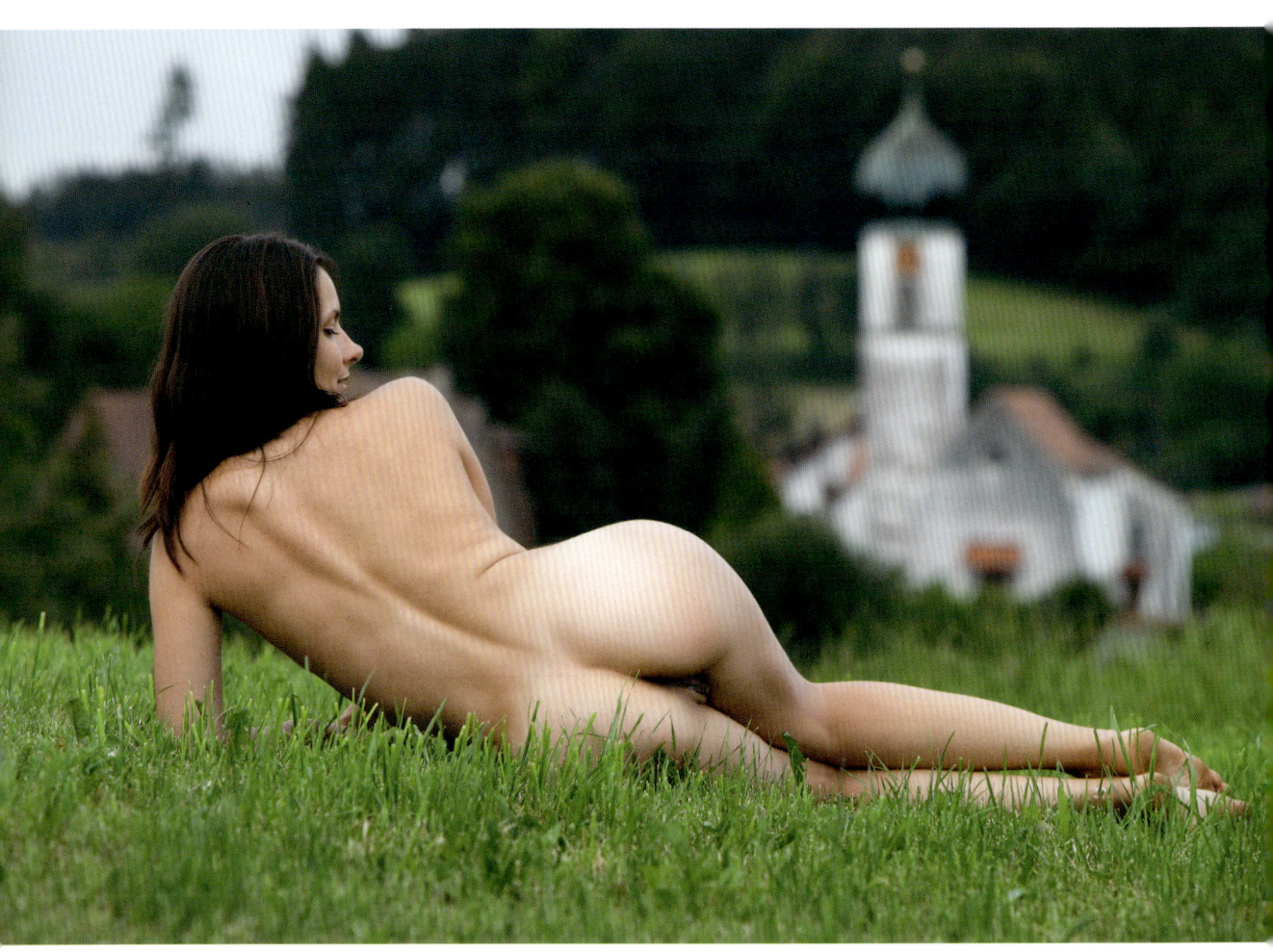

(47°27'20.13"N 8°04'37.56"E)

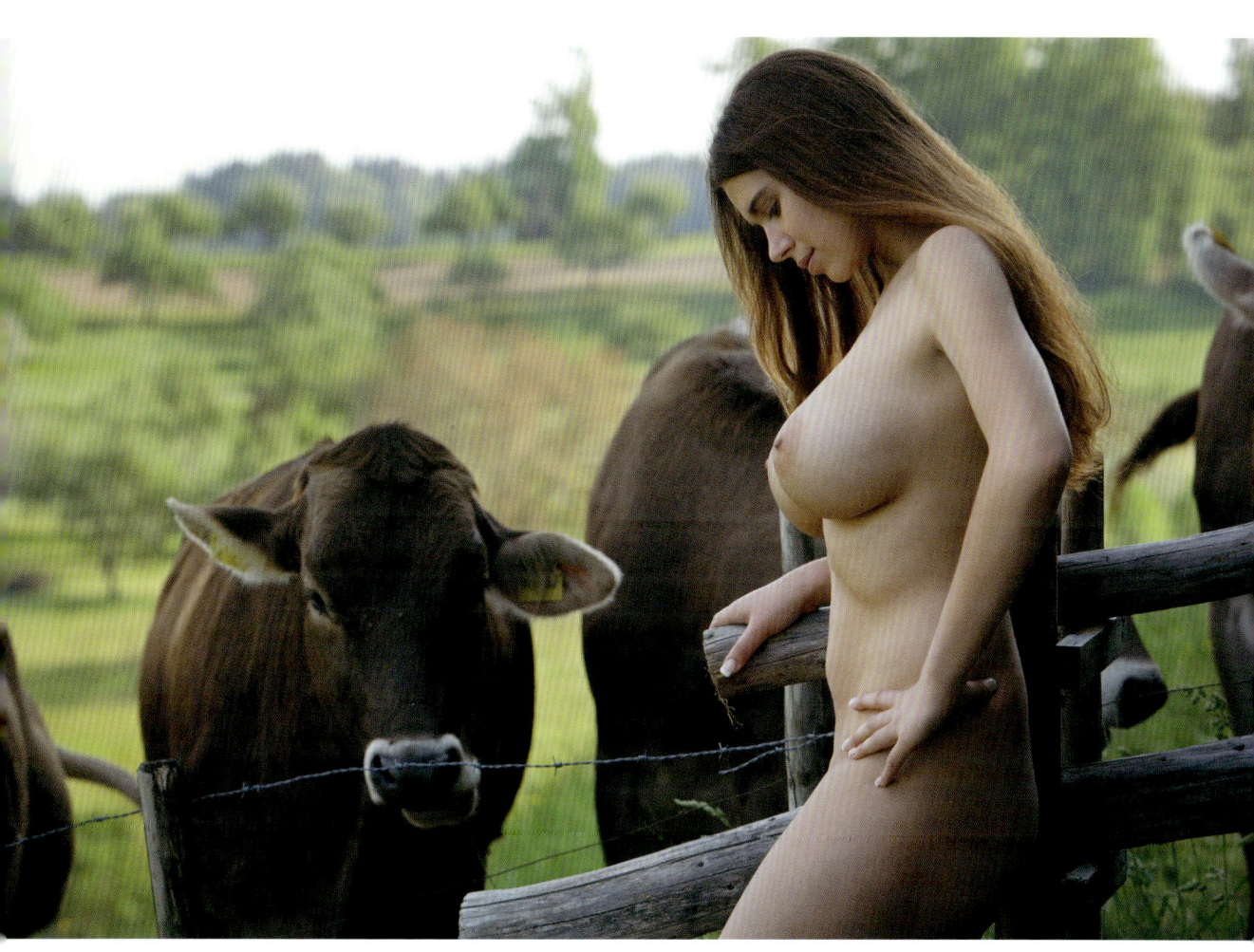

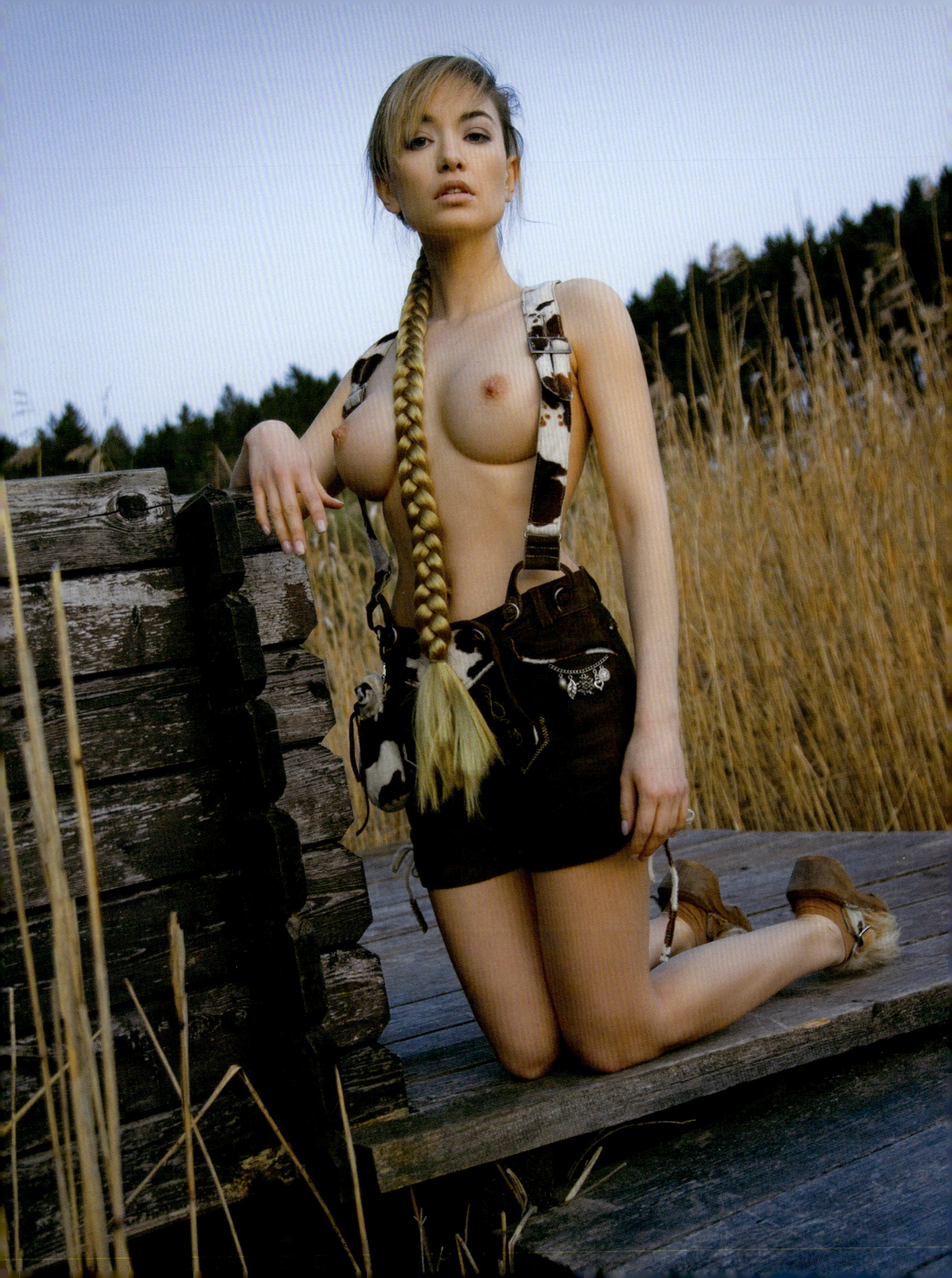

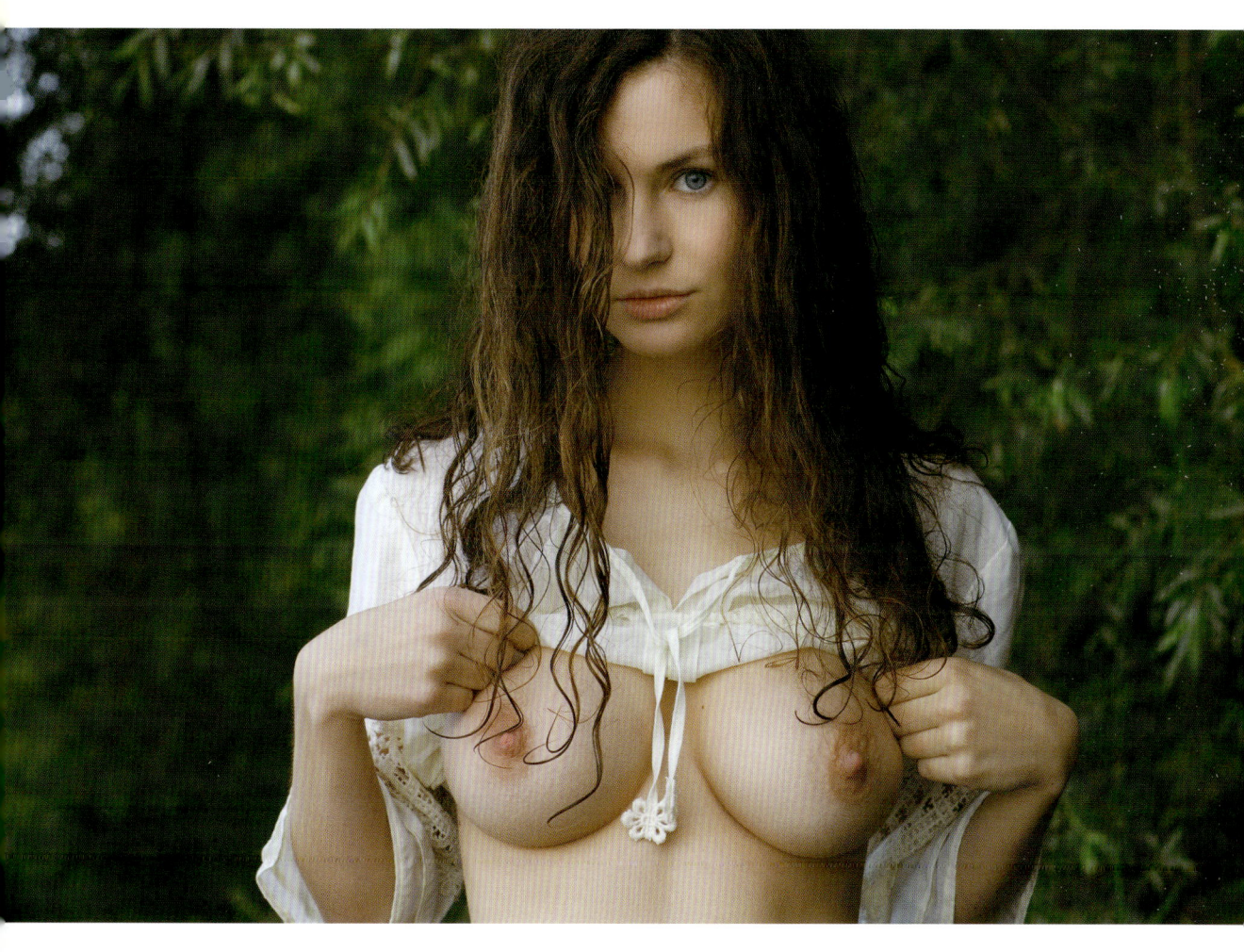

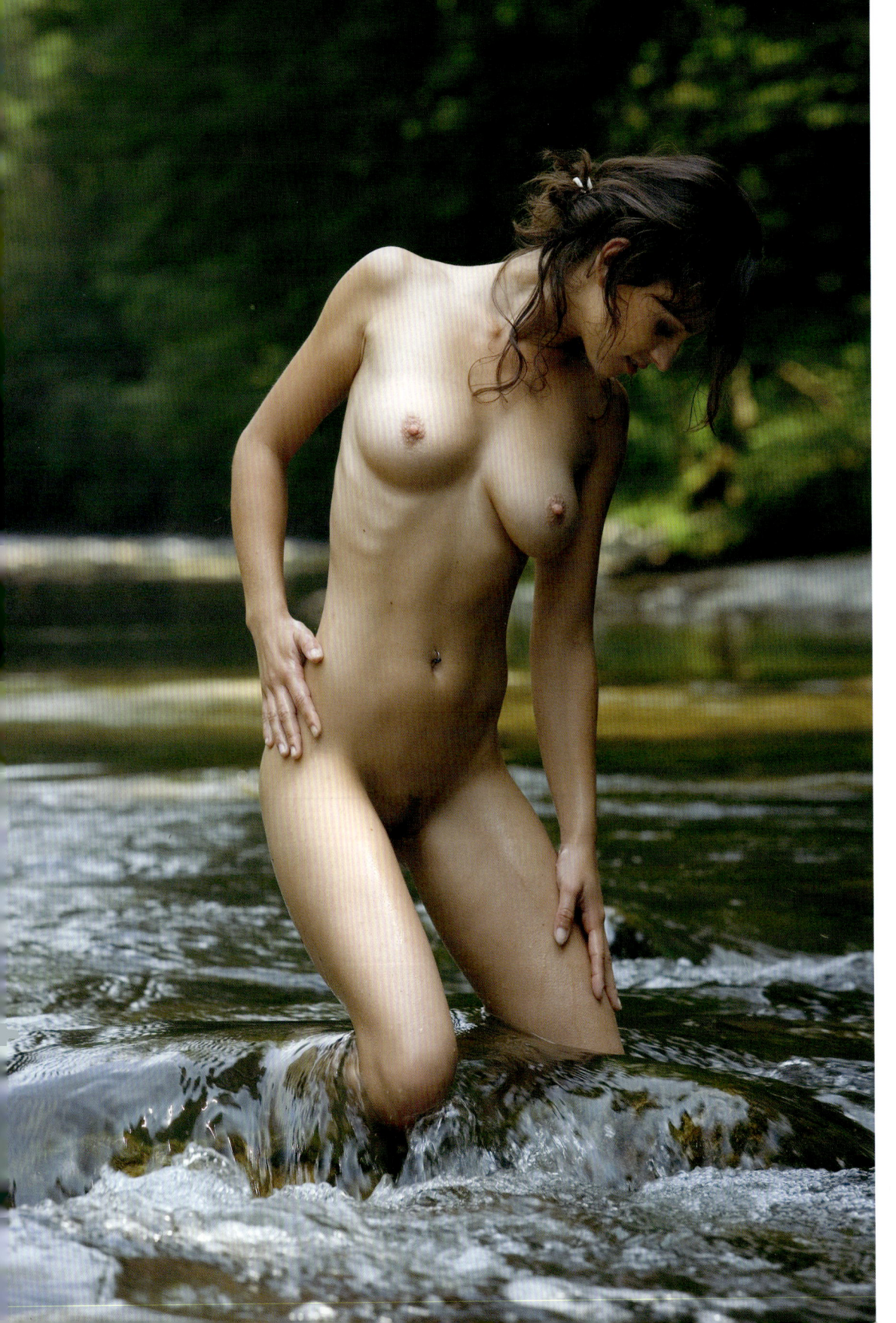

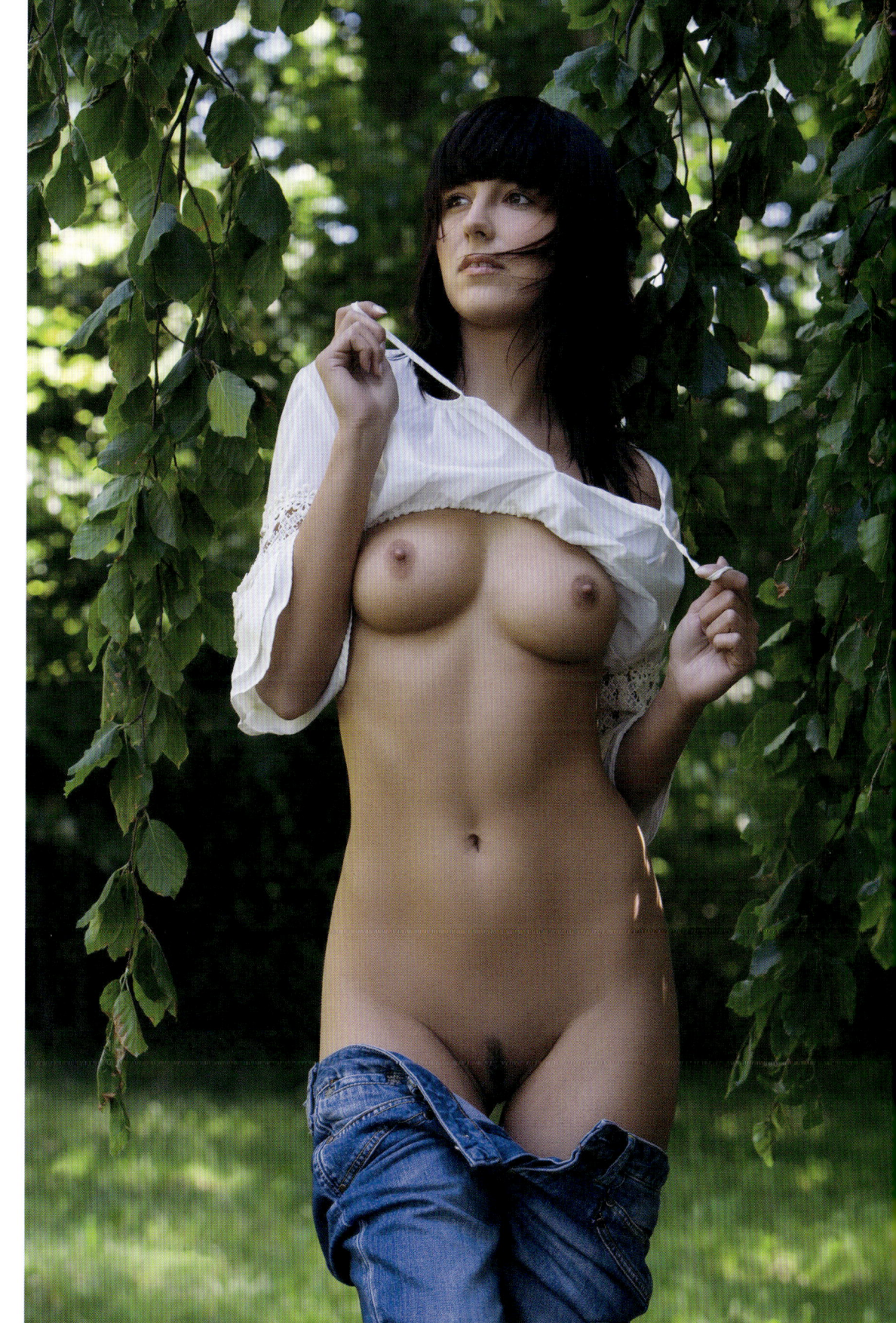

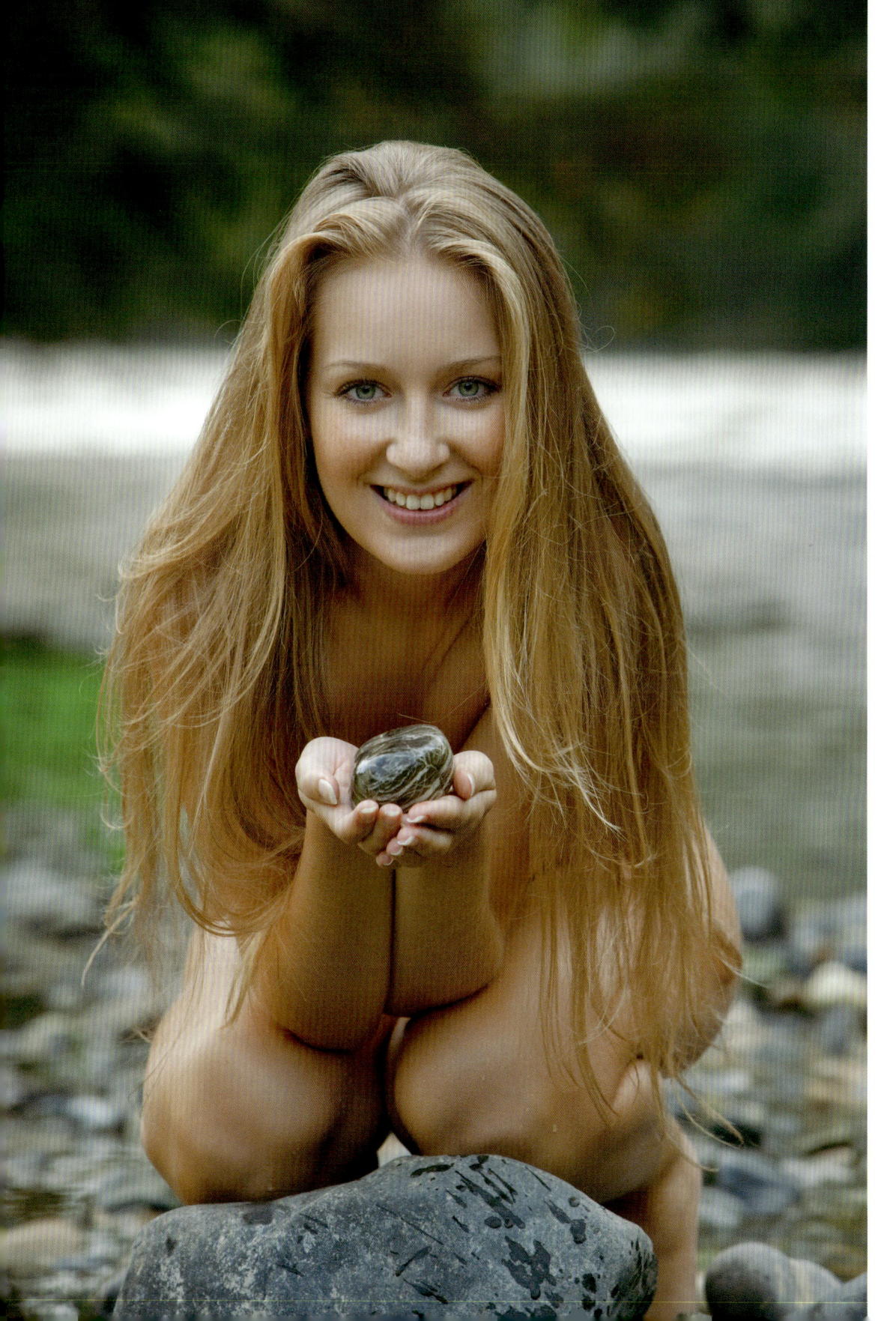

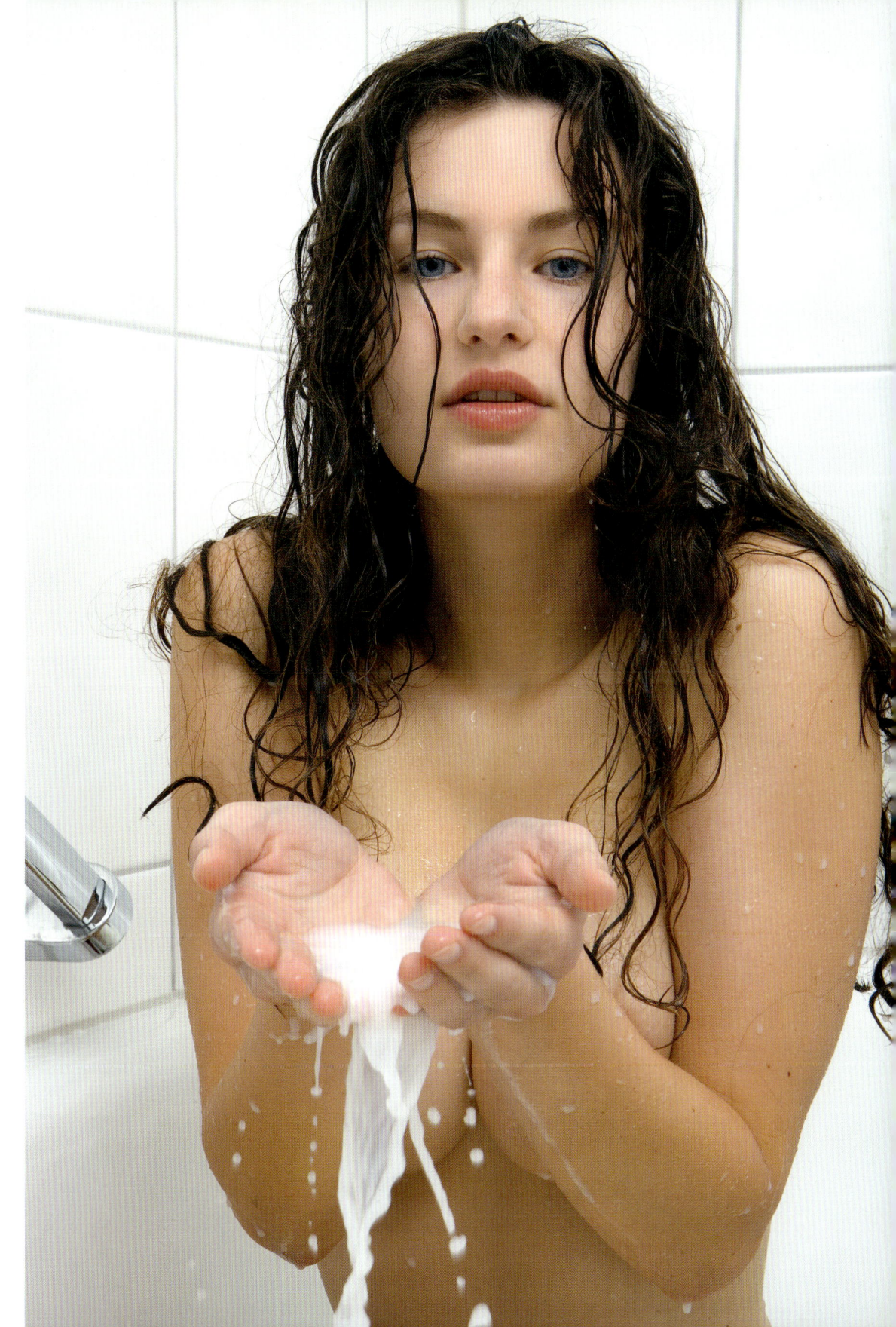

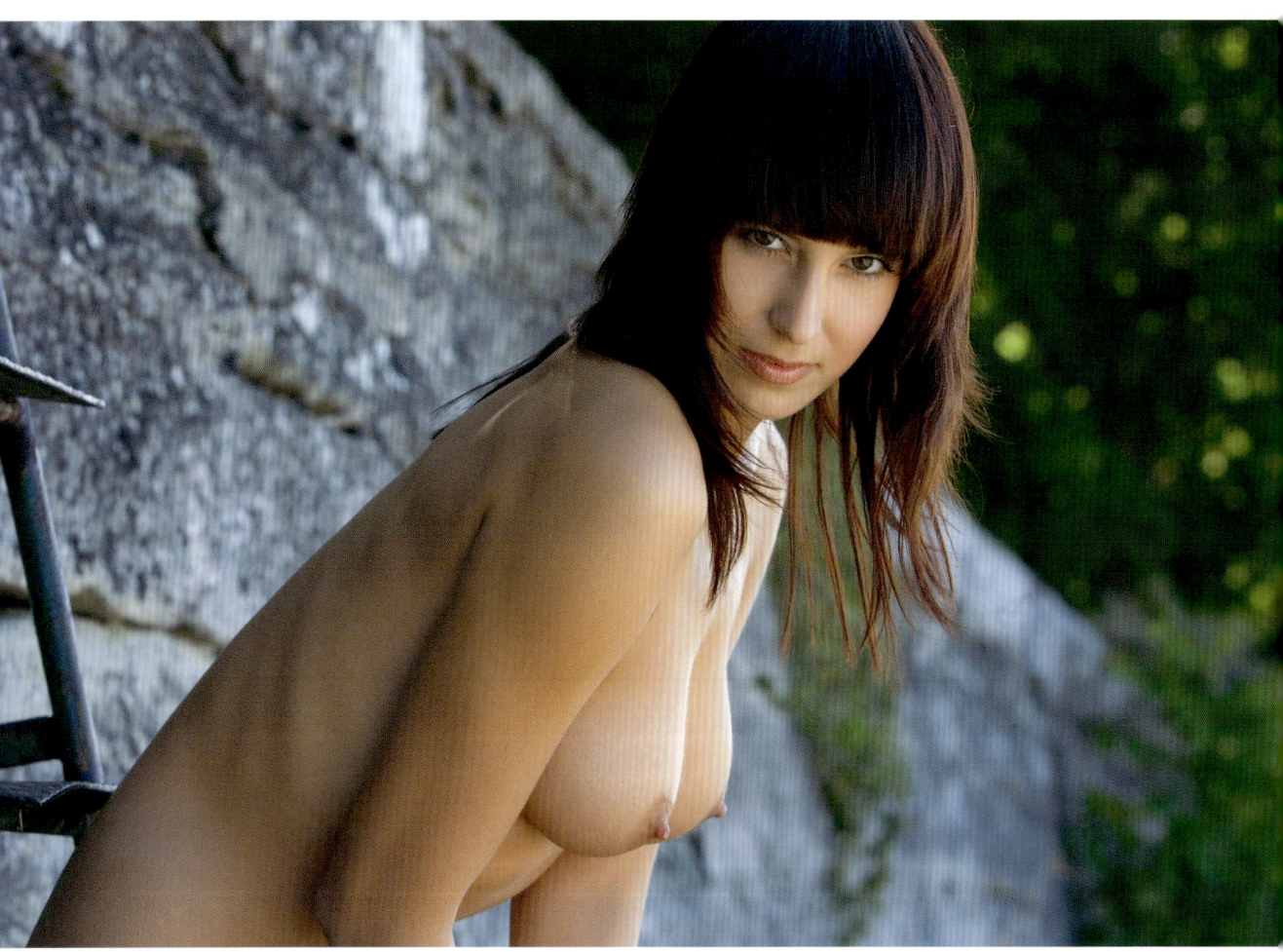

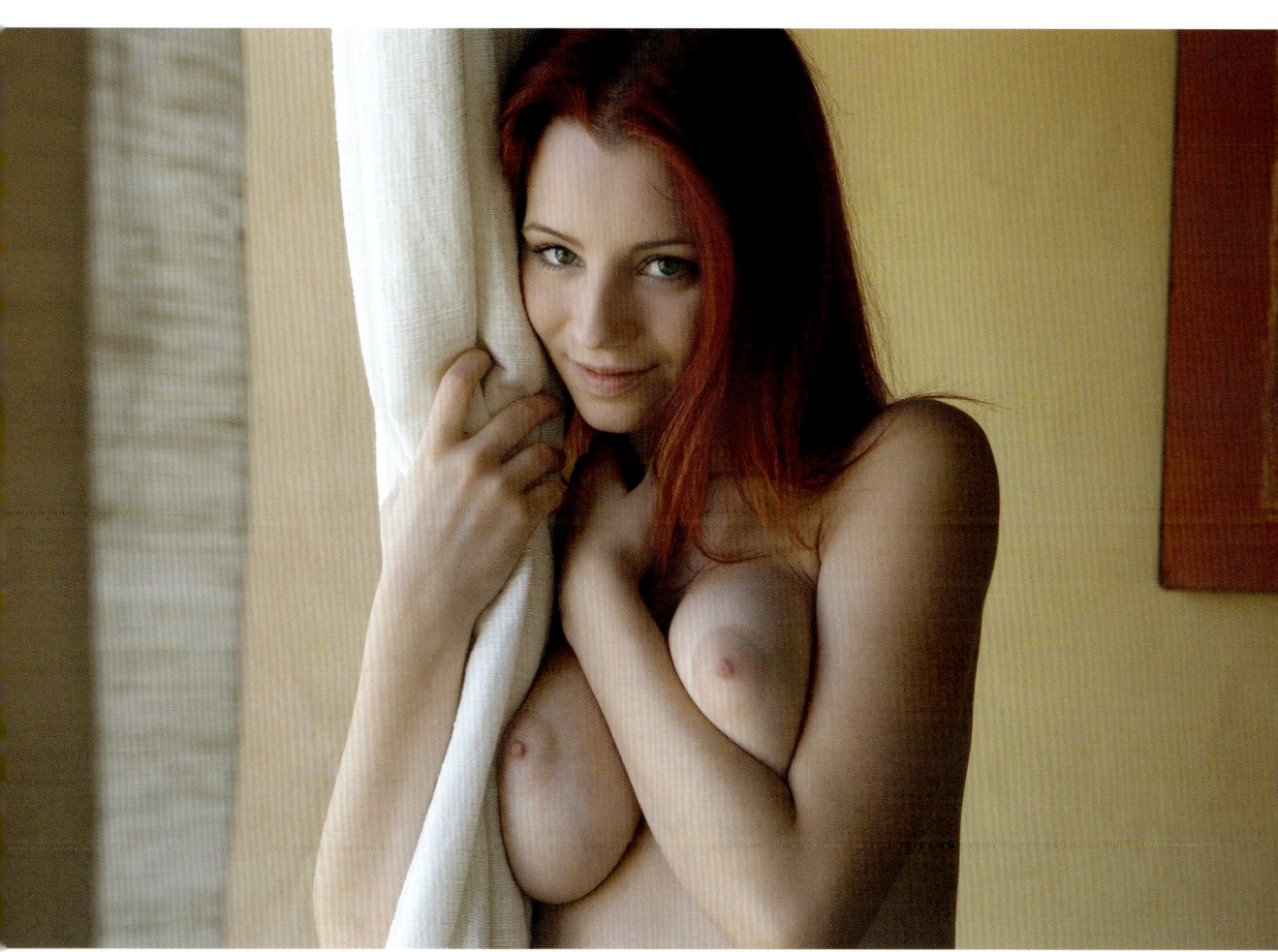

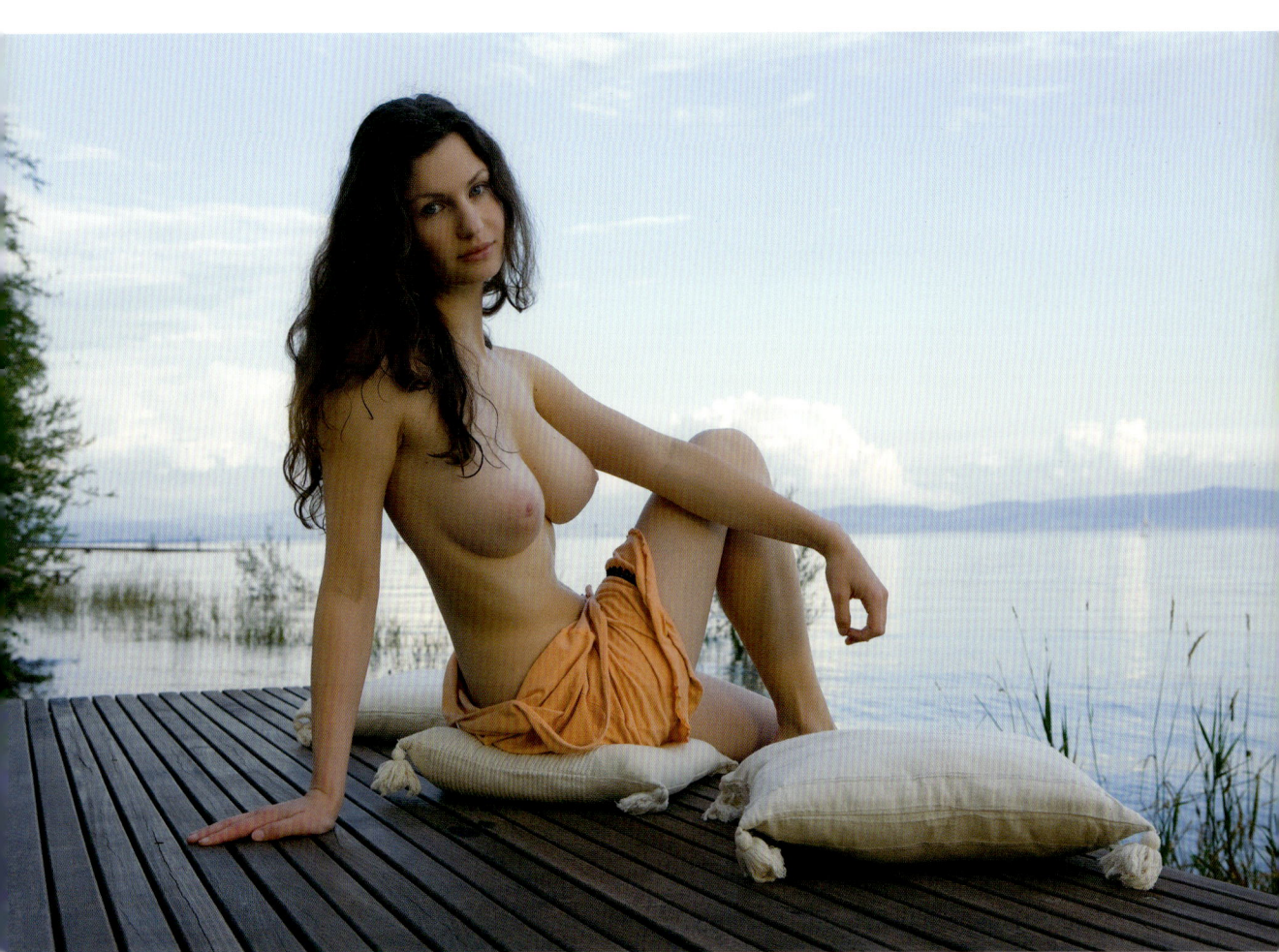

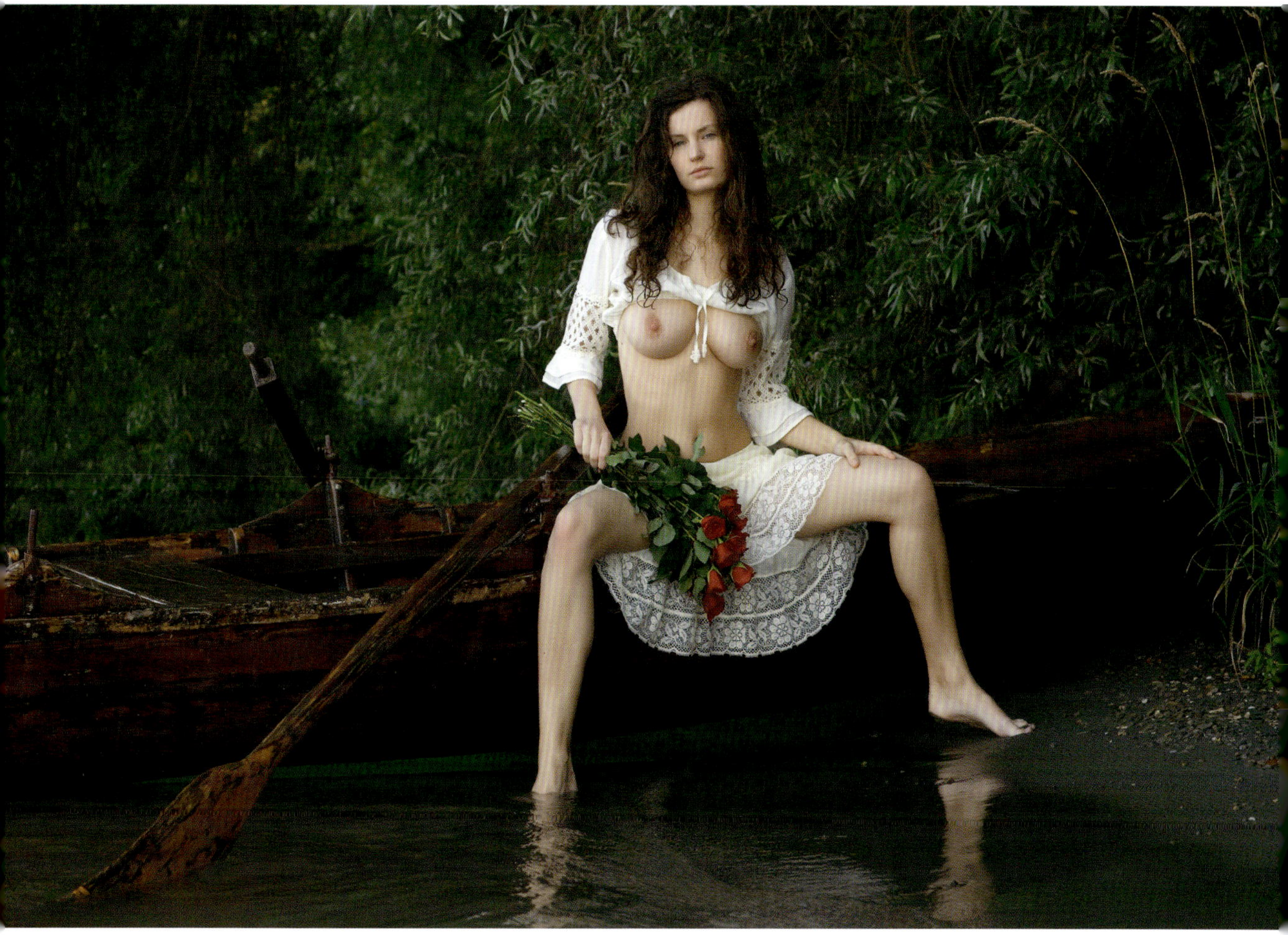

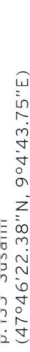

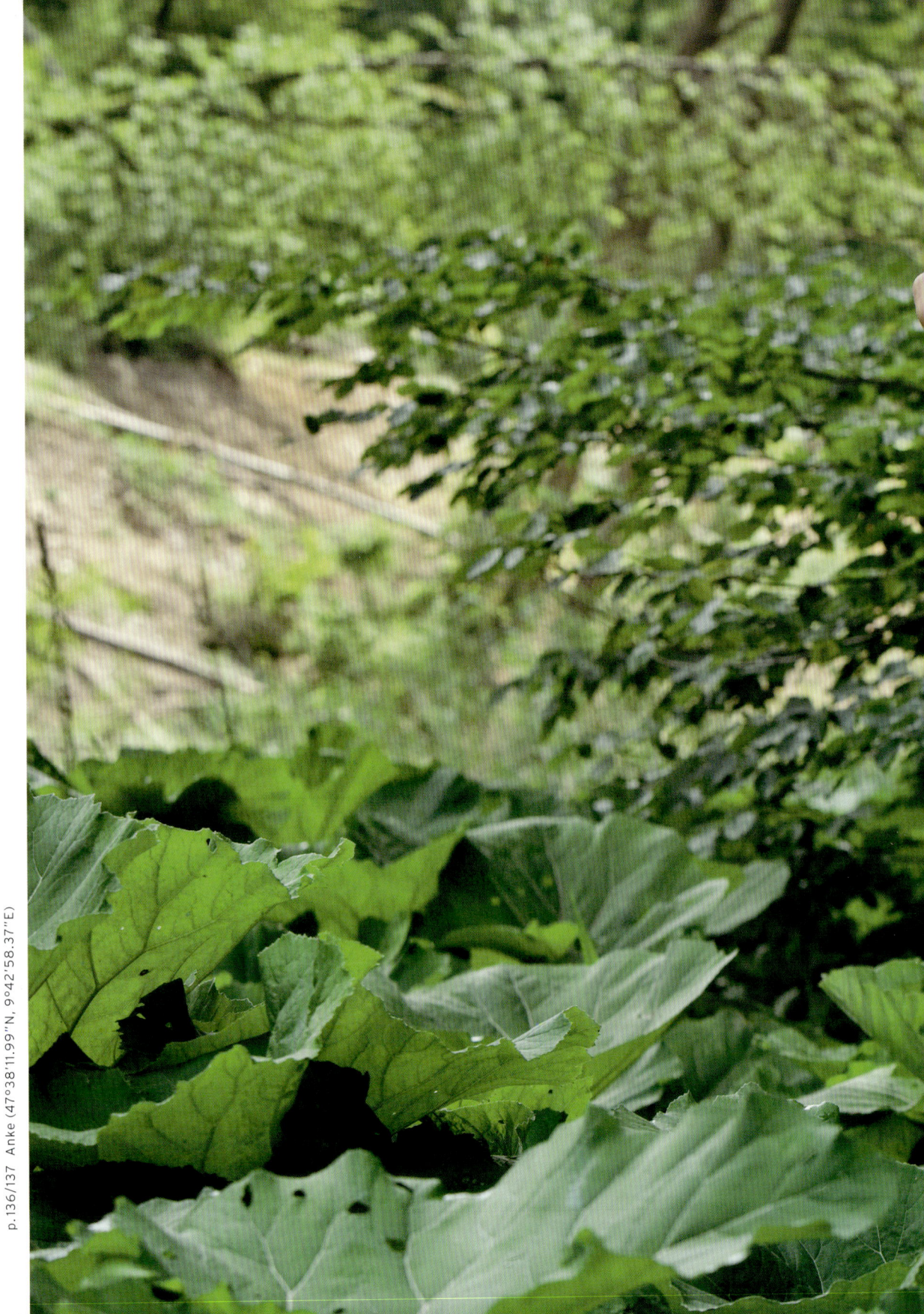

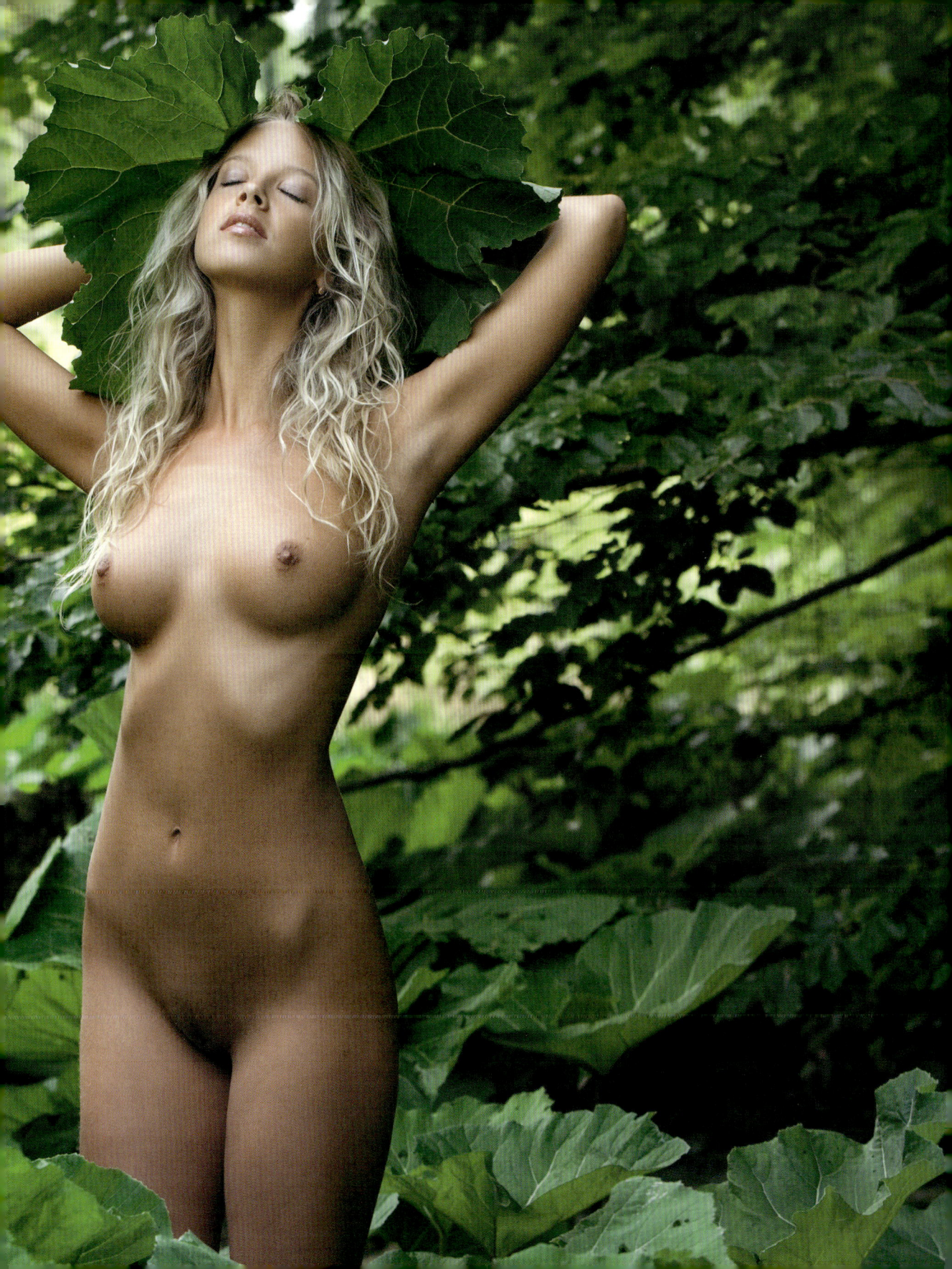

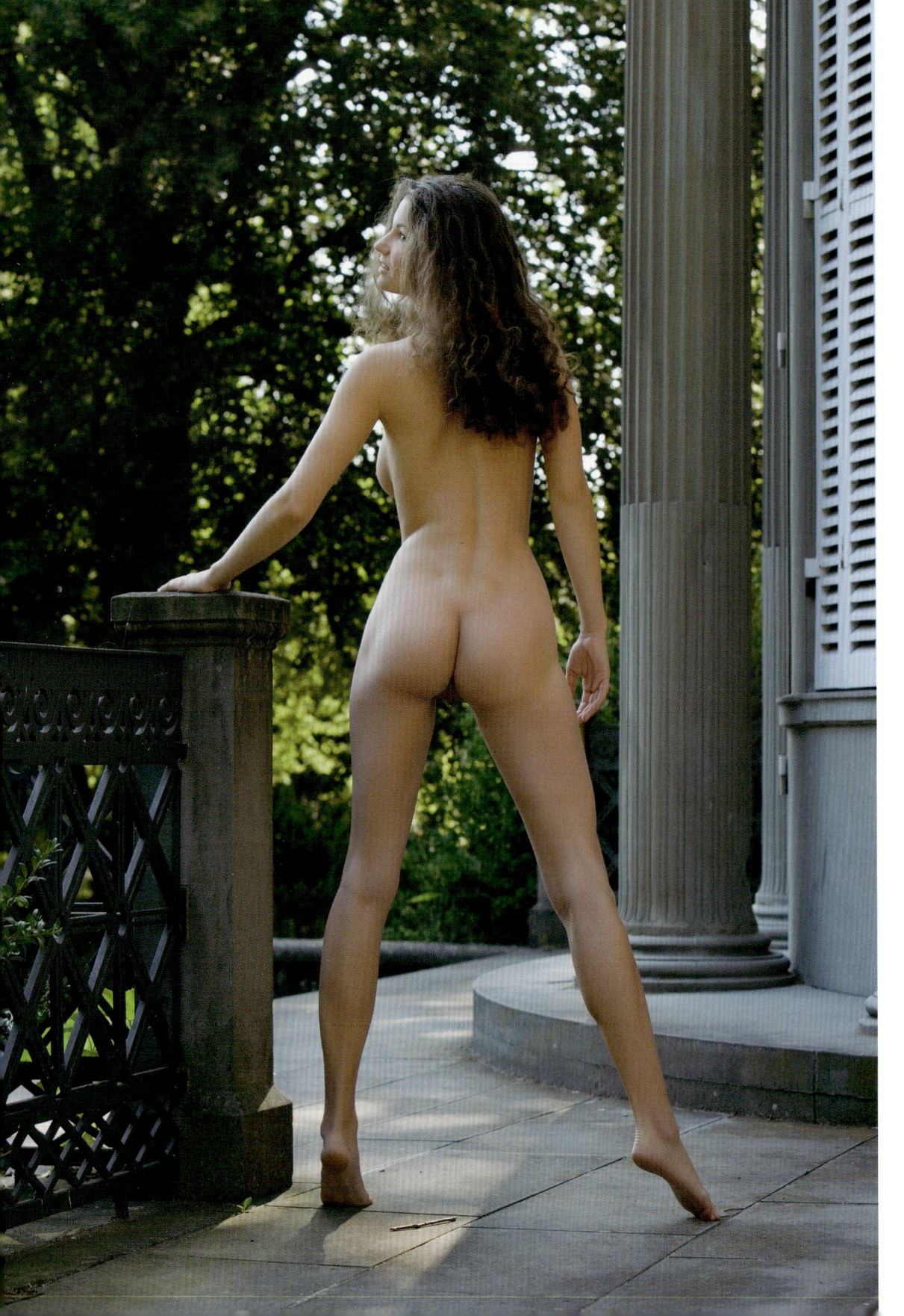

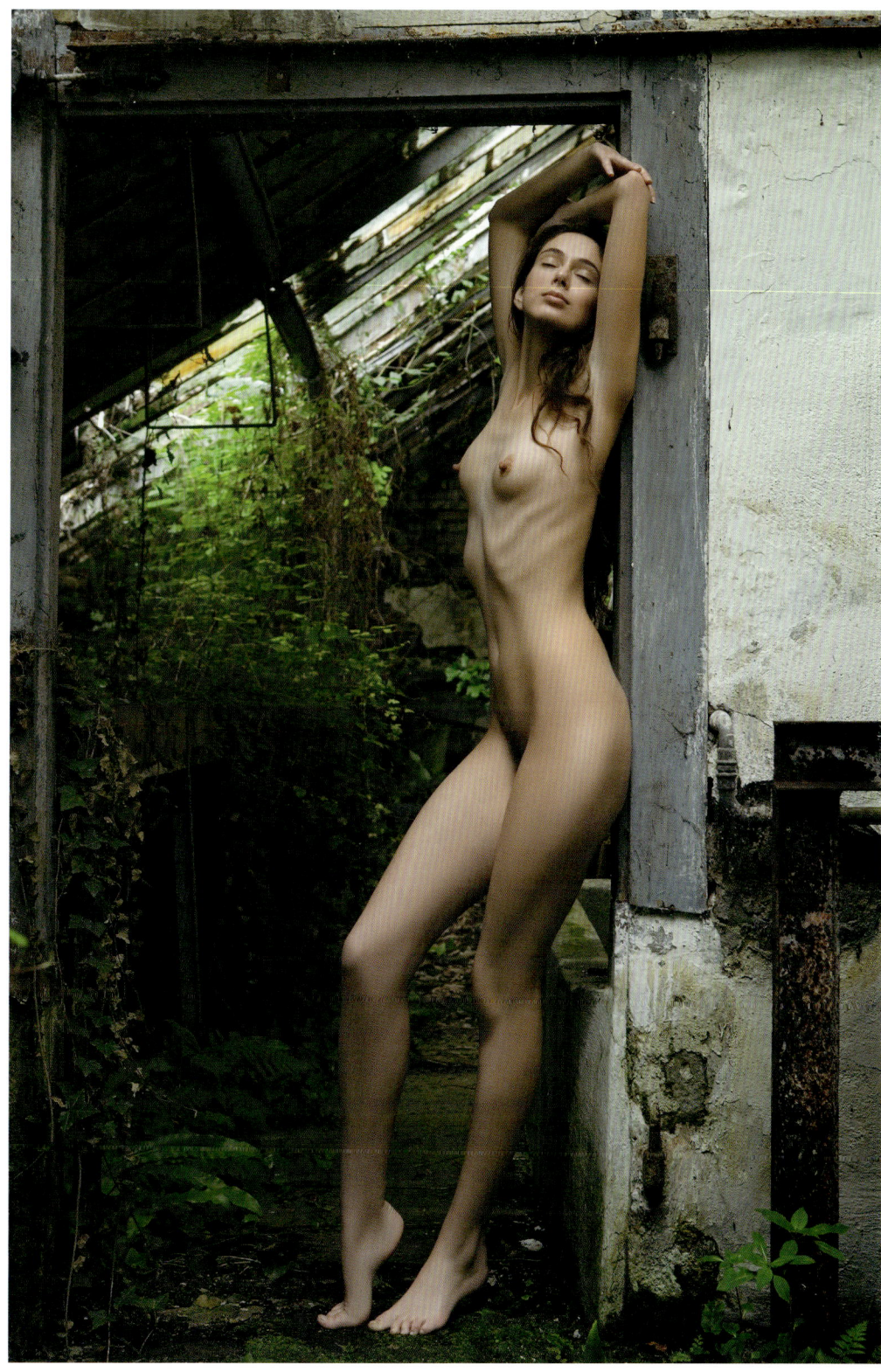

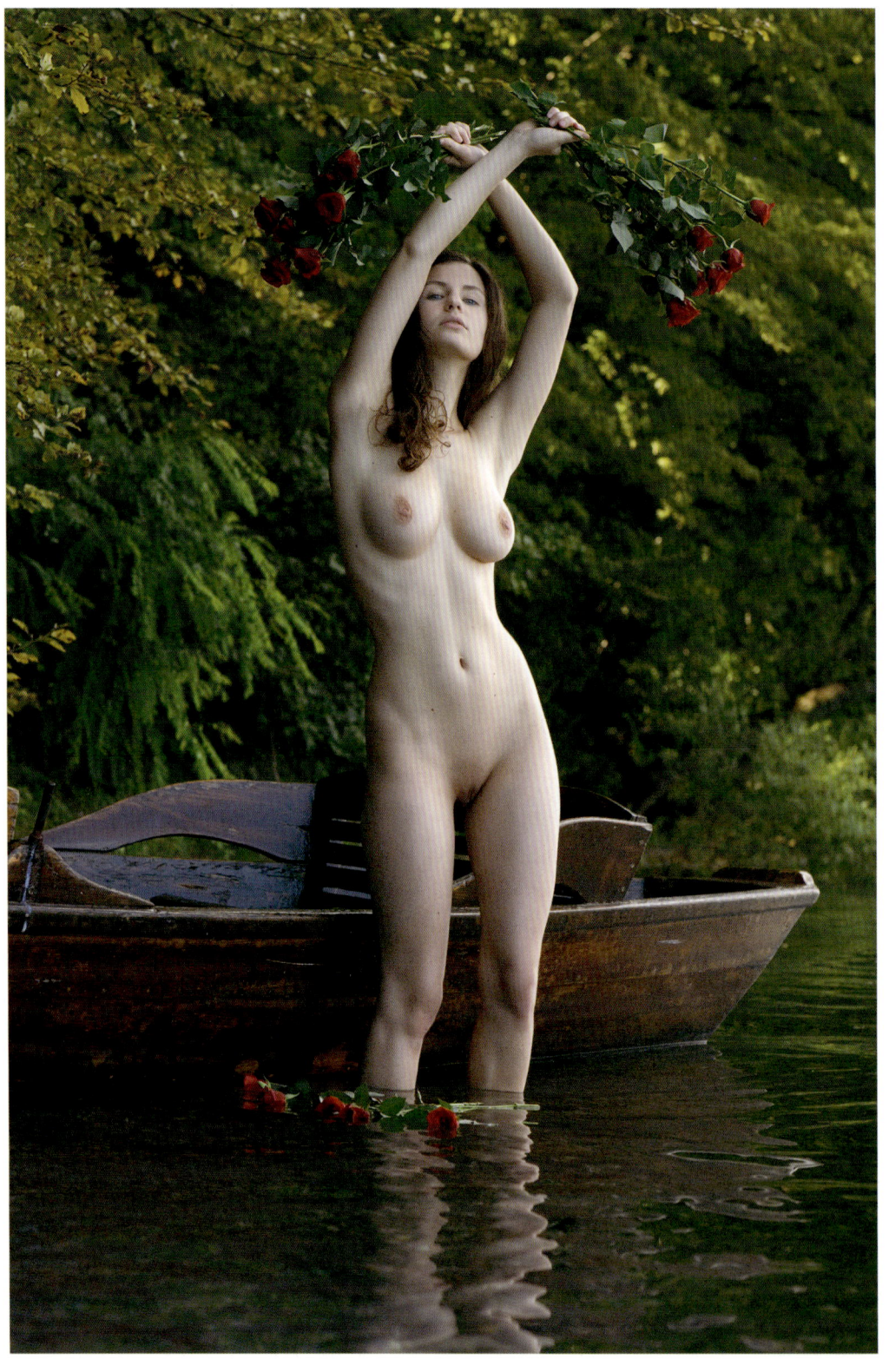

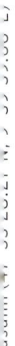

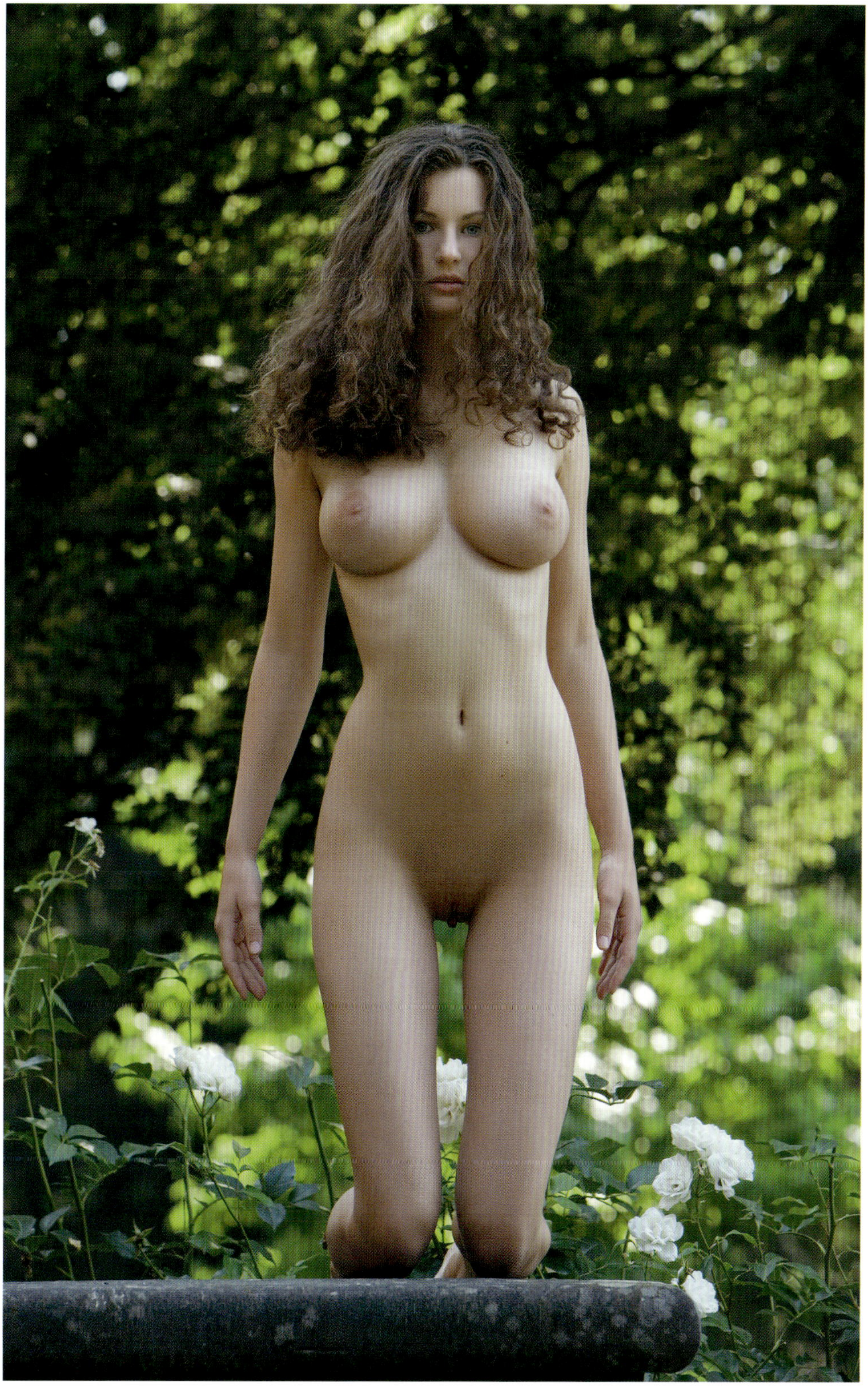

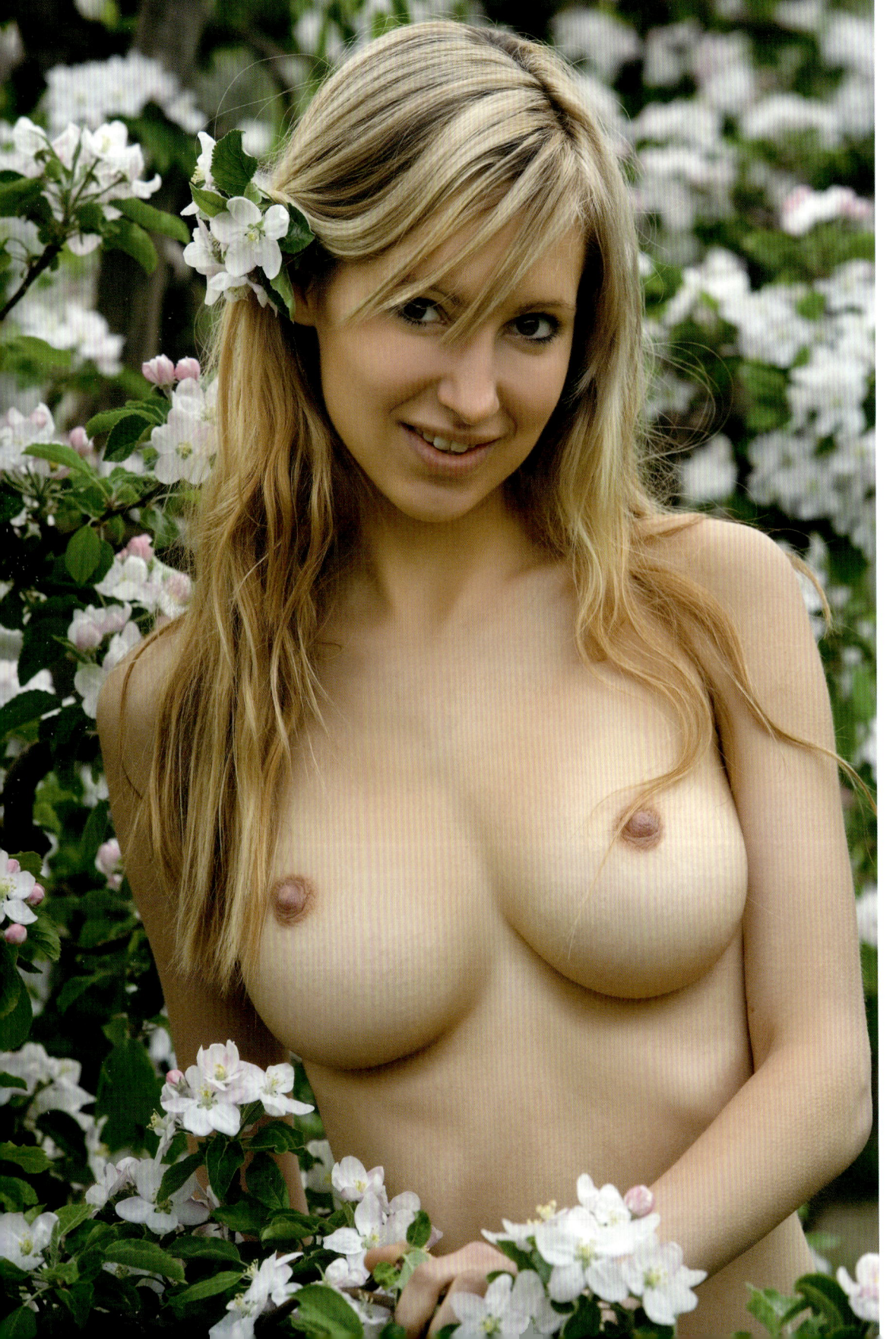

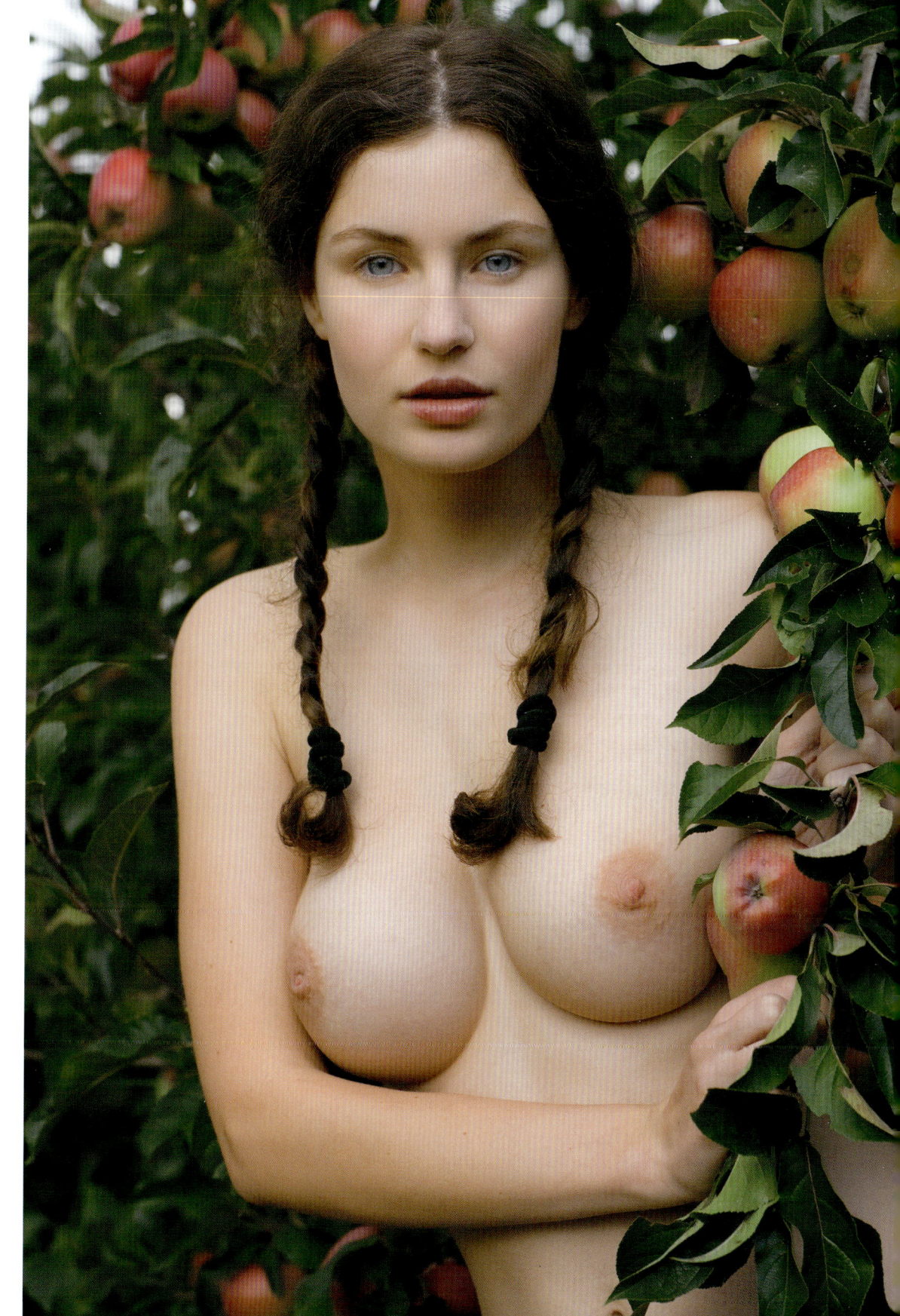

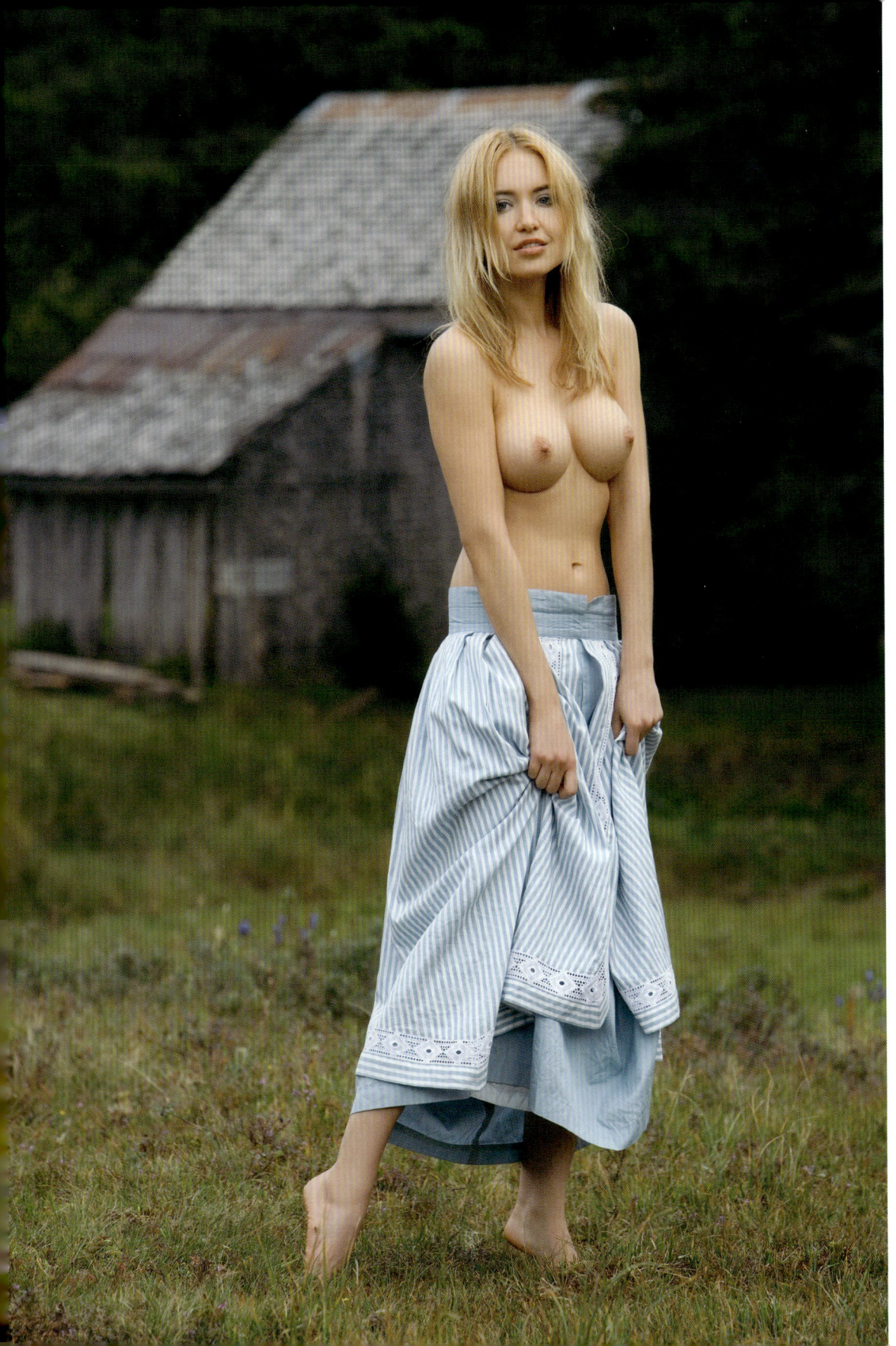

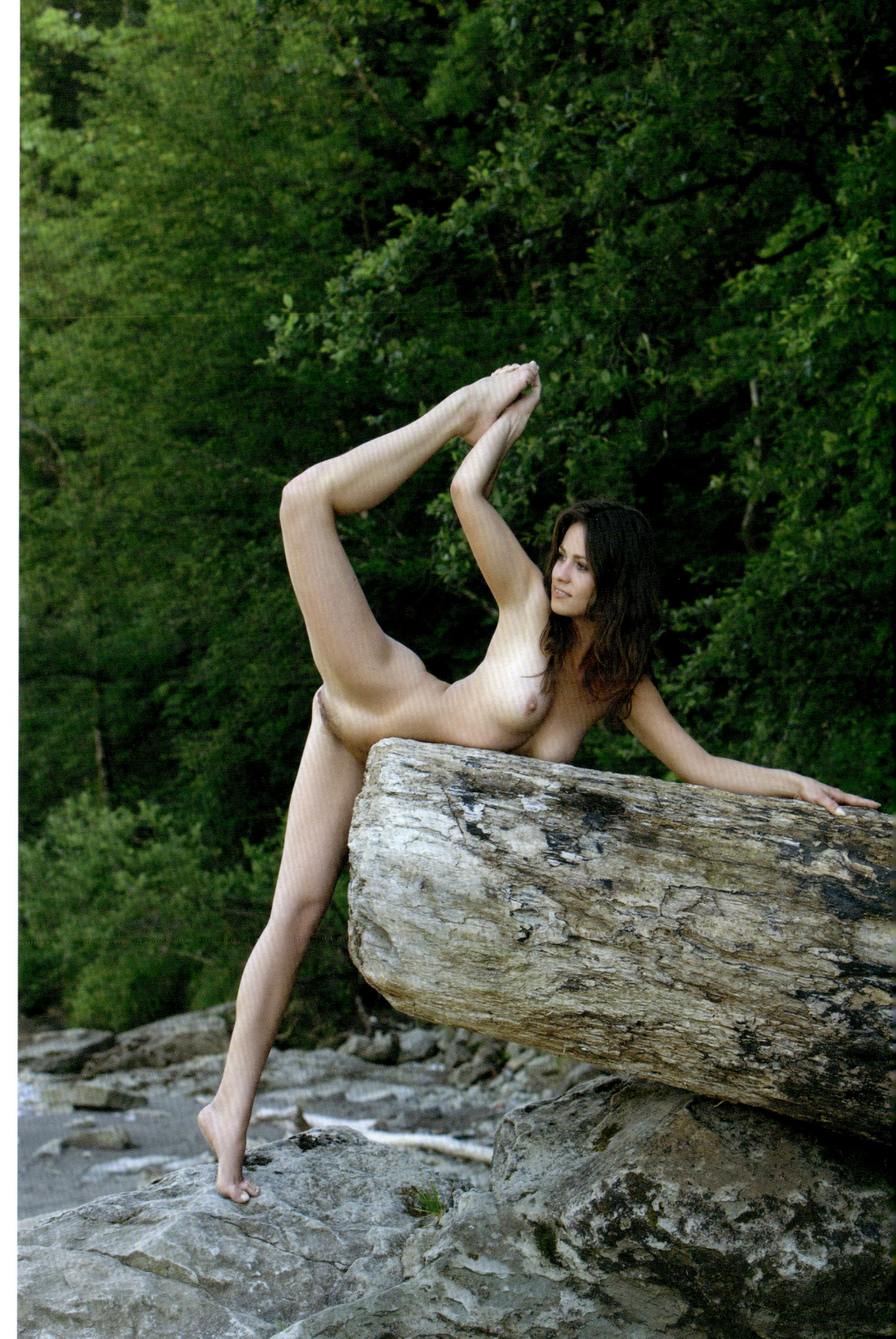

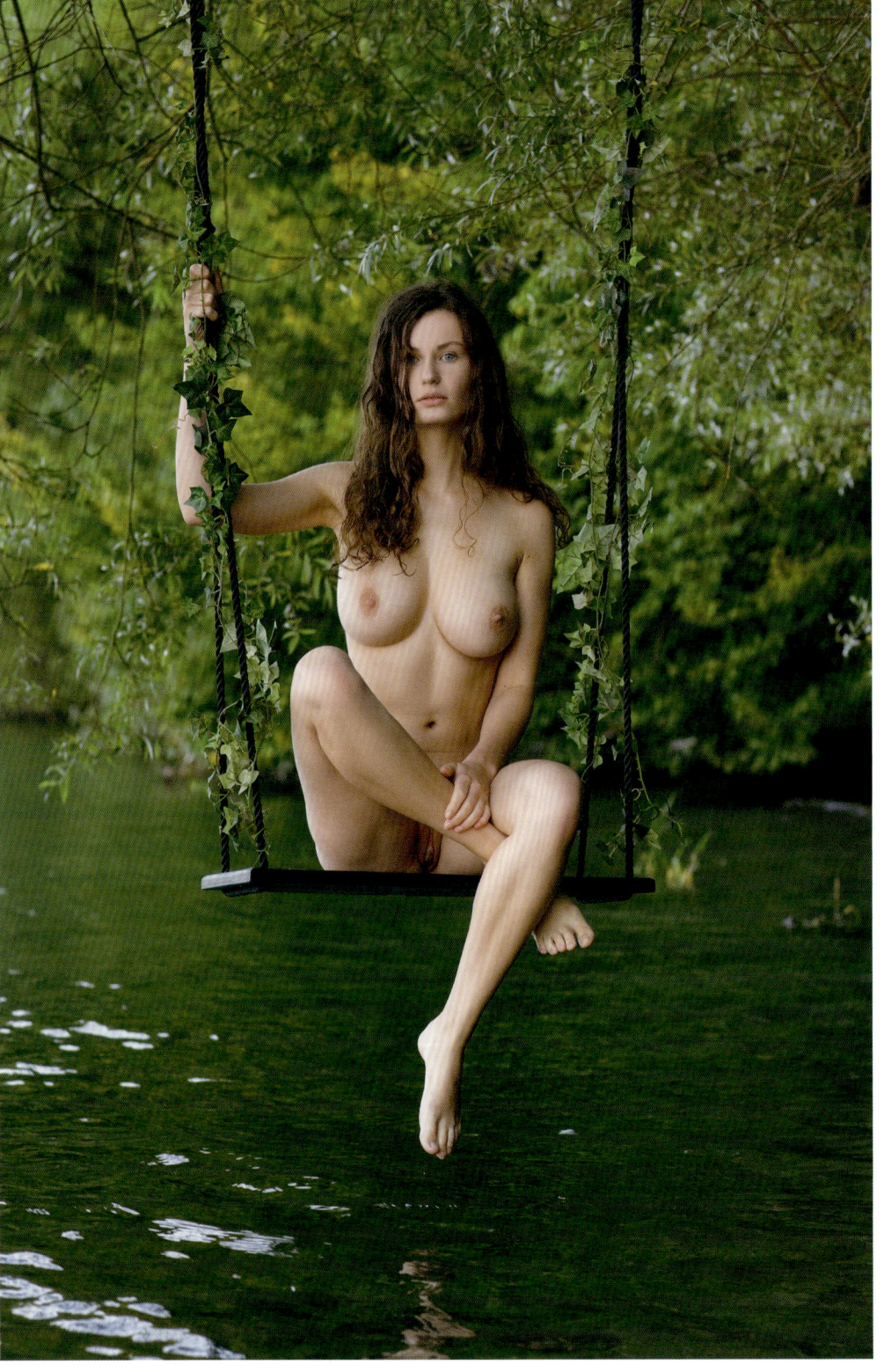

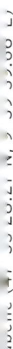

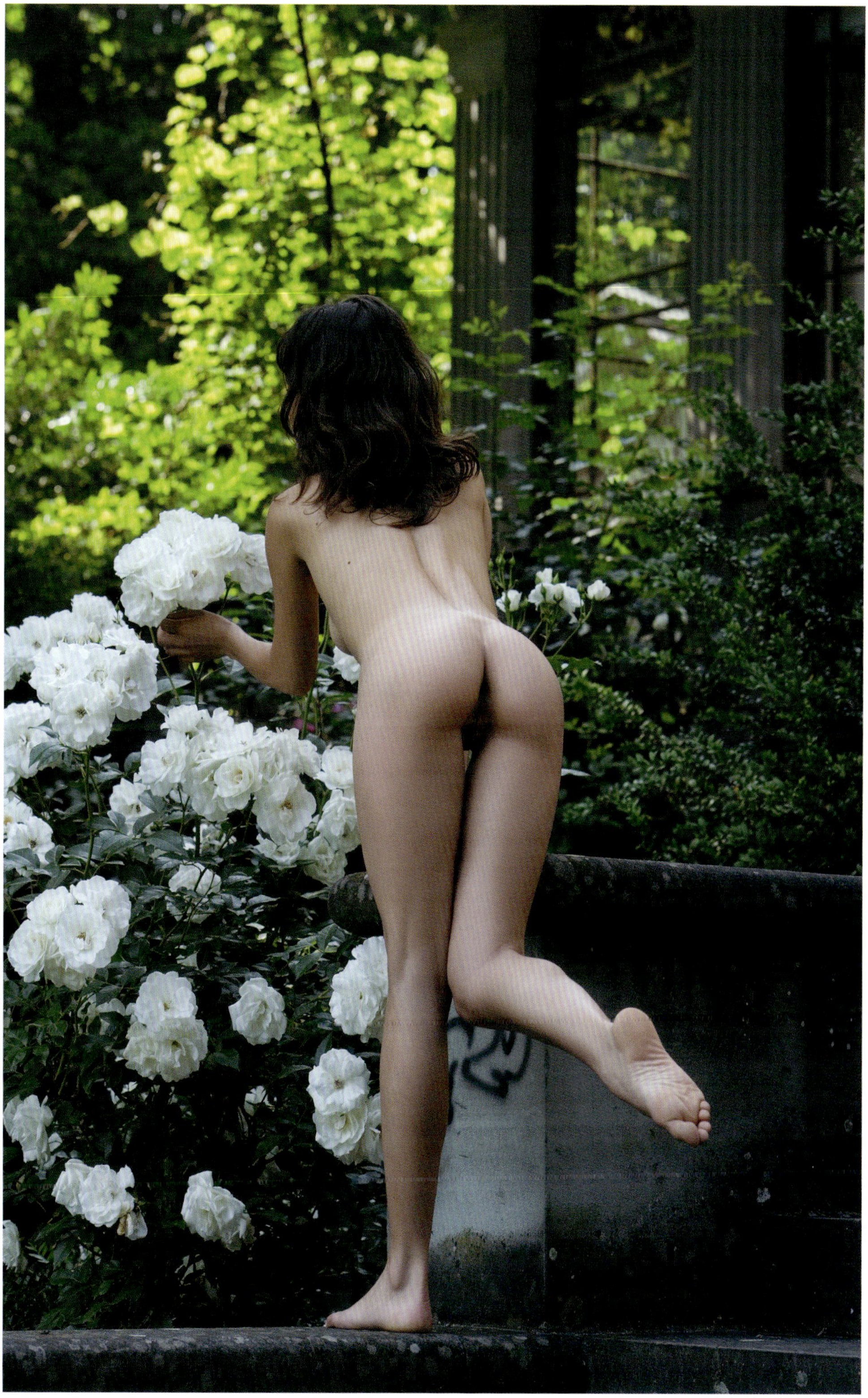

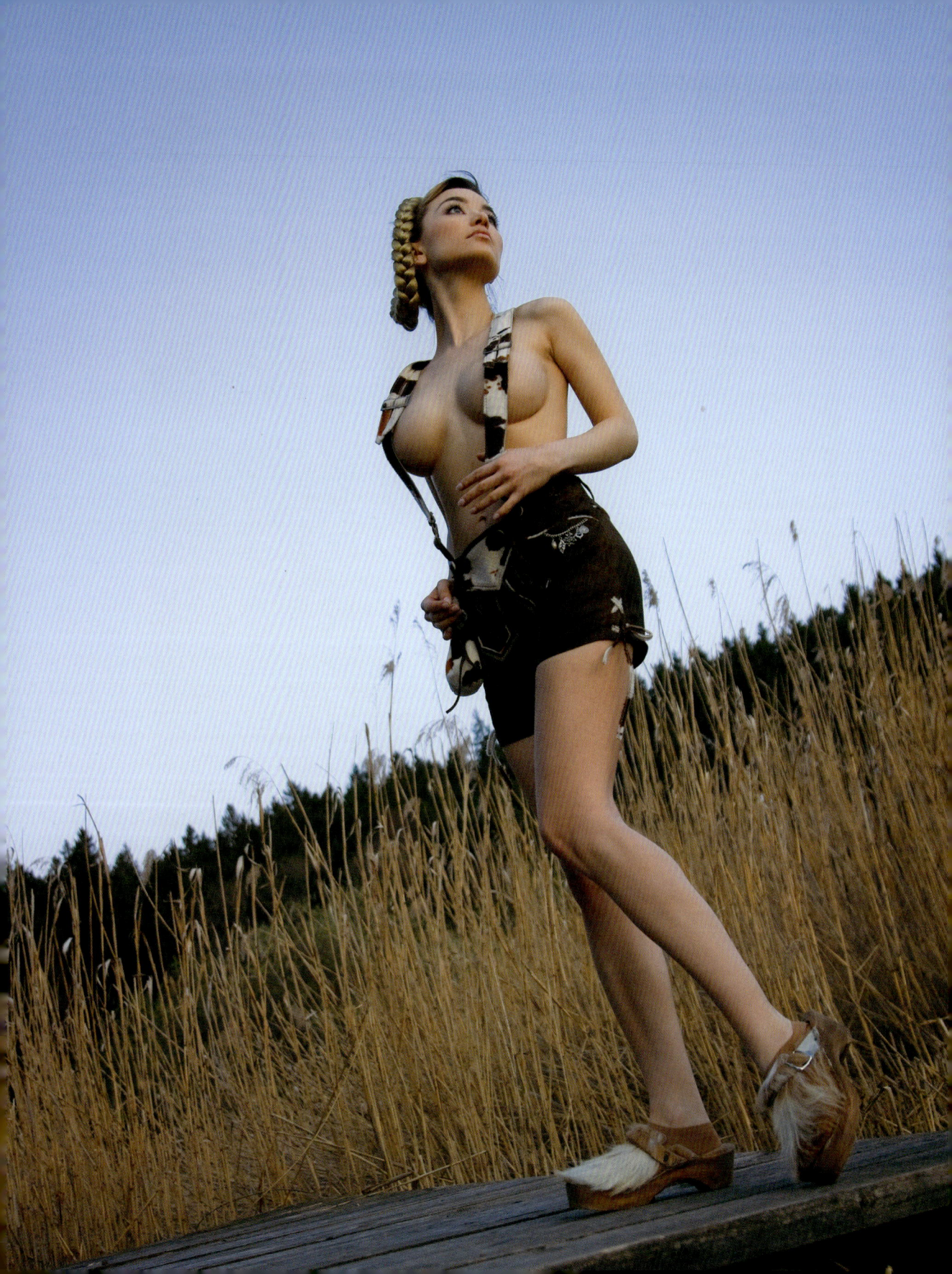

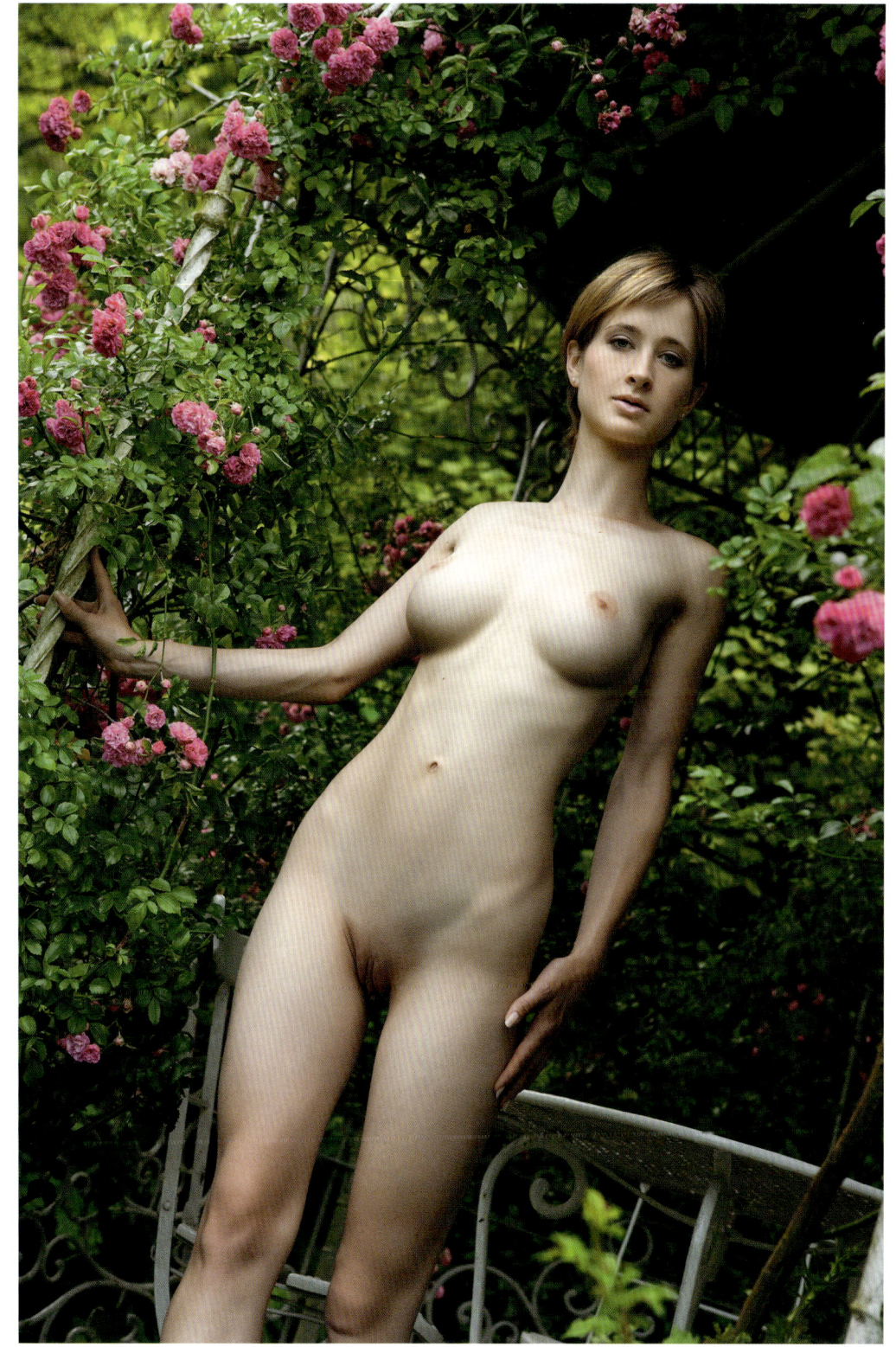

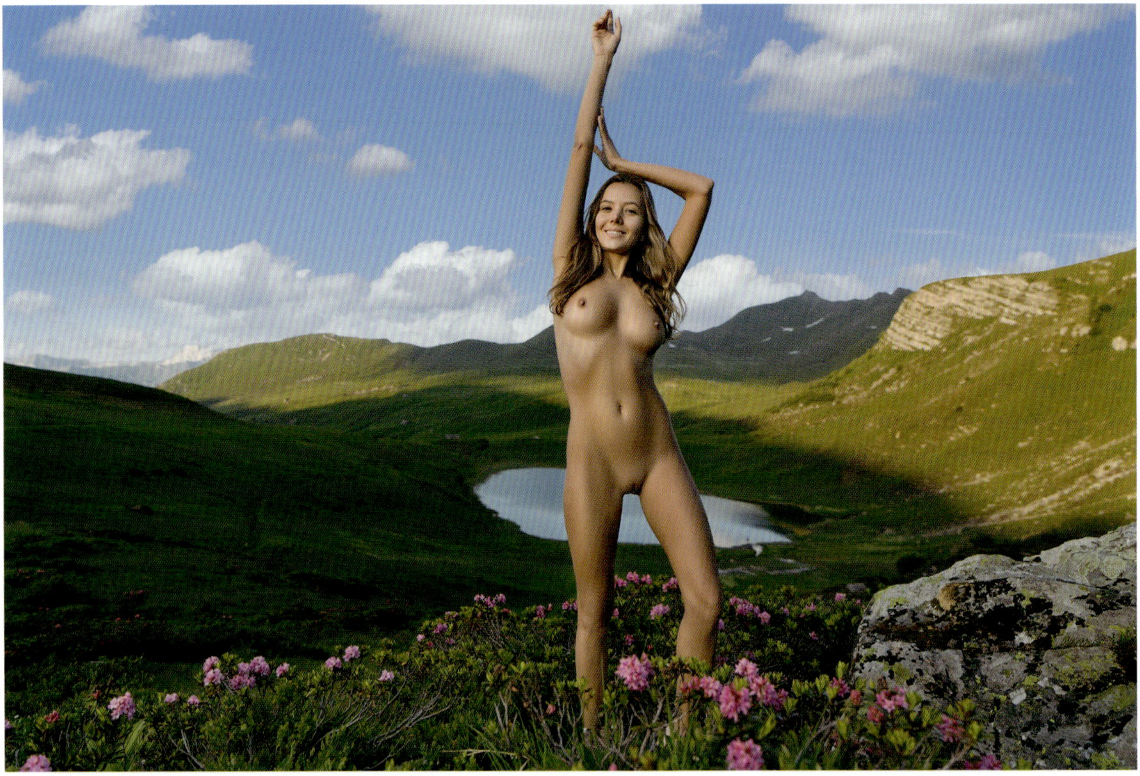

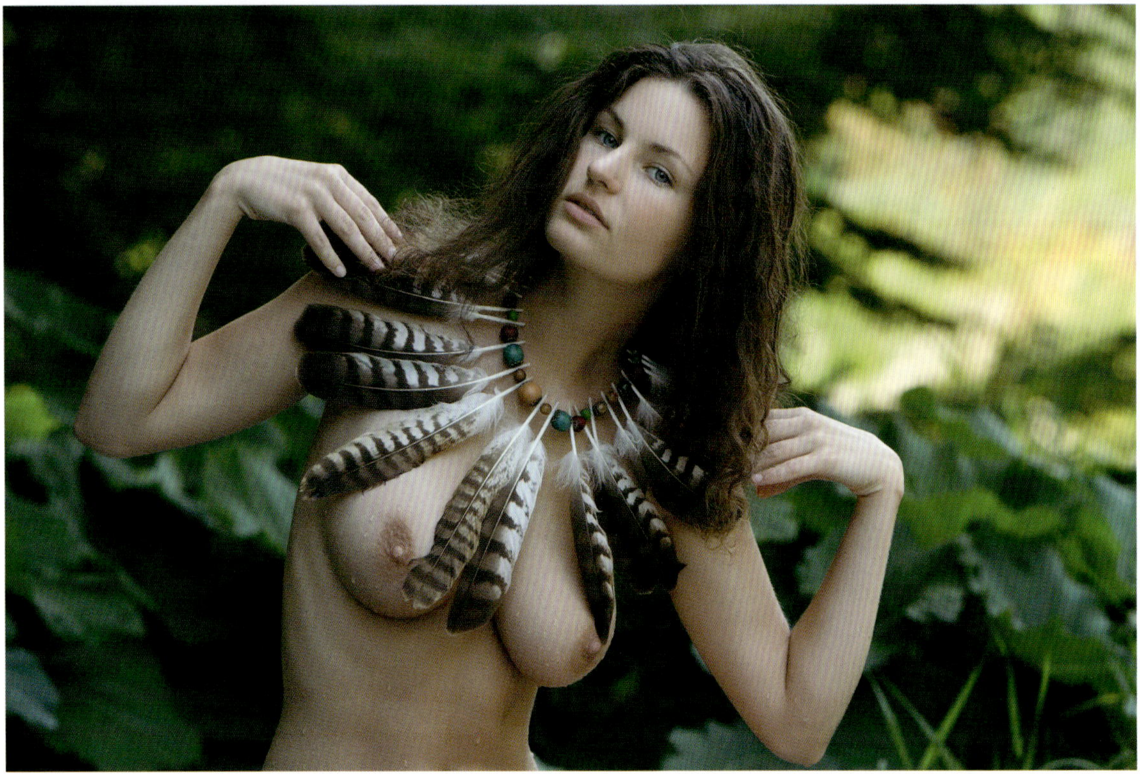

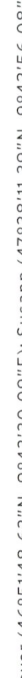

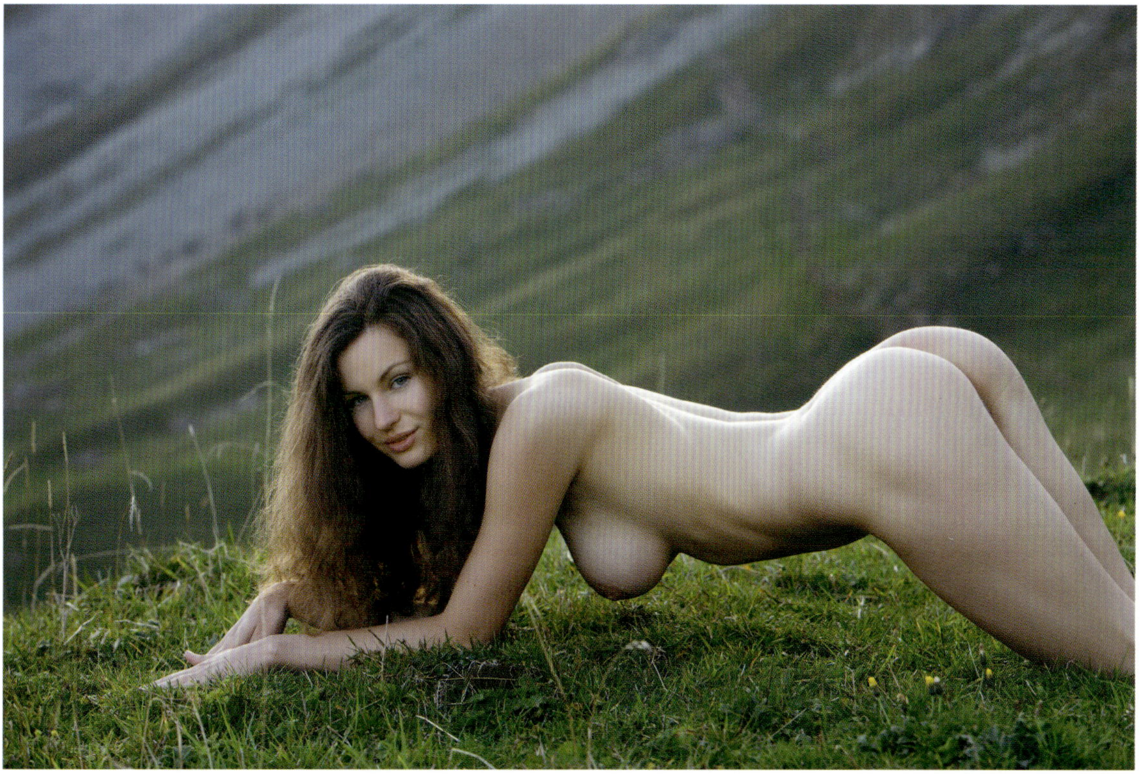

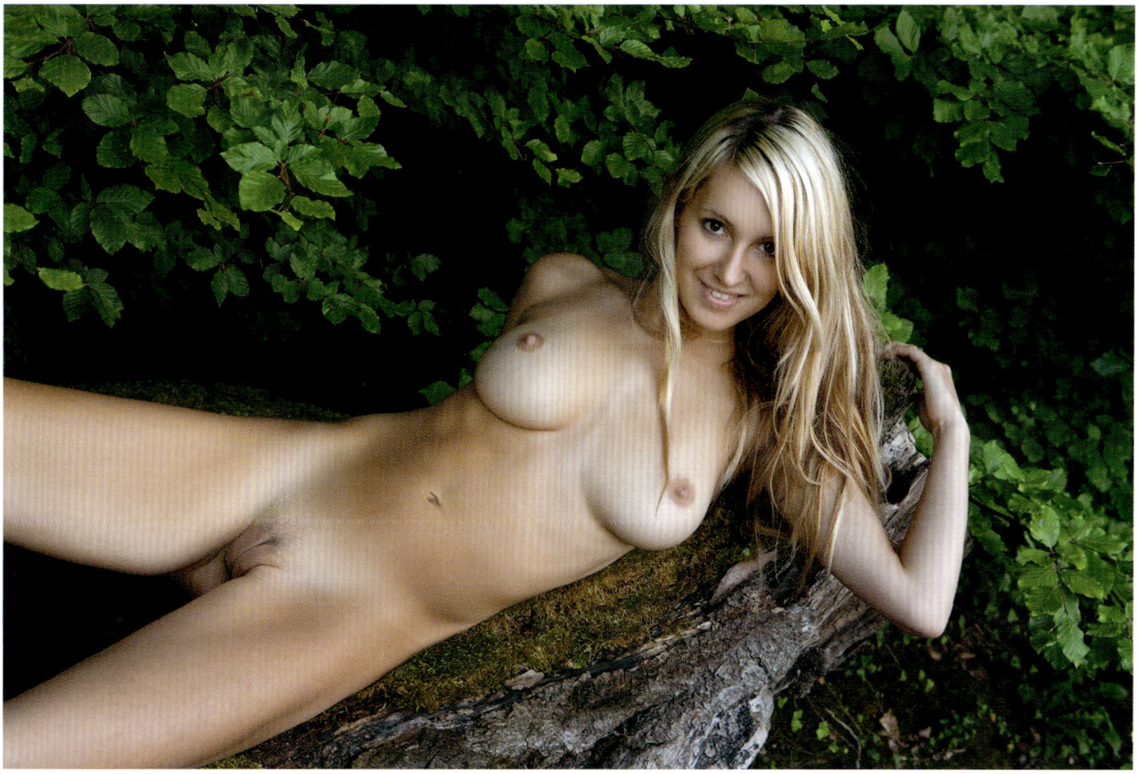

p. 151 Susann (47°16'17.81"N, 9°23'7.36"E); Corinna (47°45'41.43"N, 9°6'40.54"E)

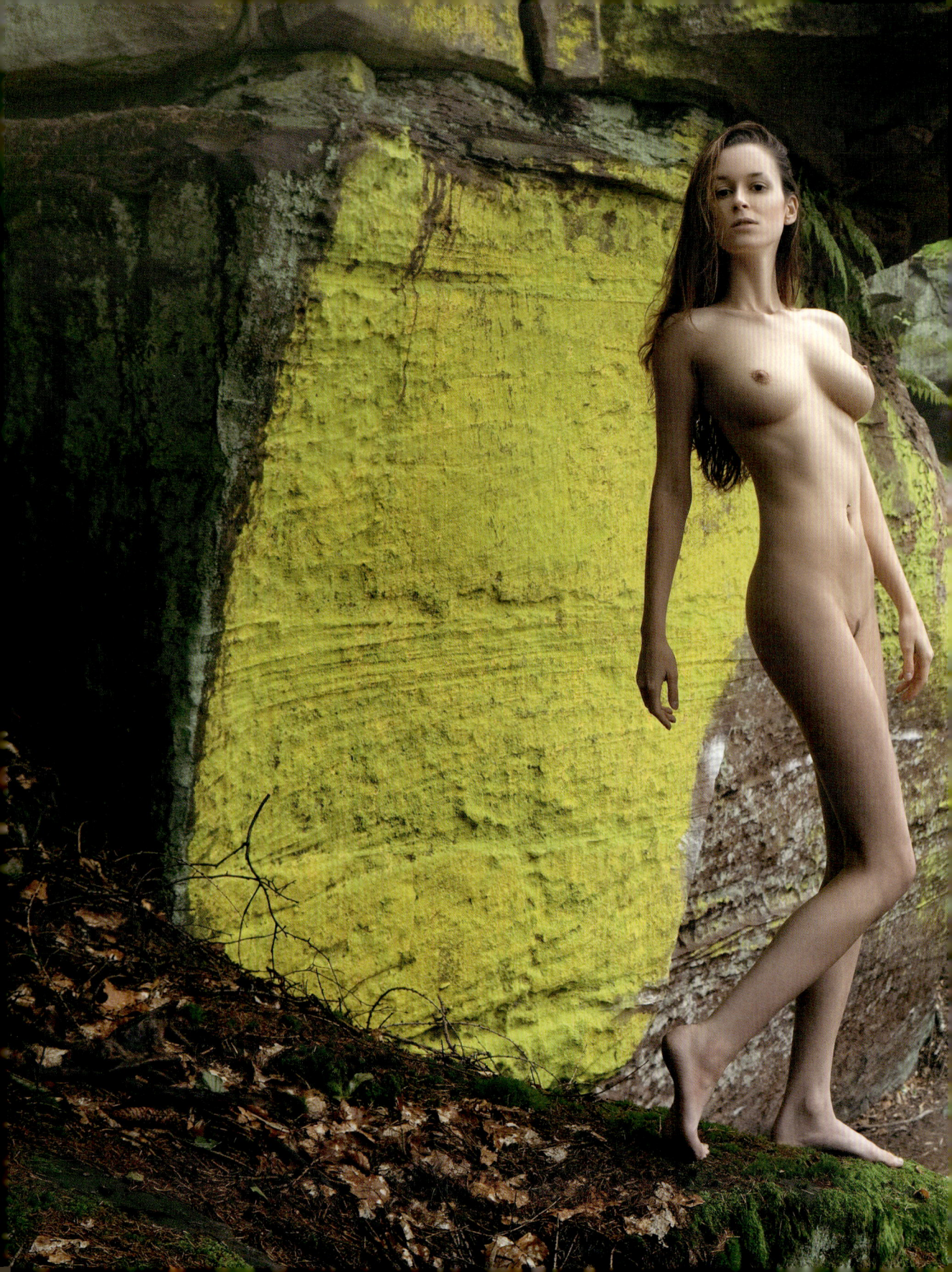

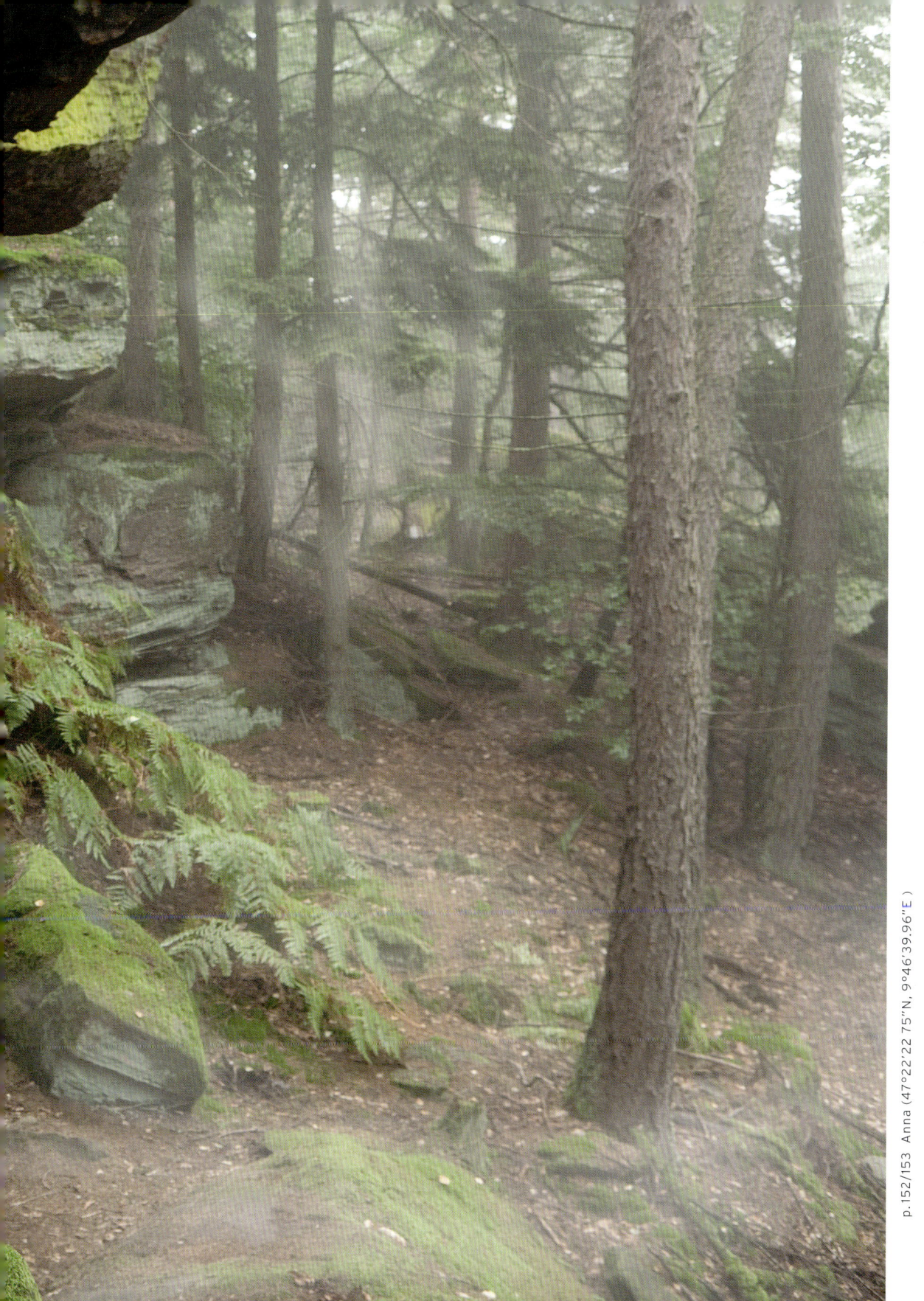

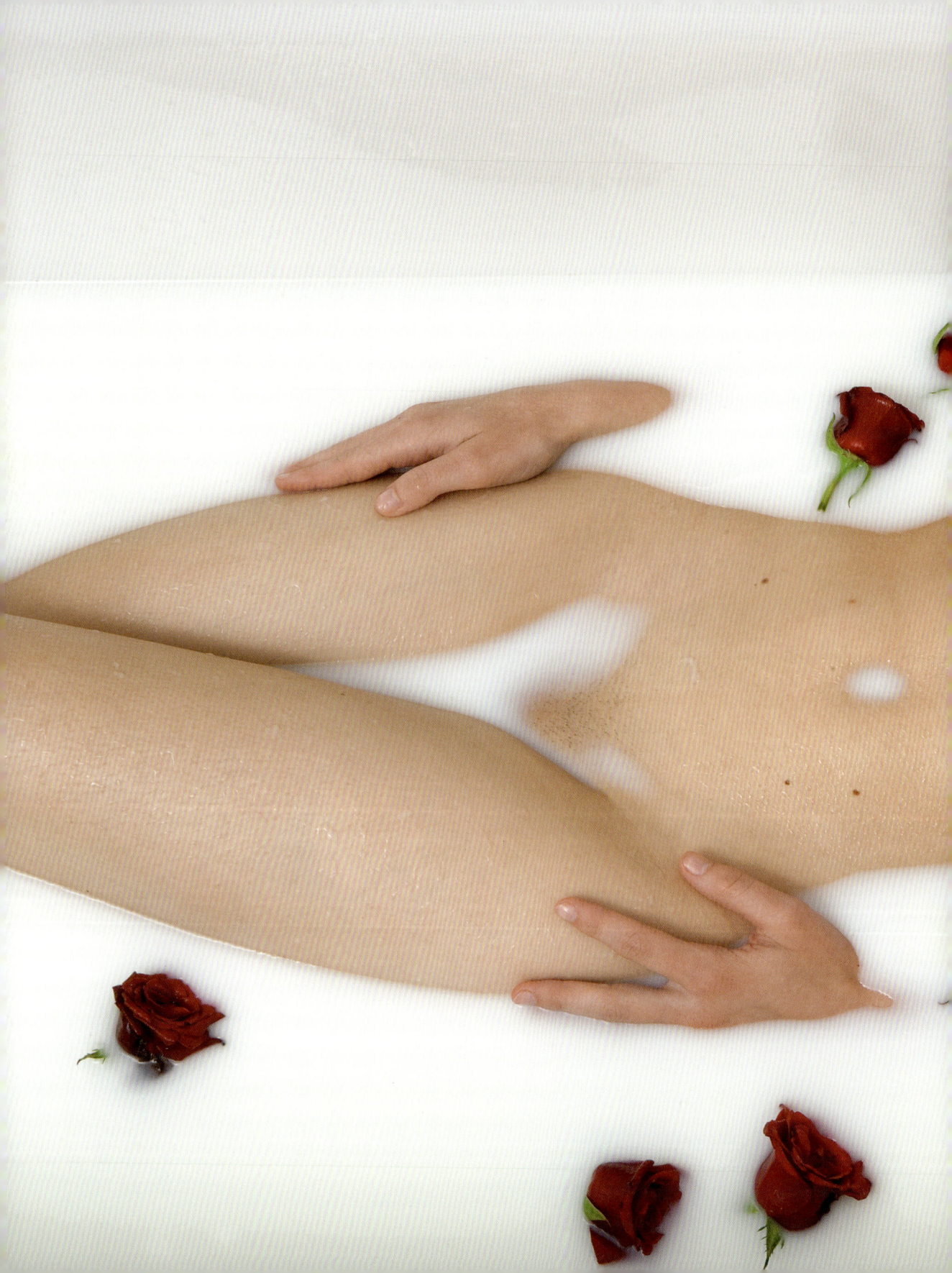

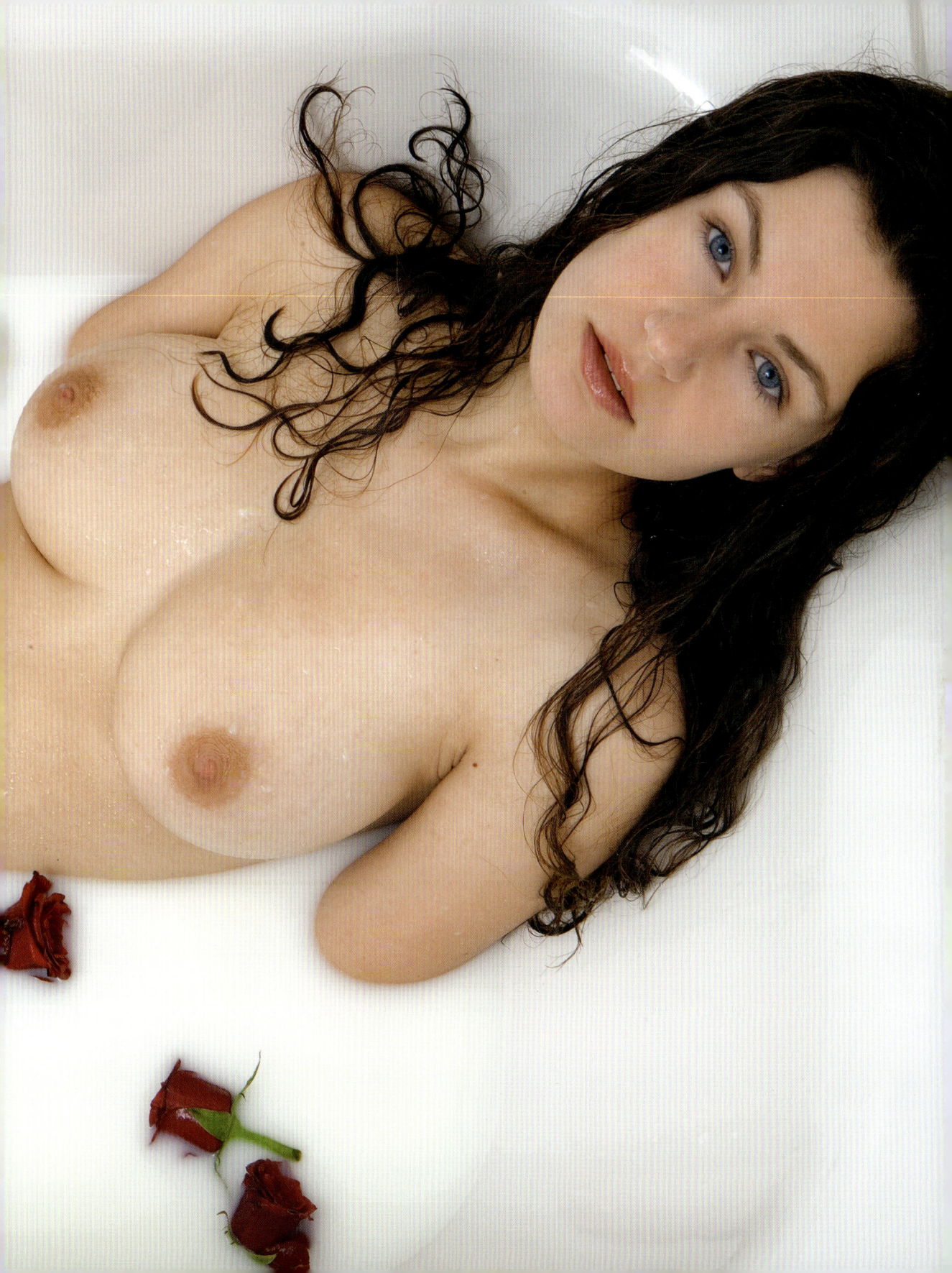

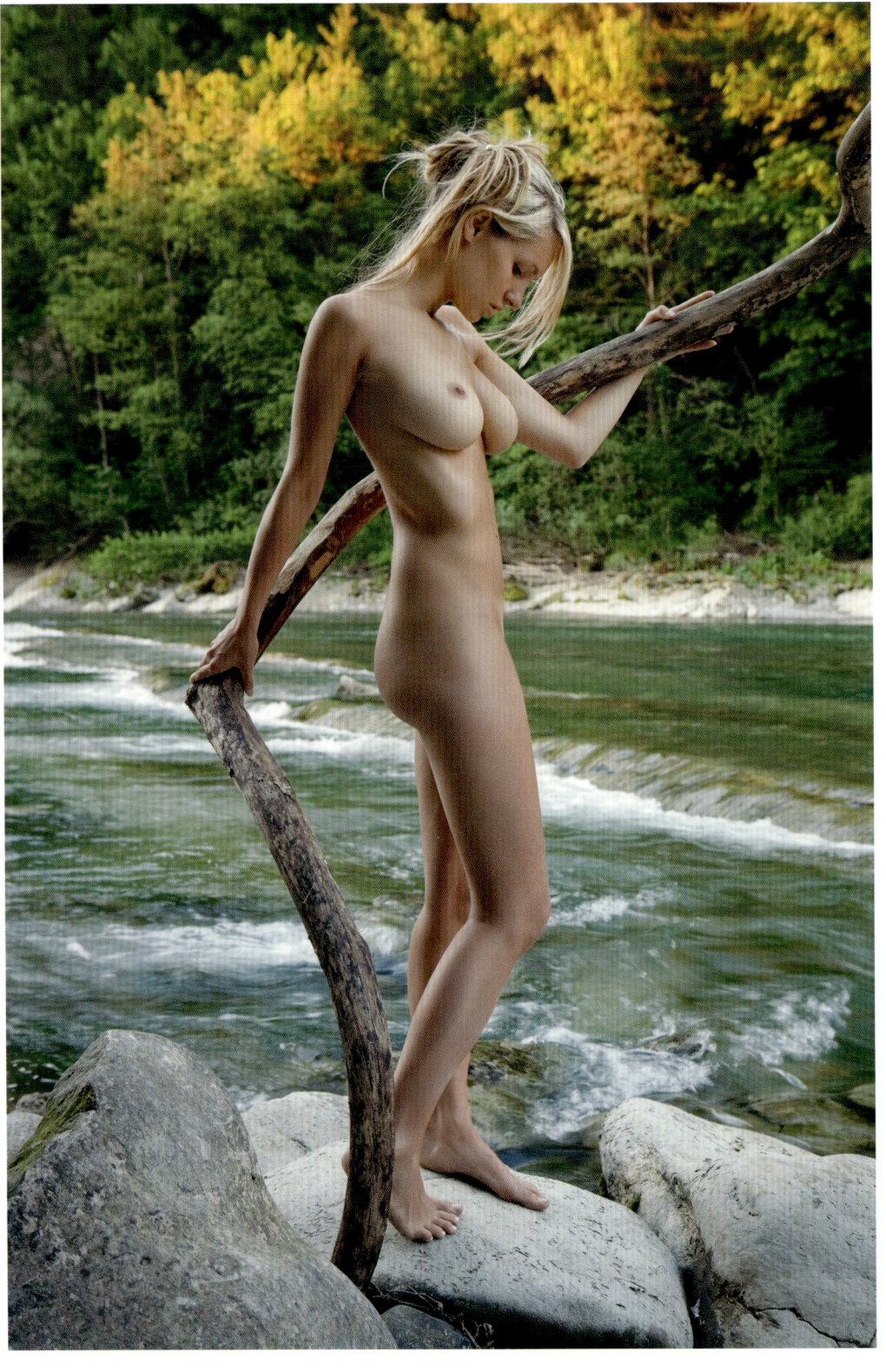

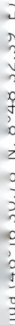

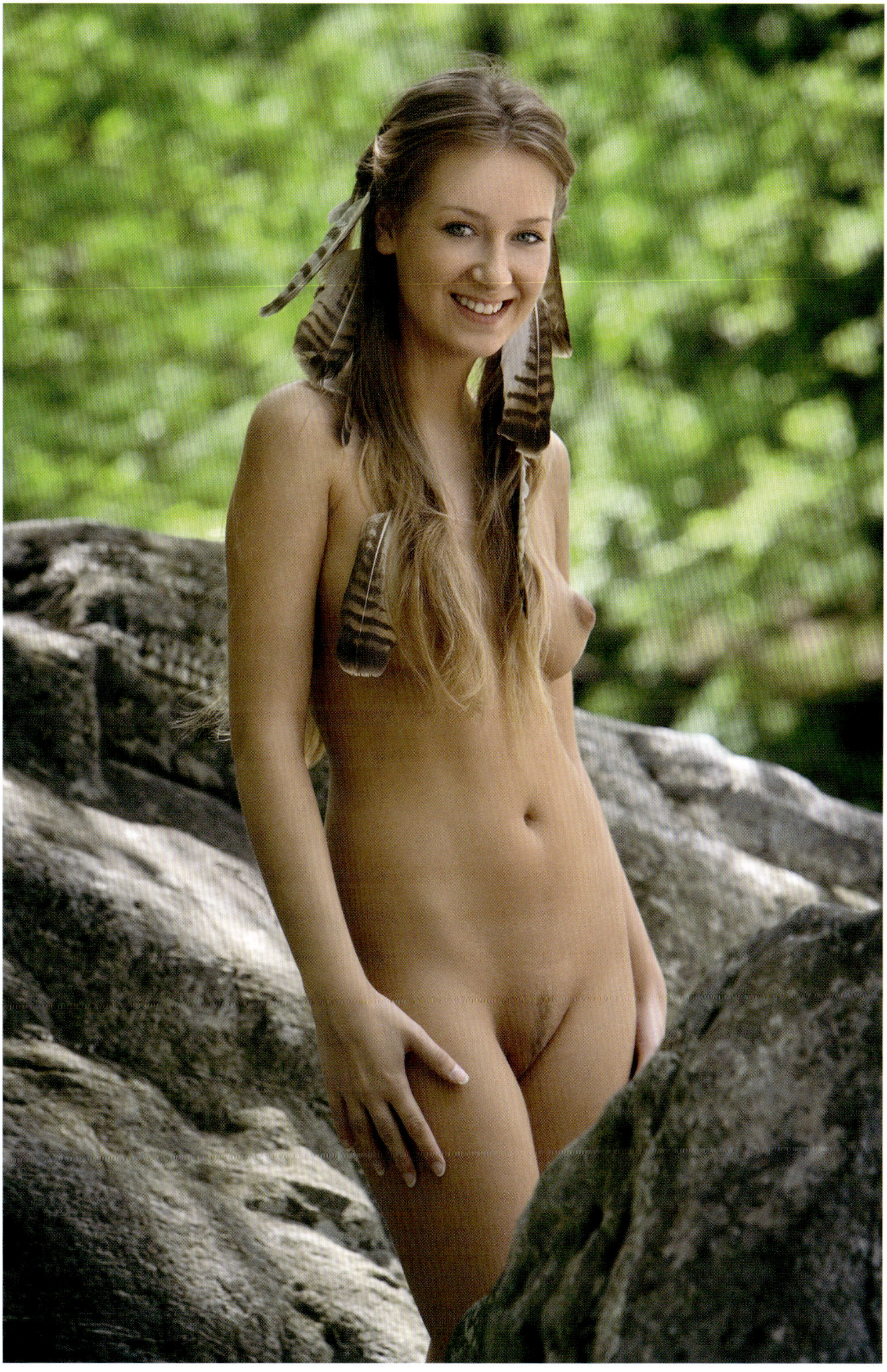

p. 157 Anhya (46°16 30.16 N, 8°48 32.39 E)

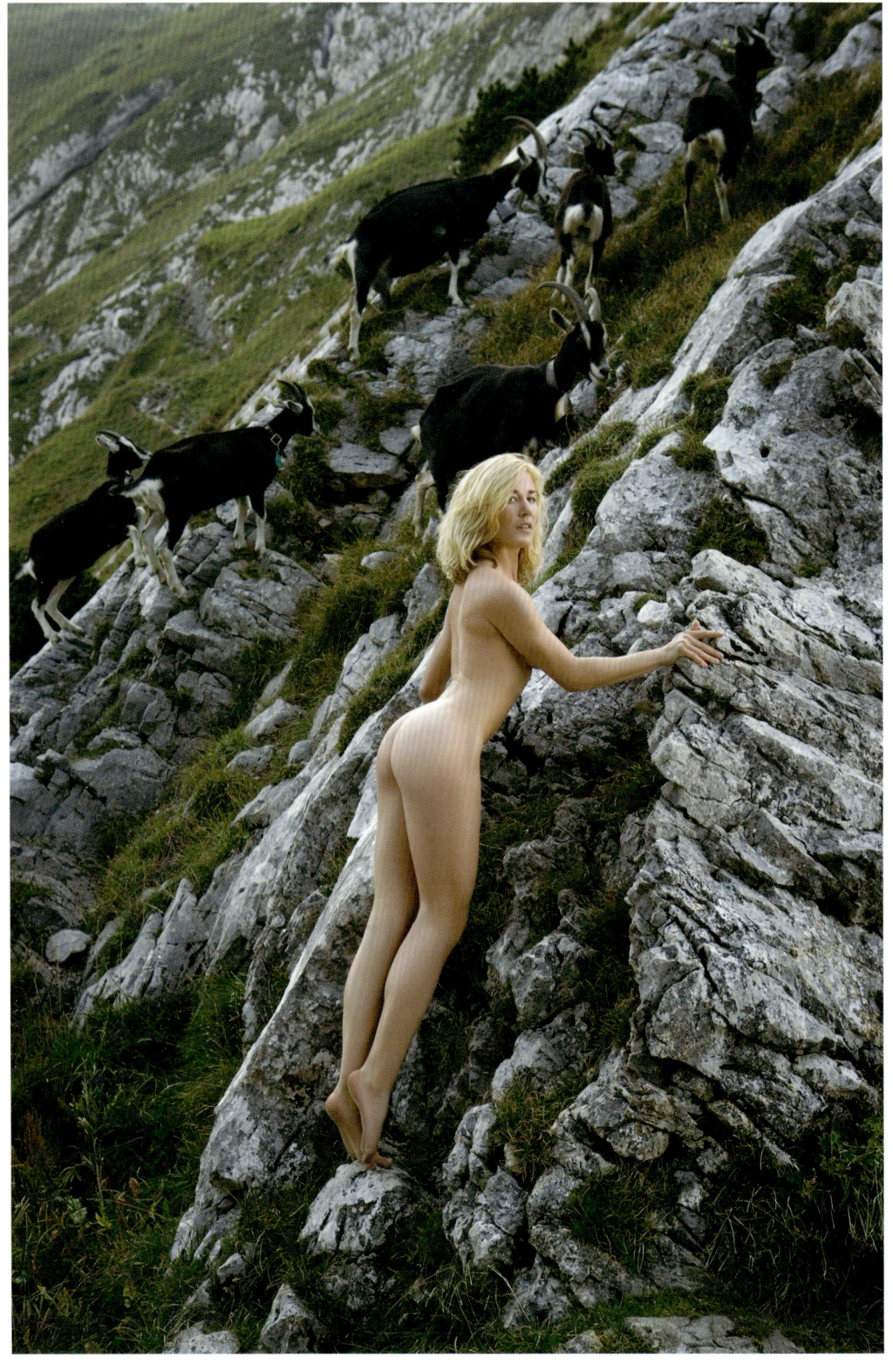

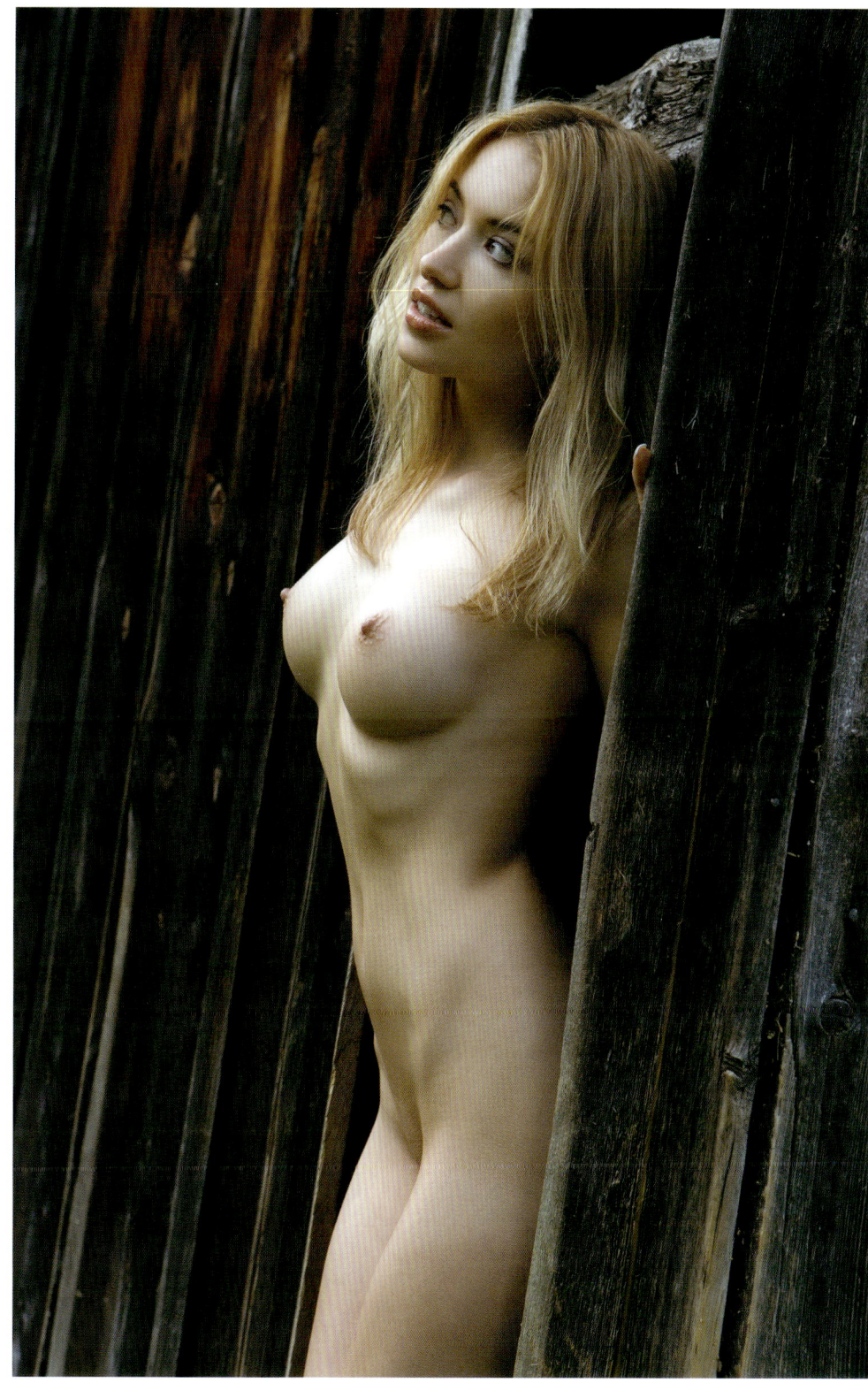

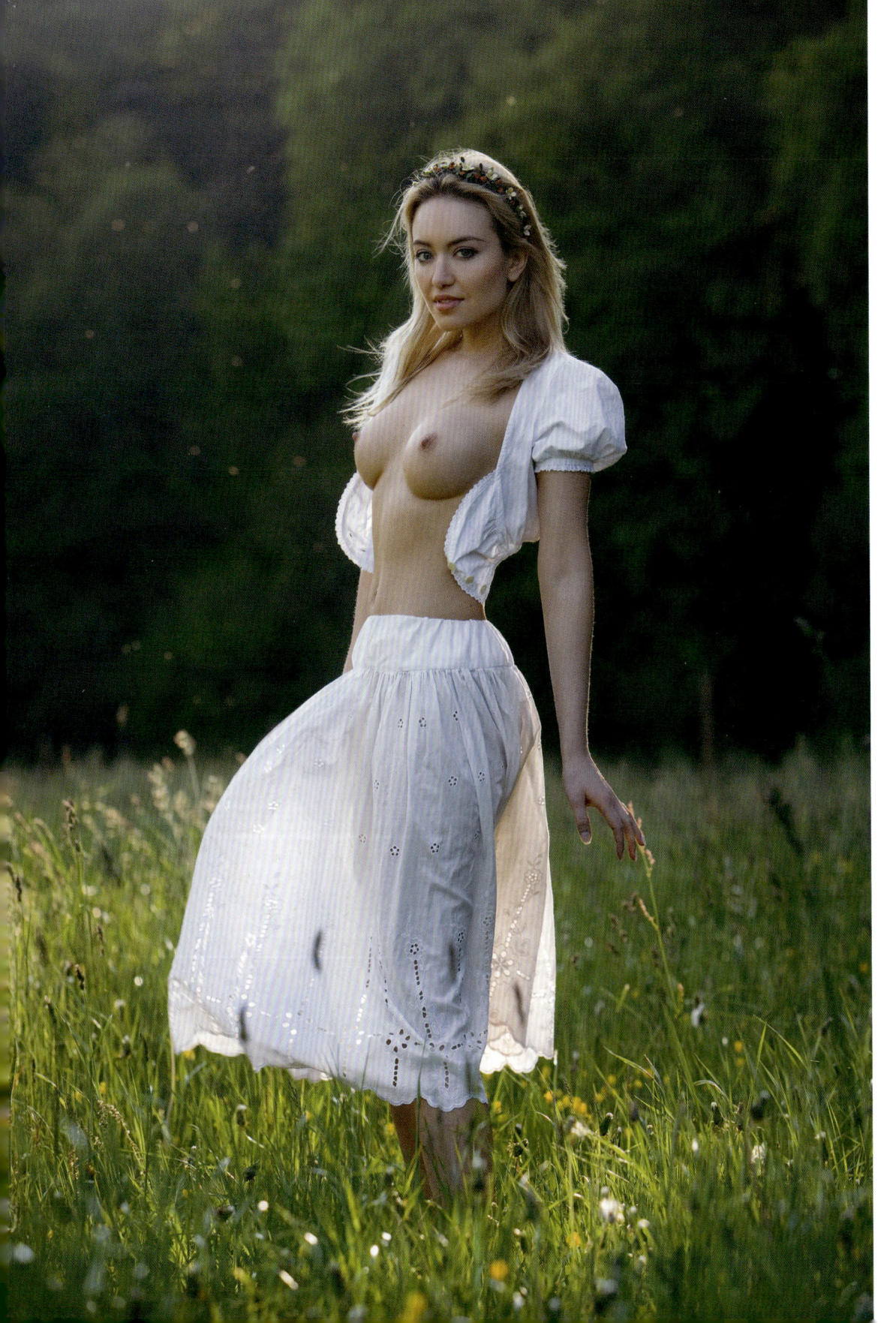

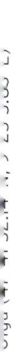

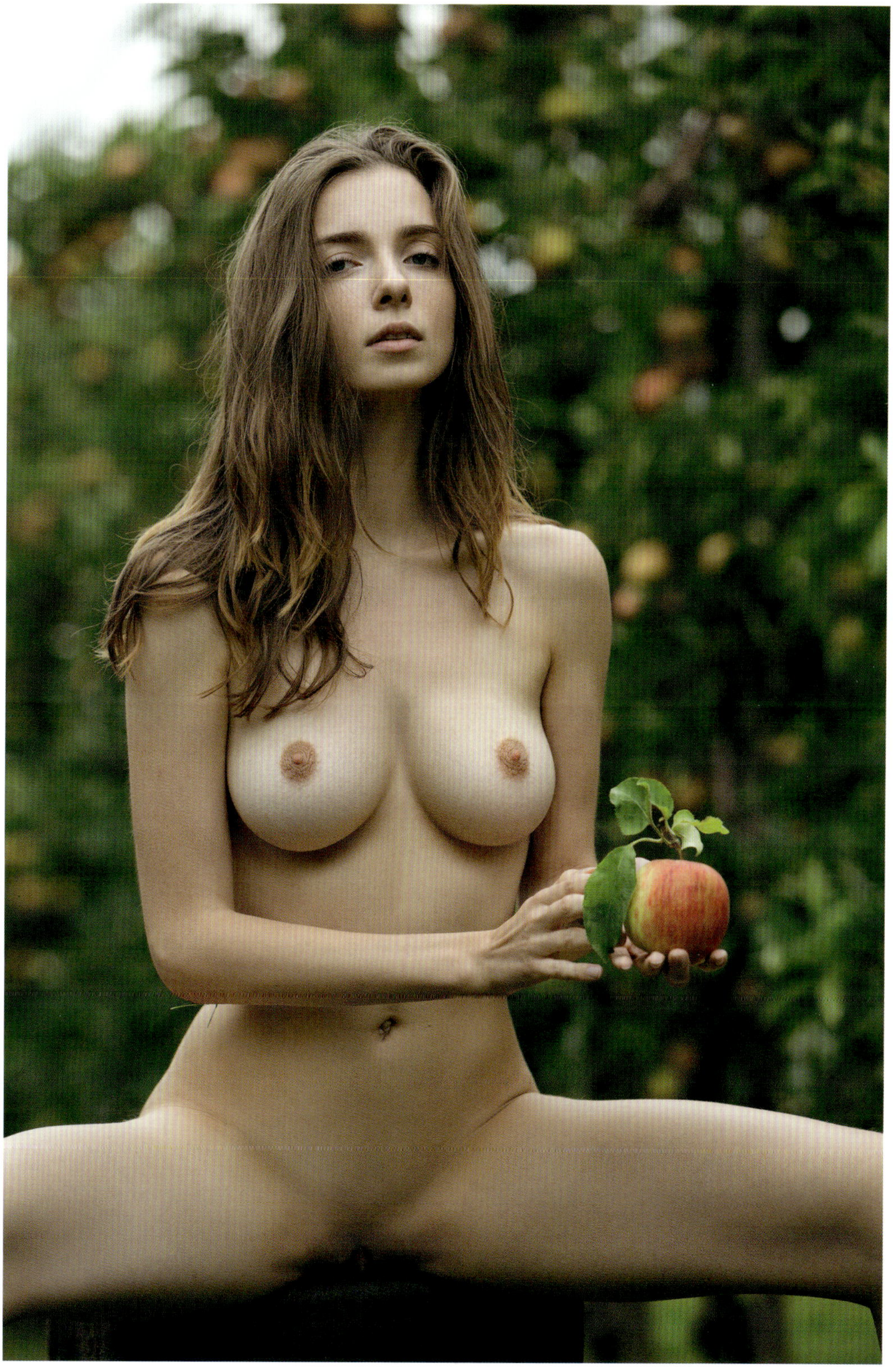

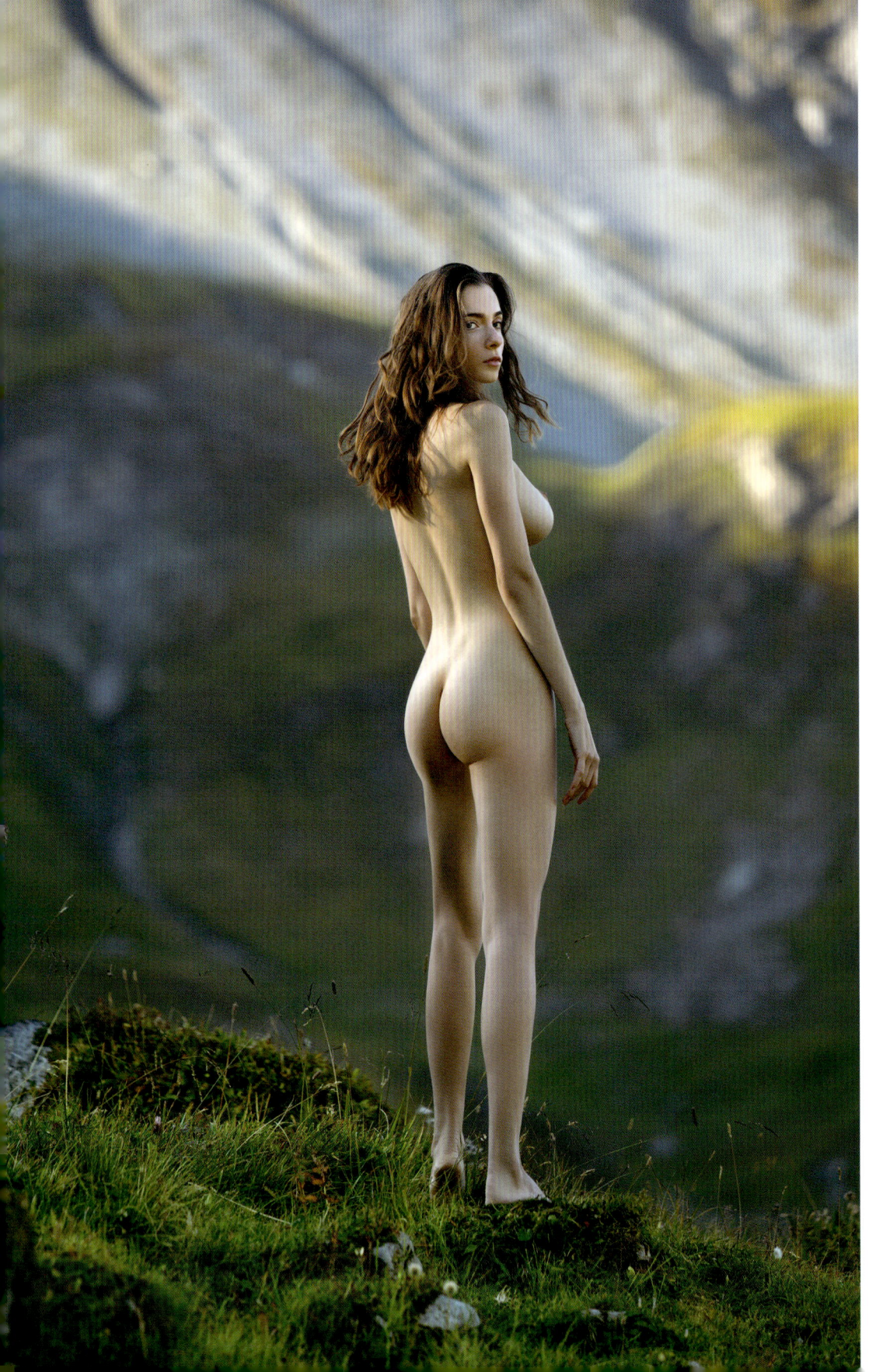

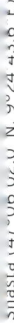

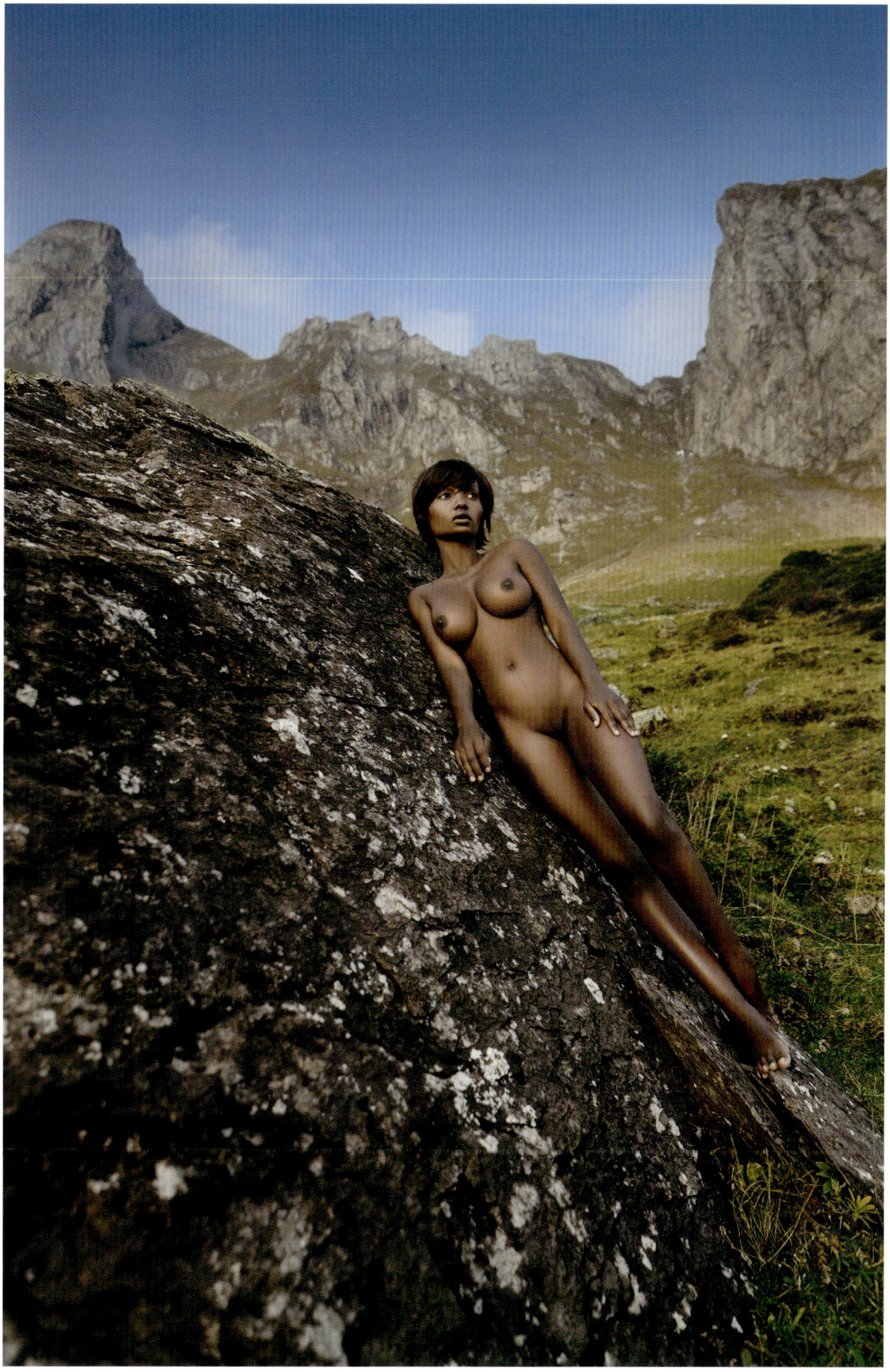

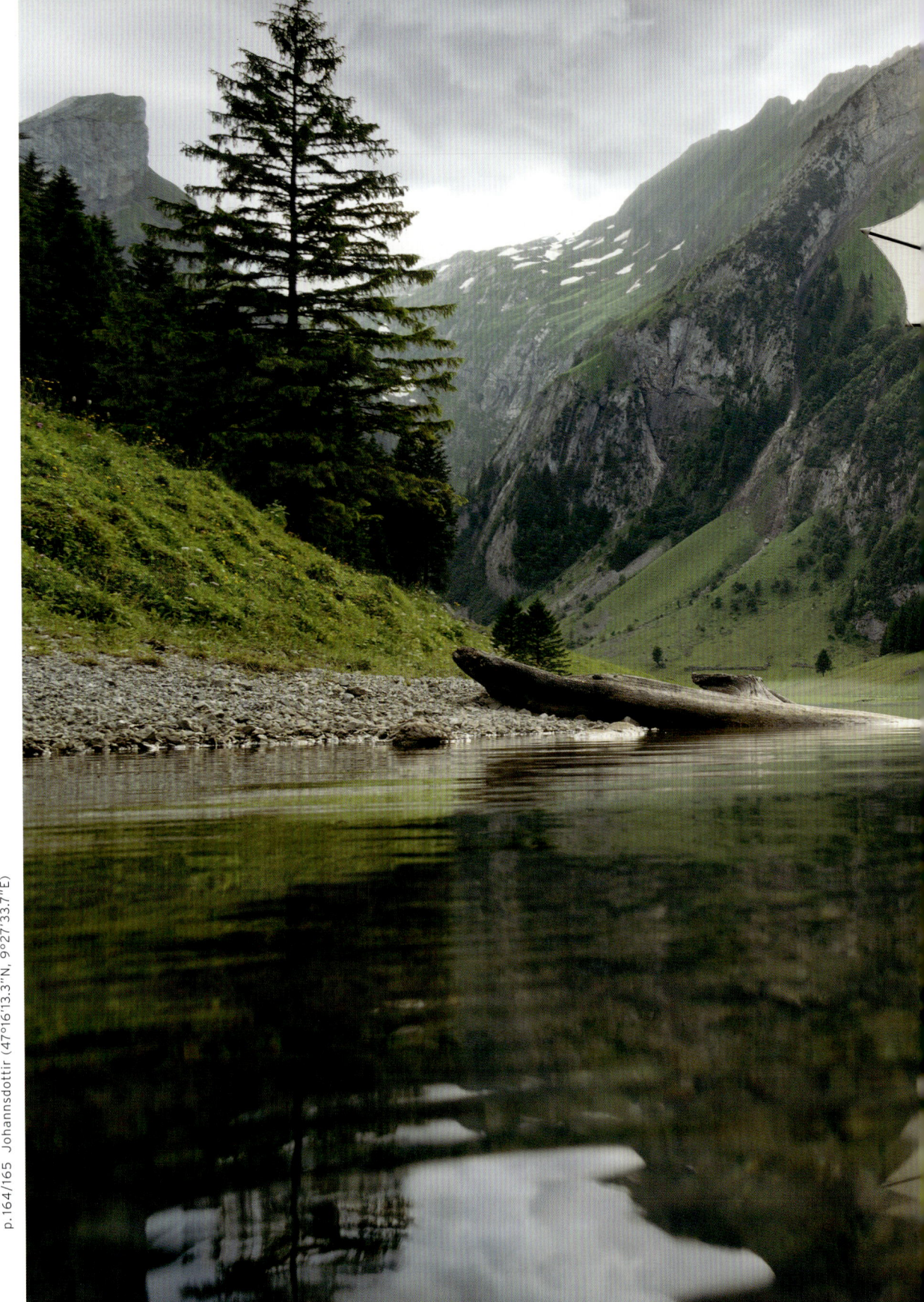

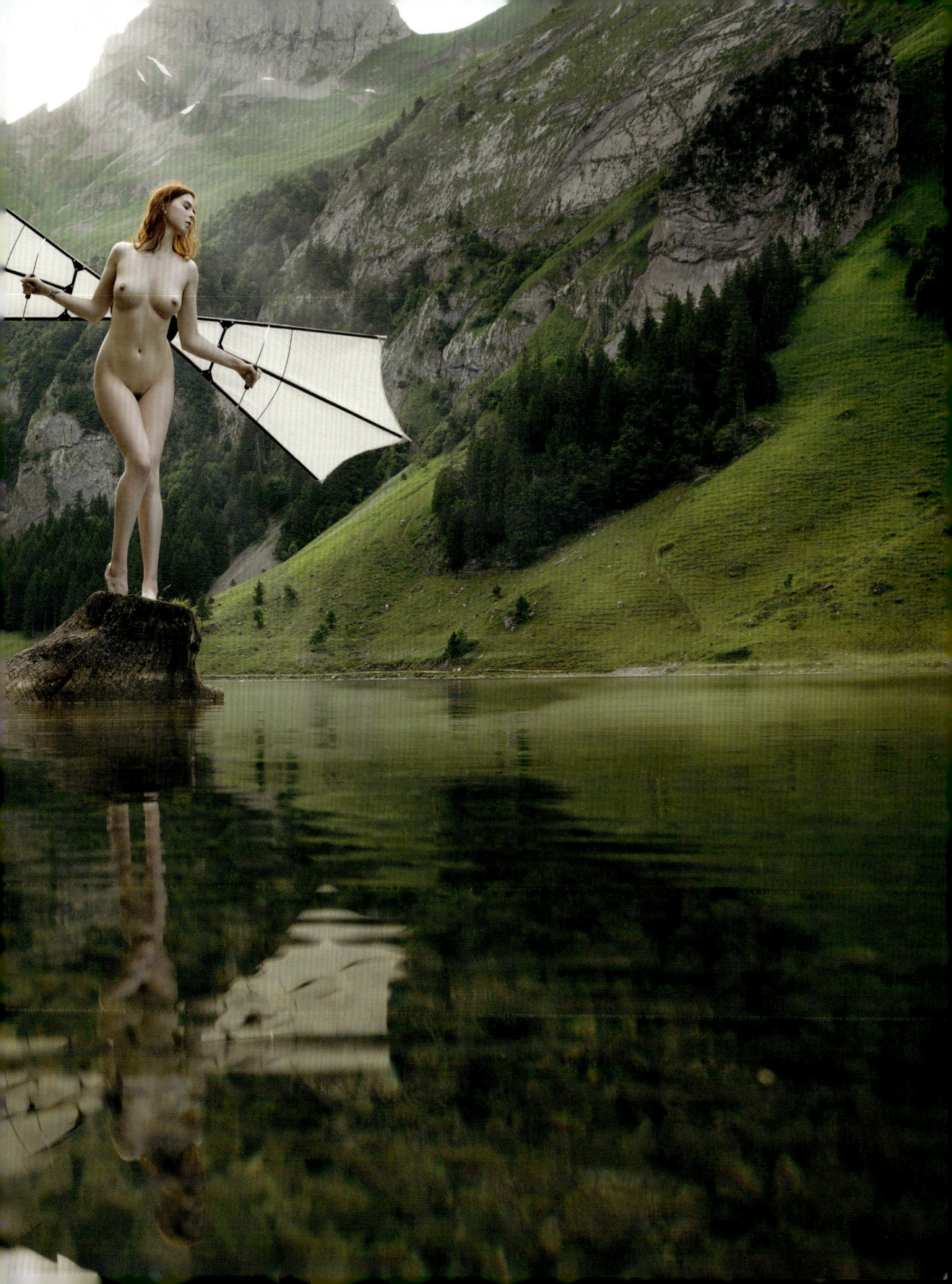

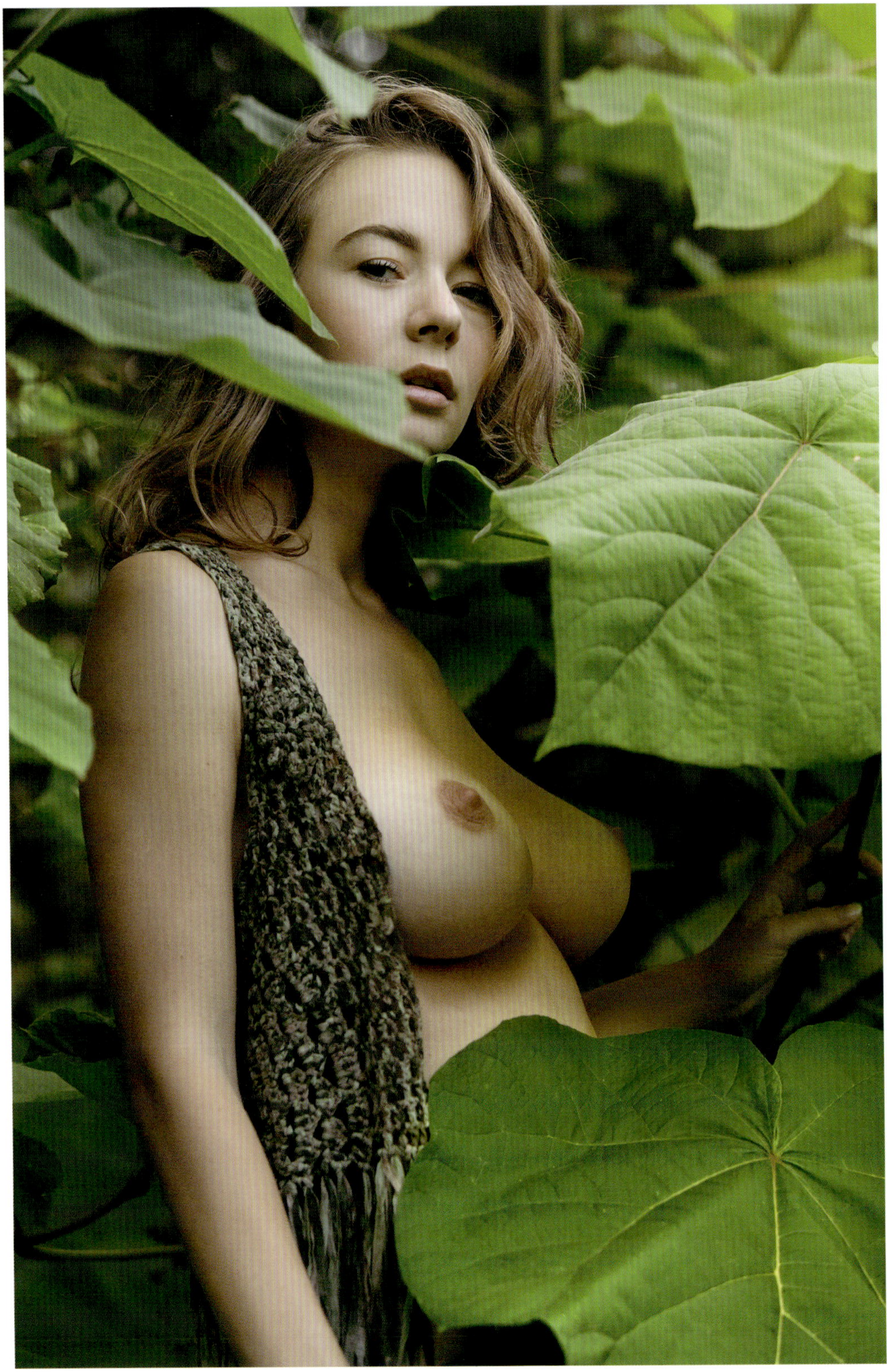

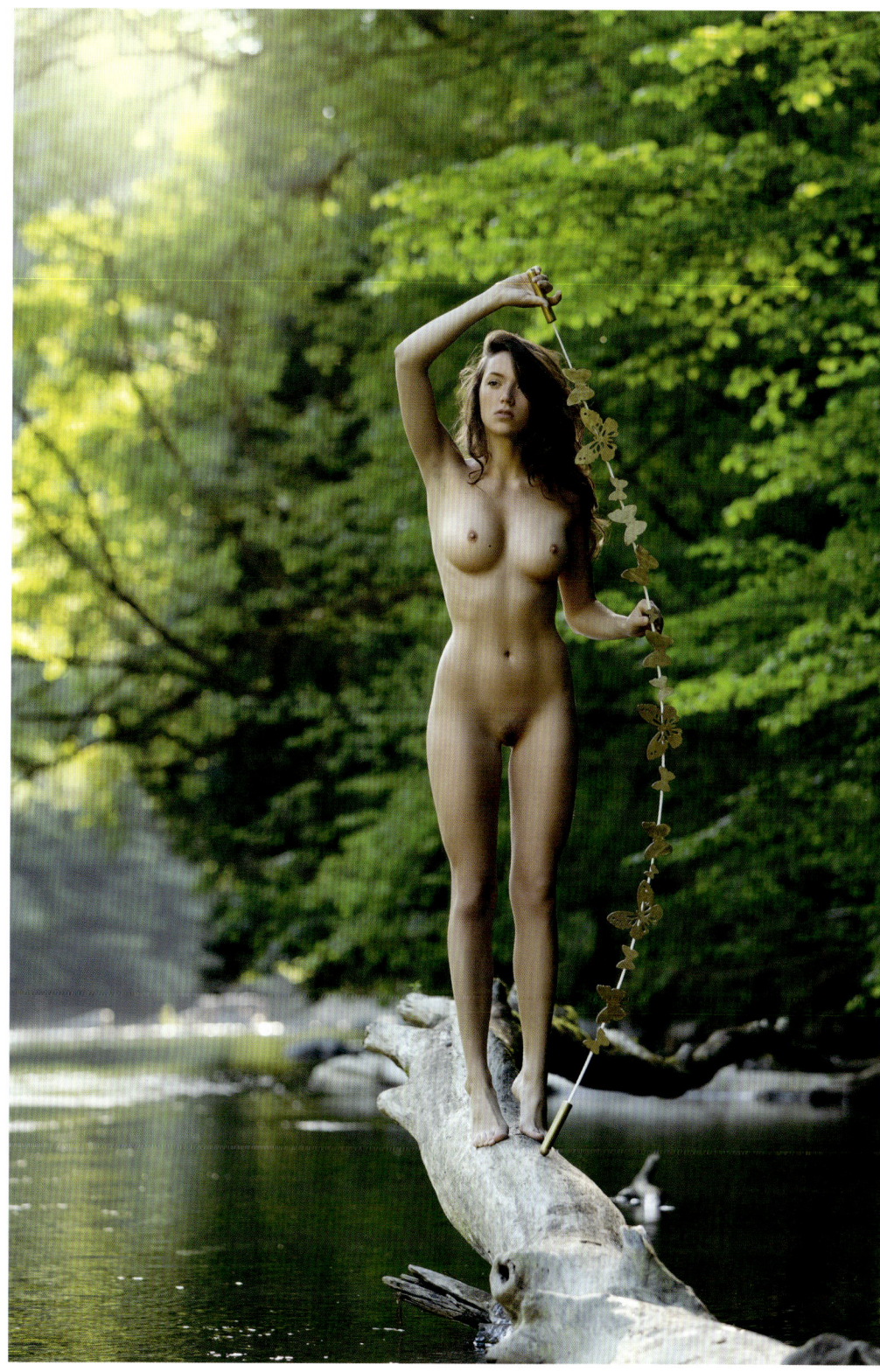

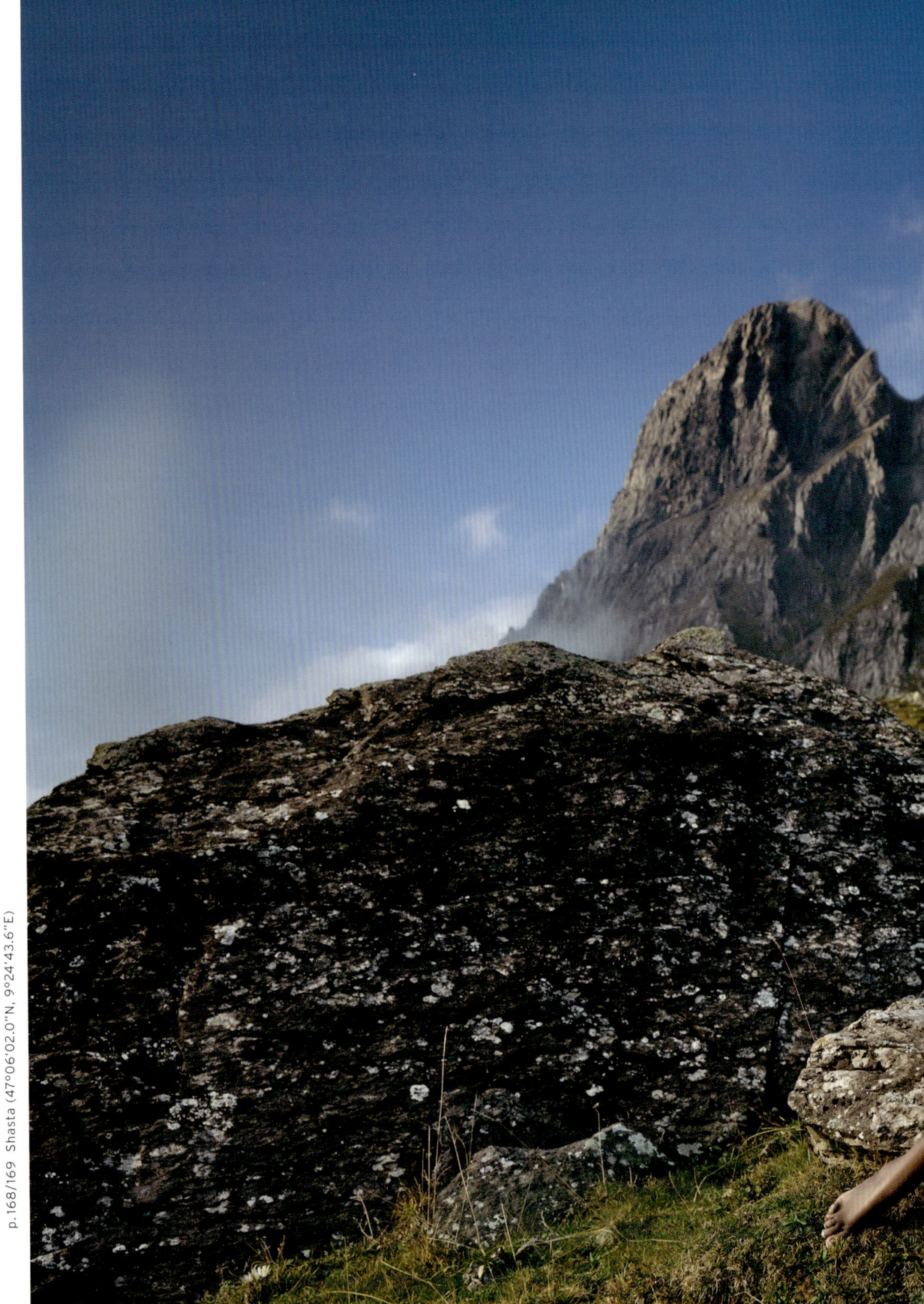

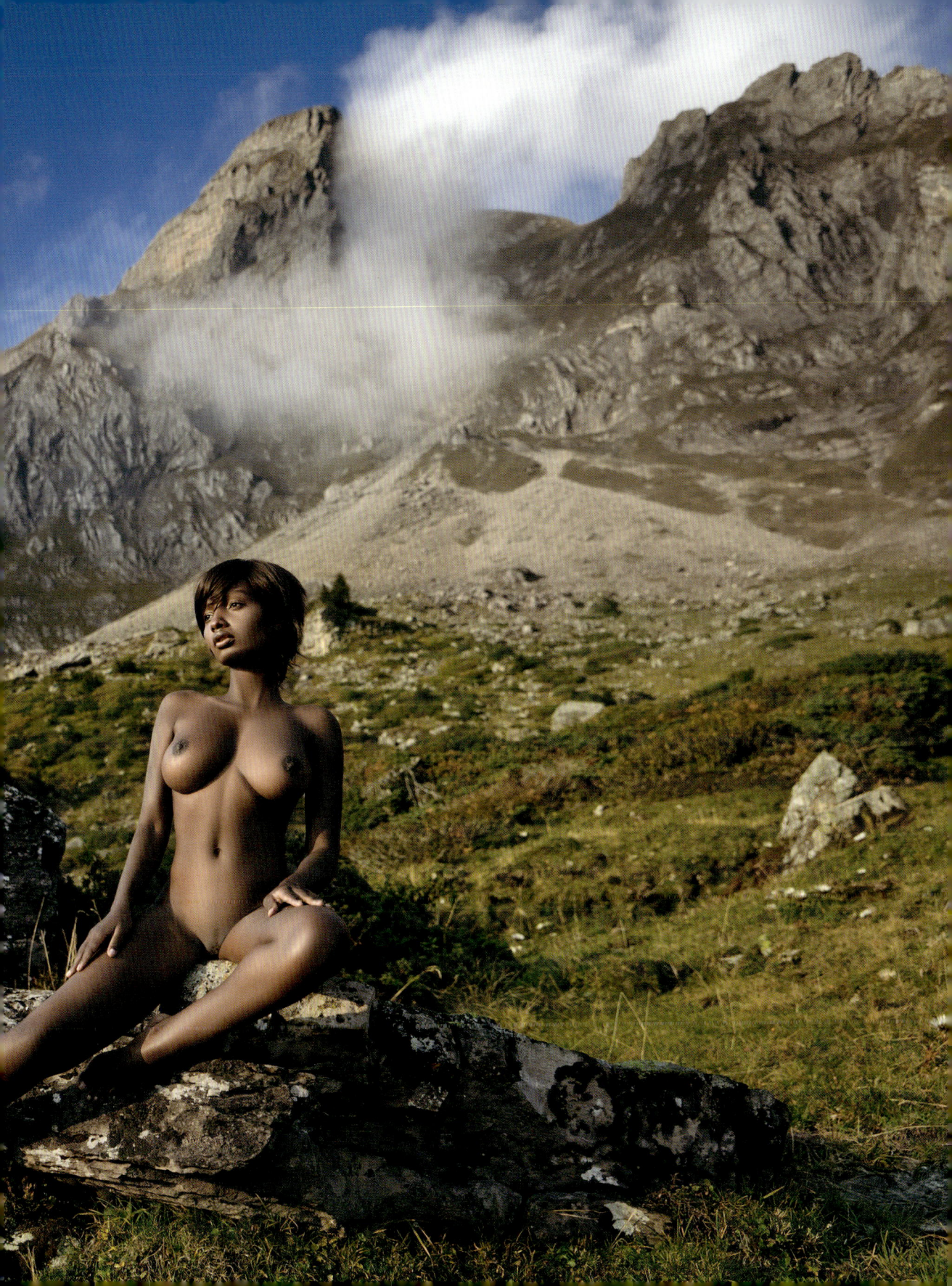

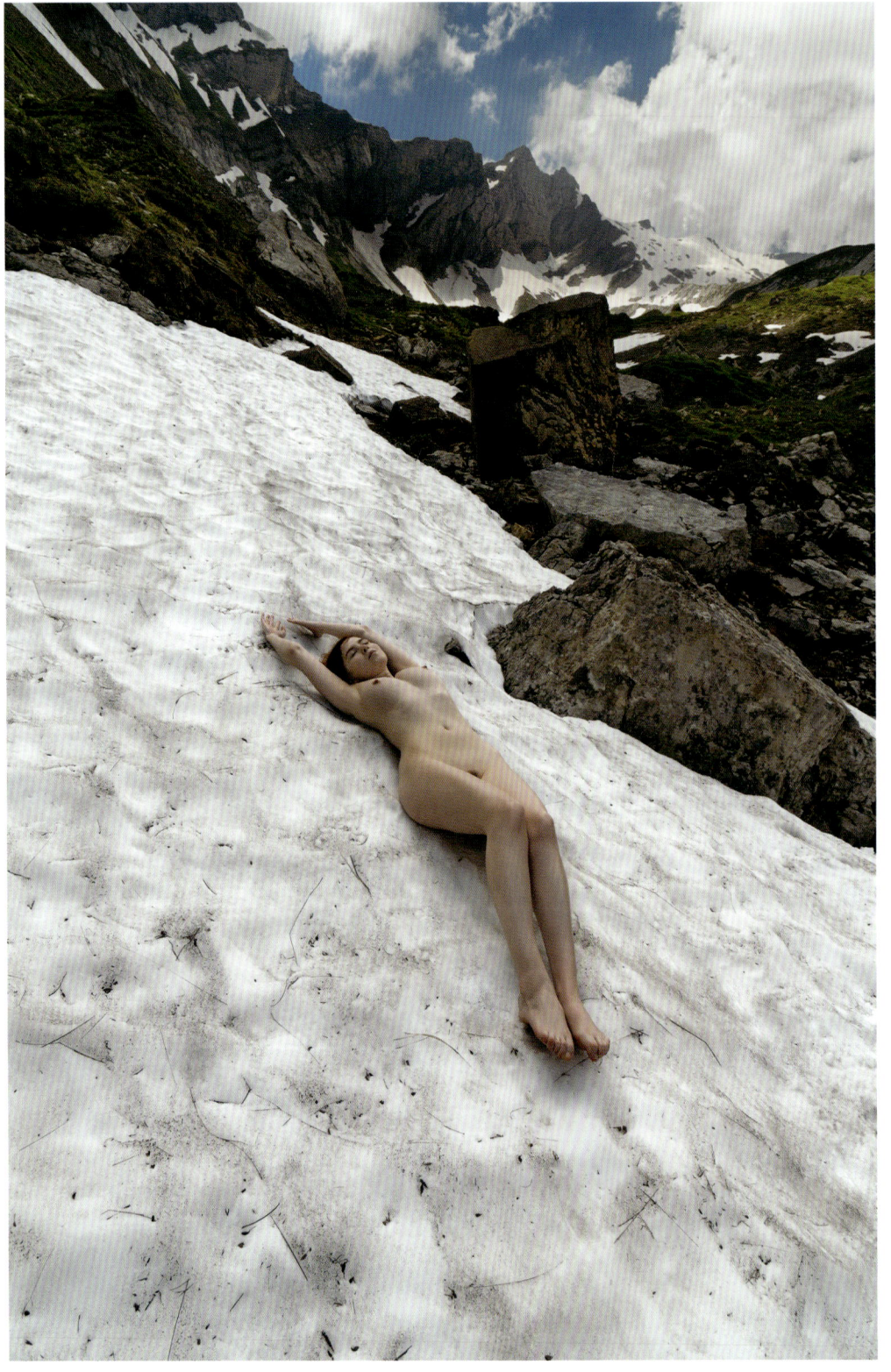

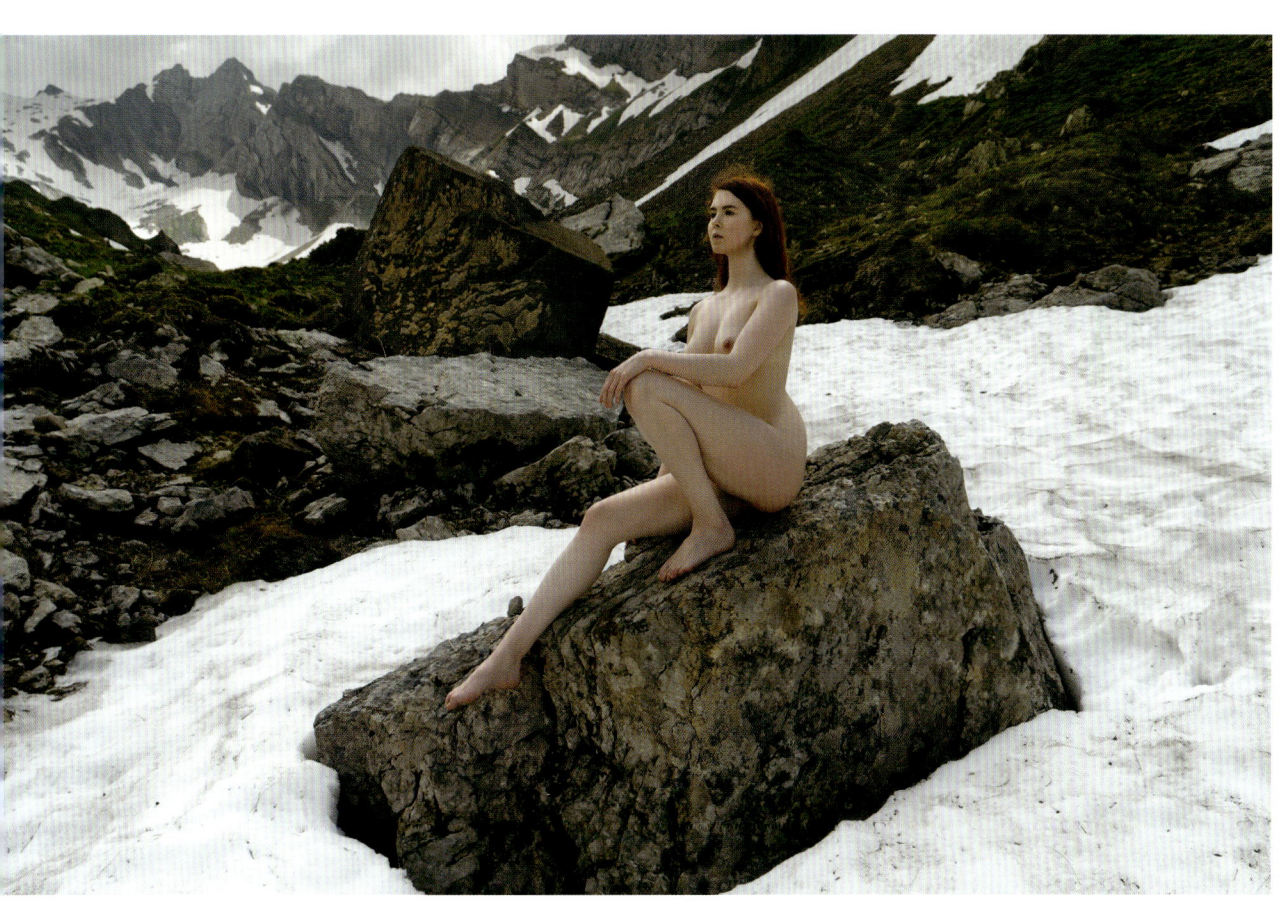

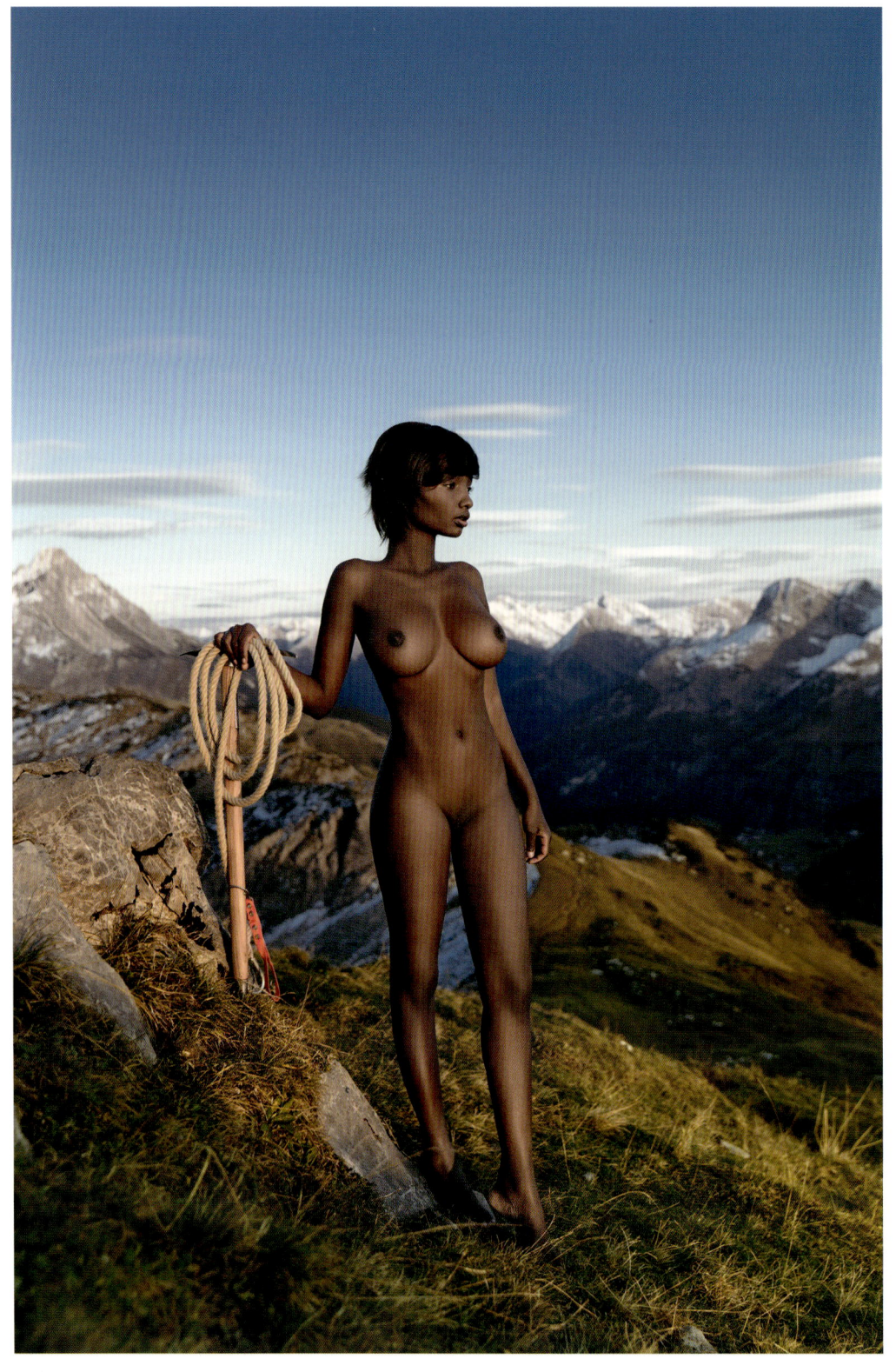

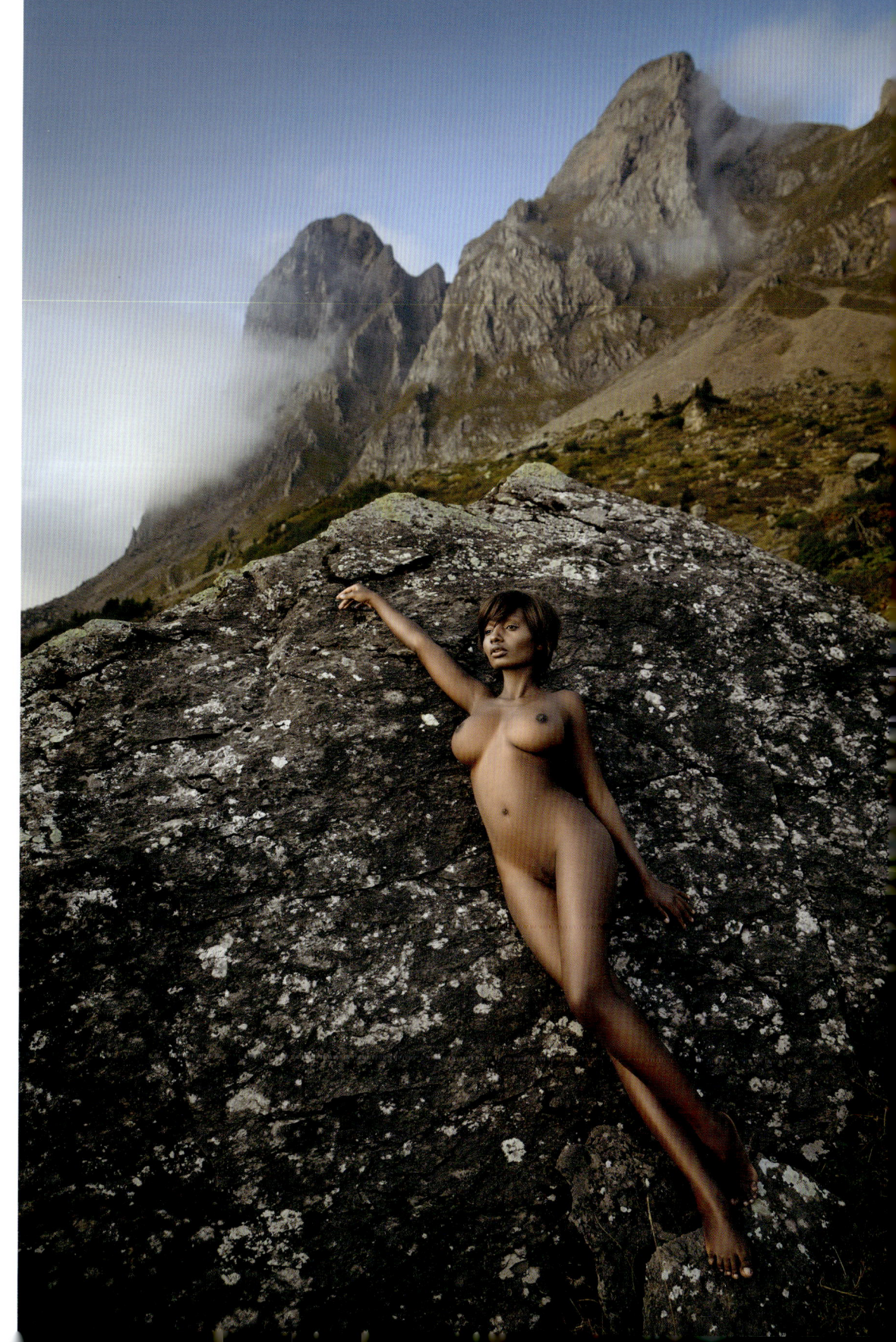

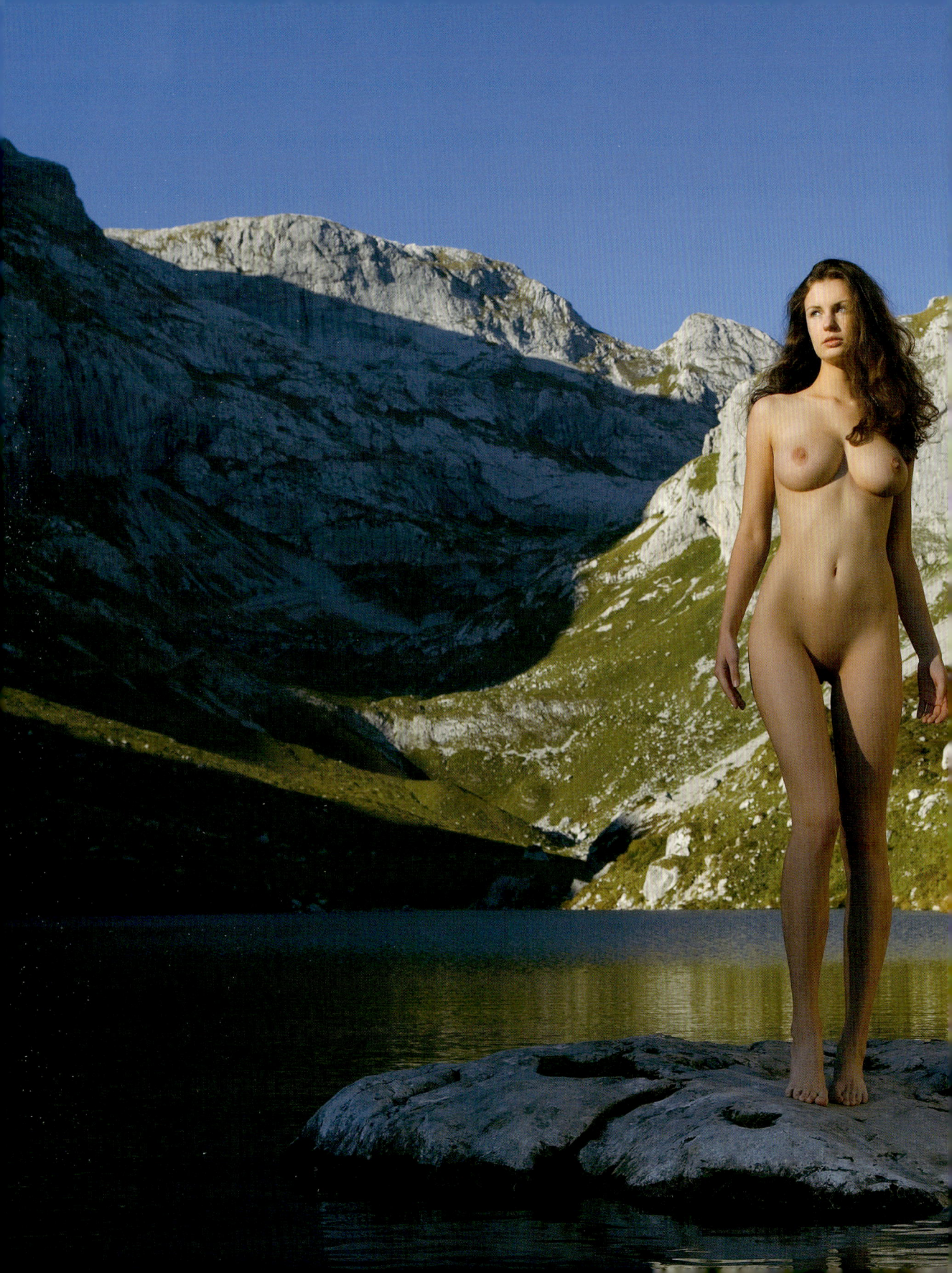

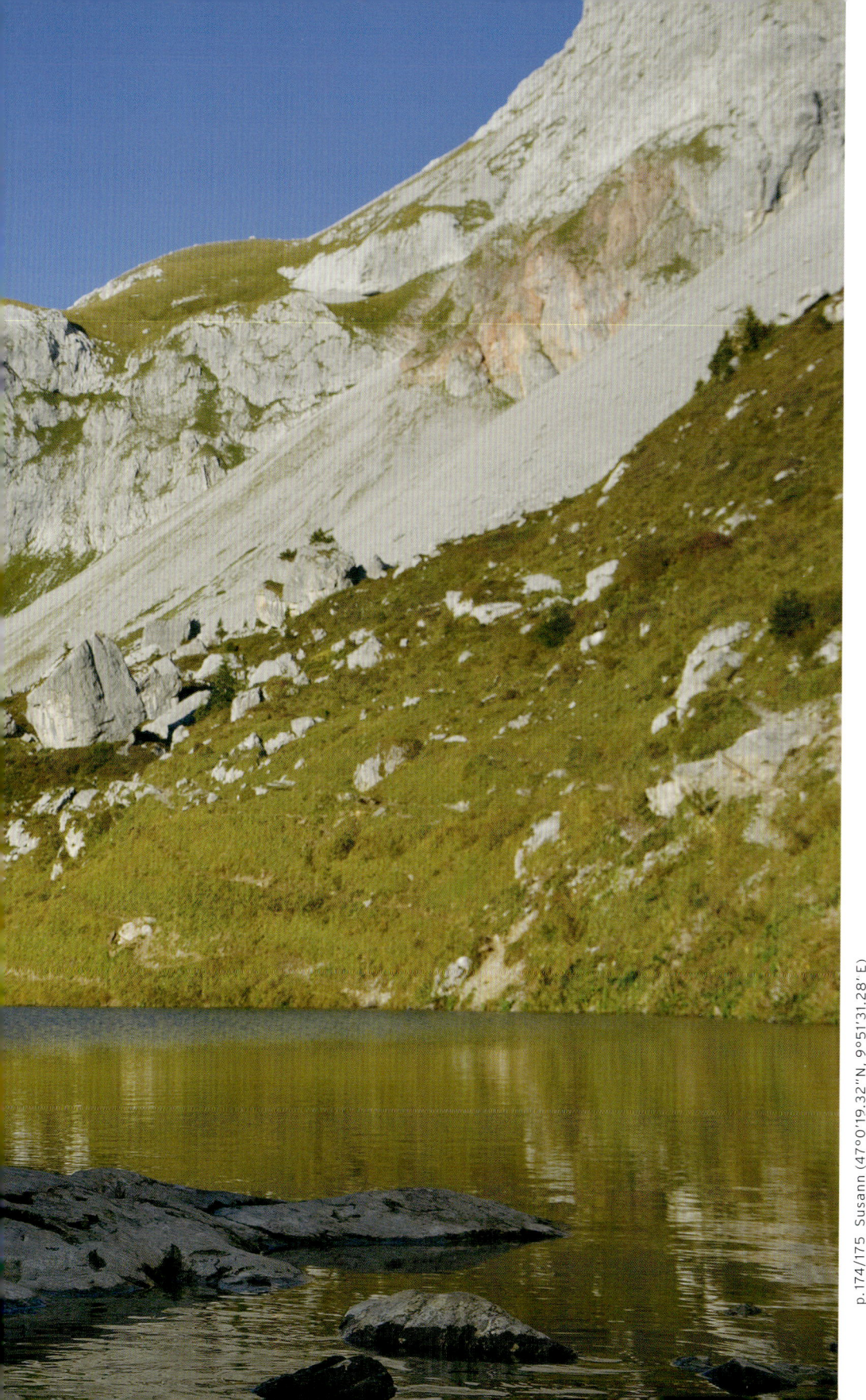

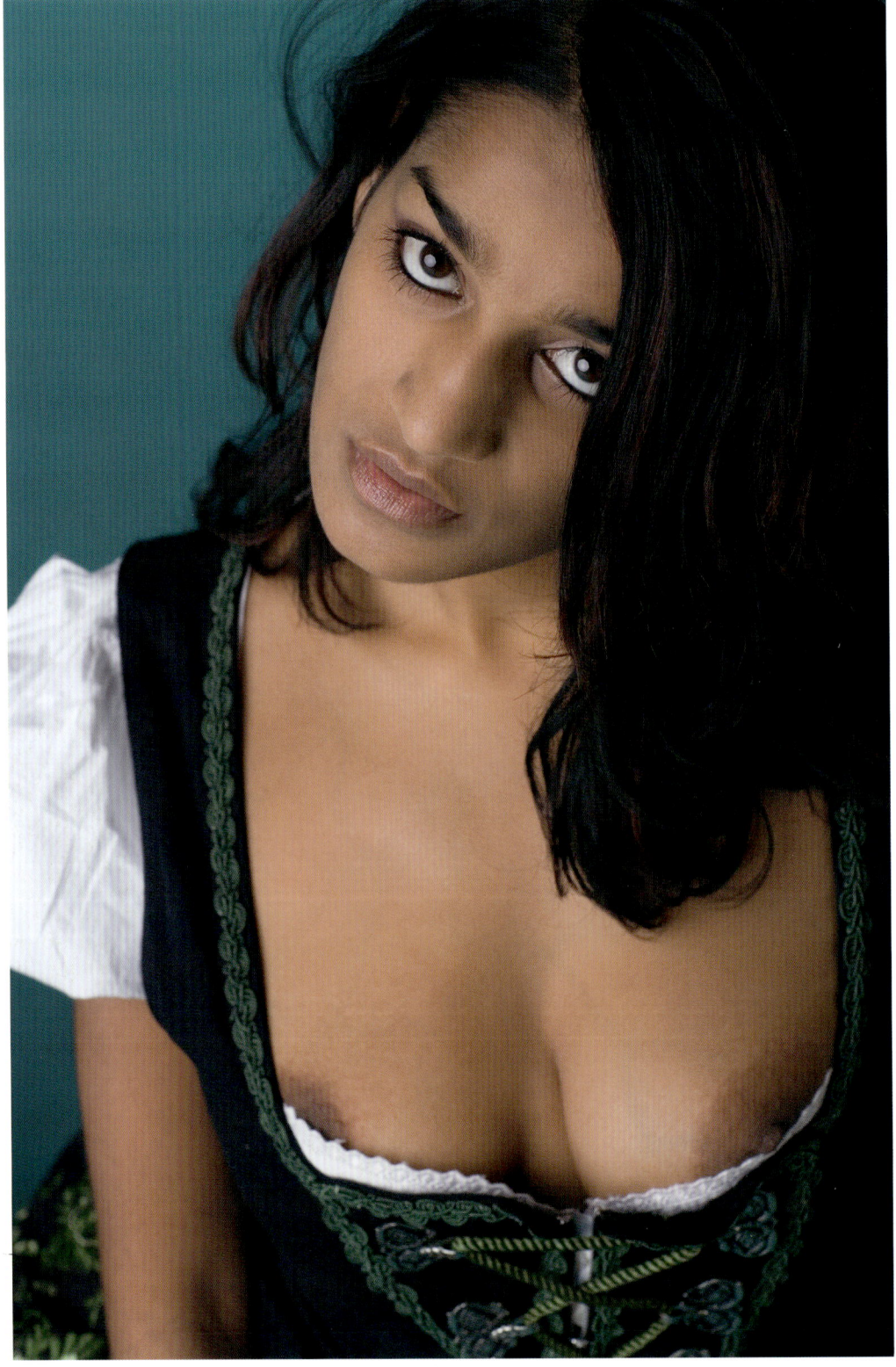

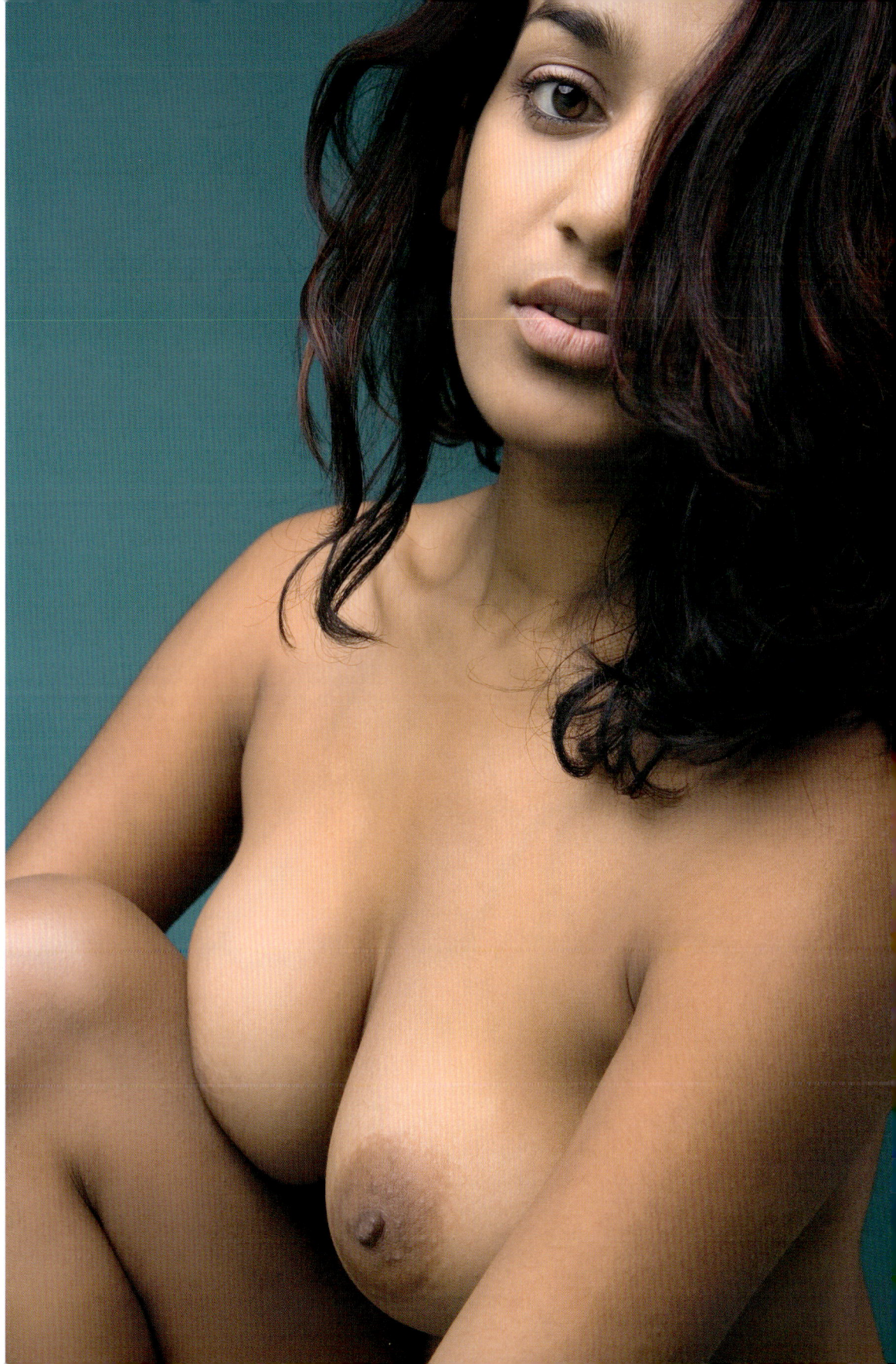

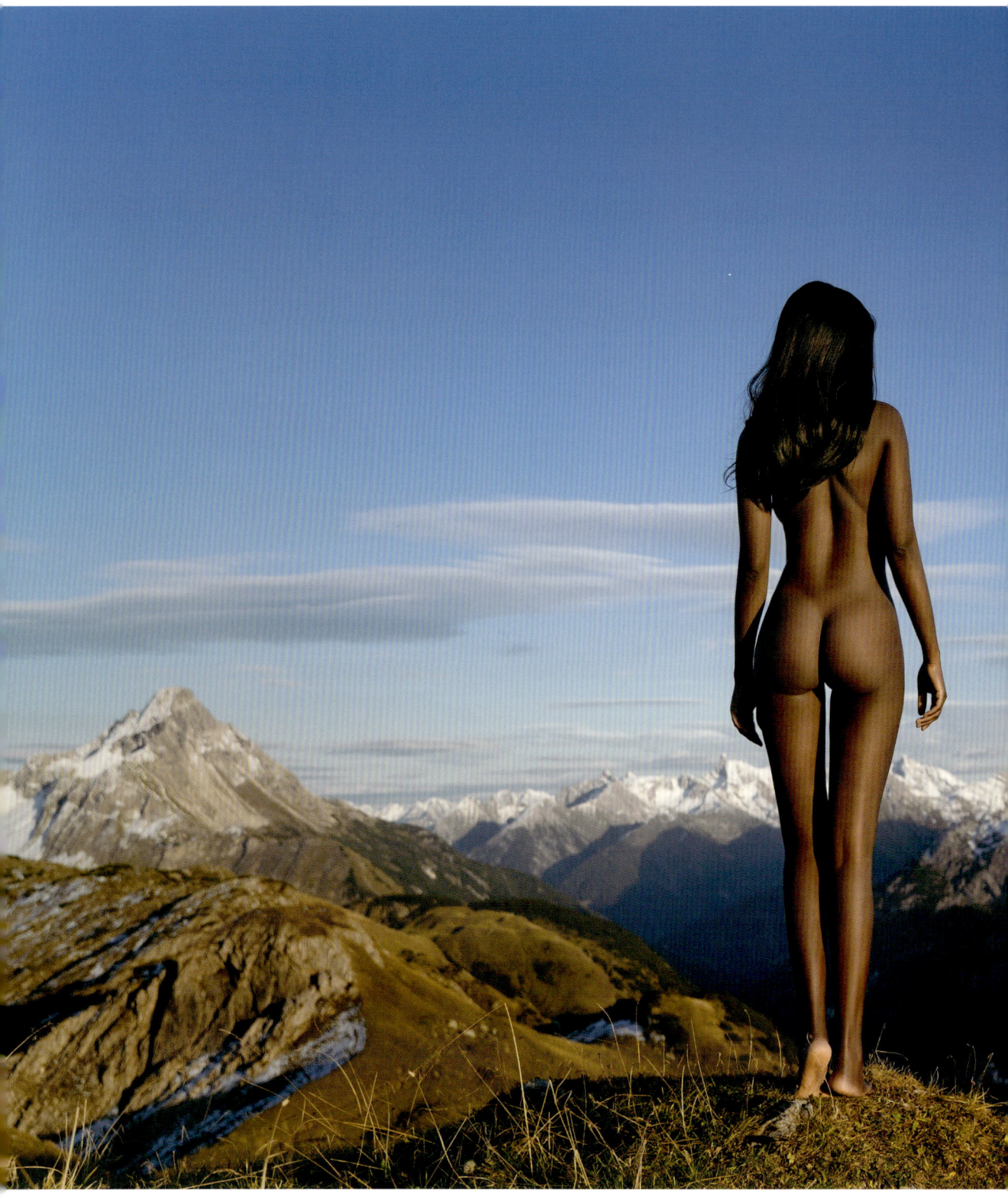

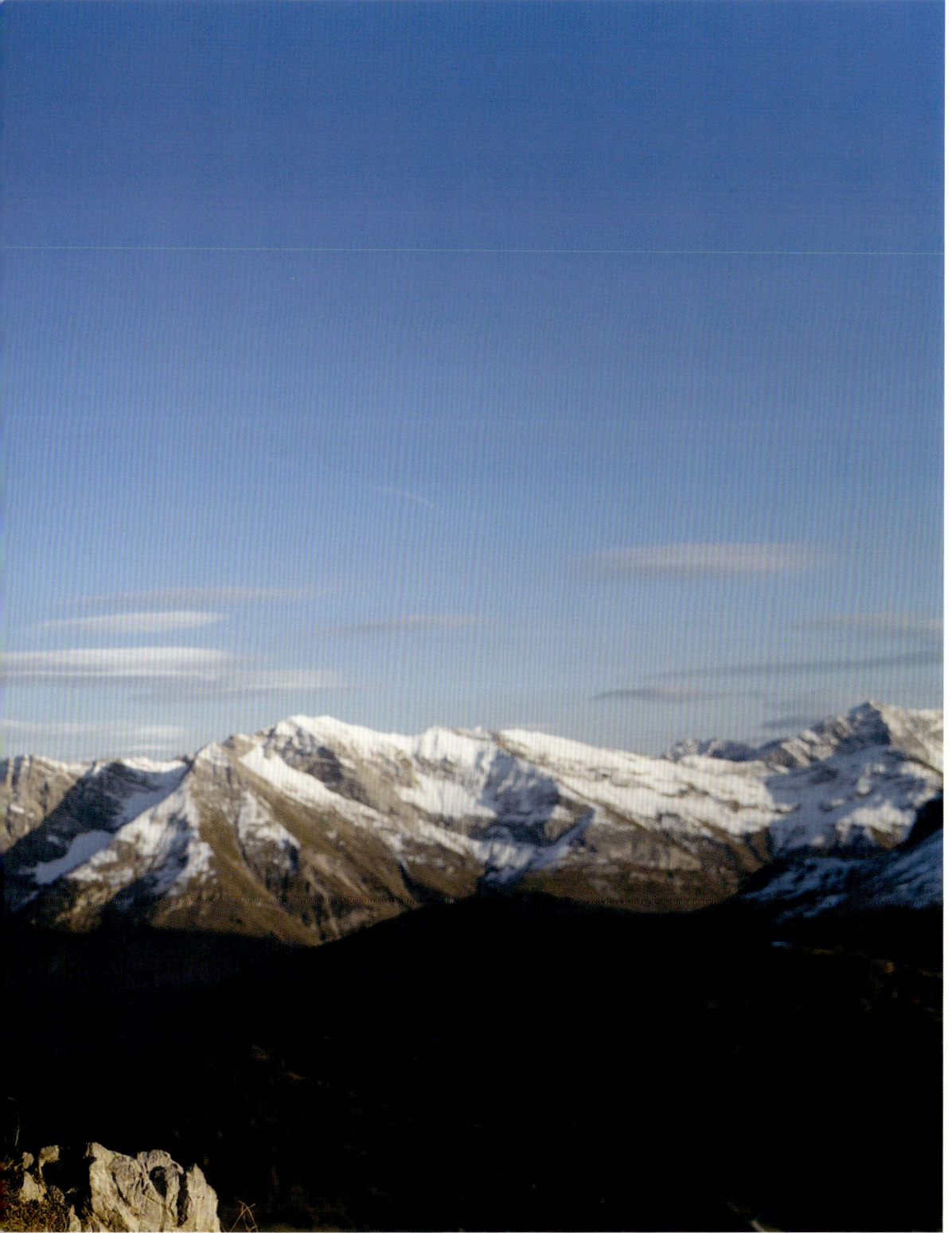

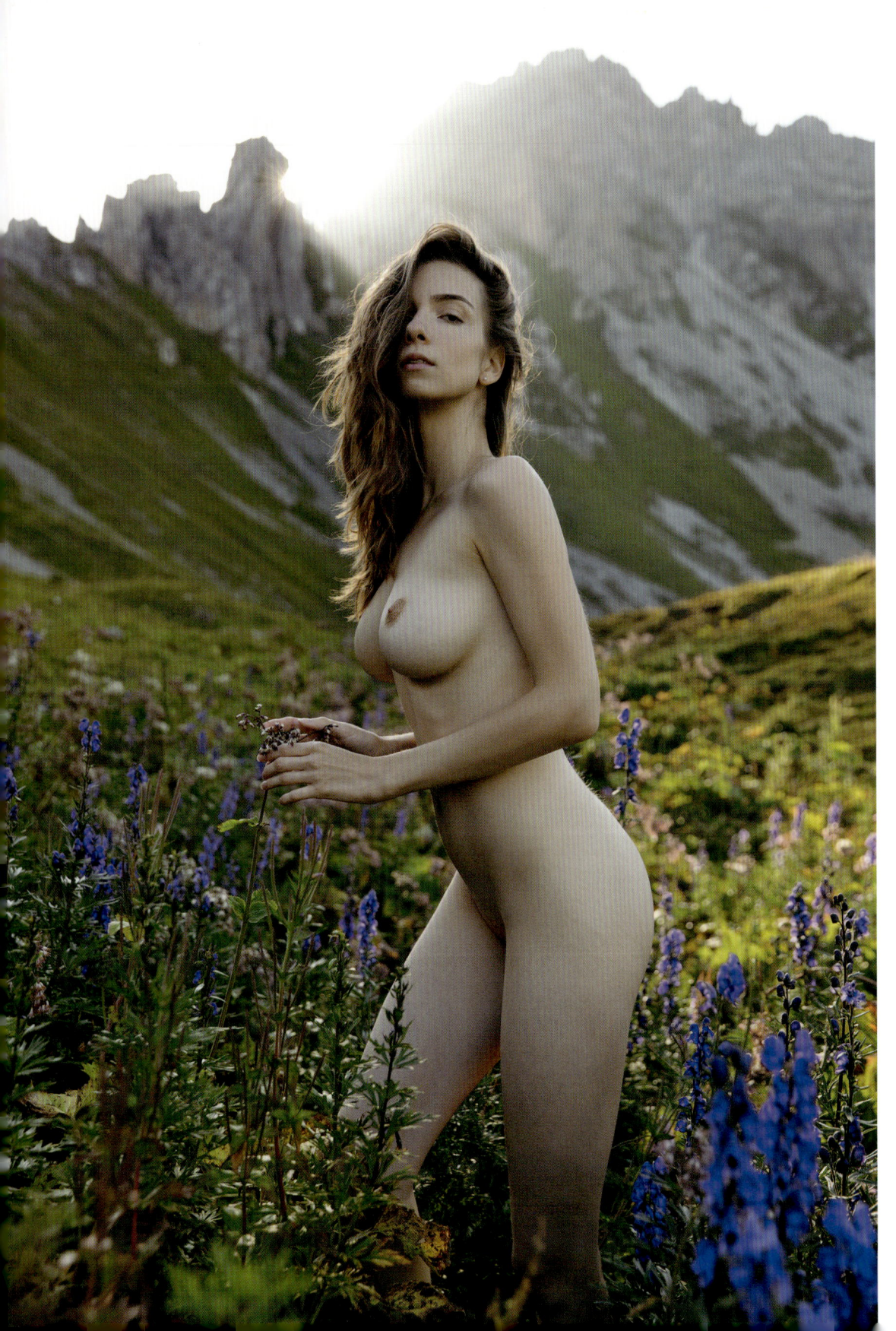

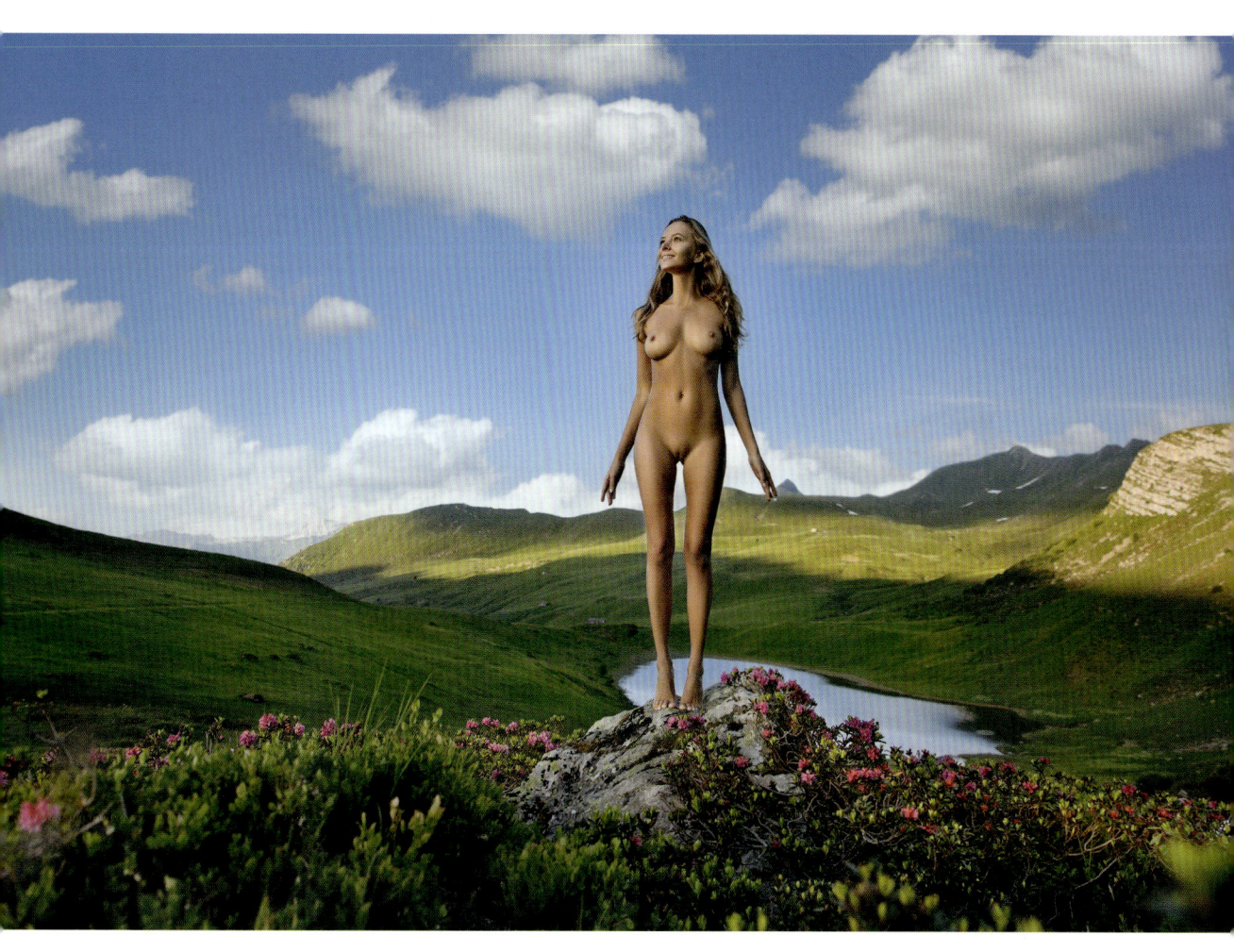

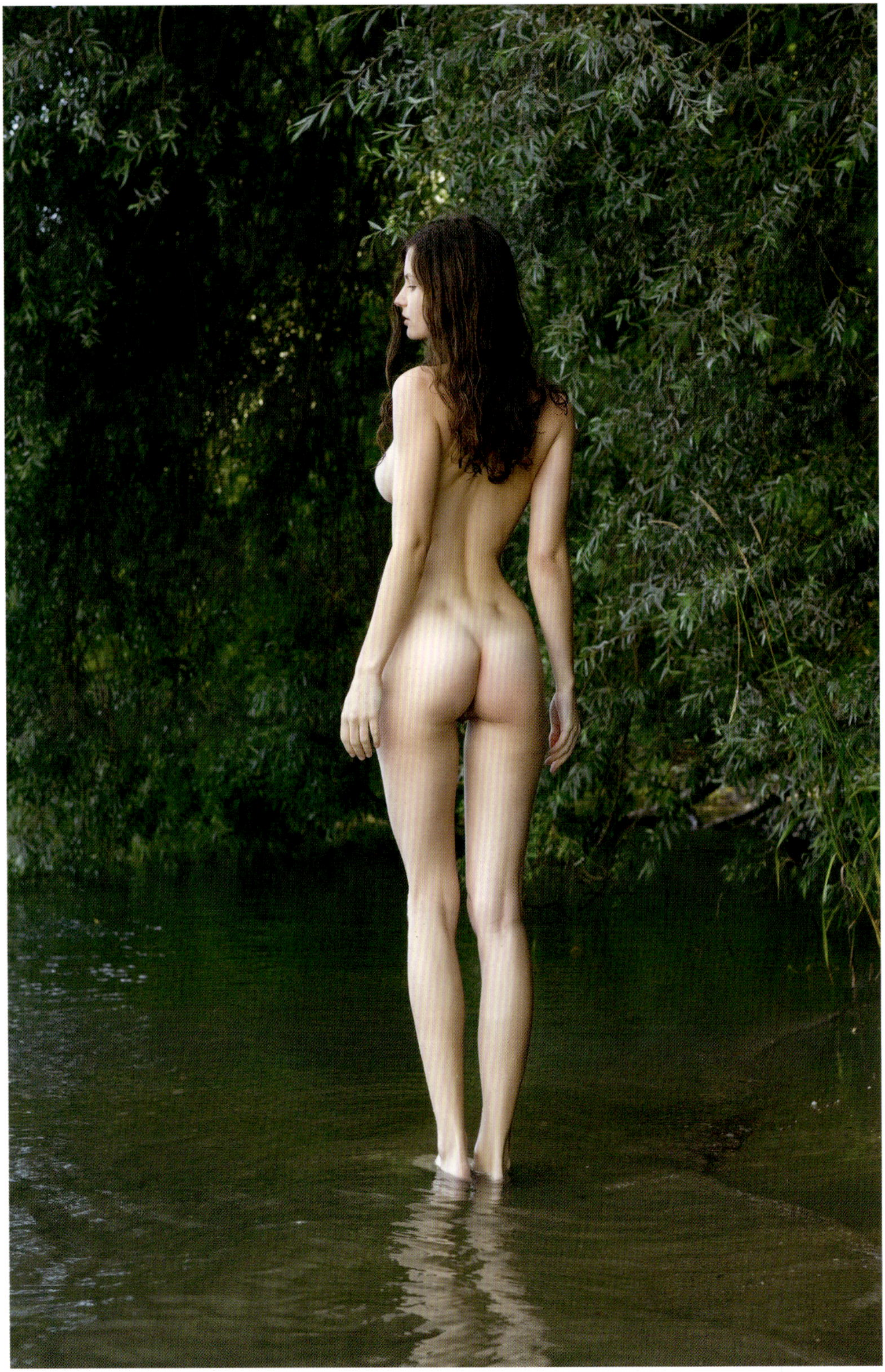

p. 182 Susanna (47°46'26.61"N, 9°04'36.52"E)

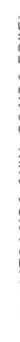

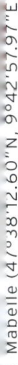

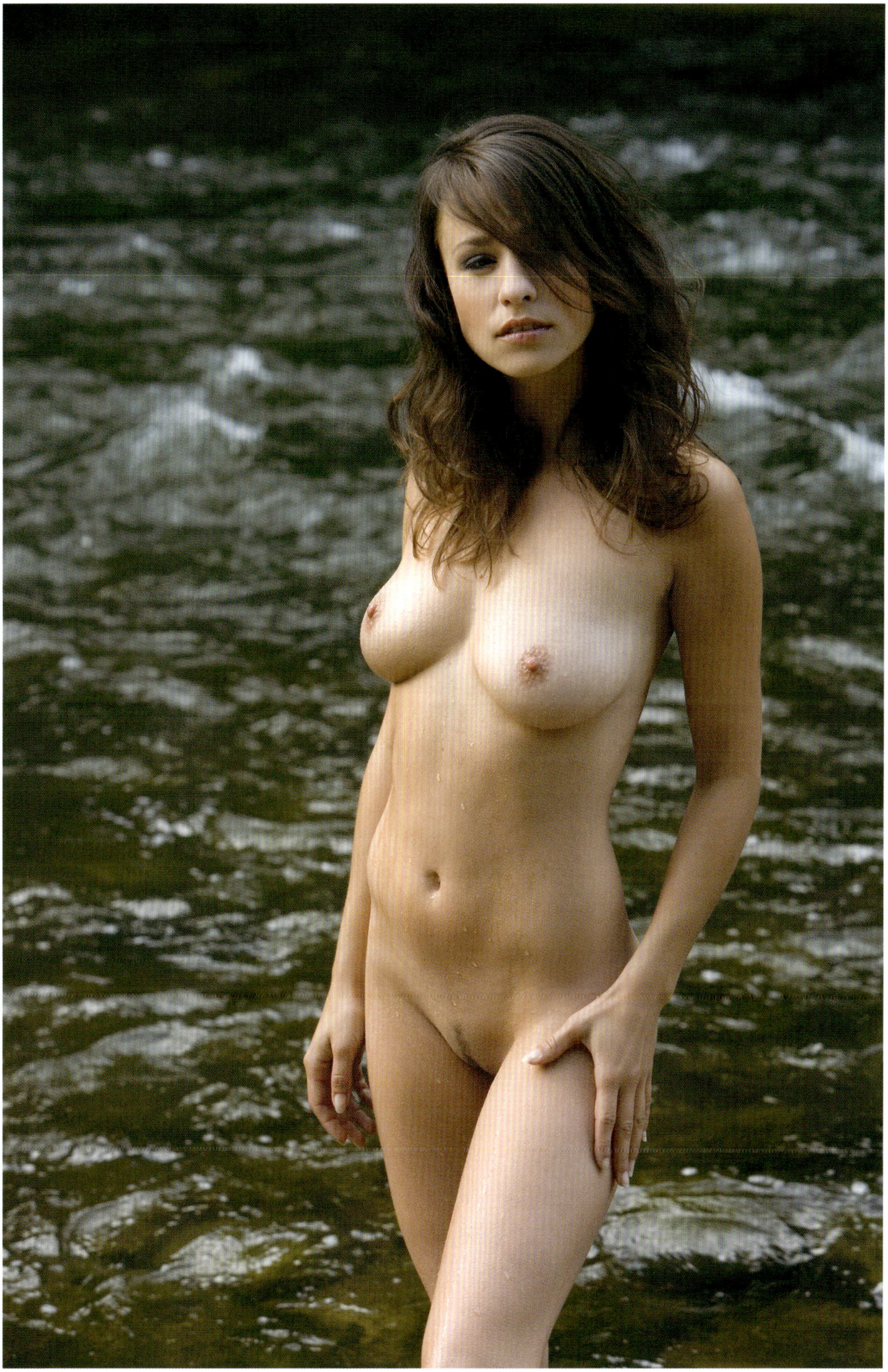

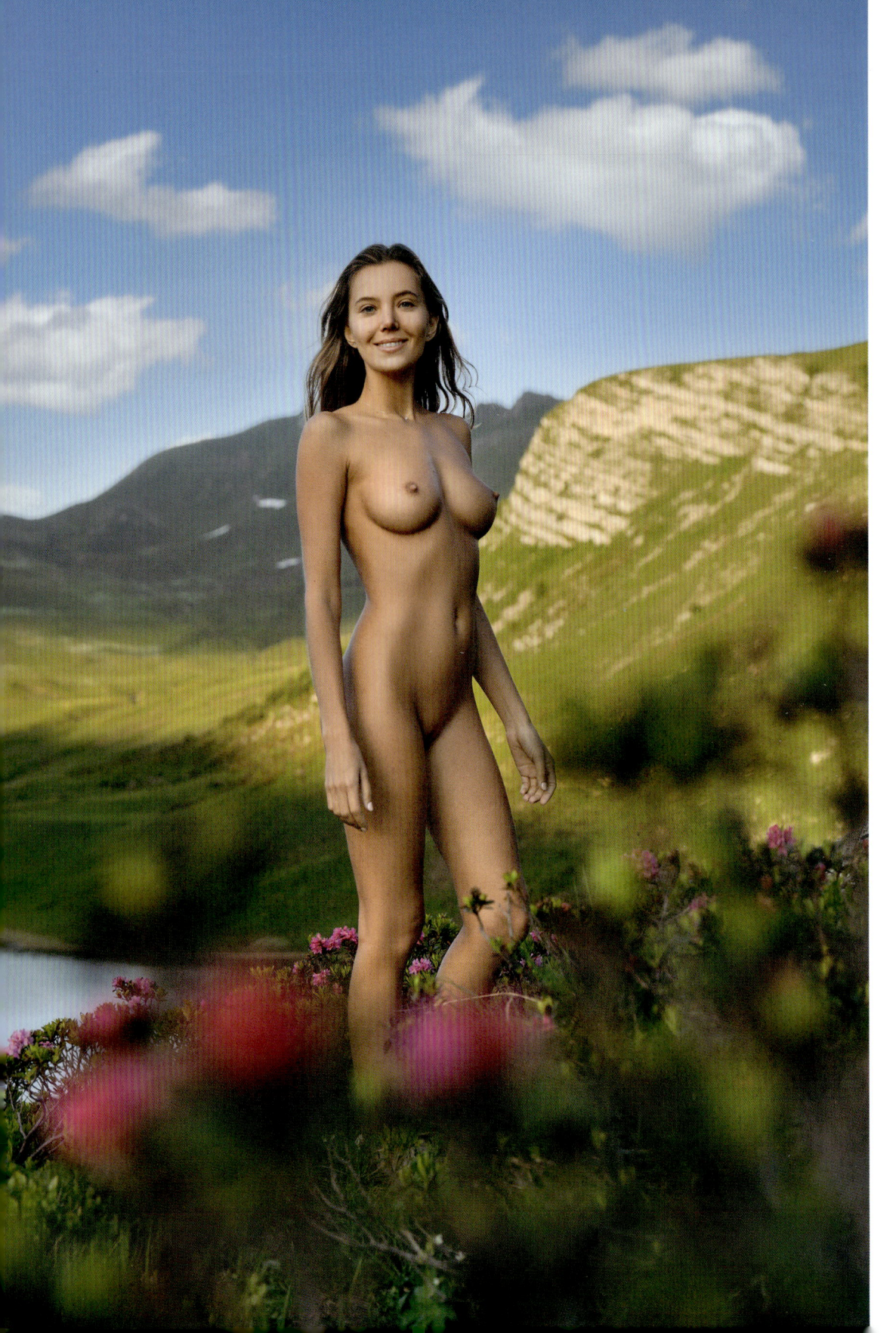

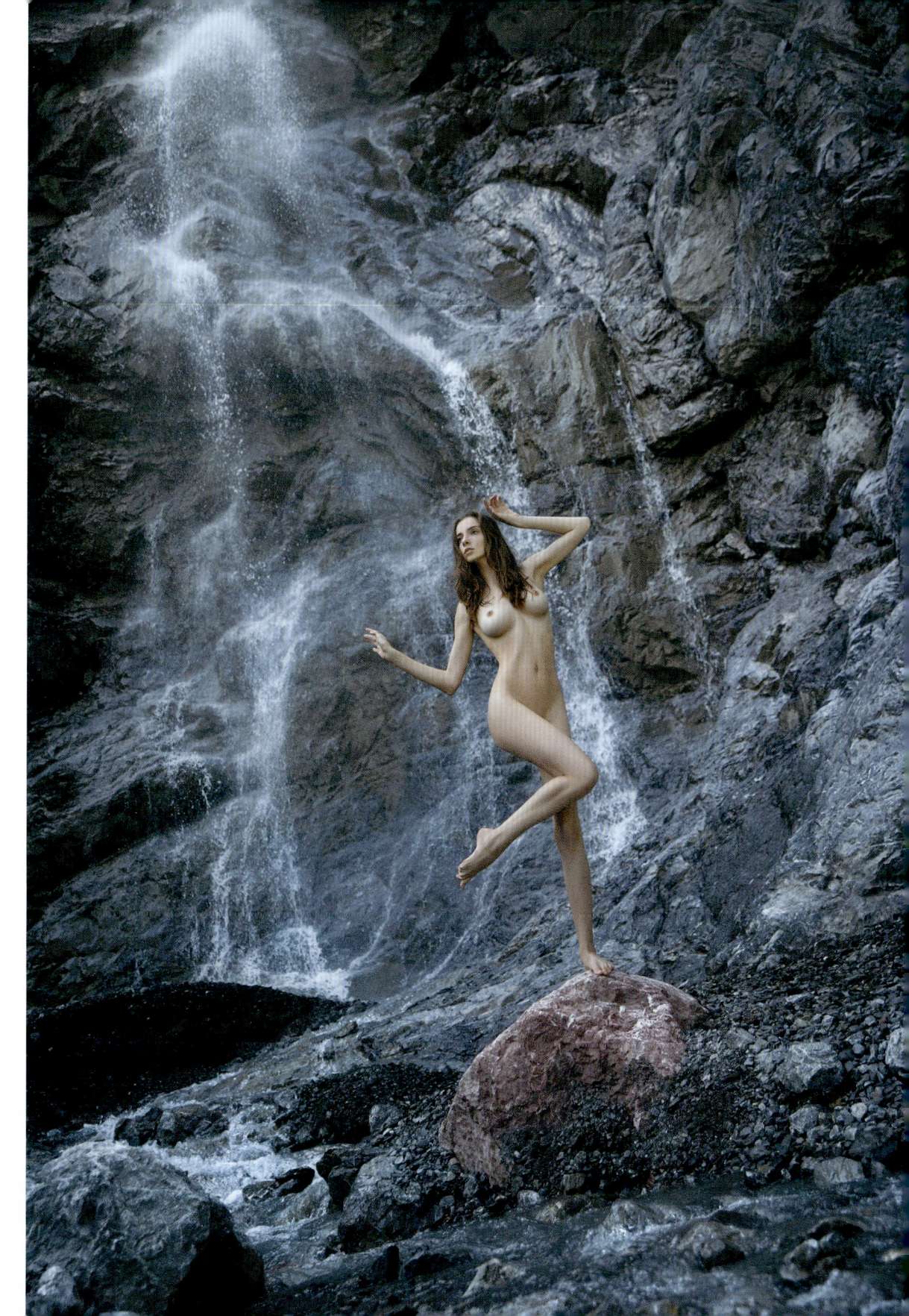

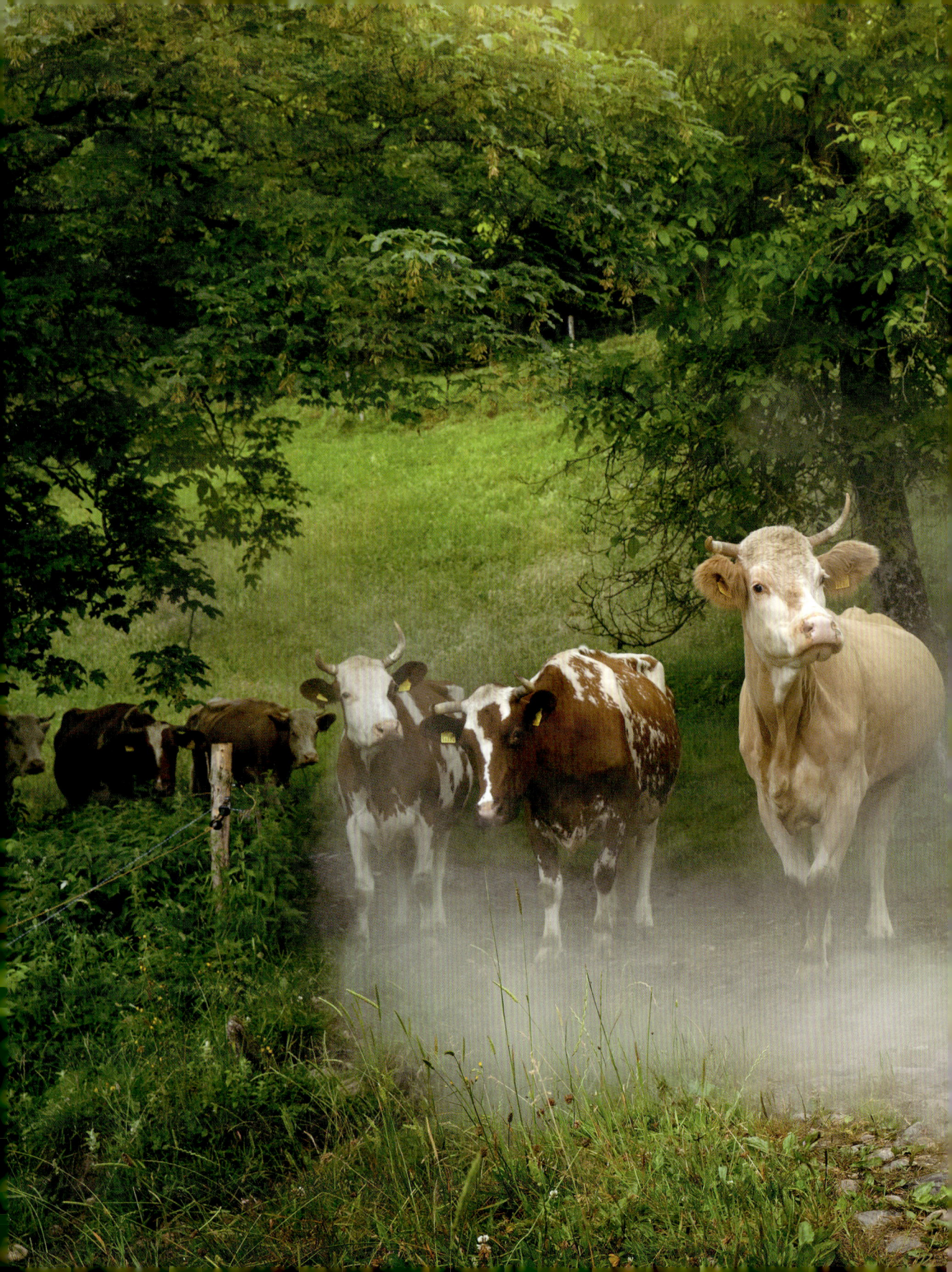

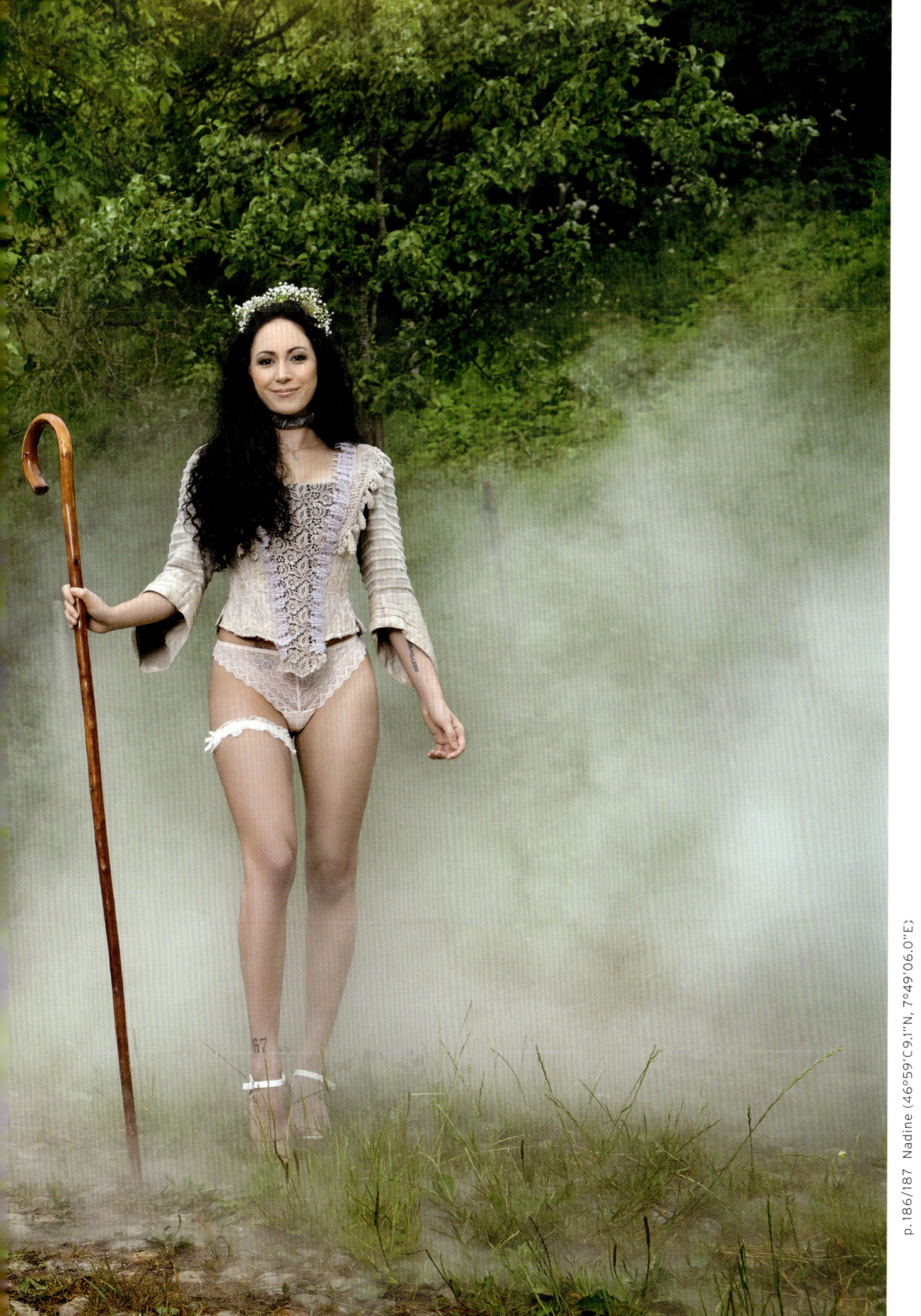

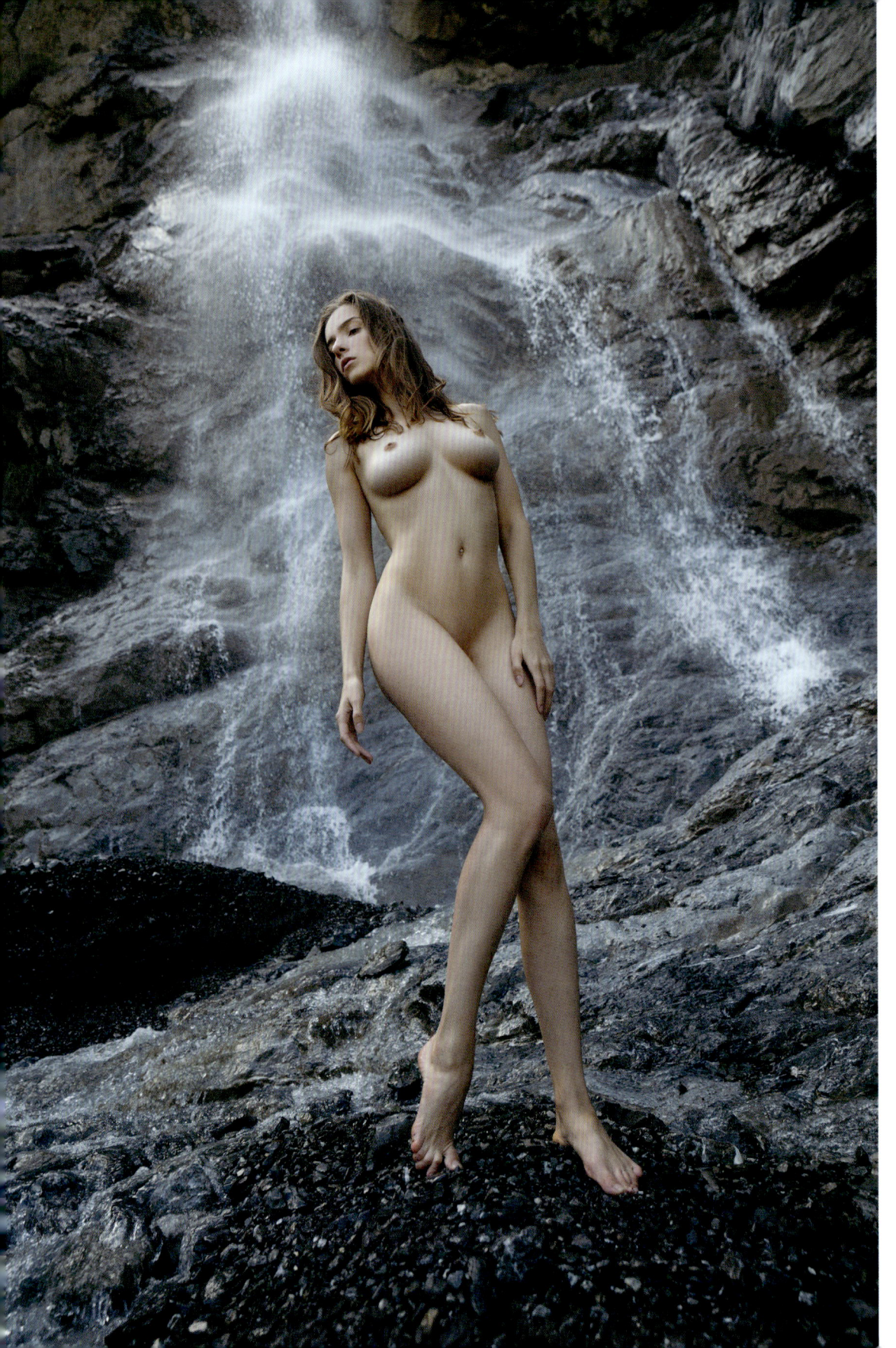

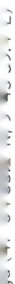

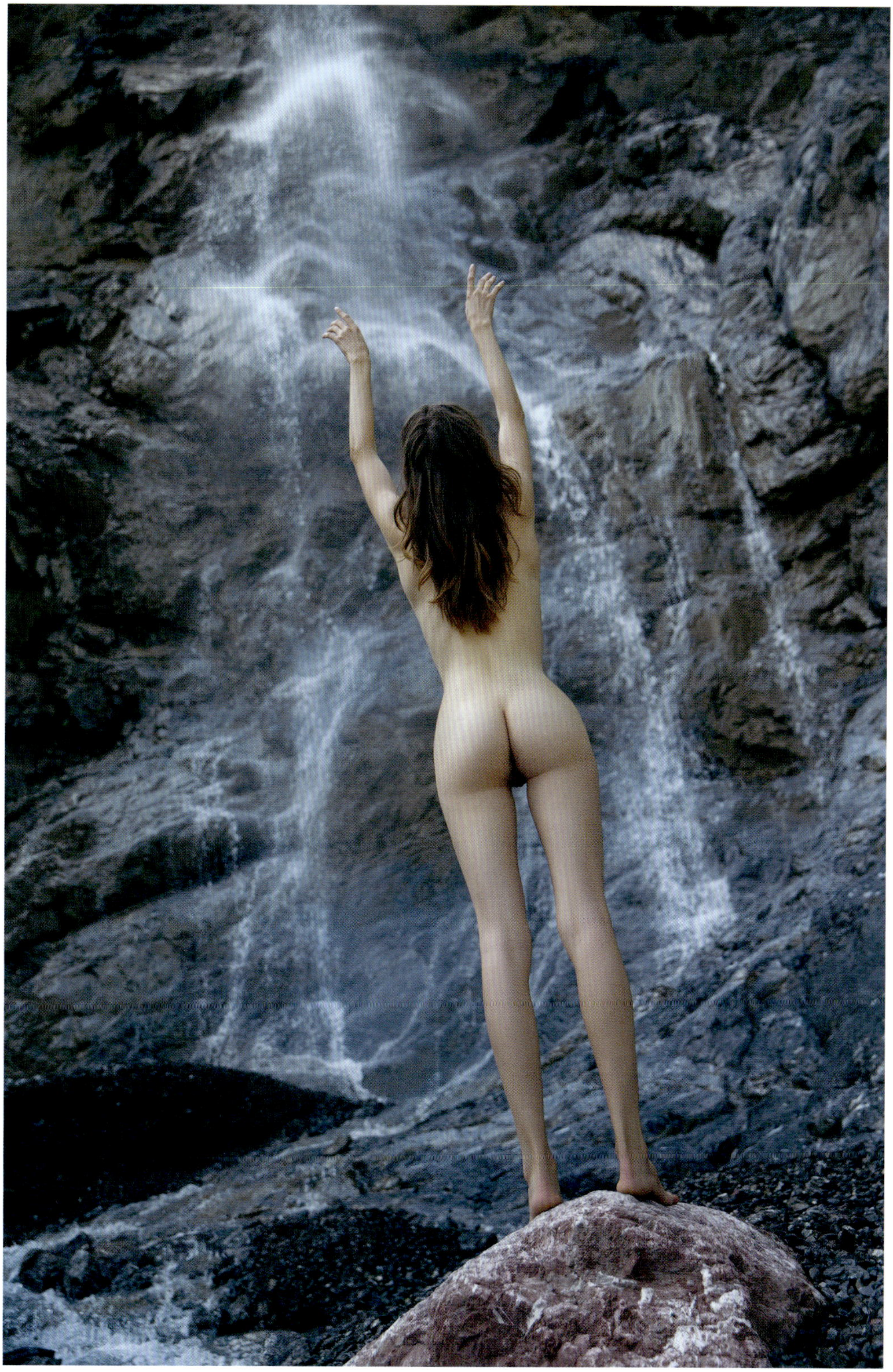

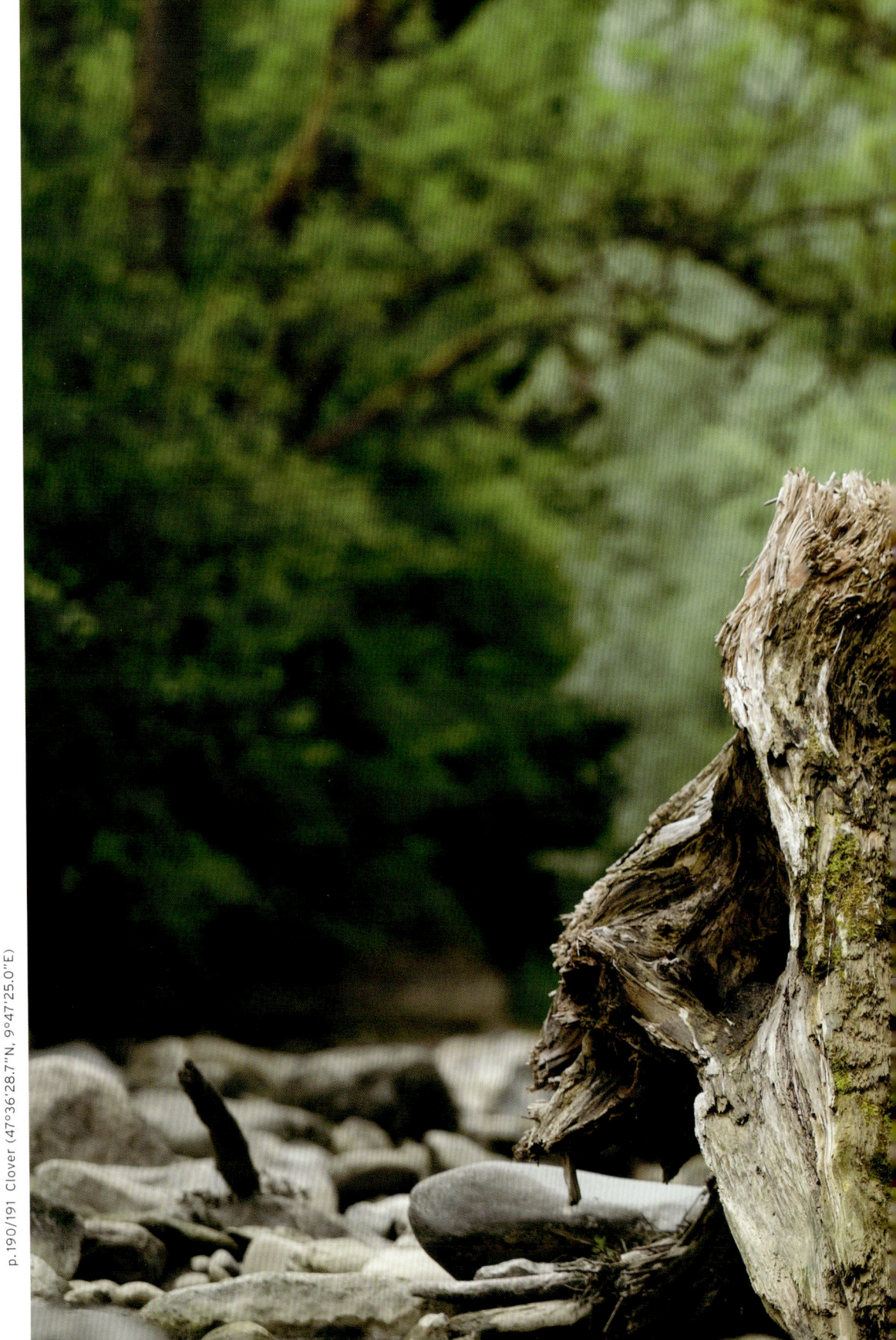